Hummingbird Plants *of the* Southwest

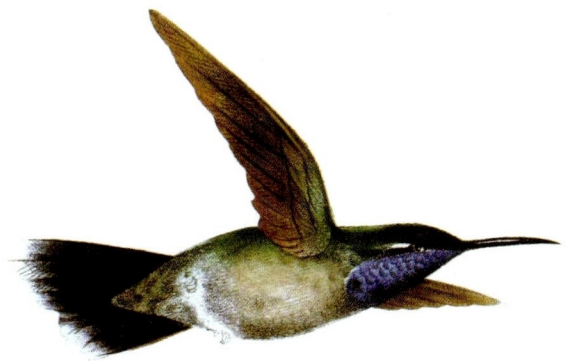

Marcy Scott

WITH PHOTOGRAPHS BY
Wynn Anderson, Dale and Marian Zimmerman,
and others

To Carolina,
Happy Hummingbirding!
Marcy Scott

RIO NUEVO PUBLISHERS

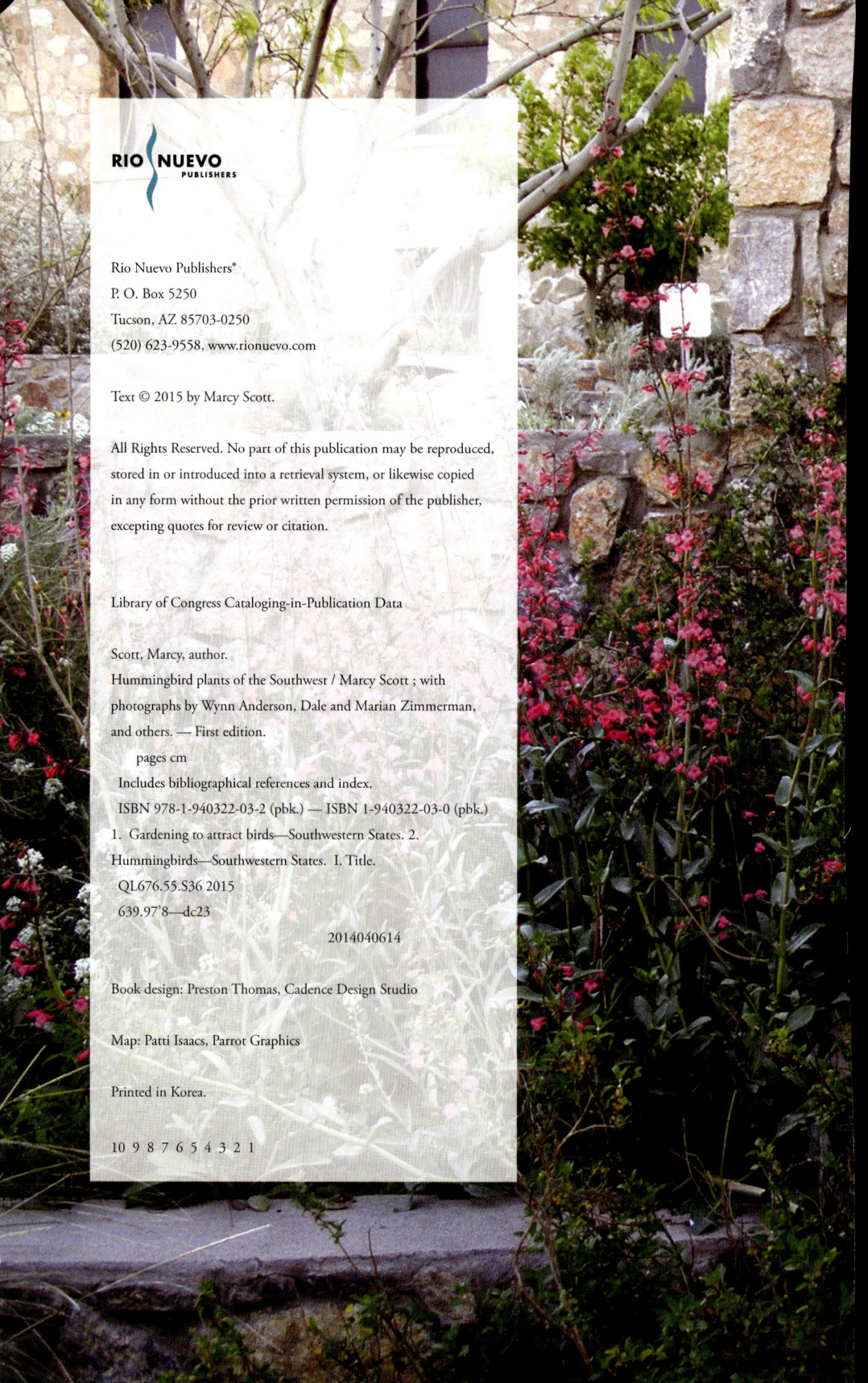

RIO NUEVO PUBLISHERS

Rio Nuevo Publishers®
P. O. Box 5250
Tucson, AZ 85703-0250
(520) 623-9558, www.rionuevo.com

Text © 2015 by Marcy Scott.

All Rights Reserved. No part of this publication may be reproduced, stored in or introduced into a retrieval system, or likewise copied in any form without the prior written permission of the publisher, excepting quotes for review or citation.

Library of Congress Cataloging-in-Publication Data

Scott, Marcy, author.
 Hummingbird plants of the Southwest / Marcy Scott ; with photographs by Wynn Anderson, Dale and Marian Zimmerman, and others. — First edition.
     pages cm
  Includes bibliographical references and index.
   ISBN 978-1-940322-03-2 (pbk.) — ISBN 1-940322-03-0 (pbk.)
 1. Gardening to attract birds—Southwestern States. 2. Hummingbirds—Southwestern States. I. Title.
  QL676.55.S36 2015
  639.97'8—dc23
                                       2014040614

Book design: Preston Thomas, Cadence Design Studio

Map: Patti Isaacs, Parrot Graphics

Printed in Korea.

10 9 8 7 6 5 4 3 2 1

CONTENTS

Introduction ... v

CHAPTER 1 Hummingbirds and Their Flowers: A Short Primer ... 1
- A GLIMPSE INTO THE WORLD OF THE HUMMINGBIRD ... 2
- A BIRD'S-EYE VIEW OF PLANT POLLINATION ... 6
- MIGRATORY CORRIDORS AND OTHER CRITICAL NATURAL AREAS ... 9

CHAPTER 2 Hummingbirds of the Southwest ... 13

CHAPTER 3 Creating a Hummingbird Habitat ... 43
- GETTING ORIENTED ... 44
- STRUCTURAL ELEMENTS ... 45
- SUCCESSION OF BLOOM ... 47
- WATER FEATURES ... 49
- ARTIFICIAL FEEDERS ... 50
- SAFETY CONCERNS ... 51

CHAPTER 4 Gardening with Native Plants, Southwestern Style ... 55
- MICROCLIMATES OF THE LANDSCAPE ... 56
- JUST ADD WATER ... 58
- SOIL TYPES OF THE REGION ... 60
- "IT'S A DRY HEAT" ... 60
- WHERE TO FIND NATIVE PLANTS ... 61
- PLANTING BASICS ... 62

CHAPTER 5 Hummingbird Plants of the Southwestern United States and Northern Mexico ... 65

Acknowledgments ... 308
Appendix: Fifteen Ways to Help Hummingbirds and Their Flowers ... 311
Glossary ... 313
Resources ... 316
Bibliography ... 319
Index ... 326

Introduction

Hummingbirds are creatures that can put a twinkle in the eye of even the crustiest of curmudgeons. They mesmerize us with their high-octane antics and take our breath away with their scintillating colors. Their appearance after a long absence quickens our heartbeats and in an instant animates our garden. It is as if their presence is an affirmation that all is still well with the world, or at least a tiny part of it.

We who dwell in the American Southwest are extremely fortunate when it comes to hummingbirds. We still enjoy—for the near future, anyway—the luxury of having many open spaces where we may encounter them in the wild, whether as lone birds defending a desert territory from atop an ocotillo or in large concentrations in high mountain meadows sipping on blooms borne of the summer monsoons.

We also typically don't have to go to great lengths to entice hummingbirds into our backyards so that we can view them on a more regular basis. Not only are they widespread across the region, in some locations occurring year-round, but most are also fairly comfortable around human habitations and quick to notice our offerings. Folks living near natural areas may need only to hang up a feeder or plant a penstemon or two for hummingbirds to appear, but even city dwellers can learn what flowering plants they might add to their gardens to make the detour worthwhile, and their efforts will usually be rewarded in time. Virtually everyone can find ways to improve the hummingbird habitat in his or her own backyard, and by doing so not only attract hummingbirds in the short term but also make a truly meaningful investment in their future. The more of us who create and maintain hummingbird gardens, the more stepping-stones of habitat across the Southwest there will be. As wildfires and development swallow up more natural areas in the future, our habitat clusters may well become increasingly valuable havens for both the birds and plants.

Much of the reason that hummingbirds frequent the areas they do is because of some remarkable flowering plants that have come to be associated with them. While many plants feature what might be considered classic hummingbird flowers, bright red in color and tubular in shape, the value of others may be much more subtle, such as providing nectar during times of seasonal shortage. Each is valuable to hummingbirds in some respect, and some largely depend upon the birds to pollinate them. In the wild, these plants tend to concentrate along drainages in the deserts and in sunny openings in mountain forests, many of them flowering in the breeding season or during migration. Whether naturally occurring or nestled in a similar niche in one's garden, the majority are veritable beacons to hummingbirds, advertising prime nectar for the taking.

The all-star hummingbird plants profiled here occur from southern California northeastward through the southern portions of Nevada, Utah, and Colorado and southward through Arizona, New Mexico, the western half of Texas, and the Mexican border states of Sonora, Chihuahua, and Coahuila. While the area covered is vast, taking in the Sonoran, Mojave, and Chihuahuan deserts together with their mountain ranges, locations throughout the region tend to share several climatic features, notably low rainfall, low humidity, intense sunlight, drying winds, and lean alkaline soils. Our commonalities within the region, along with its stark contrasts with the rest of the country, almost require a reference that focuses exclusively on our hummingbird species and their plants, and the stage on which this magnificent ballet between bird and blossom has been taking place for millennia.

Preceding the plant profiles are several informational chapters, the first an intimate glimpse into the lives of these remarkable little dynamos and the flowering plants that sustain them. Here you will learn what constitutes the ideal hummingbird flower and discover some truly special natural areas that attract hummingbirds by the thousands.

Following this primer are short life histories of each of the fourteen hummingbird species that regularly occur in the Southwest, namely Berylline, Violet-crowned, Black-chinned, Lucifer, Anna's, Costa's, Broad-billed, Magnificent, White-eared, Blue-throated, Calliope, Broad-tailed, Rufous, and Allen's Hummingbirds. (Note that the common names of the birds are capitalized, following the standards of the American Ornithologists' Union, whereas no such consensus about common plant names currently exists within the professional botany community.) Each hummingbird profile details where in the region the species can be found and at what time of year,

what special habitat needs it may have, its most important nectar plants, and its current conservation status.

Covered in the next chapter is everything you need to know about creating a hummingbird habitat. You will learn how to make any yard, whether townhouse patio or sprawling ranch, irresistible to hummingbirds, often just by adding a few plants or a lookout perch. Next, for those who may have a less-than-green thumb, is a short section about gardening with native plants that addresses finding and acquiring plants, planting and subsequent care, and coping with some of the unique challenges of gardening in the Southwest.

The gallery of native hummingbird plants follows, with in-depth profiles of 120 species from the southwestern United States and northwestern Mexico. Each features at-a-glance facts on mature size, bloom season, water use, and climate zone, a brief discussion of the plant's usefulness to hummingbirds, a description of its natural habitat, and detailed information on cultivation.

Included in the back matter are a glossary of terms, an appendix featuring a list of ways to help hummingbirds, and a brief directory of resources to consult for more information about hummingbirds and their flowers. My sincere hope is that, whether you initially picked this book up as a gardener, hiker, naturalist, or bird watcher, you will come away with a greater appreciation of our remarkable hummingbirds and their flowering plants—along with the realization that we must champion them both in order for either to thrive.

Hummingbirds and Their Flowers

CHAPTER 1

Hummingbirds *and* Their Flowers

A SHORT PRIMER

Hummingbirds have been capturing imaginations as long as there have been imaginations to capture. "Glittering fragment[s] of the rainbow," John James Audubon dubbed these most marvelous creatures, and indeed it is next to impossible to entertain a discussion about hummingbirds without waxing poetic. Many folks chart the seasons by the comings and goings of these feathered gems, and we expectantly await the first sound of whirring wings in our garden as an official proclamation of spring's arrival.

Occurring solely in the Americas, the family Trochilidae comprises about 340 species, the vast majority of which dwell in the Central and South American tropics. The most northerly hummingbirds are thought to be comparatively recent colonists that gradually followed the two predominant mountain ranges of the Sierra Madre of Mexico northward. Fourteen of the sixteen species that now regularly occur in the United States either breed in or migrate through the Southwest, and a few are year-round residents in parts of southern California and Arizona.

Long before we humans came on the scene with our artificial feeders and exotic plantings, these birds enjoyed a natural bounty of nectar from an extensive array of native plants that evolved over the course of millennia to meet their needs. Many of these specialized flowers have developed barriers to other potential pollinators such as bees and now largely depend upon hummingbirds in order to reproduce. Their fate is thereby intricately interwoven with the habits of their avian pollinators.

For hummingbirds, human beings have been a decidedly mixed blessing. Artificial feeders have enabled many birds to spend the winter in areas they formerly did not, where cold temperatures are inhospitable to many insects as well as flowering plants. Exotic plantings have had an even larger impact on geographic range. Tree tobacco (*Nicotiana glauca*) from South America and eucalyptus (*Eucalyptus* spp.) from Australia are the two most notable of these, offering winter nectar during a time of natural shortage. Both have naturalized in parts of the Southwest, and eucalyptus in particular has become invasive in some locations, choking out less assertive native plants; at the very least these exotics compete with some of the rarer natives for pollinator services.

While at first glance the birds might seem to profit from their relationship with humans, frequenting feeders and garden plantings is by no means cost-free. Pesticide poisoning, predation by domestic cats, window collisions, and bacterial infection from spoiled feeder solutions are among the potential risks associated with human habitation. Add to these concerns the vast acreage of natural habitat we devour daily—whether directly by logging and bulldozing or indirectly by overgrazing and mismanagement of water resources—and by any measure humanity's cumulative toll on the overall landscape has been substantial and far-reaching.

Perhaps hummingbirds can and will adapt to the many challenges before them. What is much easier to ascertain is that without the benefit of hummingbird pollination, many hummingbird-adapted flowers would face a grim future. As fellow inhabitants of the Southwest, we bear the responsibility to learn about its treasures, to protect remaining natural habitat for both flora and fauna, and to nurture these special plants and their pollinators, both where they occur naturally and in our gardens. By so doing, and with very little money or effort invested, we may purchase front-row seats to what must surely be one of the most fascinating spectacles in all of nature.

A GLIMPSE INTO THE WORLD OF THE HUMMINGBIRD

"Everything about a hummingbird is a superlative," Tom Colazo, a nineteenth-century naturalist, quite aptly observed. These winged wonders appear to defy physics with their astonishing aerial feats: hovering in place

for prolonged periods of time, zipping straight up, down, or sideways at will, wildly arcing courtship maneuvers, and the unique ability, even among birds, to fly backwards. In some species the sheer distance covered in migration is astounding. Whether calibrated in grams of body weight per mile or in total number of body lengths, the Rufous Hummingbird's semiannual trek between its northerly breeding limits in southern Alaska and its southern Mexican wintering grounds outdistances that of all other avian migrants.

As one might imagine, such dazzling capabilities require a tremendous amount of energy. In forward flight the wings may beat up to 80 times per second, in courtship aerobatics as much as 200 times per second. The heart is the largest in relation to body size of any bird, and depending upon ambient temperature and the bird's activity level beats from 420 to 1,250 times per minute, the fastest in the animal kingdom with the exception of some shrews. To conserve energy, particularly during long cold nights or periods of food shortage, hummingbirds have the unique ability to become torpid. That is to say, their respiration and heart rate are lowered and the body temperature drops. Come morning the bird gradually comes out of the torpor and, understandably, makes a beeline for the nearest refueling spot.

The fuel that it seeks comes in the form of high-sucrose nectar obtained from flowering plants along with the protein and other nutrients provided by small insects, the latter mostly gleaned from foliage, plucked from spider webs, or hawked in the air. Accessing nectar with a grooved, fork-tipped tongue that is about one-and-a-half times the length of the bill, a hummingbird may consume as much as two to three times its body weight in fluids each day, the liquid food fully digested in as little as twenty minutes. To meet its daily nutritional needs, an Anna's Hummingbird must catch thirty to forty small flies and visit over 1,000 flowers! If energy demands are light and nectar is abundant, the bird may rest between feeding bouts, a luxury that territorial males or incubating females may not often enjoy. In the evening or with approaching inclement weather, birds tend to feed more heavily, consuming up to a milliliter or so of nectar that is stored in a crop-like pocket in the throat and slowly digested overnight.

Gender is everything to a hummingbird. If one happens to be born a female, she can look forward to the harried life of a single mother, with sole responsibility for building a nest, incubating her typically two eggs (managing to feed herself while she does so), and rearing nestlings. The young are fed a diet consisting almost exclusively of partly digested insects at first, with nectar added as the time to leave the nest approaches. Each cycle, from egg laying to fledging, takes thirty to forty-five days depending upon the species, after which the young usually remain dependent upon their mother for two to three weeks. During this orientation period they first learn the art of catching insects and then the particulars of garnering flower nectar. Females of most species usually rear two broods per season, some even three, although farther north one clutch is more typical. Observers have reported instances of fledglings from the first brood being fed by their mother as she incubates eggs at a second nest.

A male, on the other hand, need not be concerned with such mundane duties, focusing wholly on defending a feeding territory for himself and wooing potential females with extravagant dive displays, typically mating with numerous partners over the course of a breeding season. Essentially, the male serves as a gene pool enhancement machine, his fundamental purpose being to spread his own DNA around as liberally as possible. Being a male also means one gets to wear the full dress uniform, the glittering regalia of the species. The iridescent patch of plumage on the male's throat known as the gorget is usually the showiest part of the bird, and depending upon how the feathers are angled can work magic with refracted light to create a shimmering kaleidoscope of color.

Breeding male hummingbirds are notoriously pugnacious, brooking no interlopers on their proclaimed territory. Occasionally, individual males may become so intent on driving away other birds that they themselves have little chance to feed and may go hungry. Even after the breeding cycle has ended and birds move southward, males of some species may defend patches of nectar-bearing plants along the way. Adult females and then immature birds tend to follow a few weeks later, all flying solo during the daytime hours and congregating only where unavoidable at especially rich or concentrated food sources. Depending upon the species and the resources available at a particular stopover, birds may linger from one or two days to a couple of weeks before continuing their journey. Rufous Hummingbirds, which travel the longest distances, prepare for each leg of their trip by feeding almost constantly for about two weeks, often nearly doubling their body weight in stored fat.

In western North America, large numbers of southbound migrants tend to concentrate along several main corridors—the Sierra Nevada and Coast ranges of California (which see even more traffic in spring), the Southern Rocky Mountains, the Sierra Madre Occidental, and to a lesser extent the Sierra Madre Oriental—where they take advantage of flower-filled meadows birthed by summer rains. Many birds also track southward along river valleys or cross expanses of desert to get from one mountain range to another, appearing at garden plantings throughout the region during these late summer peregrinations. These clusters of productive albeit artificial habitat, especially those that serve as stepping stones across the desert, can loom large in importance for migrating hummingbirds.

For most of the species that breed north of the Mexican border, the eventual destination in autumn is central southwestern Mexico. There they must compete with resident hummingbirds for nectar resources until the lengthening days of late winter trigger hormones that urge them to return to the breeding grounds and begin the whole cycle anew.

With good fortune, the average individual can expect a life span of about three to five years, although records exist of recaptured banded birds up to twelve years old. While eggs and nestlings commonly fall prey to snakes and a variety of birds, including jays, ravens, and orioles, adult hummingbirds have virtually no common natural predators and away from human habitations are more likely to succumb to weather-related events such as droughts, freezes, or severe storms. Among the relatively few documented instances of natural predation mentioned in the scientific literature are American Kestrel, Merlin, Sharp-shinned Hawk, Brown-crested Flycatcher, Loggerhead Shrike, Greater Roadrunner, Green Heron, and Acorn Woodpecker, with orb-weaver spiders, praying mantises, and frogs known to take an occasional victim as well.

Hummingbirds are blessed with excellent memories, not only returning to the exact spot on their breeding grounds each year (and often on the same

date) but also visiting many of the very same flower patches and feeding areas along their migratory route. This remarkable consistency is no doubt one of the more important operative traits interlaced with the parallel evolution of our magnificent array of hummingbird-pollinated flowers.

A BIRD'S-EYE VIEW OF PLANT POLLINATION

The sole purpose of a flower is reproduction, to perpetuate the species by creating seeds that will disperse and populate some plot of earth. To achieve this end requires a bit of assistance from wind, winged creatures, or ants. Wind pollination, the only method that existed until true flowering plants evolved, is fairly straightforward: the wind blows, thereby transferring pollen from the stamen, or male organ, of a plant to the pistil, or female organ, of that or another plant. Once pollination has occurred the ovary of the plant then initiates the production of seeds. Palms, coniferous trees, and grasses are examples of this ancient but rather haphazard system of reproduction. As pollinators, winged creatures are much trickier to entice but generally a great deal more thorough in their execution. The idea is to finagle the helper into contacting the flower's stamen in such a way that the flier departs bearing pollen on its body that it will deposit on the pistil of the next flower it visits.

The vast majority of flowering plants is pollinated by insects, notably bees, wasps, butterflies, moths, beetles, and flies, with a relatively few pollinated by bats or birds. Bees are by far the most important insect pollinators, and many familiar flowering plants have evolved specifically to ensnare their services, with a profusion of blossoms, bright colors, sweet fragrances, landing platforms, and lavish markings that direct them to their nectar reward. Plants that depend on other insects or animals for pollination have features specifically targeted to their particular pollinator's preferences. Examples are the flat clusters of short-tubed flowers such as milkweeds and verbenas that are adapted to butterflies, or the fragrant, pale-petaled blooms of tufted evening primrose that are pollinated by sphinx moths.

Hummingbird-pollinated plants are comparatively new on the scene, originating in and most developed in South America and still in the process of evolving in North America. As pollinators, hummingbirds have several inherent advantages over insects. Not only can they travel great distances in the course of a day, thereby distributing pollen to a wider genetic pool of plants, but they are also extremely dependable and can be counted on to be at a given place at a certain time of year. Moreover, because they are warm-blooded—unlike insects—they feed throughout the daylight hours regardless of rainy or cloudy weather.

A number of our plant families favored by hummingbirds were originally bee-pollinated, such as the penstemons (*Penstemon* spp.), with a large segment of its membership now fully adapted to hummingbirds. Indeed, these maverick penstemons serve as excellent examples of what constitutes the ideal hummingbird flower. The bee-pollinated penstemons tend to be in the pink-purple-blue end of the spectrum, while their hummingbird-pollinated counterparts are red or orange, colors that are not readily visible to most insects but that hummingbirds can easily spot. Flowers pollinated by bees tend to be either very small or, if larger, puffy enough for a bee to climb into, with flat lips that serve as a landing surface; they are often sweetly fragrant. Hummingbird-adapted penstemons, on the other hand, have relatively narrow tubular flowers, with petal lips that are often recurved to prevent insects from landing. They are typically held horizontally or are pendulous, so the nectar sipper must be able to hover while feeding, and they rarely have any fragrance, an unnecessary trait as hummingbirds have little to no olfactory sense. Often the stamens and the stigma (the receptive end of the pistil) extend past the flower, so that pollen will collect on the hummingbird's forehead or bill as it probes the flower tube and then dust the necessary parts of another flower.

Perhaps the most important distinguishing characteristic of hummingbird-pollinated flowers is their copious nectar. Not only is it typically much more abundant than in those pollinated by bees or other insects, but it is veritably packed with sucrose, at syrupy-sweet concentrations that generally range between twenty and thirty percent sugar by weight, with a few to forty percent and beyond. The remainder of the solution consists of water and small amounts of electrolytes.

Given an array of flower choices, hummingbirds demonstrate a decided preference for those with the highest concentration of sucrose and most abundant yield over all other factors. While they certainly partake of many flowers with lower nectar concentrations, particularly when other sources are scarce, their daily lives do not tend to revolve around them as much as with prime sugar spigots such as the red sages (*Salvia*), columbines (*Aquilegia*), penstemons (*Keckiella, Penstemon*), Indian paintbrushes (*Castilleja*), and certain larkspurs (*Delphinium*).

Some of the other genera with multiple classic hummingbird-adapted plants are desert-honeysuckle (*Anisacanthus*), monkeyflower *(Diplacus, Mimulus)*, gilia (*Aliciella, Ipomopsis*), hyssop (*Agastache*), justicia (*Justicia*), honeysuckle (*Lonicera*), currant (*Ribes*), ocotillo (*Fouquieria*), and lobelia (*Lobelia*). Many of these plants flower during times of critical need for particular hummingbirds, such as during the breeding season or in winter, while others time their bloom to coincide with when a great number of individuals are passing through, such as in late summer. In some cases two or more plant species sharing a habitat have even evolved to flower sequentially over the course of a season, thereby concentrating the pollinators' efforts at each respective species when it is in peak bloom.

Flowers that are primarily pollinated by bats, such as many agaves, crank out huge quantities of nectar in comparison to hummingbird-adapted plants, but rather than sucrose the main component is glucose. While hummingbirds ordinarily demonstrate a decided preference for sucrose-dominated nectars, they are by no means so persnickety as to ignore the glucose wellspring of a blooming agave. The smorgasbord of small insects that such plants offer is a powerful attractant as well. Indeed, many recorded sightings of hummingbirds visiting atypical flowers such as bluebonnets or sunflowers that produce comparatively little nectar may well be instances of the birds gleaning insects from the plants. Hummingbirds are said to be least fond of fructose, the primary component of the nectar of many Old World flowers pollinated by sunbirds and other passerines, but particularly in winter may use fructose producers like aloes heavily.

The quintessential hummingbird flower, in summary, will usually be red, reddish-pink, orange, or yellow (and yes, there exist a number of blue, purple, and even white exceptions to this rule). It will be tubular in shape and will dangle or be held horizontally, and it may have petal lobes that reflex backward to prevent insects from landing. It will produce nectar with a concentration of at least 20 percent sugar by weight, with the sugar composition averaging about 75 percent sucrose. The daily yield typically will be between two and four milligrams of sugar, or from five to fifty microliters of solution. Large patches of any such flowers are likely to draw a profusion of hummingbirds during peak migration.

MIGRATORY CORRIDORS AND OTHER CRITICAL NATURAL AREAS

The conduits that probably ushered hummingbirds into the United States in the first place, namely the north–south cordilleras of the Sierra Madre of Mexico, continue to be important travel corridors today. The border species in particular, whose ranges barely tiptoe into Arizona, New Mexico, and

Texas, are present-day examples of birds that have followed these mountain ranges to their northern limits and continued no farther.

The Arizona sky islands that many of these northerly ranks of their species call home are also rich in breeding birds of their own. Jutting abruptly above the desert to elevations of 10,000 feet, these border ranges are among the most diversely vegetated places in our entire country. The watered canyons of these mountains support staggering numbers of hummingbirds and all fourteen species in this book either breed in them or pass through on a yearly basis. Ramsey and Miller Canyons in the Huachuca Mountains, Madera Canyon in the Santa Rita Mountains, and Cave Creek Canyon in the Chiricahua Mountains are unquestionably the crown jewels of these and should be musts on the itinerary of any hummingbird enthusiast who visits southeast Arizona. Much of the prime habitat here lies within national forests so largely benefits from that protection.

The same cannot be said for riparian corridors in the area, nor of those in the entire Southwest for that matter. Like all creatures attempting to eke out a living in the desert, we humans must congregate around water for our very survival. If we continue to insist on having our sod and our sprinklers as well, however, once-great rivers such as the San Pedro will continue to dry up and the few remaining riparian gallery forests will eventually fall—along with the understory plants that they cradle. As if dropping water tables were not enough, many potentially still verdant streamsides must also contend with livestock trampling vegetation, compacting soil, and causing bank erosion. If one is lucky enough to find a yet unspoiled creek somewhere, where veritable hedgerows of flowering plants offer a bounty of nectar for hummingbirds, the point is suddenly driven home. Violet-crowned Hummingbirds, along with other species that depend on these dwindling riparian habitats, face some worrisome challenges unless human attitudes and practices change dramatically.

Coastal areas of southern California are also under siege, their once-extensive coast sage scrub habitat already all but eliminated and the interior valleys quickly being swallowed up by development. Hummingbird-adapted plants such as fuchsia-flowering gooseberry (*Ribes speciosum*) may soon become rare in the wild, setting the stage for a sorry twist of irony whereby the early-breeding Anna's Hummingbird may eventually have to depend on exotic plantings of tree tobacco and eucalyptus rather than the natives with which it coevolved. The Coast, Transverse, and Peninsular ranges, wherever they are either protected or impractical to develop, continue to provide essential habitat for breeding birds, spring migrants, and post-breeding wanderers. Unfortunately, prolonged extreme drought and devastating wildfires are an increasing and oft-looming threat to these vital remnant native plant communities.

Of all the corridors used by hummingbirds in the United States, the southern Rocky Mountains rank foremost in the number of travelers they accommodate, with thousands of birds at a time reported in late summer at feeding stations from Colorado to southern New Mexico and Arizona. A great many birds stick to the high ground, leapfrogging from one mountain meadow to another, whereas others exploit gardens and feeders in foothills and valleys. Many plants that are specifically adapted to hummingbirds synchronize their peak bloom with this huge influx of their pollinators, such as scarlet gilia (*Ipomopsis aggregata*), beardlip penstemon (*Penstemon barbatus*), and Mexican catchfly (*Silene laciniata*). Much of the high elevation habitat in the southern Rockies lies within national forests, but such areas are often at the mercy of fire suppression policies that are likely eventually to result in a locally catastrophic fire. Overgrazing by livestock is also an issue in many locations. Fortunately the vast size of this corridor helps somewhat to mitigate such threats, but rare plants with restricted ranges are especially vulnerable.

Researchers at the Arizona-Sonora Desert Museum have been working for a number of years to identify and inventory areas south of the border in Sonora, Mexico, that are important to migrating hummingbirds, particularly the Rufous Hummingbird. They have found that the birds tend to use five main routes, three in early spring and two in late summer, and have catalogued the predominant hummingbird plants that characterize each of these "nectar corridors." Habitat types vary widely, from Sonoran Desert scrub in the lowlands to high-elevation spruce-fir forest in the Sierra Madre Occidental, but what they all seem to share is an uncertain future. Clearing of land for development and the widespread planting of the highly invasive African buffelgrass (*Pennisetum ciliare*) for livestock grazing are mentioned as some of the more far-reaching threats to hummingbird habitat in parts of northern Mexico, where many landowners unfortunately seem to be following in some of our own misguided footsteps.

The more compromised and fragmented the landscape becomes, in both the United States and Mexico, the more difficult it is for hummingbirds to find enough suitable stopover habitat to be able to complete their yearly migrations, and some biologists believe that these pressures may be adversely affecting hummingbirds even more than changes on either their breeding or wintering grounds. Especially during times of severe drought, even a tiny oasis of habitat offering flowering plants that provide nectar can mean the difference between life and death to a migrating hummingbird—particularly when crossing broad expanses of mostly barren desert.

We human beings hold most if not all of the cards, and are in a position if we so desire to make decisions that can positively impact the future of these critical habitats and the fascinating birds they support. To spiritual people through the ages, the hummingbird has signified joy, and indeed that is what they bring us. We can make an effort to encourage their favored plants in our gardens so that they might continue to grace us with their magic, but we can never truly duplicate the delicate dance between bird and flower that happens naturally in the very special wild places that cry out for our protection. Our grandchildren—and theirs—deserve the opportunity to appreciate it too.

CHAPTER 2

Hummingbirds *of the* Southwest

The profiles that follow cover all fourteen of the hummingbird species that breed in or regularly occur in the southwestern United States, and are arranged in alphabetical order by their currently accepted taxonomic name. Each profile begins with a description of the bird's geographic range, migratory habits, and time of the year when it is most likely to be seen. Next is a discussion of preferred breeding habitat, with detailed information on plants used for nesting, followed by a comprehensive breakdown of nectar plants used by season. Concluding each profile are notes on the conservation status of each hummingbird species.

BERYLLINE HUMMINGBIRD—*Amazilia beryllina*

VERY FEW OF US HAVE A PRAYER OF HOSTING THIS RUFOUS-WINGED, emerald-throated beauty in the garden, as it just barely occurs in the United States. Its stronghold here (if it can even be called that) is in the Huachuca, Santa Rita, and Chiricahua mountains of southeast Arizona, where it has been known to breed, but it has also been recorded in Guadalupe Canyon on the Arizona–New Mexico–Sonora border and in the Animas and Mimbres valleys of southwestern New Mexico. Outside of this limited area it is observed very rarely north of Mexico, those sightings all from the Davis Mountains and Big Bend National Park in west Texas.

These northern pioneers of the species are migratory, departing for their Mexican wintering grounds in September and returning in May or June, but most of the population is fairly sedentary, from southern Sonora and

Chihuahua southward to Honduras and El Salvador. In Mexico, the Berylline is usually encountered in oak or pine–oak woodlands in the foothills of the Sierra Madre Occidental, but in the United States is most often seen in canyons lined with Arizona sycamore (*Platanus wrightii*) and bigtooth maple (*Acer grandidentatum*). Males are quite territorial, perching on an exposed twig in the subcanopy to vocalize. The majority of the few nests that have been located in Arizona have been in Arizona sycamores, with one noted in an alligator juniper (*Juniperus deppeana*), and are typically affixed to bare twigs and sheltered from above by overhanging branches. In Mexico, oaks (*Quercus* spp.), pines (*Pinus* spp.), and a variety of shrubs are also commonly used. The exterior of the nest is thickly decorated with bits of lichen as camouflage, sometimes in varying shades of green and others in multiple colors that give the appearance of confetti. After breeding, birds often descend to lower elevations, where they linger a few weeks before migrating southward.

Very little information is available about particular plants used by Beryllines in the United States, but firecracker bush (*Bouvardia ternifolia*), Arizona thistle (*Cirsium arizonicum*), Palmer's agave (*Agave palmeri*), coral bells (*Heuchera sanguinea*), sage (*Salvia* spp.), and New Mexico locust (*Robinia neomexicana*) have been mentioned. While the species reportedly consumes a relatively large number of insects, doubtless many additional nectar plants are visited as well.

In Sonora, birds have been observed at limita (*Anisacanthus andersonii*), wild jícama (*Ipomoea bracteata*), and scarlet betony (*Stachys coccinea*) in early spring; hierba del piojo (*Mandevilla foliosa*) and pea vine (*Cologania angustifolia*) in summer; Lemmon's sage (*Salvia lemmonii*), bat-faced cuphea (*Cuphea llavea*), bonita zinnia (*Zinnia peruviana*), and stevia (*Stevia plummerae*) in late summer and fall; and pineapple sage (*Salvia elegans*) and tree morning glory (*Ipomoea arborescens*) in late fall and winter.

Plants important to Berylline Hummingbirds dwelling even further south are cinnabar sage (*Salvia cinnabarina*), powder puff (*Calliandra anomala*), tropical mistletoe (*Psittacanthus calyculatus*), Turk's cap (*Malvaviscus arboreus*), pochote (*Ceiba aesculifolia*), and tarritos (*Lemairocereus thurberi*).

Within its broad geographical range, the Berylline seems to be fairly stable, and fortunately most if not its entire known nesting habitat in our country lies within protected forests. Its attraction to feeding stations, however, while certainly helpful in times of natural nectar shortages, does carry with it the associated risks of cat predation, window collision, and exposure to toxic pesticides.

VIOLET-CROWNED HUMMINGBIRD—*Amazilia violiceps*

THE VIOLET-CROWNED HUMMINGBIRD IS ANOTHER SOUTHEAST ARIZONA species that rarely ranges far from the sycamore-lined canyons where it prefers to breed. There it occurs regularly, albeit in small numbers, from Sonoita Creek in Arizona eastward to Guadalupe Canyon on the border of southeast Arizona and southwestern New Mexico, with the bulk of the population residing along the Pacific slope of the Sierra Madre Occidental in Mexico. Most Arizona birds retreat southward in the winter, usually departing in September, but a few may overwinter at area feeding stations and rare birds have been known to turn up at feeders as far west as California and east to the Texas Gulf Coast. The bird's immaculate white underparts and red-orange bill are often more easily seen than the blue-violet crown for which it is named. These sprightly birds love to bathe and may visit a garden to take advantage of a mist sprayer or other water source.

Whereas individuals in the Patagonia, Arizona, area regularly arrive in February, most of this northern contingent of the population does not return until May or June, the nesting cycle timed to coincide with the summer monsoons that will bring to life a cornucopia of nectar plants and associated insects. In Mexico, birds frequent a variety of habitats but are most commonly found in dense scrub along streams in canyons or foothills. Both males and females vigorously defend feeding territories, making use of lookout posts such as spent flower stalks of agaves to watch for interlopers. In the United States, all nests discovered thus far have been built on a horizontal branch or fork of Arizona sycamore (*Platanus wrightii*). The lichen-camouflaged nest is composed of various plant fibers, often including feathery plumes from the seed heads of Apache plume (*Fallugia paradoxa*) or western virgin's bower (*Clematis ligusticifolia*). The northern population rears only one brood each summer, afterward remaining in the region several weeks before moving southward to southern Sonora.

In June and July a primary source of nectar is Schott's agave (*Agave schottii*), whose blooms begin opening as birds arrive on the breeding grounds. Parry's and Palmer's agaves (*A. parryi, A. palmeri*) start flowering shortly thereafter and are likewise heavily used throughout the summer.

Other natives visited by northern Violet-crowneds include scarlet betony (*Stachys coccinea*), desert-honeysuckle (*Anisacanthus thurberi*), superb penstemon (*Penstemon superbus*), ocotillo (*Fouquieria splendens*), firecracker bush

(*Bouvardia ternifolia*), southwest coral bean (*Erythrina flabelliformis*), Huachuca Mountain paintbrush (*Castilleja patriotica*), Arizona thistle (*Cirsium arizonicum*), and Lemmon's sage (*Salvia lemmonii*).

In Mexico, birds have also been recorded at limita (*Anisacanthus andersonii*), tree ocotillo (*Fouquieria macdougalii*), Maycoba and pineapple sages (*Salvia betulifolia, S. elegans*), tree morning glory (*Ipomoea arborescens*), wild jícama (*Ipomoea bracteata*), bat-faced cuphea (*Cuphea llavea*), hierba del piojo (*Mandevilla foliosa*), bonita zinnia (*Zinnia peruviana*), palo chino (*Havardia mexicana*), and wild tobacco (*Nicotiana obtusifolia*).

In Arizona and New Mexico, the species is listed as threatened, its limited occurrence dependent upon the continued availability of suitable riparian habitat. While populations in Mexico currently appear to be fairly stable, overgrazing, development, forest fires, and human-associated risks such as cat predation are among the potential threats to the future of this dapper and energetic bird in our own country.

17

BLACK-CHINNED HUMMINGBIRD—*Archilochus alexandri*

This jaunty little dynamo reigns over much of the Southwest, that is, until the Rufous Hummingbird comes to town. Not at all shy toward humans, it will breed in well-treed residential areas if proper habitat exists and is a familiar patron of feeders and garden plantings in late summer throughout much of the region. Most numerous in southern Arizona and New Mexico and far west Texas, the Black-chinned can be found from coastal California northward to just past the Canadian border, and eastward through Utah, western and southern Colorado, and the western half of Texas.

Wintering almost exclusively in central and western Mexico, birds begin to return to the breeding grounds in March, not reaching the northern states until late April or early May. Males quickly establish territories along riparian corridors and desert washes, often on slopes where spent flower stalks of agave (*Agave* spp.), yucca (*Yucca* spp.), or sotol (*Dasylirion* spp.) provide superior vantage points from which to survey a favorite feeding patch. Females arrive soon afterward and get right down to the business of nest building. Preferred sites include Arizona and California sycamores (*Platanus wrightii, P. racemosa*), boxelder (*Acer negundo*), Arizona cypress (*Cupressus arizonica*), alligator juniper (*Juniperus deppeana*), native willows (*Salix* spp.), and various oaks (*Quercus* spp.). Where sycamores are available, the nest is composed almost entirely of plant down from the undersides of their leaves. According to biologists, about two out of three nesting attempts do not succeed, owing largely to nest predators. After the breeding season individuals make their way southward, some first moving to higher elevations to forage in montane meadows. Most depart the United States by late October.

Because these birds occur over such a broad geographic range, the list of nectar plants visited is predictably gargantuan, but some generalizations are possible. Important spring flowers include the early-blooming penstemons (*Penstemon centranthifolius, P. eatonii, P. havardii, P. parryi, P. superbus*), desert-honeysuckle (*Anisacanthus thurberi*), hummingbird sage (*Salvia spathacea*), chuparosa (*Justicia californica*), ocotillo (*Fouquieria splendens*), New Mexico thistle (*Cirsium neomexicanum*), manzanita (*Arctostaphylos* spp.), and wolfberry (*Lycium* spp.).

Locally significant are Sierra Madre lobelia (*Lobelia laxiflora*), Mexican buckeye (*Ungnadia speciosa*), desert ironwood (*Olneya tesota*), palo verde (*Parkinsonia* spp.), desert-willow (*Chilopsis linearis*), Indian warrior (*Pedicularis densiflora*), and claretcup cacti (*Echinocereus* spp.).

Heading the list of late spring and summer staples are the early-blooming agaves (*Agave havardiana, A. lechuguilla, A. schottii*) and Indian paintbrushes, particularly southwestern paintbrush (*Castilleja integra*), followed by scarlet gilia (*Ipomopsis aggregata*), scarlet larkspur (*Delphinium cardinale*), scarlet creeper (*Ipomoea cristulata*), and Arizona thistle (*Cirsium arizonicum*).

From late summer to fall, birds especially seek out Palmer's and Parry's agaves (*Agave palmeri, A. parryi*), narrowleaf desert-honeysuckle (*Anisacanthus linearis*), the summer-blooming penstemons (*Penstemon barbatus, P. pinifolius*), Lemmon's and mountain sages (*Salvia lemmonii, S. regla*), firecracker bush (*Bouvardia ternifolia*), cardinal flower (*Lobelia cardinalis*), and Rocky Mountain bee plant (*Peritoma serrulata*).

In Sonora, researchers have also recorded Black-chinneds at Huachuca Mountain paintbrush (*Castilleja patriotica*) and Maycoba and pineapple sages (*Salvia betulifolia, S. elegans*) in the fall, and at uvalama (*Vitex mollis*) and scarlet betony (*Stachys coccinea*) in spring.

Although the Black-chinned Hummingbird may demonstrate a preference for riparian habitats that face increasing pressures from development and long-term drought, its supreme adaptability and apparent tolerance of human habitation would seem to bode well for its future.

LUCIFER HUMMINGBIRD—*Calothorax lucifer*

O CCURRING IN THE UNITED STATES REGULARLY only in the Chisos and Davis Mountains of west Texas and in desert mountains of southeast Arizona and southwest New Mexico, this handsome fellow sports a rakish, purple-plated gorget and a long, downward-curving bill. In both locales it is present only during the breeding season, sometimes lingering at higher or lower elevations in the vicinity until late summer but generally departing for its wintering grounds in central Mexico—where the bulk of the population resides—by October. Though not prone to wandering far, and in fact to date no individuals have been known to venture beyond the borders of the three U.S. states in which they normally occur, vagrants have been recorded at feeders in Tucson, Silver City, El Paso, and east to Rockport.

These northern birds arrive on their breeding grounds in late March or April, the Texas birds following the Sierra Madre Oriental northward and their Arizona–New Mexico counterparts hugging the Sierra Madre Occidental. Foothill canyons, seasonal washes, and steep slopes are among the preferred habitats, where the female builds a nest over which the male will perform display flights. In Texas, the most common nest sites are the horizontal stems of tree cholla (*Cylindropuntia imbricata*), the dried pods on spent stalks of lechuguilla (*Agave lechuguilla*), and later in the season the leafy stems of ocotillo (*Fouquieria splendens*). All three plants are nectar sources as well. In New Mexico and northeastern Sonora, nests have been recorded in walkingstick cholla (*Cylindropuntia spinosior*), Arizona sycamore (*Platanus wrightii*), and oak (*Quercus* spp.). Birds often roost in the shade of spiny hackberry (*Celtis pallida*), a low, spreading tree. Whether perching or feeding, the Lucifer Hummingbird generally frequents middle to lower level vegetation.

Upon their arrival in early spring, Texas birds often visit the small but profuse flowers of Mexican buckeye (*Ungnadia speciosa*) until more favored plants begin to bloom. Havard's penstemon (*Penstemon havardii*) and woolly paintbrush (*Castilleja lanata*) then furnish most of the nectar in April and May. Ocotillo (*Fouquieria splendens*) is widely visited but of varying importance because in some locations the nectar reserves are depleted by carpenter bees. Havard's agave (*Agave havardii*) comes into bloom in May at lower elevations, a veritable spigot of nectar and associated insects until midsummer,

when narrowleaf desert-honeysuckle (*Anisacanthus linearis*) and then flame acanthus (*A. quadrifidus*) are important staples depending upon location.

Some other plants visited at various times include southwestern and bracted paintbrushes (*Castilleja integra, C. latebracteata*), desert-willow (*Chilopsis linearis*), yellow bells (*Tecoma stans* var. *angustata*), snapdragon vine (*Maurandella antirrhiniflora*), cardinal flower (*Lobelia cardinalis*), firecracker bush (*Bouvardia ternifolia*), mountain sage (*Salvia regla*), desert savior (*Echeveria strictiflora*), thistle (*Cirsium* spp.), and prairie larkspur (*Delphinium virescens*).

Information on additional plants important to Arizona and New Mexico birds is thin, but Parry's and superb penstemons (*Penstemon parryi, P. superbus*) and New Mexico and Arizona thistles (*Cirsium neomexicanum, C. arizonicum*) are mentioned, and Schott's and Palmer's agaves (*Agave schottii, A. palmeri*) are presumed. Sierra Madre lobelia (*Lobelia laxiflora*), espinosilla (*Loeselia mexicana*), and Mexican sage (*Salvia mexicana*) are widely visited in Mexico.

The Lucifer Hummingbird enjoys a measure of insulation from human encroachment in Big Bend National Park, where about one hundred birds reside, but populations in other areas may be more vulnerable to disturbance.

ANNA'S HUMMINGBIRD—*Calypte anna*

California is this strapping bird's stronghold, but it also occurs northward along the Pacific Coast to British Columbia and increasingly from southern Arizona to west Texas as well, there largely in irrigated residential areas with lush plantings of exotic flowers. In good light, the signature fluorescent rose-pink cowl of the male is distinctive. Often heard before seen, it is quite vocal in its defense of feeding territories. Breeding begins remarkably early, in October in Arizona, November in California, and February in the Pacific Northwest. In some locations birds may nest nearly year-round. Afterward, individuals range widely and through fall regularly appear both north and east of the breeding range, in Nevada, central and southeast Arizona, southern New Mexico, and west Texas, with vagrants recorded from Alaska to New York.

The Anna's Hummingbird rules the chaparral and coast sage scrub communities, where it establishes territories with up to ten conspicuous perches that afford strategic views of flower banks. Southern California females strongly prefer coast live oaks (*Quercus agrifolia*) for their nests, with California sycamore (*Platanus racemosa*) occasionally used, while birds farther north in Santa Cruz use exotic eucalyptus trees (*Eucalyptus amygdalina*) almost exclusively. Arizona birds typically nest in blue palo verde (*Parkinsonia florida*), velvet mesquite (*Prosopis velutina*), or sweet acacia (*Acacia farnesiana*), with assorted shrubs and vines used on occasion. In the Phoenix metro area, birds often use exotic pines (*Pinus* spp.). The nest is composed of plant fibers from a variety of sources including cattail (*Typha* spp.), willow (*Salix* spp.), sycamore (*Platanus* spp.), and thistle (*Cirsium* spp.).

During late fall and early winter, chaparral currant (*Ribes malvaceum*) is the primary native nectar source for California birds, with fuchsia-flowering gooseberry (*Ribes speciosum*) taking over that role when it begins to bloom in December or January. Many biologists believe that this hummingbird-pollinated gooseberry, offering abundant nectar just as young birds are fledging, might have coevolved with the unusual winter breeding cycle of Anna's Hummingbird, who also relies heavily on insects.

Other important winter nectar sources worthy of mention are bigberry manzanita (*Arctostaphylos glauca*), bladderpod spiderflower (*Peritoma arborea*), and Indian warrior (*Pedicularis densiflora*).

In spring, fuchsia-flowering gooseberry continues to provide important nectar, but in addition birds rely heavily on southern bush monkeyflower (*Diplacus longiflorus*), hummingbird sage (*Salvia spathacea*), and the bee-pollinated sages (*Salvia apiana, S. leucophylla, S. mellifera*).

Heart-leafed penstemon (*Keckiella cordifolia*) and woolly blue curls (*Trichostema lanatum*) become of major importance in late spring and early summer, with scarlet bugler (*Penstemon centranthifolius*), Mexican catchfly (*Silene laciniata*), California figwort (*Scrophularia californica*), and Indian paintbrush (*Castilleja* spp.) also widely visited.

In midsummer and fall, hummingbird trumpet (*Epilobium canum*) ranks first in importance, followed by western columbine (*Aquilegia formosa*), scarlet monkeyflower (*Mimulus cardinalis*), and scarlet keckiella (*Keckiella ternata*).

Arizona birds are known to use pointleaf manzanita (*Arctostaphylos pungens*), Parry's penstemon (*Penstemon parryi*), and Palmer's agave (*Agave palmeri*), and in Sonora have been recorded at scarlet betony (*Stachys coccinea*), tree ocotillo (*Fouquieria macdougalii*), and tree morning glory (*Ipomoea arborescens*).

Its adaptability to human habitats may ensure a rosy future for the Anna's Hummingbird, but with what little remains of its chaparral habitat, the same cannot be said for the native plants that depend upon it for pollination.

COSTA'S HUMMINGBIRD—*Calypte costae*

THIS FAMILIAR SPRITE OF SONORAN DESERT WASHES MANAGES TO EKE out a living in the harshest of habitats, the males bedecked with a long, extravagantly flaring, purple gorget. Most common in southwestern Arizona, southeastern California, and Mexico from Baja California to northwestern Sonora, breeding birds can also be found along the California coast north to about Monterey, in the Mojave Desert of southern Nevada and northwest Arizona, and locally in southeast Arizona and southwest New Mexico. Sonoran Desert birds typically exit their breeding territories during the summer months, some moving northward along the Pacific Coast and others heading southward, further inland, and/or up in elevation. Rarely, vagrants have strayed as far northward as Alaska and eastward to Kansas.

The breeding season varies somewhat according to location, but most populations tend to nest from February or March to May or June. Choice territories include several lookout perches, such as foothills palo verde (*Parkinsonia microphylla*), desert ironwood (*Olneya tesota*), saguaro (*Carnegiea gigantea*), or acacia (*Acacia* spp.), and an abundance of favored flowering plants. This opportunistic species has been known to nest in a dizzying variety of trees and shrubs, but the most preferred are foothills palo verde, blue palo verde (*Parkinsonia florida*), and jojoba (*Simmondsia chinensis*). Desert ironwood, ocotillo (*Fouquieria splendens*), cholla (*Cylindropuntia echinocarpa, C. ramosissima*), catclaw acacia (*Acacia greggii*), and desert-willow (*Chilopsis linearis*) are other commonly used plants.

At the very top of the list of important nectar plants is chuparosa (*Justicia californica*), flowering stands of which are vigorously defended by males in early spring as well as being a critical source of nectar in midwinter. Ocotillo ranks a close second among other key spring bloomers, followed by penstemon (*Penstemon eatoni, P. parryi, P. pseudospectabilis, P. subulatus, P. superbus*), wolfberry (*Lycium parishii* in January, *L. exsertum* in February, *L. andersonii* in March), bladderpod spiderflower (*Peritoma arborea*), desert lavender (*Hyptis emoryi*), desert agave (*Agave deserti*), and pink fairy duster (*Calliandra eriophylla*).

Other plants widely visited during the nesting season include desert-honeysuckle (*Anisacanthus thurberi*), desert milkweed (*Asclepias subulata*), foothills palo verde, saguaro, desert-willow, ironwood, agave (*Agave chrysantha, A. palmeri*), southwest coral bean (*Erythrina flabelliformis*), and cholla (*Cylindropuntia acanthocarpa, C. fulgida*).

California coastal birds depend on some different plants, the most important being woolly blue curls (*Trichostema lanatum*), the bee-pollinated sages (*Salvia apiana, S. leucophylla, S. mellifera*), scarlet bugler (*Penstemon centranthifolius*), bush monkeyflower (*Diplacus aurantiacus, D. longiflorus*), and scarlet larkspur (*Delphinium cardinale*).

In Sonora, researchers have recorded birds visiting tree morning glory (*Ipomoea arborescens*), wild jícama (*Ipomoea bracteata*), red justicia (*Justicia candicans*), Mexican desert lavender (*Hyptis albida*), palo chino (*Havardia mexicana*), tree ocotillo (*Fouquieria macdougalii*), scarlet betony (*Stachys coccinea*), galloping and organ pipe cacti (*Stenocereus alamosensis, S. thurberi*), cardón (*Pachycereus pringlei*), rama parda (*Ruellia californica*), agave (*Agave angustifolia*), uvalama (*Vitex mollis*), and honey mesquite (*Prosopis glandulosa*).

Costa's Hummingbirds definitely face some challenges in the future. Development has swallowed up most of their coast sage habitat in California, with Sonoran Desert habitat in southern Arizona going much the same way, and in many sprawling metropolitan areas the dominant and more people-friendly Anna's Hummingbirds have supplanted them.

BROAD-BILLED HUMMINGBIRD—*Cynanthus latirostris*

Fortunate is the soul whose garden is graced by this energetic and jewel-toned beauty, with its perpetually flicking, deeply notched tail. Widespread and common in a variety of habitats in central Mexico, in the United States the Broad-billed Hummingbird is found primarily in rocky watered canyons and outcroppings of desert mountains in southeast Arizona, southwest New Mexico, and less frequently west Texas. Individuals are also rarely but regularly reported at feeders and plantings well to the north, occasionally west to San Diego, and with increasing frequency east to the Gulf Coast.

Populations in central and southern Mexico are sedentary, but those that breed within our borders return from their winter haunts in March and early April. Nests are placed on a drooping branch and often above a stream, sometimes camouflaged with bits of leaves and bark, looking much like flotsam left by high water. Lichen, a customary finishing touch to the nests of many hummingbirds, is almost never used. Favored nesting plants include netleaf hackberry (*Celtis reticulata*) and red barberry (*Mahonia haematocarpa*), with Arizona sycamore (*Platanus wrightii*), Fremont cottonwood (*Populus fremontii*), soapberry (*Sapindus drummondii*), honey mesquite (*Prosopis glandulosa*), Goodding's willow (*Salix gooddingii*), and even poison ivy (*Toxicodendron radicans*) used on occasion. Once the second brood of young fledges in August, birds range widely before making their way southward to their wintering grounds in northern Mexico. Most depart by October, but a few individuals may winter at feeding stations in southern Arizona.

These engaging and relatively even-tempered birds tend to forage widely rather than defend particular patches of flowers. Early in the season, Broad-billeds rely heavily on the spring-blooming penstemons (*Penstemon parryi, P. superbus, P. pseudospectabilis*). Also widely visited in the spring months are ocotillo (*Fouquieria splendens*), desert-honeysuckle (*Anisacanthus thurberi*), southwest coral bean (*Erythrina flabelliformis*), scarlet betony (*Stachys coccinea*), New Mexico and Arizona thistles (*Cirsium neomexicanum, C. arizonicum*), and desert-willow (*Chilopsis linearis*).

In the summertime, agaves (*Agave schottii, A. parryi, A. palmeri*) are by far the most important source of nectar. Beardlip penstemon (*Penstemon barbatus*), various Indian paintbrushes (*Castilleja* spp.), firecracker bush (*Bouvardia ternifolia*), and tiny flying insects round out the summer fare. Hummingbird trumpet (*Epilobium canum*) provides valuable nectar in early fall.

Among the many plants reportedly used by birds wintering in Sonora are pineapple sage (*Salvia elegans*), red justicia (*Justicia candicans*), tree morning glory (*Ipomoea arborescens*), wild jícama (*Ipomoea bracteata*), and trumpet tree (*Tabebuia impetiginosa*).

Nectar sources in late winter and early spring include tree ocotillo (*Fouquieria macdougalii*), palo adán (*Fouquieria diguetii*), limita (*Anisacanthus andersonii*), Sierra Madre lobelia (*Lobelia laxiflora*), rama del toro (*Tetramerium abditum*), Anderson's thornbush (*Lycium andersonii*), uvalama (*Vitex mollis*), and galloping and organ pipe cacti (*Stenocereus alamosensis, S. thurberi*).

The future of the population of Broad-billed Hummingbirds breeding in the United States appears to be of twofold concern. Although some of the riparian thickets where it nests enjoy a measure of protection in national forests, other areas continue to be trampled and drained as the human population in the region balloons, and its wintering grounds in northwestern Mexico are rapidly being converted to rangeland for cattle. Resident populations in Mexico have thus far not been widely studied.

MAGNIFICENT HUMMINGBIRD—*Eugenes fulgens*

MAGNIFICENT IS AN UNDERSTATEMENT FOR THIS SPECIES, one of the two largest hummingbirds regularly occurring in our region and one of the most colorful as well with its iridescent teal to emerald-green gorget and purple crown. Its geographic range is huge, with populations occurring south to Panama, but in the United States it is confined to southeast Arizona, more rarely in southwest and south central New Mexico, and west Texas. There it is locally common in the sky islands where it can generally be found from March or April through September. A few individuals regularly overwinter at feeding stations in southeast Arizona. In early spring and especially in late summer, migrants often move through the foothills and may visit feeders and garden plantings en route to or from their Mexican wintering grounds. Most birds do not stray far from the borderlands, but vagrants have been recorded from California to Georgia and north as far as Wyoming and Minnesota.

Home for the Magnificent Hummingbird is typically above 5,000 feet in elevation, in pine-oak woodlands, mixed coniferous forest, or sycamore-maple groves. A variety of trees are used for nest sites, including bigtooth maple (*Acer grandidentatum*), Arizona sycamore (*Platanus wrightii*), red fir (*Abies magnifica*), Douglas-fir (*Pseudotsuga menziesii*), Mexican alder (*Alnus oblongifolia*), Arizona walnut (*Juglans major*), and various pines. Prominent perches overlooking forest openings or creeks are an essential habitat component. This species is highly insectivorous, particularly during the spring dry season when few flowers are in bloom, frequently foraging near the foliage of sycamores and the long needles of Apache pines (*Pinus engelmannii*) to glean a variety of small insects and spiders. When the summer rains turn mountain meadows into nectar bars, birds move in to take advantage of the bounty.

Among the few spring-blooming plants that the birds are known to visit are claretcup cactus (*Echinocereus coccineus*), New Mexico thistle (*Cirsium neomexicanum*), twinberry (*Lonicera involucrata*), golden columbine (*Aquilegia chrysantha*), desert beardtongue (*Penstemon pseudospectabilis*), Parry's penstemon (*P. parryi*), and scarlet betony (*Stachys coccinea*), this last also blooming in fall.

In summer and fall commonly visited plants include Parry's and Palmer's agaves (*Agave parryi, A. palmeri*) for both nectar and associated insects, beardlip penstemon (*Penstemon barbatus*) and others, Mexican catchfly (*Silene laciniata*), Huachuca Mountain paintbrush (*Castilleja patriotica*) and others, Lemmon's and mountain sages (*Salvia lemmonii, S. regla*), Chiricahua Mountain columbine (*Aquilegia desertorum*), firecracker bush (*Bouvardia ternifolia*), giant trumpet (*Macromeria viridiflora*), Arizona thistle (*Cirsium arizonicum*), snapdragon vine (*Maurandella antirrhiniflora*), pine trumpets (*Polemonium pauciflorum*), and Sierra Madre lobelia (*Lobelia laxiflora*). The Sierra Madre lobelia is strongly associated with Magnificent Hummingbirds in Colima, Mexico.

Other Mexican natives visited include penstemons (*Penstemon kunthii, P. roseus*), agaves (*Agave americana, A. salmiana*), pineapple and Mexican sages (*Salvia elegans, S. mexicana*), najicoli (*Lamourouxia viscosa*), Santa Catalina paintbrush (*Castilleja tenuiflora*), Turk's cap (*Malvaviscus arboreus*), butterfly bush (*Buddleja cordata*), thistles (*Cirsium anartidlepis, C. mexicanum*), night-blooming jessamine (*Cestrum terminale*), tropical mistletoe (*Psittacanthus calyculatus*), and gooseberry (*Ribes ciliatum*).

In the United States, much of this bird's habitat lies within national forests, where fires may temporarily affect populations in the short term but where fire suppression policies may pose an even greater threat to habitat in the long run. At feeding stations birds are exposed to increased risks such as cat predation and pesticide poisoning.

WHITE-EARED HUMMINGBIRD—*Hylocharis leucotis (Basilinna leucotis)*

Rare in the United States but quite common in the Sierra Madrean highlands of Mexico, this feisty hummingbird has recently become an almost regular summer resident in its few known haunts in the border sky islands, including the Huachuca and Chiricahua mountains of southeast Arizona and the Animas Mountains of southwest New Mexico. Here it is strongly associated with pine-oak and coniferous forests of middle to upper elevations, where the species probably nests, although birds are more likely to be observed at canyon feeding stations after the breeding season. Most records are from June to August and within this immediate vicinity, but individuals have been recorded nearly every month and (very rarely) as far away as Mississippi. In west Texas the species is considered a casual visitor.

The White-eared Hummingbird occurs southward through Mexico and into Nicaragua, so not surprisingly occupies a wide variety of habitats, from grassy montane meadows to cloud forests. Strategic perches are an important amenity, with birds using high exposed branches as well as those in dense thickets fairly low to the ground. Shrubby oaks (*Quercus* spp.), particularly in areas with dense undergrowth, are favored nest sites in Mexico, and the soft down from the undersides of the leaves is typically a key component of nest construction. Also used are woolly insect galls that are associated with oak leaves. A reported nest in the Huachuca Mountains was found in a New Mexico locust (*Robinia neomexicana*). In the United States, breeding birds arrive in late April, nest in May and June, and then may depart for wintering grounds in Mexico as soon as late July or may linger in the region through September.

Relatively little is known about the feeding habits of this species north of the Mexican border, with agaves (*Agave* spp.), pineleaf penstemon (*Penstemon pinifolius*), New Mexico locust, and madrone (*Arbutus arizonica, A. xalapensis*) among the few native plants mentioned in the literature.

Field biologists in New Mexico have observed birds also visiting Rocky Mountain bee plant (*Peritoma serrulata*), southwestern paintbrush (*Castilleja integra*), many-flowered ipomopsis (*Ipomopsis multiflora*), and Arizona thistle (*Cirsium arizonicum*).

In northern Mexico, some of the nectar plants used that also occur in the United States include red justicia (*Justicia candicans*), scarlet betony (*Stachys coccinea*), cardinal flower (*Lobelia cardinalis*), Huachuca Mountain and Santa Catalina paintbrushes (*Castilleja patriotica, C. tenuiflora*), pointleaf manzanita (*Arctostaphylos pungens*), and Madrean star thistle (*Plectocephalus rothrockii*).

Limita (*Anisacanthus andersonii*), espinosilla (*Loeselia mexicana*), pineapple and Mexican sages (*Salvia elegans, S. mexicana*), penstemon (*Penstemon* spp.), hierba del piojo (*Mandevilla foliosa*), gooseberry (*Ribes dugesii*), agaves (*Agave salmiana, A shrevei*), and tree morning glory (*Ipomoea arborescens*) are some of the other plants that the birds are known to visit in Mexico.

In southern Sinaloa, White-eared Hummingbirds defend patches of Indian paintbrush (*Castilleja* sp.) from all other species, even successfully driving away larger birds such as Blue-throated and Magnificent Hummingbirds. White-eareds have also been observed taking advantage of holes punched by carpenter bees in flowers that would otherwise be too long to access.

Because this species enjoys a huge geographical range and is a generalist feeder, exploiting a wide variety of flowers, its future seems optimistic. Its status as rare in the United States, however, will probably continue for the foreseeable future.

BLUE-THROATED HUMMINGBIRD—*Lampornis clemenciae*

THE APPEARANCE OF THIS IMPOSING COMMANDO IN ONE'S BACKYARD IS apt to cause heart palpitations in all but the most seasoned of avian aficionados. This, our largest regularly occurring hummingbird, is most commonly encountered in the sky islands of southeast Arizona, southwest New Mexico, and west Texas, but its post-breeding travels occasionally take it well away from this home turf, with scattered records from interior California north to North Dakota and east to South Carolina. In central and southern Mexico the Blue-throated Hummingbird is a permanent resident, but the northern population is largely migratory, departing in September for its wintering grounds in southern Chihuahua, Sinaloa, and Durango. A few individuals may winter at southeast Arizona feeding stations.

The breeding season begins in April, as returning birds stake out prime feeding territories in shady watered canyons lined with Arizona sycamores (*Platanus wrightii*) and bigtooth maples (*Acer grandidentatum*). Males tend to occupy territories at slightly higher elevations than females. The nest is commonly located near flowing water but rarely placed in a tree, more often being tucked into a cranny in a stream bank, cliff face, or building eave and almost always sheltered from above by a rock overhang or similar structure. Nests are typically lined with soft plant down from the leaves of oaks (*Quercus* spp.) or Arizona sycamores. Lichen is rarely used. Females may rear up to three broods per year and typically use the same nest, adding fresh materials each time. During the spring dry season, the birds are highly insectivorous, frequently hawking insects over creeks and forest openings. They are vocal and aggressively territorial, dominating all other hummingbird species at flowers and feeders. Unlike most hummingbirds, Blue-throateds commonly feed within banks of blooms, when the only clue to their presence may be their distinctive high-pitched call note.

Early spring returnees find few nectar plants in bloom but will make use of flowering heaths such as pointleaf manzanita (*Arctostaphylos pungens*) and madrone (*Arbutus arizonica, A. xalapensis*). Later in the spring they are known to visit desert-honeysuckle (*Anisacanthus thurberi*), scarlet betony (*Stachys coccinea*), golden columbine (*Aquilegia chrysantha*), claretcup cactus (*Echinocereus coccineus*), New Mexico locust (*Robinia neomexicana*), Sierra Madre lobelia (*Lobelia laxiflora*), and twinberry (*Lonicera involucrata*) if available.

Most important of the summer nectar sources are beardlip penstemon (*Penstemon barbatus*), Lemmon's and mountain sages (*Salvia lemmonii, S. regla*), and various agaves (*Agave havardiana, A. parryi. A. palmeri*). Other summer bloomers often patronized include scarlet monkeyflower (*Mimulus cardinalis*), scarlet gilia (*Ipomopsis aggregata*), Arizona thistle (*Cirsium arizonicum*), Madrean star thistle (*Plectocephalus rothrockii*), and coral bells (*Heuchera sanguinea*).

Of plants used by resident populations farther south in central Mexico, Mexican cardinal sage (*Salvia fulgens*) appears to be the most important, and may in fact have coevolved with the Blue-throated Hummingbird. Kunth's penstemon (*Penstemon kunthii*) and pineapple sage (*Salvia elegans*) are also widely used.

Like all southwestern creatures that are dependent upon riparian groves, the U. S. population of this species faces an uncertain future. Much of its habitat is somewhat protected by national forest but as such is vulnerable to fire suppression policies that may inhibit wildflower proliferation. Its penchant for feeders exposes it to the various human-associated hazards.

CALLIOPE HUMMINGBIRD—*Selasphorus calliope* *(Stellula calliope)*

IN THE SOUTHWEST THIS TINY CREATURE WITH ITS ROSY-PURPLE STARBURST gorget breeds only in Utah and a few locations in the Coast Ranges of southern California, its range extending northward from there into British Columbia and Alberta in Canada. After the nesting season it leisurely makes its way southward from one mountain meadow to another, often visiting feeders and garden flowers at lower elevations along the way. Most common in July and August, the birds typically follow the southern Rockies southward and then along the Sierra Madre Occidental. Most individuals spend the winter in pine-oak woodlands in foothills and mountains of central Mexico, but numbers of birds wintering along the Gulf Coast are increasing and vagrants have been recorded north to New York and Minnesota. In the springtime migration is chiefly through California and western Arizona.

The heart of the breeding range is in the northwestern states, where birds dwell in cool coniferous forests of the mountains, often along streams. Male feeding territories typically include several sentinel posts such as dead twigs atop willows (*Salix* spp.) or alders (*Alnus* spp.) that afford views of a forest clearing or meadow. Trees commonly used by females for nest sites include various pines (*Pinus contorta, P. ponderosa, P. jeffreyi*), grand fir (*Abies grandis*), Douglas-fir (*Pseudotsuga menziesii*), Engelmann spruce (*Picea engelmannii*), and western red cedar (*Thuja plicata*). Plant down from the seeds of cottonwoods (*Populus* spp.) or willows (*Salix* spp.) is often used to line the nest, which is usually sheltered from above by an overhanging bough.

In early spring as the birds are returning from Mexico the nectar pickings can be slim but northbound birds take it wherever they can find it, often from wax and red-flowering currants (*Ribes cereum, R. sanguineum*), manzanita (*Arctostaphylos* spp.), and snowberry (*Symphoricarpos albus, S. oreophilus*). Like many other hummingbird species, they also are known to feed from wells that sapsuckers excavate on tree branches.

During the breeding season the most important nectar sources are scarlet gilia (*Ipomopsis aggregata*), giant red paintbrush (*Castilleja miniata*) and others (*C. applegatei, arachnoidea, linariifolia*), two-lobed larkspur (*Delphinium nuttallianum*), Barbey's delphinium (*Delphinium barbeyi*), columbine (*Aquilegia elegantula, A. formosa*), and penstemon (*Penstemon davidsonii, P. leiophyllus, P. newberryi, P. rostriflorus*). Orange honeysuckle (*Lonicera ciliosa*), pink corydalis (*Corydalis caseana*), lousewort (*Pedicularis semibarbata*), and snow plant (*Sarcodes sanguinea*) are also much used in some locations. Several of these continue to provide nectar through summer to help fuel the southbound migration.

Other widely visited late summer bloomers include Rocky Mountain bee plant (*Peritoma serrulata*), hummingbird trumpet (*Epilobium canum*), yellow monkeyflower (*Mimulus implexus*), beardlip penstemon (*Penstemon barbatus*), Rincon Mountain paintbrush (*Castilleja austromontana*), larkspur (*Delphinium geraniifolium, D. scopulorum*), scarlet betony (*Stachys coccinea*), and bubblegum mint (*Agastache cana*). Unlike other species, Calliope Hummingbirds do not object to feeding close to the ground; they also frequently feed within banks of flowers.

This species apparently benefits somewhat from logging, which opens up the canopy and promotes both nectar-producing wildflowers and the dense vegetation preferred for nesting. While fire management policies may impact local populations, the broad geographic range of the species ought to help mitigate most such casualties. Their comfort with feeding at low flowers does put them at increased risk of cat predation in human-inhabited areas.

BROAD-TAILED HUMMINGBIRD—*Selasphorus platycercus*

THE FAMILIAR HUMMINGBIRD OF MOUNTAINS FROM THE CENTRAL AND southern Rockies to west Texas, the Broad-tailed is frequently heard before it is seen, the rose-throated male creating a distinctive trilling sound with its wings. Females can be quite richly colored as well, their cinnamon flanks contrasting smartly with their bottle-green backs. With a range extending southward through Mexico to Guatemala, the Broad-tailed Hummingbird is most common in the Rocky Mountains and Mexico's Sierra Madre Occidental. While the southern contingent is largely resident, the U.S. population is migratory, the birds moving up to alpine meadows after the breeding season and then drifting southward through foothills and valleys from late July through October. Most winter in high-elevation forests in central Mexico, but scattered individuals are regularly recorded in winter at feeders in the border states and along the Gulf Coast, with vagrants reported from British Columbia to Delaware.

Returning to the breeding grounds as early as February in the south and as late as May in the north, birds quickly establish territories at coniferous forest edges, in open woodlands, and along streams. Territorial males require several high perches for dive displays and to survey their domain. In the Rocky Mountains favored nest sites are ponderosa pine (*Pinus ponderosa*), Douglas-fir (*Pseudotsuga menziesii*), spruce (*Picea engelmannii, P. pungens*), fir (*Abies concolor, A. lasiocarpa*), and aspen (*Populus tremuloides*). In west Texas and New Mexico other trees used include Arizona cypress (*Cupressus arizonica*), piñon (*Pinus cembroides, P. edulis*), alligator juniper (*Juniperus deppeana*), and oaks (*Quercus* spp.), while in eastern California birds typically construct nests in singleleaf piñon (*Pinus monophylla*), California juniper (*Juniperus californica*), or willows (*Salix* spp.). Nests are almost always sheltered by overhanging vegetation.

In late winter birds take sap from sapsucker wells and use whatever nectar is available, with pointleaf manzanita (*Arctostaphylos pungens*) the most widely distributed of the few plants in flower at that time. Limita (*Anisacanthus andersonii*) is also visited as birds move northward through Sonora and Chihuahua. Heading the list of important spring bloomers are ocotillo (*Fouquieria splendens*), two-lobe larkspur (*Delphinium nuttallianum*), penstemon (*Penstemon parryi, P. pseudospectabilis, P. eatoni*), scarlet betony (*Stachys coccinea*), and claretcup cacti (*Echinocereus coccineus, E. triglochidiatus*), with twinberry (*Lonicera involucrata*), golden and wax currants (*Ribes aureum, R. cereum*), New Mexico locust (*Robinia neomexicana*), Sierra Madre lobelia (*Lobelia laxiflora*), and Rocky Mountain iris (*Iris missouriensis*) also widely visited.

The many important late spring and summer staples include scarlet gilia (*Ipomopsis aggregata*), Chiricahua Mountain and comet columbines (*Aquilegia desertorum, A. elegantula*), beardlip penstemon (*Penstemon barbatus*) and others (*P. cardinalis, P. pinifolius, P. sepalulus, P. whippleanus*), paintbrush (*Castilleja austromontana, C. integra, C. miniata, C. patriotica*), Lemmon's and mountain sages (*Salvia lemmonii, S. regla*), Barbey's delphinium (*Delphinium barbeyi*), firecracker bush (*Bouvardia ternifolia*), Mexican catchfly (*Silene laciniata*), and various agaves (*Agave palmeri, A. parryi, A. havardiana*). Several of these continue blooming into early fall and provide valuable nectar for migrants. Mimbres figwort (*Scrophularia macrantha*) is well used in the few spots where it occurs, as is its cousin, mountain figwort (*S. montana*).

Wintering birds in Mexico visit a variety of flowers, including fuchsia sage (*Salvia iodantha*) and gooseberry (*Ribes ciliatum*).

The Broad-tailed Hummingbird is widespread enough to be fairly well insulated against localized habitat losses, but its ready attraction to feeders puts it at greater risk of cat predation and exposure to garden pesticides than in natural habitats.

RUFOUS HUMMINGBIRD—*Selasphorus rufus*

Most any westerner who has put up a feeder is familiar with this copper conquistador, whose arrival in the neighborhood is not likely to go unnoticed. Promptly claiming the most prominent perch for its command post, it assiduously chases any and all would-be interlopers from its newly decreed realm. Sunlight works color magic with the male's gorget feathers, at one moment fiery vermilion and the next glittering gold. While its breeding range lies north of our area, from Oregon and Idaho to southern Alaska, its protracted fall migration through the Rocky Mountains and southward brings it to gardens across the Southwest. Most birds winter in Mexico, but a few remain in southern California and increasing numbers head for hummingbird havens along the Gulf Coast. Vagrants can and do turn up nearly anywhere.

In spring, birds travel northward primarily along the Pacific Coast, advancing through the Coast Ranges and Sierra Nevada as nectar-producing flowers come into bloom. Reaching the breeding grounds when snow often still blankets the coniferous forests they call home, females select a nest site in a Sitka spruce (*Picea sitchensis*), Douglas-fir (*Pseudotsuga menziesii*), or western red cedar (*Thuja plicata*). The cycle is calibrated so that the young will fledge just as mountain meadows come into peak bloom. Adult males begin to drift southward in July, often establishing temporary feeding territories along the way, and are followed by females and immature birds in August. The sheer numbers of birds that sometimes congregate at feeding stations in the Southwest can be dizzying.

As birds move northward into southern California in early spring, chuparosa (*Justicia californica*) and ocotillo (*Fouquieria splendens*) are widely used wherever they occur, with manzanita (*Arctostaphylos* spp.), honeysuckle (*Lonicera* spp.), and Pacific madrone (*Arbutus menziesii*) also supplying important nectar. Birds reach the breeding grounds as red-flowering currant (*Ribes sanguineum*) begins to bloom, and biologists speculate that this major nectar source has coevolved with the Rufous Hummingbird. Several other plants endemic to the Pacific Northwest also rely heavily on the Rufous for pollination.

The birds visit a veritable host of plants on their return trip in late summer, with the most widely used being western columbine (*Aquilegia formosa*), scarlet gilia (*Ipomopsis aggregata*), paintbrush (*Castilleja austromontana, C. integra, C. linariifolia, C. miniata, C. patriotica*), penstemon (*Penstemon barbatus, P. labrosus, P. newberryi, P. rostriflorus, P. wislizenii*), firecracker bush (*Bouvardia ternifolia*), crimson and Lemmon's sages (*Salvia henryi, S. lemmonii*), and scarlet betony (*Stachys coccinea*), patches of which in Sonora may be vigorously defended.

Other favorites include Barbey's delphinium (*Delphinium barbeyi*), Rocky Mountain larkspur (*Delphinium scopulorum*), mintleaf beebalm (*Monarda fistulosa* var. *menthifolia*), fireweed (*Chamerion angustifolium*), cardinal flower (*Lobelia cardinalis*), Rocky Mountain bee plant (*Peritoma serrulata*), agave (*Agave palmeri, A. shrevei*), hummingbird trumpet (*Epilobium canum*), figwort (*Scrophularia macrantha, S. montana*), and Arizona thistle (*Cirsium arizonicum*).

Important plants in Sonora are hierba del piojo (*Mandevilla foliosa*) and pineapple and Mexican sages (*Salvia elegans, S. mexicana*) in the fall, and tree morning glory (*Ipomoea arborescens*), wild jícama (*Ipomoea bracteata*), tree ocotillo (*Fouquieria macdougalii*), desert-honeysuckle (*Anisacanthus andersonii, A. thurberi*), and to a lesser extent agave (*Agave angustifolia*), Sierra Madre lobelia (*Lobelia laxiflora*), and desert beardtongue (*Penstemon pseudospectabilis*) in early spring.

The future might seem bright for such a stalwart and adaptable hummingbird, but in fact annual Breeding Bird Surveys coordinated by the U. S. Geological Survey have documented an accelerating population decline of nearly 3 percent per year. While more study is needed, loss of breeding habitat is a primary concern for this hummingbird species considered most at risk.

ALLEN'S HUMMINGBIRD—*Selasphorus sasin*

THIS HUMMINGBIRD OF THE CALIFORNIA COAST ALSO OCCURS RARELY but regularly in southern Arizona and occasionally southwestern New Mexico during migration in late summer. Female and immature birds are virtually impossible to distinguish in the field from Rufous Hummingbirds, making generalizations about vagrancy elsewhere difficult. Even the flashy male Allen's, with its typically bright green back, can be hard to distinguish from the occasional green-backed Rufous Hummingbird. Hummingbird banders, who during the banding process can closely inspect tail feathers, have provided much of the limited information available on the movements of Allen's Hummingbird. Two subspecies exist, one of which is sedentary, residing year-round on the Channel Islands, the adjacent California mainland of the Palos Verdes Peninsula, and inland through the coastal slope of Orange and Los Angeles counties. The other subspecies is migratory, breeding on west slopes of the mountains along the Pacific Coast from near Santa Barbara north to southern Oregon and wintering from Baja California southward to Jalisco in central Mexico. These birds are typically present from February through July or August, but males may depart as early as May.

Misty coastal forests and riparian woodlands are the preferred breeding habitat, where males establish feeding territories on shrubby slopes with a variety of prominent sentinel perches, particularly bare twigs atop willows (*Salix* spp.). Females tend to build nests in the more thickly vegetated ravines, where thickets of blackberry (*Rubus* spp.) or brackenfern (*Pteridium aquilinum*) are favorite nest sites, but willows, coast live oak (*Quercus agrifolia*), and non-native eucalyptus (*Eucalyptus* spp.) are also commonly used. The resident population of Allen's Hummingbird, historically restricted to sage scrub of the islands and nearby coastline, now occupies a wide variety of habitats in the vicinity, including parks, backyards, and university campuses.

Channel Island birds depend heavily upon a very few endemic plants that in turn rely on them almost entirely for pollination. Among these are island bush snapdragon (*Gambelia speciosa*), island paintbrush (*Castilleja lanata* var. *hololeuca*), and island monkeyflower (*Diplacus flemingii*). Mainland birds naturally have a more varied menu. Important late winter and early spring flowers include fuchsia-flowering gooseberry (*Ribes speciosum*), Indian warrior (*Pedicularis densiflora*), Pacific madrone (*Arbutus menziesii*), and manzanita (*Arctostaphylos* spp.).

Spring staples include California Indian pink (*Silene californica*), Mexican catchfly (*Silene laciniata*), twinberry (*Lonicera involucrata* var. *ledebourii*), wild lilac (*Ceanothus* spp.), and hummingbird sage (*Salvia spathacea*).

Orange bush monkeyflower (*Diplacus aurantiacus*) heads the list of important summer plants, with paintbrush (*Castilleja applegatei, C. linariifolia, C. miniata*), western columbine (*Aquilegia formosa*), penstemon (*Penstemon newberryi, P. rostriflorus*), bush penstemon (*Keckiella* spp.), and scarlet larkspur (*Delphinium cardinale*) also widely used. North of our range, the endangered western tiger lily (*Lilium occidentale*) is pollinated primarily by Allen's Hummingbirds.

In late summer and fall, birds visit scarlet monkeyflower (*Mimulus cardinalis*) and hummingbird trumpet (*Epilobium canum*) extensively. The introduced and widely naturalized eucalyptus (*Eucalyptus* spp.) is often used by wintering birds, as is the non-native tree tobacco (*Nicotiana glauca*), and the two may have had a hand in the species' range expansion.

In some ways benefited in the short term by exotic plantings as more and more of its habitat is paved, Allen's Hummingbirds may eventually be squeezed out by the more dominant and urban-adaptable Anna's Hummingbird. The several plants reliant upon Allen's Hummingbirds for pollination probably face an even grimmer future.

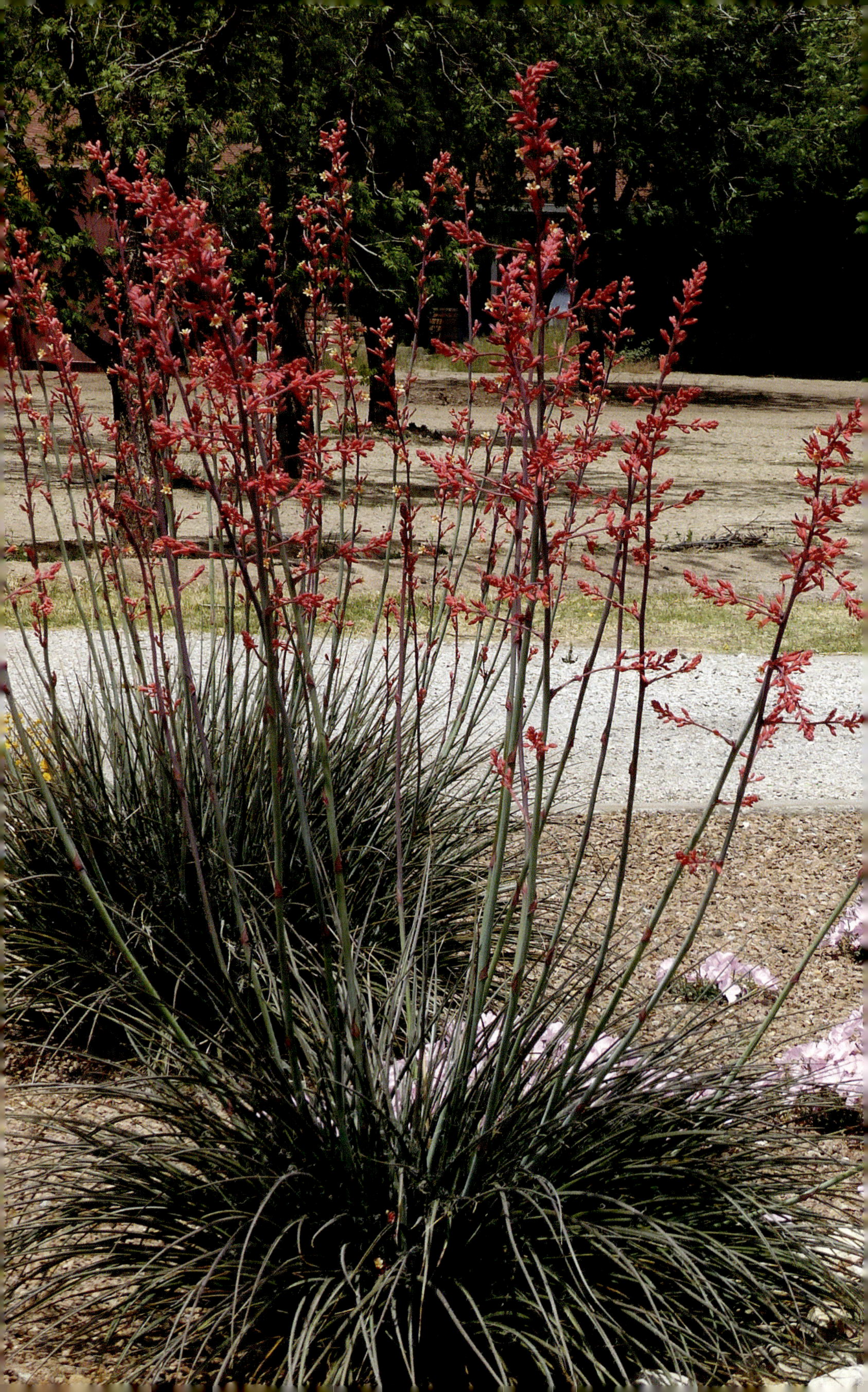

CHAPTER 3

Creating a Hummingbird Habitat

As the human population in the Southwest grows, more and more pressures will doubtless come to bear upon natural areas, particularly the riparian corridors and watered canyons that also comprise optimum habitat for a number of hummingbird species and their attendant flowers. Beyond directly acquiring such properties—not something within the financial means of most of us—we may feel powerless to do very much. But as this chapter will demonstrate, although we can never truly duplicate the wild in our own backyards, we can certainly maximize the potential of whatever bit of land we do have and often make a truly meaningful difference, especially if we can inspire our neighbors to get on board as well. Particularly when prolonged drought or wildfires temporarily displace populations, our thoughtfully landscaped yards can serve as a viable Plan B for both hummingbirds and their flowers.

A hummingbird habitat is much more than a profusion of red flowers, although the more of these the merrier as far as the birds are concerned. The ultimate garden will offer a calendar of flowering plants that will bloom over the course of the season in which hummingbirds are expected to be present, in some locations year round, and will be particularly eye-catching during migration. Certainly, feeders can help fill any voids in flower availability while the garden is developing, but a number of other features are important as well. As field biologists will confirm, natural habitats are often quite sparse on blooms for much of the time, but they provide other amenities that are less obvious but just as necessary, such as places to forage for tiny insects, prominent perches from which to monitor a territory, open spaces for courtship flights, roosting spots to spend the night, and secretive places to build nests. All of these considerations will be detailed in the following pages.

GETTING ORIENTED

Whether you are seeking to add a few plants that will appeal to the neighborhood hummingbirds or transform an entire landscape into a hummingbird haven, you will likely have the most success in the long run by first looking over your property as a prospective hummingbird visitor might. Identify the type of habitat that most closely resembles your yard and the surrounding environs. Most of us are at least loosely linked to one of the deserts (Chihuahuan, Sonoran, Mojave, or Great Basin), the chaparral and coast sage scrub habitats of California, or one of the various mountain habitats (piñon-juniper, pine-oak, or spruce-fir). Within these may be assorted features such as rivers, canyons, arroyos, and seasonal washes that further define the habitat. The better understanding you have of the natural landscape—the soil types, the local climatic peculiarities, and the native vegetation—the smarter plant choices you will inevitably make, even in developed residential areas. Make an effort to identify the mature trees and shrubs in the immediate area, as well as where pockets of nectar-producing flowers occur and when they are in bloom, and then as you learn about the needs of the locally occurring hummingbird species you will be able to pinpoint the most glaring gaps in the existing vegetation. By the same token, if the neighbor next door has a dozen desert-willows, say, then you won't necessarily need another in your own yard (although they are such pretty trees that space for one more can nearly always be justified). A bird's-eye sketch of the neighborhood illustrating these various features can be quite helpful for those planning elaborate hummingbird gardens.

Next, consult the hummingbird profiles in this book to determine which species of hummingbirds might be expected in your area and at what time of year, and then concentrate most of your efforts on providing for these. Rest assured that once one hummingbird has discovered your plantings, others will soon follow. The idea is not so much to replicate natural habitats in your landscape but rather to choose selected plants from those habitats that seem most appropriate for your site and the surrounding vicinity. In many cases all that is needed is to fill in some gaps, such as a few cover plants for nesting or roosting, a source of water for drinking and bathing, or some flowering plants that offer nectar during a particular season.

STRUCTURAL ELEMENTS

The ideal layout for a hummingbird habitat includes open expanses with flowering plants and sentinel perches, along with more densely vegetated areas for roosting and nesting. A naturalistic landscape, with some untended weedy areas that will attract aphids and other small insects essential for rearing young, is much more likely to persuade breeding hummingbirds to make themselves at home than a manicured lawn with clipped hedges. Large properties with abundant vegetation may be able to support more than one family of breeding birds, particularly if groups of flowering plants are located in separate areas of the yard. Newer or highly developed neighborhoods with few mature trees might not provide sufficient cover for nesting birds but can still catch the attention of passing migrants. Even a small patio garden, featuring a well-timed profusion of flowers in large pots or planters, can serve as a welcome way station.

Massing multiple plants of a species makes more of a visual splash than the polka-dotted look of many types of single plants (and the flowers stand the best chance of being pollinated this way), but hummingbirds will not ignore a favored flower just because it stands alone, so feel free to experiment as space allows. To maximize density in narrow areas, try stair-stepping plants by height with trees, tall shrubs, and vines in the back and shorter shrubs and perennials in front. Just leave enough room between mature plants for hummingbirds to maneuver while feeding, and be sure to locate at least one flower bed next to a favorite seating area so you will be able to enjoy the fruits of your labors up close. Most hummingbirds are quite active around humans and seem remarkably unperturbed by our quiet presence.

During breeding, male hummingbirds require broad open expanses for their dazzling courtship displays, as well as a number of tall perches interspersed within these expanses to survey their territory and watch for intruding males. Some commonly used plants employed for such sentinel perches include the spent flower stalks of agaves (*Agave* spp.), yuccas (*Yucca* spp.), and sotols (*Dasylirion* spp.); the thorny stems of ocotillo (*Fouquieria splendens*), cholla (*Cylindropuntia* spp.), saguaro (*Carnegiea gigantea*), and spiny hackberry (*Celtis pallida*); and leafless twigs atop a variety of shrubs and trees (remember the latter when pruning). One of the simplest improvements you can make to a landscape is "planting" a few spent agave stalks for instant lookout posts. Property owners who are not trying to attract hummingbirds are usually delighted to have spent agave stalks carted off, but note that large stalks can be extremely heavy and may require a year or more to dry out before they are very portable.

Between their feeding forays, female hummingbirds typically choose a less prominent roosting spot that offers protection from sun and wind. Evergreen trees and shrubs are ideal for this purpose, particularly those with a horizontal branching structure. With their extremely short legs and tiny feet, hummingbirds have difficulty perching on angled stems and tend to gravitate toward plants that feature level perches.

Some native evergreens repeatedly mentioned as being favored for roosting are red barberry (*Mahonia haematocarpa*), Arizona rosewood (*Vauquelinia californica*), jojoba (*Simmondsia chinensis*), Texas sage (*Leucophyllum frutescens*)—also an occasional nectar source, evergreen sumac (*Rhus virens*), Wright's silktassel (*Garrya wrightii*), manzanita (*Arctostaphylos* spp.), oak (*Quercus* spp.), juniper (*Juniperus* spp.), Arizona cypress (*Cupressus arizonica*), toyon (*Heteromeles arbutifolia*), and California buckthorn (*Frangula californica*).

Semi-evergreen or deciduous plants that are frequently used for roosting include willow (*Salix* spp.), hackberry (*Celtis reticulata, C. pallida*), desert ironwood (*Olneya tesota*), foothills palo verde (*Parkinsonia microphyllya*), catclaw acacia (*Acacia greggii*), and mesquite (*Prosopis glandulosa, P. pubescens, P. velutina*).

Check with your county extension agent (usually listed in the local government pages of the phone book) to determine which of these may be native or adapted to your area and site conditions.

Female hummingbirds demonstrate some slightly different preferences when it comes to selecting a nest location. While both individual birds and different species vary tremendously in their habits, some trees bear mentioning because they are selected so consistently. Among the highly preferred broad-leaved evergreens are coast live oak (*Quercus agrifolia*), jojoba (*Simmondsia chinensis*), and red barberry (*Mahonia haematocarpa*)—these last two also preferred roosting spots. Arizona sycamore (*Platanus wrightii*) by far leads the list of deciduous trees favored for nesting, known to be used by no fewer than nine of the hummingbird species profiled in this book; its cousin, California sycamore (*Platanus racemosa*), is also quite popular within its range. An additional benefit of sycamores is that many hummingbirds use the downy fibers from the undersides of the leaves in constructing their nests.

Other highly preferred nest trees include Fremont cottonwood (*Populus fremontii*), Rio Grande cottonwood (*Populus deltoides* ssp. *wislizenii*), foothills palo verde (*Parkinsonia microphylla*), netleaf hackberry (*Celtis reticulata*), western soapberry (*Sapindus drummondii*), boxelder (*Acer negundo*), various oaks (*Quercus* spp.), willows (*Salix* spp.), and alders (*Alnus* spp.).

At upper elevations virtually any tree species may be used, with alligator juniper (*Juniperus deppeana*), ponderosa pine (*Pinus ponderosa*), Engelmann spruce (*Picea engelmannii*), white fir (*Abies concolor*), Douglas-fir (*Pseudotsuga menziesii*), Arizona cypress (*Cupressus arizonicus*), and quaking aspen (*Populus tremuloides*) the most frequently mentioned.

Hummingbird nests ordinarily are not easily found, although with a little bit of knowledge and some patience you stand a somewhat better chance. To discourage the approach of heavier predators, females often locate their nests toward the terminal end of a branch, where the smaller twigs won't support a predator's weight, and to provide optimal protection from the elements they usually select a site beneath overhanging vegetation. From my own experience, the most productive way to find a hummingbird nest is to spend some time watching an adult female during the nestling stage, when for most of the daylight hours she will be hurriedly gathering insects and making frequent beelines to the nest. Should you be fortunate enough to spot a nest, please enjoy it respectfully from a distance and do not disturb any surrounding vegetation, and from the time of your discovery to the day when the fledglings depart the nest you will be treated to a truly awesome unfolding of events.

SUCCESSION OF BLOOM

Some readers may be lucky enough to host hummingbirds year-round, whereas those at the northern fringe of our region may enjoy them for only a few months during the breeding season. For most Southwesterners, the hummingbird calendar commences in early spring with the first migrants, settles into the nesting period through early summer, erupts in midsummer with large numbers of eventually southbound birds, and finally peters out entirely in fall. To provide for hummingbirds, you need to offer an assortment of nectar plants that will flower sequentially throughout this period of time. Gardeners in frost-free climates will need to continue the cycle through winter as well. The rest of us can then take a break from our gardens or, if we wish to try to entice a stray hummingbird, tend a few winter-flowering shrubs or perennials in containers that can be moved about as the temperatures dictate.

The bloom season listed within each plant profile should be taken only as a rough indication of the possible flowering period, as individuals and even populations may actually flower only a portion of this time in a given locale. For instance, many widely distributed species bloom in early spring at low elevations and in late spring or early summer in the mountains. If budget and space allow, provide two or more types of plants that will be in bloom at any given time, and at least twice as many for periods when large numbers of migrating hummingbirds are likely to be moving through the area. Locations that host hundreds to thousands of migrants cannot have too many flowering plants in July and August. Remember to consider flowers in adjacent yards as well, and first focus your efforts on adding plants that will bridge a current gap in the neighborhood bloom schedule. Occasionally, individual plants may disappoint, whether they wither and die for whatever reason or fail to bloom at a particular time, so plant two or more of a species to help ensure that some flowers will appear at the expected time.

For beginners especially, penstemons are great starter plants for the hummingbird garden and, given a mostly sunny spot and good drainage, they are easily grown most anywhere in the Southwest. Choose a spring- or summer-blooming penstemon native to your locale, water until established, and welcome the hummingbirds back in style next year. Once you have experienced the sublime satisfaction of having a hummingbird take notice of your offerings, you'll likely be encouraged to plunge onward with some additional plantings to bloom at other times.

Many other creatures are likely to visit your nectar garden as well, including other birds such as orioles and Verdins, some types of bats, and a variety of insects, especially butterflies, day-flying sphinx moths, and bees. Occasionally gardeners may become frustrated with carpenter bees (*Xylocopa*), which can damage and deplete the nectar of large quantities of hummingbird flowers in a short time, typically in spring, when the bees slit open the long narrow blooms at their bases in order to access the nectar. They do so in order to provision their nursery, a series of excavated chambers in a snag, or standing dead wood, each of which will hold one egg and enough collected pollen and nectar to nourish the larva from hatching to adulthood, when it finally emerges from the hole. Thus, the harm the bees cause to hummingbird flowers is usually a temporary occurrence in springtime, and if expected can possibly be mitigated by adding more spring-blooming plants. These same bees, one might keep in mind, are the critters that are chiefly responsible for pollinating the lovely desert-willow (*Chilopsis linearis*), a flower whose nectar hummingbirds happily "steal," or consume without pollination taking place, so some turnabout is conceivably fair play.

WATER FEATURES

All birds appreciate a source of water, and while hummingbirds normally obtain sufficient water from the nectar they ingest, they particularly seem to enjoy bathing. In natural habitats, hummingbirds typically bathe by flitting in and out of small waterfalls, dunking themselves in shallow pools, or fluttering against leaves wet from rain or dew, all scarce phenomena in the desert most of the time. In the garden, they can be easily enticed to birdbaths with trickling, dripping, or misting water, and a number of mechanisms to produce these effects are available from specialty stores and mail-order catalogs that deal in bird feeders and garden products. Hummingbirds also readily bathe in sprinklers, flying in and out of the spray before heading to a perch to preen and dry off. Only occasionally do they use traditional bowl-shaped birdbaths, which are usually much too deep for the tiny birds. Sometimes adding flat, rough-textured rocks to make a portion of the water a half-inch or less in depth will make this type of birdbath more attractive to hummingbirds, but purchasing or fashioning a dripper or mister is much more effective. Especially during migration, large numbers of hummingbirds may avail themselves of such water features, whether elevated or at ground level, and a great many other birds will be drawn to the sounds of moving water as well. In times of severe drought, when area ponds and rivers go dry, any reliable water source can be a critical lifeline for wildlife.

Ideally, birdbaths should be situated in the open, where birds can spot approaching predators with plenty of time to escape, and with dense or thorny cover several feet away where they can hide or preen out of danger. Check all birdbaths frequently to see that the water is fresh and clear.

ARTIFICIAL FEEDERS

People have been putting out nectar feeders for hummingbirds for over a hundred years, and have experimented with innumerable contraptions and concoctions to lure them into their gardens. Because this book is primarily concerned with native plants, I would heartily advise the interested reader to consult the excellent references in the bibliography for information on recommended types and brands of feeders, where to procure them, and their use and care.

Feeders can be particularly handy for supplying nectar during periods when flowering plants are scarce or when great numbers of hummingbirds are moving through. Unlike a low-maintenance garden, however, a feeding station requires frequent attention. Making and storing sugar water solution, cleaning and replenishing feeders, and keeping ants and bees from the syrup can be time-consuming during busy periods and should not be undertaken unless you are committed to following through for the duration of the season. Breeding or wintering birds in particular may become reliant on your food source and have difficulty if it is suddenly cut off. Try to arrange for a neighbor to monitor your feeders if you go away during such times, or determine in advance that you will not put up a feeder at all that season.

What to serve in the feeder is equally important. Use only granulated white cane or beet sugar to make the solution. Honey that begins to ferment can make birds ill and sugar substitutes lack the sucrose that hummingbirds need for energy. Red food coloring is also not recommended as it is unnecessary if there are red parts on the feeder and it is known to be detrimental to the birds' health. Simply add four parts boiling water to one part sugar, stir to blend, let cool to room temperature, and serve. Note that this 4:1 ratio of water to sugar, which closely approximates the concentration of natural flower nectar, can be strengthened to 3:1 if desired, but solutions any stronger are much more likely to attract bees and may cause dehydration in the birds. Any leftover solution can safely be stored for a week or so in the refrigerator.

Fill feeders only to a level that will be consumed in two to three days because the solution is quite prone to spoilage, particularly during hot weather. Feeders should be rinsed out thoroughly with hot water at least this often and scrubbed well with a bottle brush if any mold or film develops. Avoid using detergents, which leave a residue that is unhealthy for the birds to ingest. If some type of cleaning agent is necessary, white vinegar or a 10:1 bleach solution is recommended, along with rinsing well after scrubbing.

SAFETY CONCERNS

If we are to genuinely welcome hummingbirds into our gardens, it is incumbent upon us to at least do them no harm. Associating in our midst can be quite costly for the birds if our carelessness or ignorance results in situations that put them unfairly at risk. Because of their family structure, with females being the sole providers for the young from nest to fledging and a few weeks beyond, hummingbirds are extremely vulnerable to human-associated dangers—if something happens to a mother bird, her dependent young will in all likelihood die as well, typically from starvation or exposure. We must take extreme care that we are not the cause of any such unnatural fatalities, particularly during the breeding season, or we defeat the whole purpose of creating a hummingbird haven.

Spoiled feeder solutions are one potential manmade danger that can be eliminated with the scrupulous cleaning of feeders as discussed earlier. Birdbaths need to be checked regularly as well and scrubbed as needed.

Window collisions, while not as frequent an occurrence with hummingbirds as with other birds, are another threat associated with human habitation.

Typically, birds fly into windows either because the window reflects trees and sky or because it appears possible to fly through the interior and out another window. With the former situation you will need either to distract the birds (with hawk or owl silhouettes, spider web graphics, streamers, chimes, or even feeders) or to cushion their impact (with bird netting stretched several inches from the problem window). If the latter scenario seems to be the case, simply shutting the blinds or curtains of one of the windows will usually remedy the problem.

Another potential hazard to hummingbirds is pesticide poisoning, especially from exposure to chemical insecticides or fungicides. Even tiny amounts can be extremely toxic; it is important to avoid using these anywhere in the garden when hummingbirds are present, as the birds forage on many types of plants for tiny insects in addition to visiting nectar flowers. If insects on occasion do get the upper hand, they can often be plucked off the plant manually, hosed off with a sharp stream of water, or failing these measures sprayed with an environmentally friendly insecticidal soap. One of the delightful benefits of using native plants is that pests don't usually bother them and often when they do many natural controls, such as birds, lizards, and beneficial insects, are in place to respond to them. Before you reach for a pesticide, remember that to persuade hummingbirds to call your yard home you will need to have an abundance of insects. A relaxed attitude about spider webs, which are essential for constructing nests, will also help sell your property to breeding hummingbirds.

One of the most formidable dangers to hummingbirds in our gardens is that posed by free-roaming domestic cats. We might assume, watching mockingbirds dive-bomb our tabby while uttering raspy scolding calls to alert their young, that birds are pretty savvy about cats and when necessary can just fly away from danger. But in actuality mockingbirds are somewhat unusual in having evolved behaviors to cope with what is a relatively new, in evolutionary terms, predator of native birds. While birds may be born with an innate fear of some predators, such as hawks, owls, and snakes, avoidance of mammal predators is thought to be learned, necessitating that birds either gain direct experience with the type of predator (by surviving or observing an attack) or be taught by a parent. This kind of learning curve can take an extremely long time before it translates into adaptive behavior. Migrating birds unfamiliar with the surroundings, harried parents during the breeding season, and newly fledged young birds are especially easy prey for a cat on the prowl, and contrary to the popular myth a bell is not much of a deterrent as birds generally have no reason to associate the sound with danger.

Hummingbirds are particularly vulnerable to cats for several reasons. As mentioned earlier, predation of adult hummingbirds is rare in the wild; their tiny size and appreciable powers of flight probably combine to make them fairly difficult for most predators to catch. Because of this, hummingbirds generally have not developed the avoidance behaviors that come from a long predator-prey relationship. Nor do hummingbirds have a social structure that in other birds facilitates a warning system, with alarm calls or behaviors such as predator mobbing. Migrants from remote high-elevation forests may have little experience with humans, let alone their pets, and may be especially easy targets. Some hummingbird species, most notably Calliope Hummingbirds, frequently feed close to the ground and thus are at even greater risk. While we humans may be able to recognize the peril of a cat lying in wait or on the prowl, we must realize that the hummingbirds' primary focus is on responding to the various visual clues that tell them a certain flower—that we likely have planted specifically to attract them—may offer nectar. Hummingbirds desperately need us all to be responsible pet owners and keep our beloved felines indoors.

For further information on cat predation, useful tips on converting an outdoor cat to an indoor one (often not as difficult as you might imagine), and fast facts on other conservation issues that affect wild birds, please explore the excellent website of the American Bird Conservancy listed under Resources.

As habitat across the Southwest dwindles, how we decide what to replace it with becomes increasingly significant. If we think of our yards as outcroppings of habitat of which we are the current stewards and strive to manage them accordingly, we have a tremendous opportunity to make a genuine difference to hummingbirds and the extraordinary flowers they pollinate.

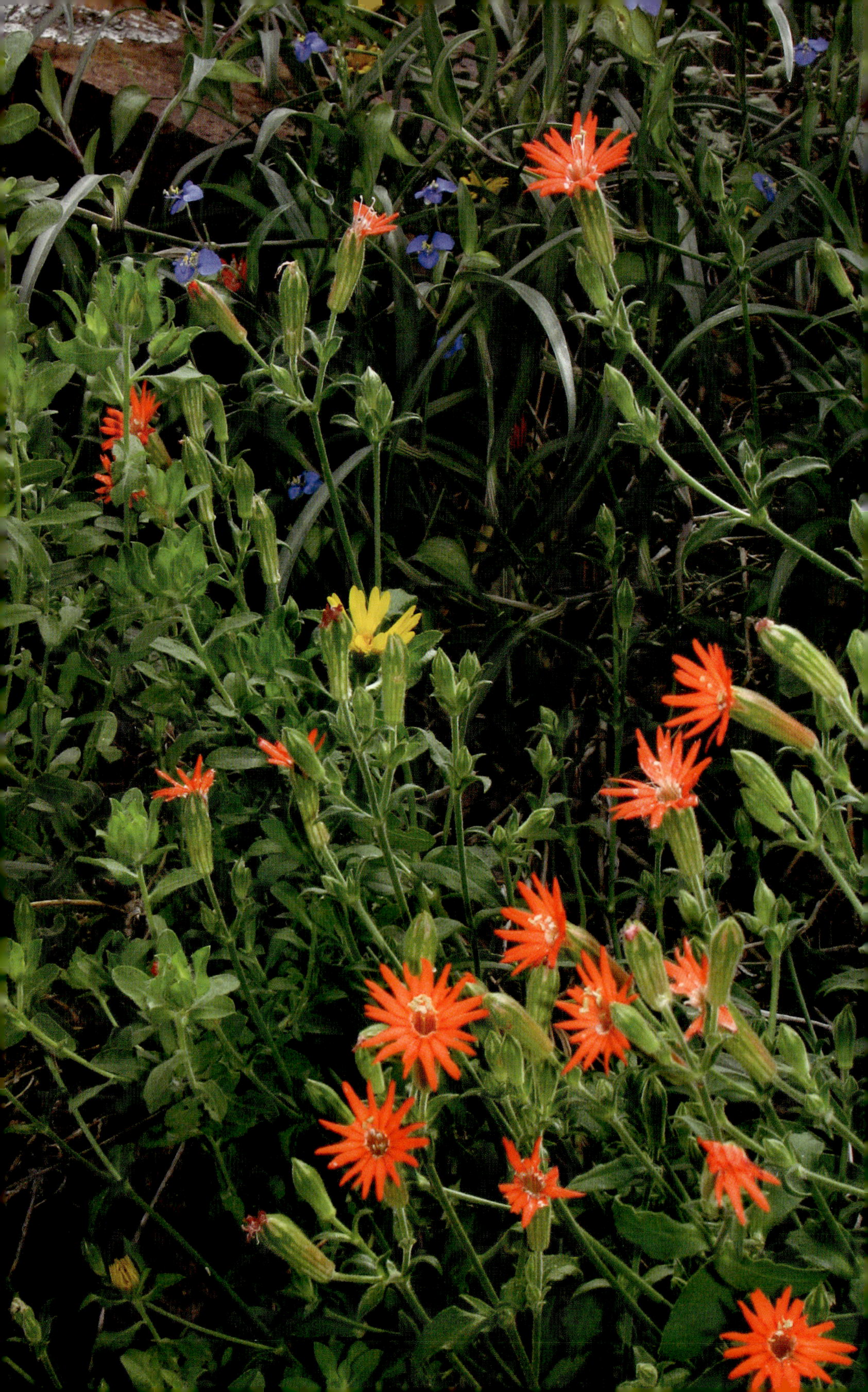

CHAPTER 4

Gardening *with* Native Plants, Southwestern Style

Just as the preceding chapter details some of the considerations that go into creating a happy and healthy environment for hummingbirds, this one focuses on doing the same for the plants we bring into our gardens. Newcomers to the Southwest and those who have only recently taken up gardening may appreciate some entry-level tips that will help make the process as simple and as rewarding as possible.

Perhaps nowhere else in the country does gardening with native plants make more sense than in the Southwest, with its extremes of temperature, desiccating winds, nutrient-poor soils, and mere dribbles of annual rainfall that together often conspire to cripple a great many plants that hail from gentler climes. Because they are better adapted to these harsh conditions, appropriately placed native plants tend to be easier to establish and require far less in the way of pesticides, soil amendments, and scarce water resources than traditional garden plantings; as such they are apt to be friendlier to the environment in the long run. Once established, most need only minimal care and maintenance to keep them looking terrific day after day, freeing up time for things like enjoying our hummingbird visitors. What's more, native plants intrinsically provide something that the generic lawn-and-hedge landscape decidedly lacks: a distinctive sense of place that anchors the garden to the surrounding region.

Another impetus for choosing native plants is that you can be reasonably sure they will not become invasive at some point in time, something that cannot be said with any degree of certainty about many exotic species. Tales abound of good plant intentions gone awry, such as the once-touted salt cedar and Russian olive. Since their innocent introduction many years ago, these two kudzus of the Southwest have choked out huge swaths of native riverside vegetation in much of the region. Similarly, aggressive non-native plants such as tree tobacco and particularly eucalyptus, both quite popular with hummingbirds, can be extremely invasive and are best avoided in native plant gardens. Our native flora, in contrast, is an integral part of the larger ecosystem, and as such benefits from natural checks and balances in the form of insects, fungi, and various pathogens that normally prevent plants from becoming a nuisance.

We who wish to put out the welcome mat for hummingbirds luckily have little need to look any further than our own region for flowering plants, for evolution has crafted a luscious cornucopia of choices that will not only be instantly recognizable to the birds but also have a decent chance of succeeding in our landscapes. We can maximize those chances of success by selecting plants that in the wild favor a habitat similar to the spot they will inhabit in the landscape or—to a point—by altering the landscape to more closely mimic a plant's natural haunts.

MICROCLIMATES OF THE LANDSCAPE

In order to make wise plant choices, you must first become at least somewhat familiar with your own property, including not only the various features within the yard but how it fits into the surrounding environs as well. The more thoroughly you are able to describe the landscape, the easier it will be to evaluate potential new plantings. In rural or lightly developed areas, the predominant ecosystem will usually be obvious and easily defined, whether desert (Chihuahuan, Sonoran, Mojave, or Great Basin), coastal sage scrub, grassland, riparian woodland, or montane coniferous forest. Piñon pines, junipers, and evergreen oaks typically reside in the lower elevations of the mountains, with ponderosa pines, Douglas-firs, spruces, and firs predominating as elevation increases. Rivers, canyons, or arroyos may further punctuate the landscape and introduce additional habitat niches for plants.

In highly developed neighborhoods, the surrounding natural landscape may seem practically irrelevant and yet the larger ecosystem will determine a great deal about growing conditions such as wet and dry seasons, annual precipitation, and temperature extremes. A plant native to ponderosa pine meadows in the Rocky Mountains, where clouds often shield the sun on summer afternoons and annual rainfall averages sixteen inches or more, will be decidedly unhappy baking away in the unrelenting June sun in the parched Chihuahuan Desert. The difference in the heat index between the two is just as palpable to plants as it is to us, though such disparate environments may be quite close in proximity to one another. When evaluating how a plant might perform in a given location, the elevation and other habitat characteristics are usually of much more relevance than the exact geographic bounds of the plant's native distribution.

Regardless of the prevailing habitat type of a particular piece of property, within it will be any number of nooks and crannies possessing unique combinations of features that replicate slightly different habitats. Thus, along the north side of a home will be a microclimate that is colder in winter than the remainder of the yard, and on the south side or against a rock wall will be warm zones that coddle more tender plants. Likewise, areas beneath overhangs provide a few degrees of frost protection. Various corners on the inside of a courtyard will be warmer or cooler depending upon exposure. An acequia or irrigation ditch resembles an arroyo, where seasonal moisture supports more vegetation than the surrounding areas. A hose bib, in-ground birdbath, or swamp cooler bleeder line mimics a seep. And so on. The ultimate in flexibility are container gardens, moveable as mood and season dictate and thus having an infinite number of possible microclimates.

Once these various habitat niches have been determined, plants being considered for the garden can be more easily appraised in terms of how closely a particular spot resembles the natural environment of the plant. While it is often possible to blur the boundaries of a habitat to some extent—for example, placing a plant that naturally occurs in a cool upland environment on the north side of a home at a lower elevation—the most success will come with as little such fudging as possible. If eventual ease of maintenance and water conservation are desired objectives, the backbone of the garden should consist of plants that are situated similarly to how they might occur naturally. Then with time, accomplishment, and growing knowledge, you may feel more comfortable experimenting with plants that require more fussing.

This vital part of the planning process can greatly minimize the frustrations that commonly result from inappropriate plant choices.

JUST ADD WATER

Plants native to the American Southwest are generally pretty frugal when it comes to the ability to subsist on trace amounts of rainfall. Annual precipitation amounts of some desert cities in the region range from a relatively ample twelve inches in Tucson, with eight to nine in El Paso and Las Cruces and seven in Phoenix, to a paltry four inches in Las Vegas and less than three in Yuma. Locations at higher elevations typically enjoy quite a bit more precipitation, as much as two or three times that of neighboring desert sites, attributable to both a more substantial snow melt and more frequent summer thunderstorms. Along the Pacific Coast, rainfall amounts increase as well, with the majority of precipitation occurring in the winter. Gardeners might note that coast-dwelling plants that are normally dormant during long summer dry periods sometimes have difficulty if planted in a location that experiences summer monsoons.

While many native plants are quite drought tolerant once mature, new transplants will need regular watering for a period of up to several years. Many desert-dwelling trees and shrubs can be excruciatingly slow-growing, first devoting the bulk of their energy toward developing the complex root systems that eventually will enable them to withstand prolonged droughts. Other plants, such as those that hail from riparian areas or higher elevations, may need some supplemental water indefinitely if planted out of their element. Even among plants considered drought tolerant, many cope with drought by going into dormancy, ceasing flowering and often dropping leaves. Plantings meant to attract hummingbirds may thus require periodic watering during the bloom period regardless of the plant's intrinsic ability to endure drought.

Many of us planning hummingbird gardens will probably find that while a number of plants may be able to make do with very little water once established, such as agaves, red yuccas, ocotillos, and claretcup cacti, the bulk of our plantings will need at least some supplemental water in order to thrive. Both for simplicity and to conserve water, try to group plants with similar water requirements together into zones whenever possible.

Drip irrigation is an efficient method to irrigate plants and is especially useful when installing new landscapes. A landscape professional can make this task much simpler and recommend a schedule of watering that is tailored toward the particular plants. The use of an automatic timer, while certainly convenient for the homeowner, is not without its pitfalls. At the very least, watering schedules need to be adjusted seasonally, and you need to know how to properly operate and reprogram the controller. If an automatic controller is used, one with a 31-day cycle is preferable; controllers with 7-day cycles force us to water at least once a week, regardless of whether the plants need it or not. The alternative to a drip system is to commit to a discipline of manual watering until plants become established, and stick to it.

Once established, most plants prefer to be watered deeply but infrequently, so that their roots have a chance to dry out somewhat between waterings. In very sandy or rocky soils this may take mere moments, whereas clay soils may hold water for several days or more. Regardless of the soil type, however, allow the water to penetrate slowly to the depth of the root ball and then some, whether with drip irrigation or a trickling hose placed near the base of the plant. Few of us enjoy standing around in triple-digit temperatures tending to new plants, but bear in mind that light sprinkling encourages shallow roots that will be much more susceptible to heat and drought. Encircling new plantings with a berm a few inches high makes deep watering relatively simple and is strongly recommended. Likewise, a covering of mulch, whether organic (like pine needles, pecan shells, bark, or hay) or inorganic (like gravel), will help keep roots cool and moist in the summer and cozy in the winter as well.

SOIL TYPES OF THE REGION

What passes for soil in much of the Southwest bears no resemblance to the rich texture and hue of the humus familiar to gardeners in other parts of the country. Typically quite low in organic matter, the stuff here is not blackish or even brown in most cases, but rather gray, tan, pink, or white. It may drain almost immediately (as does sand or gravel), slowly (as does clay), or not at all (like caliche, an impenetrable layer of calcium carbonate common in deserts). Most plants native to the region prefer fast-draining soil and many, such as the penstemons, require it; happily, this is what most of us have. Those with clay soil need to be especially mindful about drainage when choosing plants and still may find that many of the natives will perform much better in raised beds. The more energetic gardeners among us may add compost to clay soils to improve drainage over time or to sandy soils to increase the water-holding capacity; either way, compost makes a nifty soil conditioner and usually works best as a top-dressing after planting.

Whether predominantly composed of silt, sand, or clay, soils of our region share a tendency to be alkaline—that is, having a pH greater than 7.0. Most traditional garden plants, hailing as they do from the eastern United States and Europe, prefer a neutral or slightly acidic soil and are unhappy in our soils without a constant stream of amendments. Our native plants, on the other hand, need no such fussing and are usually quite content in their high-calcium, alkaline environment. The same goes for fertilizer; many southwestern plants not only prefer our lean soils but may actually languish if grown in highly enriched garden loam. Often a plant's own exuberance will surprise you, so unless you are trying to force a plant to crank out unending blooms—probably not in the long-term best interests of the plant—frequent applications of fertilizer are usually unwarranted.

"IT'S A DRY HEAT"

That's what we Southwesterners say to our dewy-faced relatives and friends from back east who are contemplating a visit. And while it may make oven-like temperatures more bearable for human beings, it's what turns plants that hail from other regions into toast in short order. For most of the year the relative humidity is negligible, less than 20 percent, and coupled with drying winds can be debilitating to plants that are not adapted to life in the desert. Our desert natives, on the other hand, have developed a variety of special mechanisms that enable them to make the most of what little moisture exists. Many woody plants go into semi-dormancy during the driest months until the summer monsoons jump-start them again, and indeed hummingbird plants that bloom reliably during the dry season are highly welcome and comparatively few.

Plants from the higher elevations are not nearly as heat tolerant as their desert counterparts, a fact that desert dwellers should keep in mind when evaluating plants to add to their gardens. Not only are ambient temperatures cooler in the mountains, but clouds often mask the summer sun as well. Plants that flourish in full sun in mountain meadows absolutely cannot take the intense sunlight of lower elevations, and will need afternoon shade if they are to stand a chance of surviving in the desert. Indeed, even desert-adapted plants appreciate some relief from the sun for a portion of the day, thriving in the dappled shade of trees such as palo verdes or mesquites.

WHERE TO FIND NATIVE PLANTS

Thanks to committed growers willing to ride out a long learning curve, native plants are becoming easier to find, some of the most popular even showing up at the mass merchants and home improvement chains on occasion. For most natives you will probably have the best luck at smaller nurseries or specialty retailers. Frequently, such places may be able to offer a lead to a particular plant even if they don't stock it themselves. For more obscure plants, check with area botanical gardens, arboreta, master gardeners, or native plant societies to inquire whether they might hold an annual or semi-annual plant sale. Such organizations are also great venues for meeting other like-minded gardeners, with whom you can exchange information on sources, cultivation tips, seeds, and even cuttings of unusual plants.

Another option is to start plants from seed yourself. The Lady Bird Johnson Wildflower Center, listed in the Resources, is one resource to check for potential seed suppliers. You can also collect seed from the wild, but care should be taken not to do so if the plants are rare or threatened. Even with common plants, please be mindful of the Rule of Thirds: Take seeds from no more than a third of the plants occurring in a given population, and harvest no more than a third of the seeds on any single plant. Always ask permission from the landowner or agency in charge of management before collecting seeds or taking cuttings. Since regimes for cleaning, storing, and germinating seeds vary widely, it is wise to familiarize yourself with these requirements prior to gathering seeds whenever possible.

Obtaining seeds of Mexican plants is more problematic, unfortunately, as Mexico requires permits to collect seeds and plant material and the USDA requires permits to bring seeds and plant material over the border; furthermore, such permits are quite restricted and reportedly difficult to obtain even for scientific purposes. Perhaps botanical gardens and nurseries that may have acquired seeds in the past and grown some of these extraordinary plants can make them more widely available to the public in the future.

The gardener with patience and a willingness to learn a few propagation techniques can grow a wonderful hummingbird garden on a remarkably tiny budget by starting with several plants that are known to either set seed readily or propagate easily from cuttings or divisions. When setting out starter plants, be sure to leave plenty of empty space for the next generation or two of youngsters. Then as cuttings develop or volunteer seedlings emerge they can be transplanted to wherever desired, whether clumped together with the mother plant or to another area of the yard. In three to four years or less an unremarkable garden can be transformed into a spectacular hedgerow of hummingbird flowers, and for a veritable song.

Please resist the temptation to dig up wild plants, unless in conjunction with an organized salvage operation to save plants from imminent destruction. Precious few will survive transplanting regardless of how careful you try to be, and our wild places face too many threats as it is. In addition, make the effort to seek out seed-grown rather than wild-collected plants such as cacti and ocotillos, unless such plants have been legitimately salvaged. In parts of the Southwest, truckloads of such plants are dug illegally—often from public lands—and perpetrators commonly evade prosecution.

PLANTING BASICS

In much of the Southwest you can plant most anytime, but early fall is usually optimal so that the new plants can have a lengthy period of time to get settled in before the rigors of their first summer. In areas that have prolonged freezing temperatures, the more tender plants should be planted in spring after the last hard frost. In most cases the least opportune time to plant is probably early summer, but if you are willing to water daily (or more if necessary) it can be attempted.

For container plants, dig a hole that is the same depth as the root ball and two to four times the diameter of the container. Avoid disturbing the soil beneath the plant, and then after placing the plant in the hole tamp the backfill down firmly around the sides. Compost can be added to the backfill, but most experts believe this is not a good idea because then the roots will be loath to go beyond the amended soil. A better idea is to apply a layer of compost to the surface of the entire planting bed, where it will gradually break down and condition the soil and also do double duty as mulch.

New plants will be much easier to water if surrounded with a berm a few inches high around the planting hole to retain water within the circle as it percolates slowly into the ground. When planting on slopes, such catch basins are particularly important for harvesting water. Also, as mentioned earlier, applying some sort of mulch will help to conserve moisture and shade the roots.

For further information on planting and cultivation of native plants please consult any of the fine references listed in the bibliography, in particular those by Mary Irish, Judy Mielke, Judith Phillips, and Sally and Andy Wasowski. *Native Plants for High-Elevation Western Gardens* by Janice Busco and Nancy Morin will be particularly useful for upland gardeners. For tips on propagation, see especially *How to Grow Native Plants of Texas and the Southwest* by Jill Nokes and *Plants for Natural Gardens* by Judith Phillips.

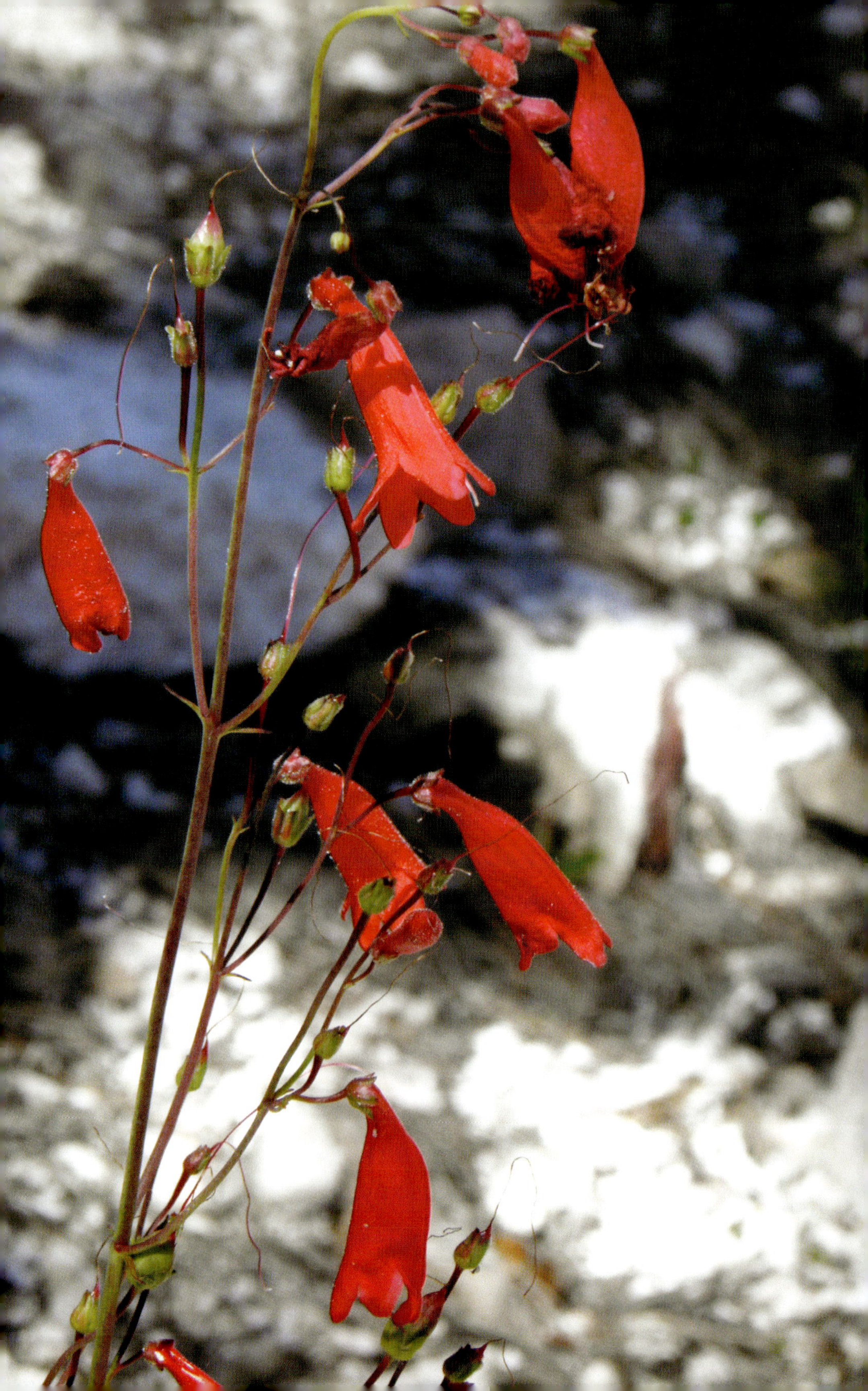

CHAPTER 5

Hummingbird Plants *of the* Southwestern United States *and* Northern Mexico

The 120 plants profiled here appear in alphabetical order by botanical name and are each organized into three (or more) paragraphs—the first highlighting the plant's special significance to hummingbirds, the second describing the native range, habitat, and appearance of the plant, and the third discussing cultivation requirements to the extent they are known. Each profile also contains an inset with at-a-glance information on several important plant characteristics:

❶ **FAMILY:** The group of plants to which the plant belongs, according to professional botanists. Such assignments may occasionally change to reflect new research findings, thus for some plants two family names will appear.

❷ **TYPE:** Tree, shrub, subshrub, vine, perennial, biennial, or succulent; also evergreen or deciduous.

❸ **SIZE:** The approximate size range of a mature plant (which can vary widely between wild and cultivated plants and the amount of water the plant receives).

❹ **BLOOM:** The typical flowering season for the plant, which may differ greatly by location and elevation. Note also that individual plants may bloom for only a portion of this period.

❺ **WATER USE:** The relative amount of water needed by established plants, with low representing extremely drought-tolerant species that can typically exist on little to no supplemental irrigation and high pertaining to those that occur near water courses and need regular watering to thrive.

❻ **COLD HARDINESS:** The lowest temperature that the plant is known to tolerate. For some plants temperatures are also given for the top growth and/or roots.

❼ **USDA ZONE:** The plant hardiness zones in which the plant might be expected to grow. Such zones are defined by the U. S. Department of Agriculture and based primarily upon average annual minimum winter temperatures. Current maps may be viewed at www.planthardiness.ars.usda.gov/PHZMWeb/.

❽ **AUTHOR CITATION:** The person(s) who first named and described the plant, sometimes along with others who later renamed the plant.

❾ **SYNONYM(S):** Additional botanical names by which the plant may be or may have been known, along with their author citations.

SAMPLE
Agastache pallida
Pale Giant Hyssop, Giant Hummingbird Mint

❶ **Family:**	Lamiaceae	❺ **Water use:**	Moderate
❷ **Type:**	Perennial	❻ **Cold hardiness:**	Roots to 0°F
❸ **Size:**	2–3' high x 1–2' wide	❼ **USDA zone:**	7–10
❹ **Bloom:**	July–October or frost		
❽ *Author citation:*	(Lindley) Cory		
❾ *Synonym:*	*Agastache barberi* (B. L. Robinson) Epling		

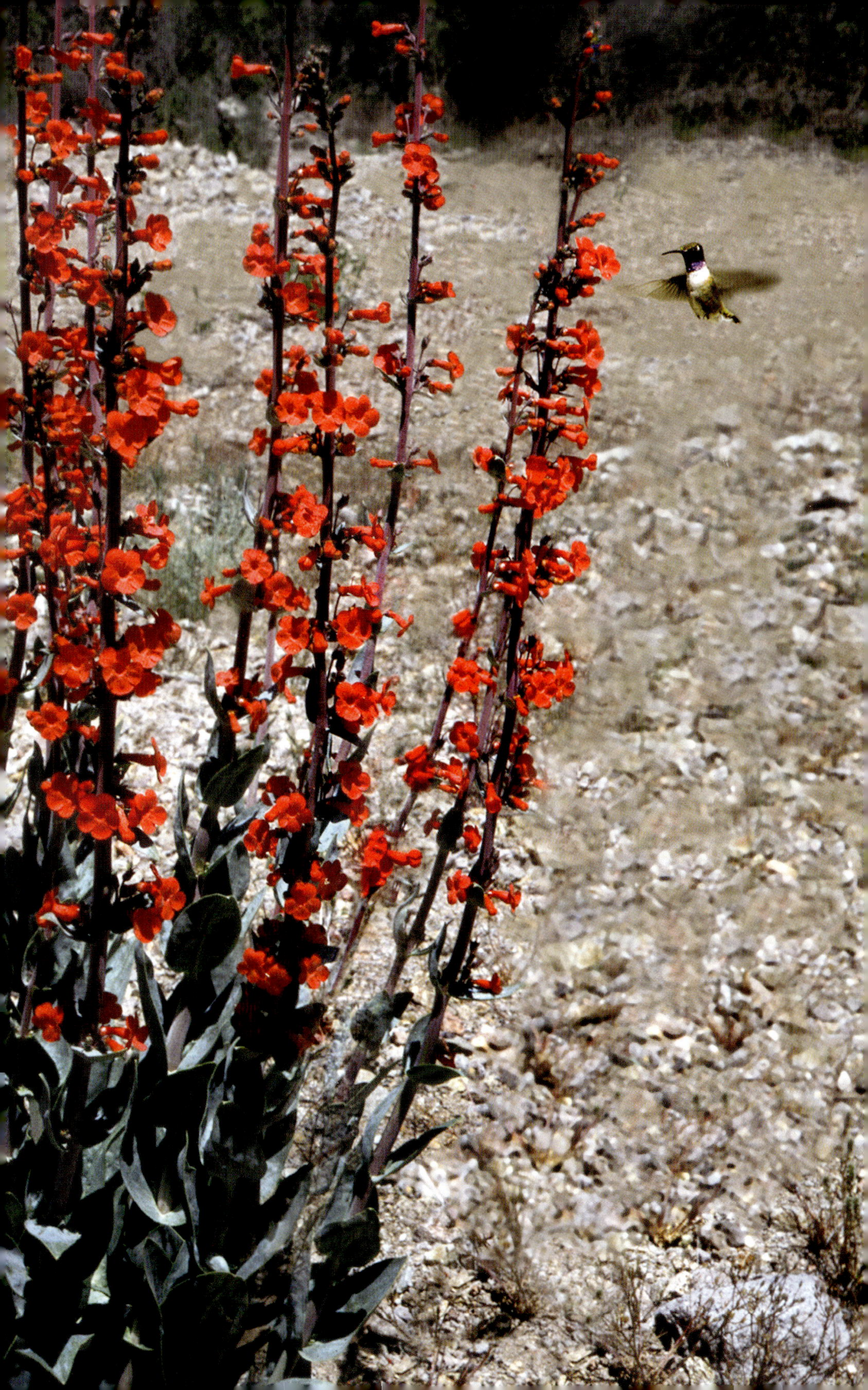

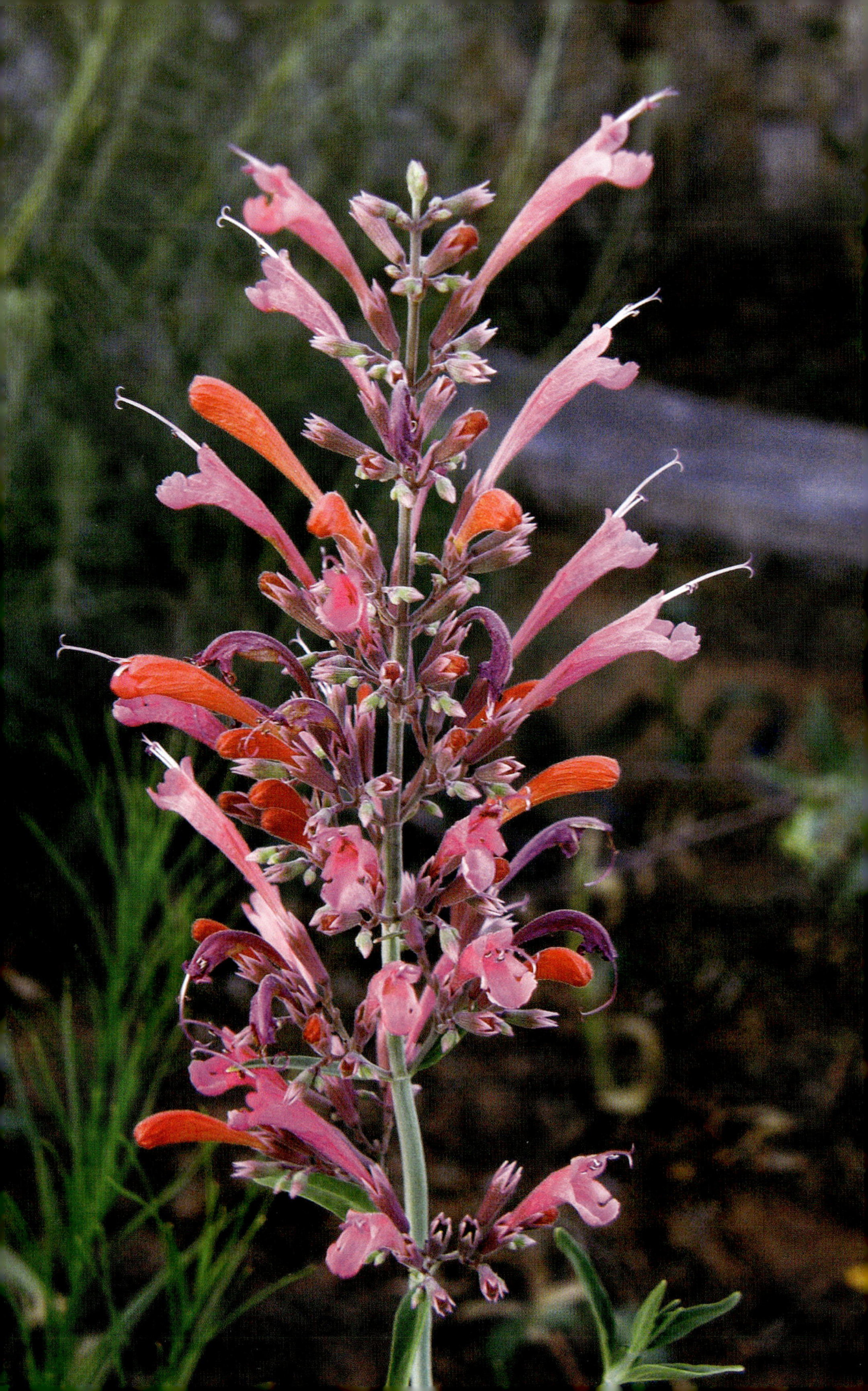

Agastache cana

Bubblegum Mint, Mosquito Plant, Giant Hyssop

Family:	Lamiaceae	**Water use:**	Moderate
Type:	Perennial	**Cold hardiness:**	Roots to -20°F
Size:	2–3' high x 1–2' wide	**USDA zone:**	5–8
Bloom:	July–October		

Author citation: (W. J. Hooker) Wooton & Standley

As they stream southward from the Southern Rocky Mountains in late summer, migrating Broad-tailed and Rufous Hummingbirds are strongly attracted to the bright rose-pink flowers of this delightful perennial, and Black-chinned and Calliope Hummingbirds take nectar from the blossoms as well. The plants are pollinated in part by hummingbirds, along with sphinx moths, and Lesser Goldfinches quickly consume the seeds that ripen in autumn.

Bubblegum mint is widely available in the nursery trade but surprisingly rare in the wild, occurring only on several scattered upland sites in central and southern New Mexico, where it is listed as endangered, and in west Texas in the Hueco and Franklin Mountains. Typically it is found in cool niches where its deep, spreading roots can find water, such as springs, seeps, and water-holding rock crevices, at elevations of 4,000 to 8,400 feet. Its square stems bear small shiny oval to heart-shaped leaves that are aromatic and said to repel mosquitoes if crushed and rubbed on the skin. The one-inch tubular flowers are densely clustered on spikes above the foliage and have a bubblegum-like scent.

This profuse bloomer can be tricky to grow at first but once established tends to be long-lived, performing the best in light, lean to moderately fertile, well-drained soils and partial or dappled shade. With supplemental water it can be rather heat tolerant, but be careful not to overwater it when dormant or in rainy months. A good rule of thumb is to give plants a deep soaking once a month during the growing season and once a week in summer if no natural rainfall occurs. Deadhead, or pinch off, spent blossoms and flower spikes to maximize flowering time. Propagation is fairly easy by rooting stem cuttings in moist sand or vermiculite or by planting seed that has been cold stratified for several weeks. Plants usually bloom the first year from seed if sown in early spring. When setting out potted plants, grower Judith Phillips recommends digging a hole that is four times wider than the diameter of the container.

This extremely showy plant enlivens the midsummer garden and is an excellent choice for mixed perennial borders, desert oasis gardens, and containers.

Agastache pallida

Pale Giant Hyssop, Giant Hummingbird Mint

Family:	Lamiaceae	**Water use:**	Moderate
Type:	Perennial	**Cold hardiness:**	Roots to 0°F
Size:	2–3' high x 1–2' wide	**USDA zone:**	7–10
Bloom:	July–October or frost		

Author citation: (Lindley) Cory
Synonym: *Agastache barberi* (B. L. Robinson) Epling

THE BRIGHT ROSY-PURPLE BLOOMS OF THIS PRIMARILY MEXICAN BEAUTY are usually anything but pale when they unfurl, and are produced over a long bloom season that just so happens to parallel the peak of hummingbird migration in the Southwest. Broad-tailed and Rufous Hummingbirds are among the many visitors. Hummingbirds, along with butterflies and bees, contribute pollination services in exchange for partaking of the nectar bounty.

In the United States, pale giant hyssop occurs naturally only in southern Arizona, where canyon bottoms in the Patagonia Mountains are among its few haunts, but in Mexico it can be found all along the Sierra Madre Occidental in Sonora, Chihuahua, and Durango southward into Michoacán. Typical habitats include moist niches within arid pine-oak forests, such as springs, watered canyons, and seeps, at elevations of 5,000 to 9,000 feet. Upright in form and woody at the base, the numerous erect stems are clothed in pale gray-green foliage that presumably inspired the species name. The pleasantly aromatic leaves are ovate to rather triangular in shape and coarsely toothed. The tubular flowers, purplish when they open and gradually fading to pink or lavender as they age, are loosely arranged on flower spikes above the foliage.

This pretty perennial is fairly adaptable, but it demands excellent drainage and seems to perform best in a loose, gravelly soil with low to moderate fertility. In the wild it grows in full sun to part shade but in hot desert locations will require mid-afternoon shade as well as regular water during the summer. Deadheading, or pinching off, faded flowers and snipping spent stalks will encourage continued bloom. Propagate by seed sown at 70°F (cold stratifying the seed first for a month or more may improve germination rates) or by stem cuttings taken in spring and placed in moist sand or other fast-draining medium. In an upland garden, this prolific bloomer would be magnificent tucked next to a water feature among rocks or massed at a woodland edge. It also works beautifully in containers but will then require more frequent watering.

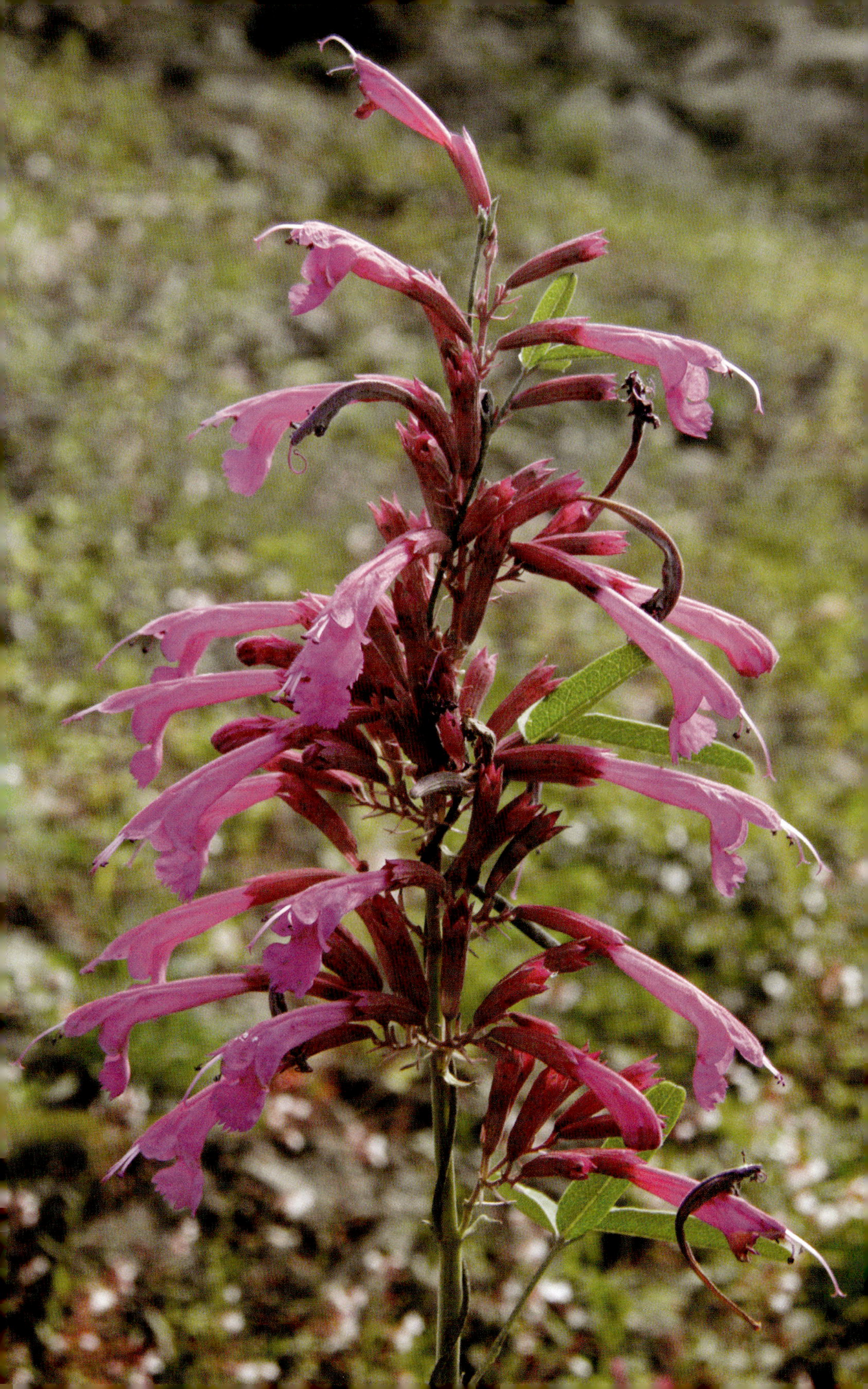

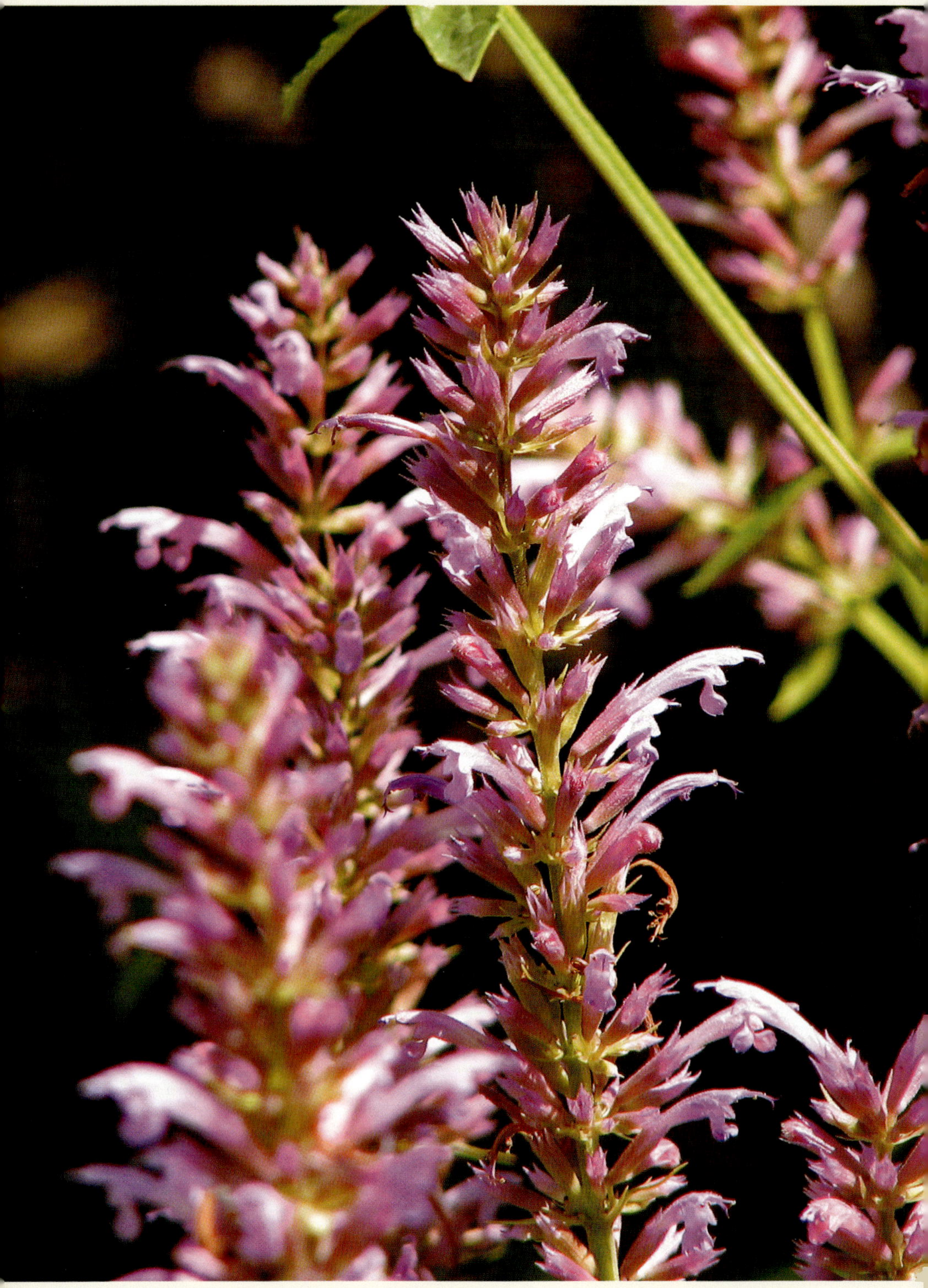

Agastache pallidiflora
Bill Williams Mountain Giant Hyssop

Family:	Lamiaceae	**Water use:**	Moderate–high
Type:	Perennial	**Cold hardiness:**	Roots to -10°F
Size:	2' high x 2–3' wide	**USDA zone:**	6–10
Bloom:	July–October		

Author citation: (A. Heller) Rydberg

While perhaps not as showy as those of some of their cousins, the lovely pastel purplish flowers of this agastache nevertheless are quite valuable to post-breeding and migrating hummingbirds in mid to late summer because of their broad distribution and abundance. Bees and butterflies are also drawn to the delicately scented blossoms and are probably the primary pollinators.

Bill Williams Mountain giant hyssop, its common moniker indicating where its type was first named, occurs over a large geographical swath that extends from the Colorado Plateau of southwestern Colorado southward through north-central and eastern Arizona, western and parts of southern New Mexico, the Trans-Pecos region of Texas, and Sonora and Chihuahua in northern Mexico. Occurring at elevations ranging from 5,000 to 10,000 feet, it can be found in a variety of habitats, including piñon-juniper slopes, ponderosa pine stands, spruce-fir forests, and subalpine meadows, but within these environments typically inhabits moist or wet niches.

Compact in form, its thick, erect stems bear opposite pairs of grayish green, prominently veined, triangular to heart-shaped leaves that are an inch or more in length and have scalloped edges. The flowers, consisting of half-inch corollas packed together in dense terminal spikes up to three inches long, appear throughout the summer and range in color from pale lavender to soft pink to rosy purple depending on the subspecies. A near-twin from northern Mexico that is often indistinguishable, San Luis giant hyssop (*A. mearnsii*), has reddish-purple blossoms.

One of the few in its family that truly tolerates wet feet and heavy soils, Bill Williams Mountain giant hyssop does beautifully in perennial beds and borders, where it will thrive in loamy garden soil that may prove lethal to other agastaches. In lower elevations it definitely prefers cool niches. Plants are reportedly easy to propagate by seed sown in spring, and one would think that cuttings should work as well. Given a sunny exposure and adequate moisture during the summer, this agastache adds a nice touch to herb, butterfly, and cutting gardens, and its subtle hues provide a lovely foil for the bold reds that tend to predominate in a hummingbird garden.

Agastache rupestris

Threadleaf Giant Hyssop, Sunset Hyssop, Licorice Mint

Family:	Lamiaceae	**Water use:**	Moderate
Type:	Perennial	**Cold hardiness:**	Roots to -20°F
Size:	2–4' high x 2' wide	**USDA zone:**	5–9
Bloom:	July–October		

Author citation: (Greene) Standley

THIS COLORFUL, LONG-BLOOMING PERENNIAL IS HEAVILY VISITED BY southbound Rufous Hummingbirds in late summer, and garden plantings are popular with Black-chinned, Broad-tailed, and Calliope Hummingbirds as well. The cantaloupe-orange flowers with their lavender calyces offer intriguing possibilities to the hummingbird gardener overwhelmed by too many reds. Hummingbirds play at least a minor role in pollination, and goldfinches take the reddish-brown seeds in autumn.

Threadleaf giant hyssop naturally occurs in southern Arizona in several scattered mountain ranges and in the Gila River Basin, in southwestern New Mexico in mountains of the Gila National Forest, and in northern Mexico in the state of Chihuahua. Common habitats in which it can be found include oak grasslands, piñon-juniper woodlands, and openings in ponderosa pine forest at elevations of about 4,000 to 7,600 feet, where it is often tucked into rock crevices or sheltered by boulders. Its hollow, square stems are dressed with narrow, grayish green, threadlike leaves that give the plant an airy look and have a pleasant anise or root beer fragrance. The slender one-inch tubular flowers are borne in clusters on spikes above the foliage.

Plants prefer a well-drained, gravelly soil that is low in organic matter. They will grow in full sun or part shade, but in low desert locations afternoon shade is recommended. Give plants a deep soaking once a month during the growing season and at least twice a month during summer dry periods. Pinching spent blossoms will maximize the bloom period. Plants flower the first year from seed if sown early. Propagation is also fairly easy by rooting stem cuttings in a light potting soil-vermiculite mix in spring or fall. Threadleaf giant hyssop lends a distinctive texture and the colors of a southwestern sky to oasis plantings, perennial borders, and containers.

Agastache 'Desert Sunrise' is a hybrid of this plant and *Agastache cana*, and is said to be extremely attractive to hummingbirds. It has bright pink and orange flowers with lavender calyces that bloom midsummer to fall and is reportedly suitable for USDA Zones 5–10.

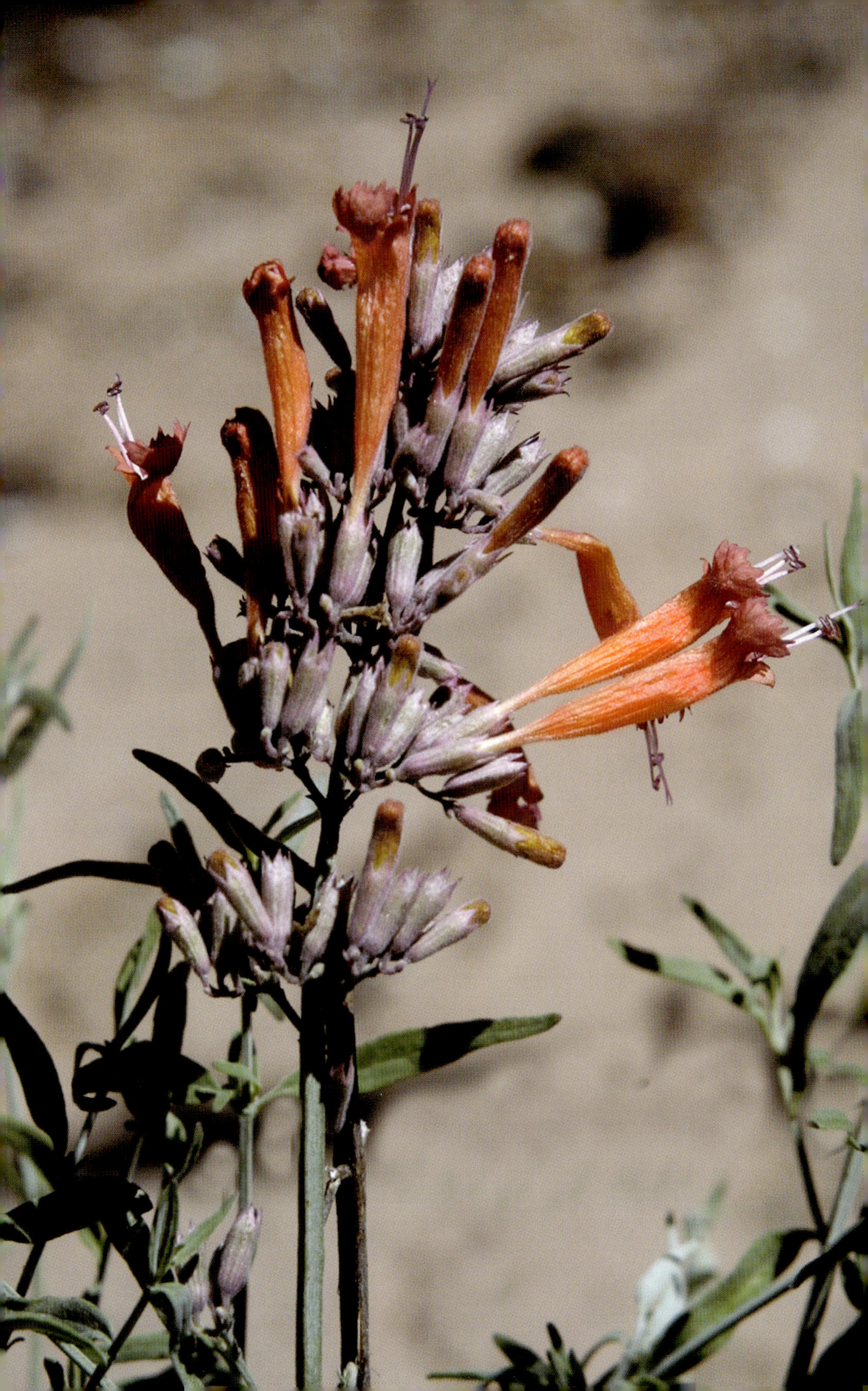

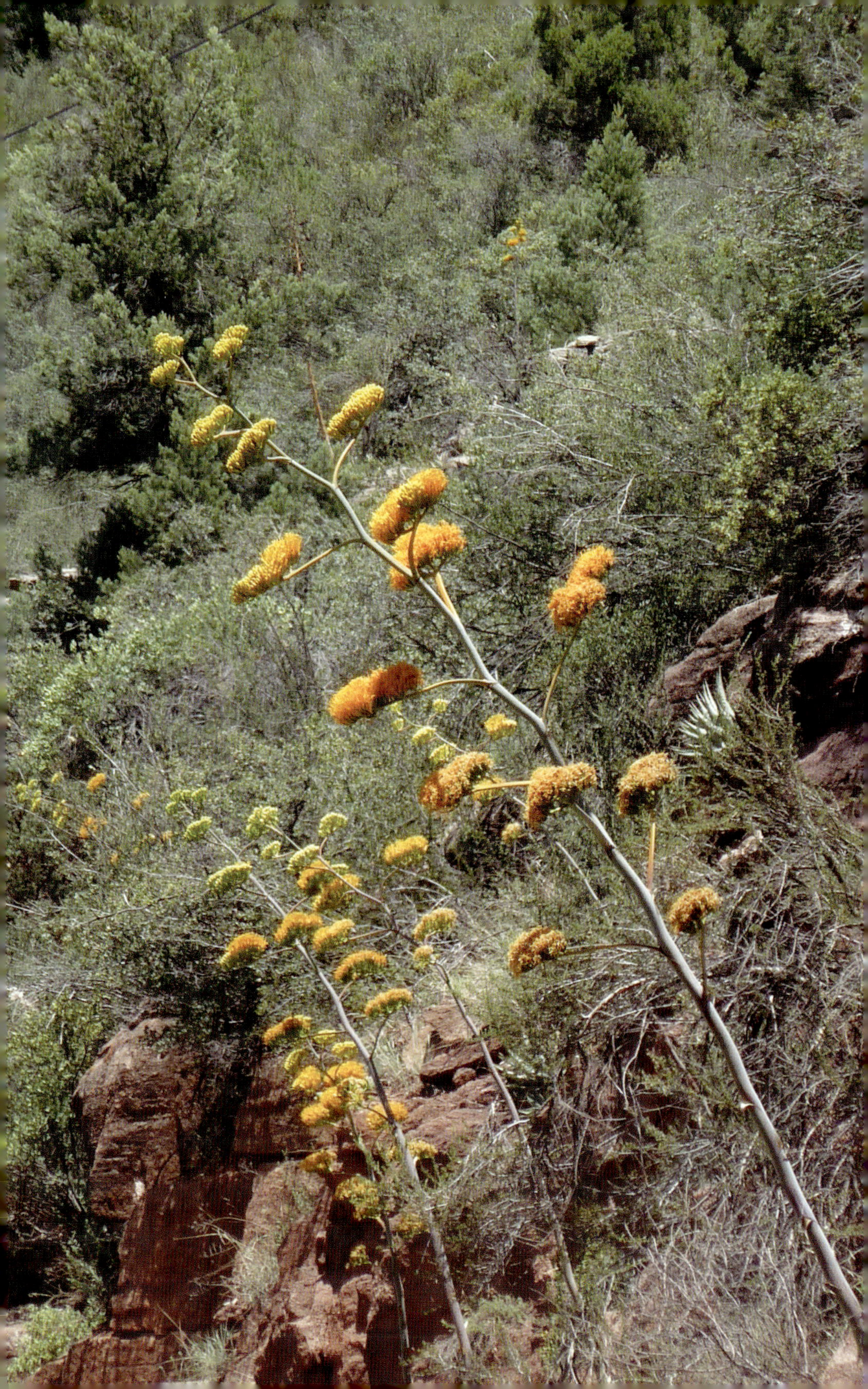

Agave chrysantha

Golden-Flowered Agave, Goldenflower Century Plant

Family:	Agavaceae (Asparagaceae)	**Bloom:**	Late May–July
Type:	Succulent	**Water use:**	Low
Size:	2–3' high x 3–5' wide, with 13–23' flower stalk	**Cold hardiness:**	To 10°F
		USDA zone:	8–10

Author citation: Peebles
Synonym: *Agave palmeri* var. *chrysantha* (Peebles) Little ex Benson

THIS LARGE AGAVE OF THE SONORAN DESERT is an important nectar source for breeding Costa's Hummingbirds, especially in May and June. The enormous candelabra-like flowering stalk will not form on the plant for many years but when it finally does, the golden yellow tubular blossoms, held in dense upright clusters at the branch tips, produce abundant nectar for hummingbirds and a huge variety of insects. The succulent leaves host the larvae of the Aryxna and Yavapai giant skipper butterflies. Spent flower stalks make excellent sentinel perches for hummingbirds and other birds and provide homes for both birds and native bees.

Golden-flowered agave is endemic to, or occurs exclusively in, south-central Arizona, where it grows at elevations of 3,000 to 7,000 feet on granitic or volcanic soils of mountain slopes and foothills, often in the company of chaparral or junipers. Its long, narrow, fleshy, silvery gray leaves are borne in a rosette, and have cat claw–like teeth along the margins and dangerously sharp spines at the tips.

Not fussy as long as it is given a lean fast-draining soil and full sun, this agave thrives in blazing heat that would shrivel most plants. Newly planted agaves need a deep watering once or twice a month and weekly during the first summer. Once established, they will look best with a monthly soaking. This agave does not always form offsets as many other agaves do, so the show may come to an end with the plant's eventual flowering and death. If you have the room, plant several of the plants for generations of enjoyment. Note that golden-flowered agave is known to hybridize with several other agave species, including *Agave murpheyi, A. palmeri, A. parryi* var. *couesii*, and *A. delamateri*, so do not plant it near these species if you want new plants to remain true to type. This slow-growing plant makes a striking accent for a naturalistic desert planting, nicely complementing the softer textures of shrubs and trees. It is particularly appropriate for areas where Costa's Hummingbirds are known to breed, but be sure to locate it a good distance from walkways.

Agave deserti

Desert Agave, Amul

Family:	Agavaceae (Asparagaceae)	**Bloom:**	May–July
Type:	Succulent	**Water use:**	Low
Size:	1–1.5' high x 2' wide, with 5–15' flower stalk	**Cold hardiness:**	To 9°F
		USDA zone:	8–10

Author citation: Engelmann

WHEN THIS AGAVE OF THE LOWER COLORADO DESERT FLOWERS IN springtime, its pale yellow flowers offer abundant nectar to breeding Costa's Hummingbirds when other flowering plants may be in short supply, particularly early in the season. The birds also occasionally nest on old flower stalks in the Anza-Borrego Desert of southeastern California. Hummingbirds and a variety of insects probably perform the lion's share of pollination services, with desert bats (*Leptonycteris sanborni*) doing so in the scattered localities where they still occur. The succulent foliage hosts the larvae of the California giant skipper butterfly and also serves as an important source of moisture for bighorn sheep during periods of drought.

Desert agave ranges from southern California and southwestern Arizona southward into Mexico from northern Baja California to northwest Sonora. True to its common name, it is a denizen of the desert, occurring on sandy flats, alluvial fans, and gravelly slopes dotted with low desert scrub at elevations that vary widely from 300 to 5,000 feet. The variety *deserti* tends to form large colonies, while the variety *simplex*, of southeastern California and south-central Arizona, does not. Its narrow, light grayish green leaves are borne in a rosette and have sharp spines at the tips and curved teeth on the margins. After up to thirty years the flower stalk finally shoots up, growing two or more inches per day and bearing clusters of short-tubed flowers with long threadlike stamens and styles on short, lateral branchlets.

This agave thrives in blistering temperatures, full and reflected sun, and poor, rocky, alkaline soils, demanding only excellent drainage. New plants should be deep watered weekly during their first summer and then once or twice a month thereafter, although they often manage fine with much less. Desert agave usually produces offsets that can be divided from the main plant. As this agave is a bit smaller than most, it is especially appropriate as an accent in residential landscapes, as long as its weapons are kept away from pathways.

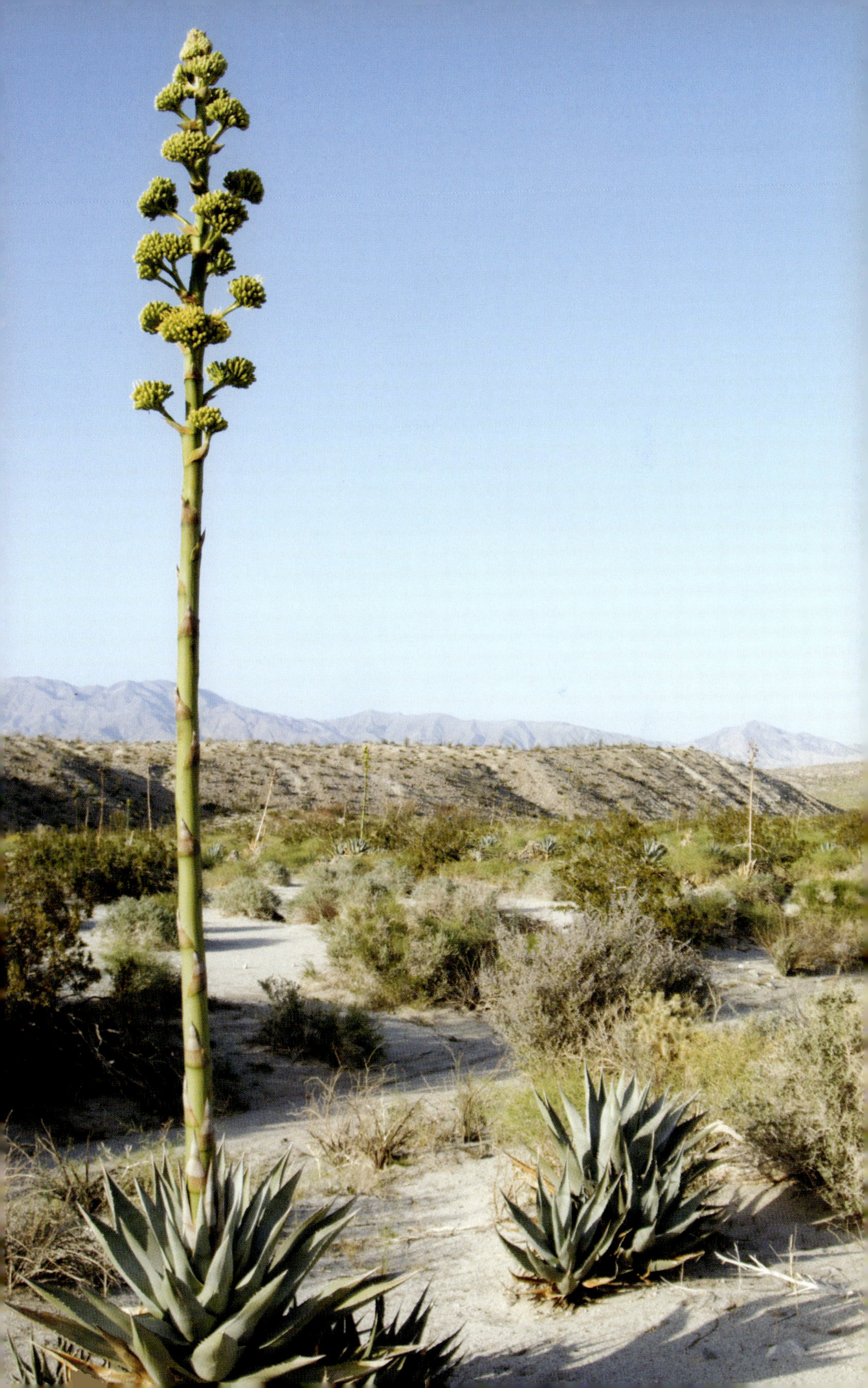

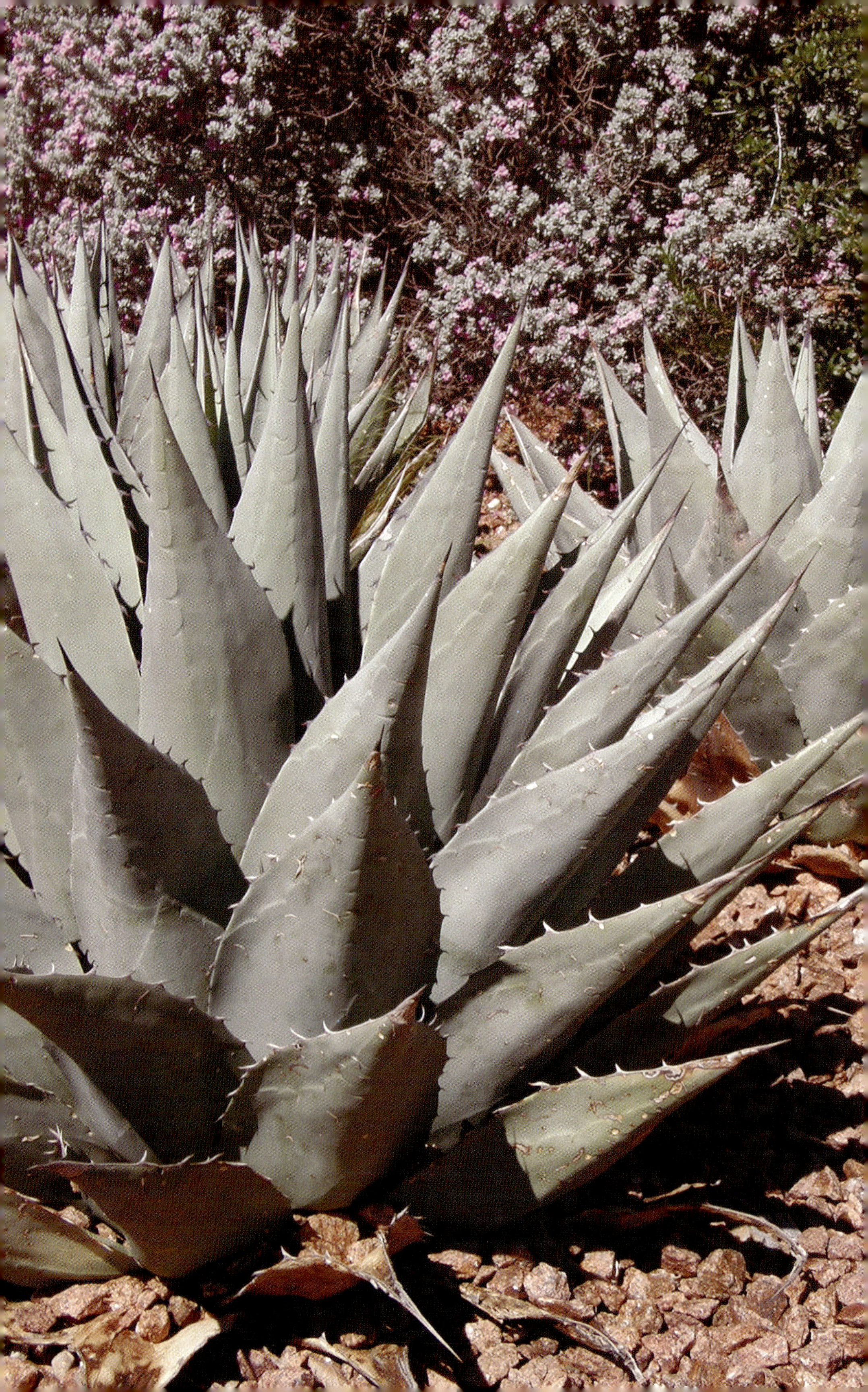

Agave havardiana

Havard's Agave, Big Bend Agave

Family:	Agavaceae (Asparagaceae)	**Bloom:**	April–June in lowlands, June–October in highlands
Type:	Succulent		
Size:	3' high x 4' wide, with flower stalk to 15'	**Water use:**	Low
		Cold hardiness:	To -20°F
		USDA zone:	5–10

Author citation: Trelease

This is the predominant large agave of the Big Bend area of Texas, often biding its time until flowering for twenty-five years or more. When the big event finally does occur, the yellow funnel-shaped blooms are borne in upright clusters on a tall candelabra-like stalk and produce copious nectar that is an important food source for Lucifer, Blue-throated, Broad-tailed, Black-chinned, and migrating Rufous Hummingbirds. While rich in glucose and fructose, each flower producing an astonishing 200 milligrams of sugar each day, the nectar is relatively low in sucrose, but with more than 2,000 flowers on a plant the sheer quantity must make up for quality. Lucifer Hummingbirds actively defend flowering plants, often using the stalk as a sentinel perch. Many insects are attracted to the blossoms, adding to the plant's appeal as a one-stop cafeteria for hummingbirds. Long-nosed bats (*Leptonycteris nivalis*) and passerine birds are reportedly the plant's main pollinators.

Havard's agave is found only in west Texas in a handful of mountain ranges, including the Chisos, Davis, and Guadalupe mountains, and in northern Mexico from Chihuahua to Coahuila. Typically, it occurs on rocky desert slopes and bajadas or on foothill grasslands, often in the company of junipers or oaks, from 4,000 to 6,500 feet in elevation. The stout, fleshy, blue-gray leaves are held in a rosette, and have claw-like teeth along the margins as well as brutally sharp spines at the tips that are up to two inches long.

Usually found on limestone soils in the wild, this agave is quite adaptive in landscapes, demanding only a well-drained soil that is low in organic matter and full sun. Water new plants deeply once or twice a month until established and weekly during their first summer. Havard's agave is one of the cold hardiest in the family, tolerating brief periods when temperatures hover below 0°F. Under favorable conditions this agave may form offsets, which will take the place of the parent plant after it flowers and dies. Otherwise, propagate by seed. This tough plant makes a handsome accent for rock gardens or corner plantings, but do keep its sharp spines away from walkways.

Agave lechuguilla
Lechuguilla, Shindagger

Family:	Agavaceae (Asparagaceae)	**Bloom:**	May–July
Type:	Succulent	**Water use:**	Low
Size:	1.5' high x 2' wide, forming clump 4–8' wide, with 8–15' flower stalk	**Cold hardiness:**	To 0°F
		USDA zone:	7–10

Author citation: Torrey

An indicator plant of the Chihuahuan Desert, lechuguilla differs from most familiar agaves in having flowers that are presented in spikes. Its shallow-tubed blossoms are packed thickly in bottlebrush-like clusters along the stalk and are greenish yellow with red or purple tinges. While not particularly showy, the blooms provide important nectar to breeding Black-chinned Hummingbirds, and are often visited by Lucifer Hummingbirds as well. South of the Mexican border in the rapidly dwindling areas where they still occur, nectivorous bats are the primary pollinators, but hummingbirds, butterflies, sphinx moths, and bees are responsible for pollination in most locations. This agave is a larval host for giant skipper butterflies. The dead stalks provide important nest sites for Lucifer Hummingbirds, who often build nests on the dried fruit pods, and homes for native bees.

Lechuguilla occurs on gravelly limestone slopes and rocky outcrops in west Texas, southern New Mexico near Las Cruces and eastward, and in north-central Mexico, from Chihuahua east to Tamaulipas and south to Hidalgo. Generally found at elevations of 3,000 to 7,500 feet, it frequently forms clumps that seem to spike entire hillsides. Its narrow, fleshy, pale or yellowish green leaves have claw-like teeth on the margins and terminal spines up to an inch-and-a-half long. The sometimes straight, sometimes curving leaves are borne in upright rosettes that are unremarkable until the plant blooms, typically at about twelve to fifteen years old.

Plants require a well-drained sandy or gravelly soil and full sun, will thrive in caliche, and once established need no supplemental water, subsisting contentedly on a mere six to eight inches of rainfall per year. New plants should be given a deep soaking once or twice a month during the growing season of their first year. This agave offsets profusely, almost guaranteeing blooms each year once the mother plant reaches maturity. Pups can be divided by cutting them off with a sharp knife, letting them air dry, and planting where a new colony is desired. Lechuguilla adds a nice texture to rock gardens and is a perfect complement to wildflowers in naturalistic plantings.

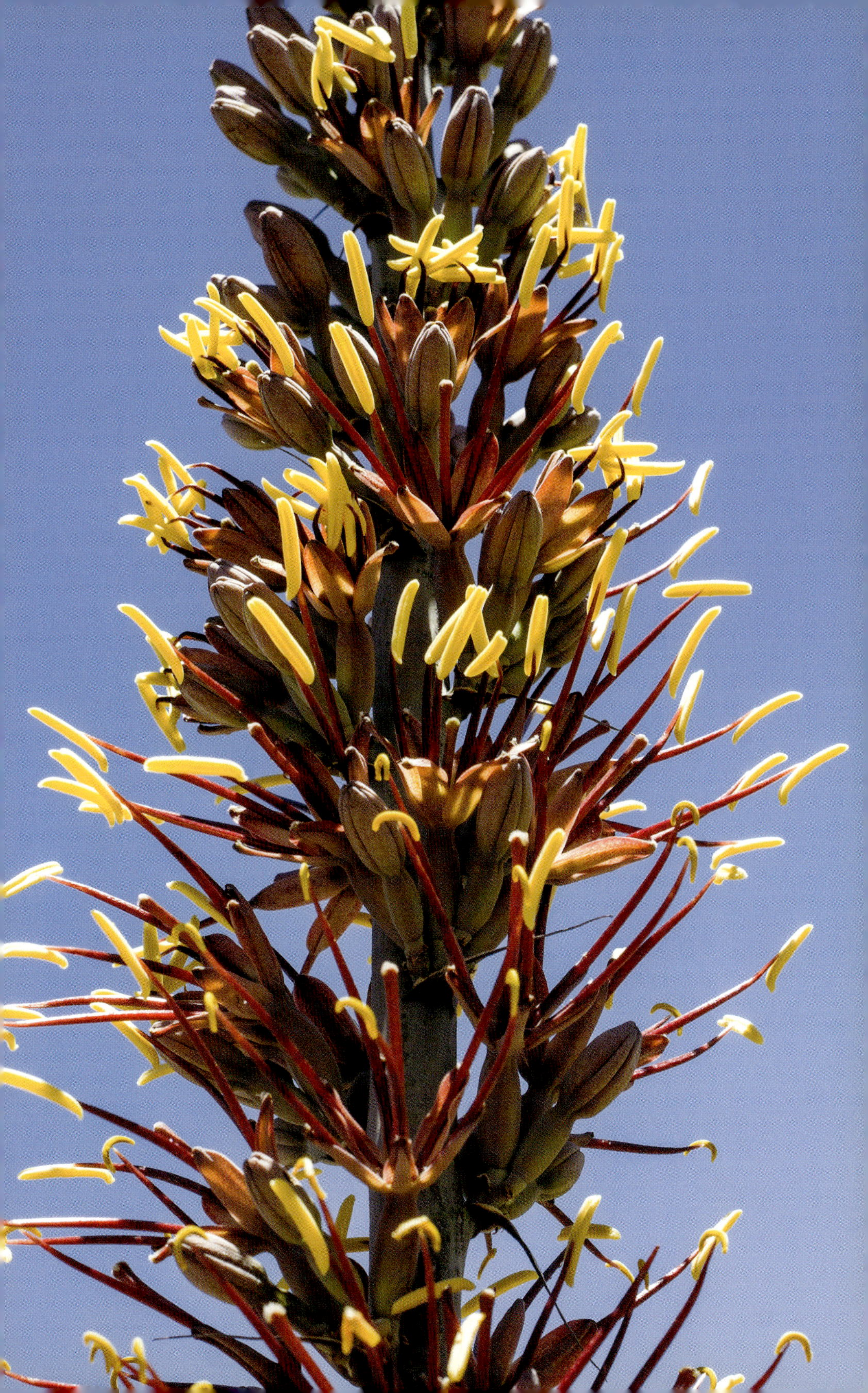

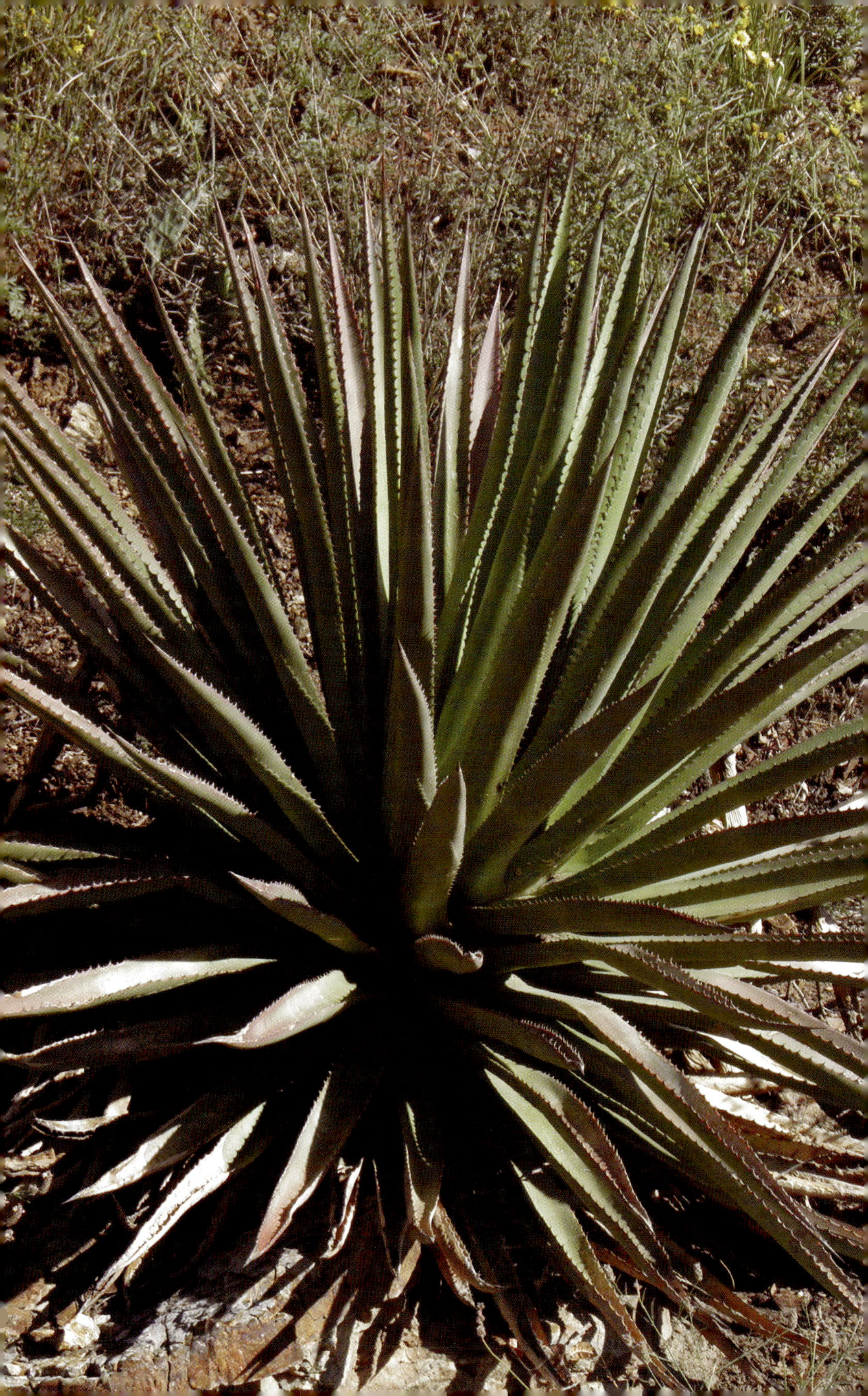

Agave palmeri
Palmer's Agave

Family:	Agavaceae (Asparagaceae)	**Bloom:**	June–August
Type:	Succulent	**Water use:**	Low
Size:	2–3' high x 3–4' wide, with 10–15' flower stalk	**Cold hardiness:**	To 9°F
		USDA zone:	8–10
Author citation:	Engelmann		

If there's a spot in your landscape begging for a medium-large native agave, the hummingbirds will applaud this choice. You may have to wait a couple of decades for the candelabra-like flower stalk to appear with its scrub brush-like clusters of greenish yellow, burgundy-tipped flowers, but the blossoms are avidly sought by Blue-throated, Violet-crowned, Black-chinned, and migrating Rufous Hummingbirds. Anna's, Costa's, Magnificent, Broad-tailed, and Broad-billed Hummingbirds and Plain-capped Starthroats, rare visitors from Mexico, are also known to visit the blossoms for both nectar and small insects, as do Hooded Orioles. Historically the plant's primary pollinators were desert bats (*Lyptonycteris sanborni*), whose numbers have plummeted since the 1950s, but fortunately hummingbirds and a variety of insects are effective pollinators as well. Band-tailed Pigeons avidly feed upon the seeds.

Palmer's agave occurs in southeast Arizona, spottily in southern New Mexico, and southward into Mexico from northern Sonora to northwest Chihuahua, at elevations of 3,000 to 6,000 feet. Found on rocky or grassy hillsides and in oak woodlands, most often on limestone soils, it is quite similar to its close relative from south-central Arizona, golden-flowered agave (*A. chrysantha*). The fleshy, relatively narrow, deep green leaves are thickest at the base and are armed with many slender reddish teeth along the margins and sharp terminal spines up to two inches long.

Plants demand a well-drained soil and need full sun to flourish. Once established, the plant is an extremely low water user, but while young should be watered deeply but infrequently. Keep its mature size in mind and do not plant it near walkways. Otherwise this slow-growing plant makes a fine accent for naturalistic gardens or corner plantings. Once the plant flowers, allow the stalk to remain standing, for many hummingbirds will use it as a lookout post and birds and native bees may dwell in woodpecker-excavated cavities. In the wild this species does not usually form offsets, but under cultivation it reportedly may do so. Like many other agaves, it is susceptible to the agave snout weevil; remove infested plants and monitor other agaves in the vicinity.

Agave parryi
Parry's Agave

Family:	Agavaceae (Asparagaceae)	**Bloom:**	June–August
Type:	Succulent	**Water use:**	Low
Size:	1–2' high x 2' wide, with 13–20' flower stalk	**Cold hardiness:**	To -20°F
		USDA zone:	5–10

Author citation: Engelmann
Synonym: *Agave neomexicana* Wooton & Standley

Parry's agave commands the attention of all hummingbirds in the vicinity when it is in bloom. Its clusters of reddish-tinged lemon yellow flowers are highly valued by Broad-billed, Magnificent, and Blue-throated Hummingbirds, and also are known to be visited by Black-chinned, Broad-tailed, Violet-crowned, and Lucifer Hummingbirds and Plain-capped Starthroats. Not only are the blossoms rich in nectar, but they also attract many small insects that are easy pickings for hummingbirds. Where nectivorous bats occur, primarily in Arizona and southward, they are said to be the plant's chief pollinators, but elsewhere hummingbirds, other birds including orioles and Northern Mockingbirds, and bees perform this task.

The several diverse varieties of this agave collectively range from central and southeast Arizona eastward through southern New Mexico and west Texas and southward into Mexico to Zacatecas, and they occur from as low as 1,500 feet to over 8,000 feet in elevation. On favored sites, such as grama grasslands or south-facing rocky slopes in oak or pine woodlands, plants typically form extensive colonies. The subspecies *neomexicana,* once considered a full species, has a shorter (6–15') flower stalk, tends to have a flat-topped instead of rounded rosette, and occurs in New Mexico, Texas, and Mexico. A particularly showy (and much more cold tender) variety from north-central Mexico, var. *truncata*, is known as artichoke agave because of its distinctive leaf shape and form. All types bear fleshy gray-green to blue-green leaves with brown-toothed margins and needlelike spines at the tips.

Plants need only a coarse, well-drained soil and full sun or light shade. Give them a deep soaking once or twice a month until established, weekly during summer dry spells. Mature plants are quite drought-tolerant, but look best when watered monthly during the growing season. This agave has a slow to moderate growth rate but is one of the cold hardiest in the family. It makes a striking accent or addition to a naturalistic desert garden, but be sure to locate it away from walkways. Parry's agave offsets freely, so even once flowering occurs and the mother plant dies, pups will be there to take its place.

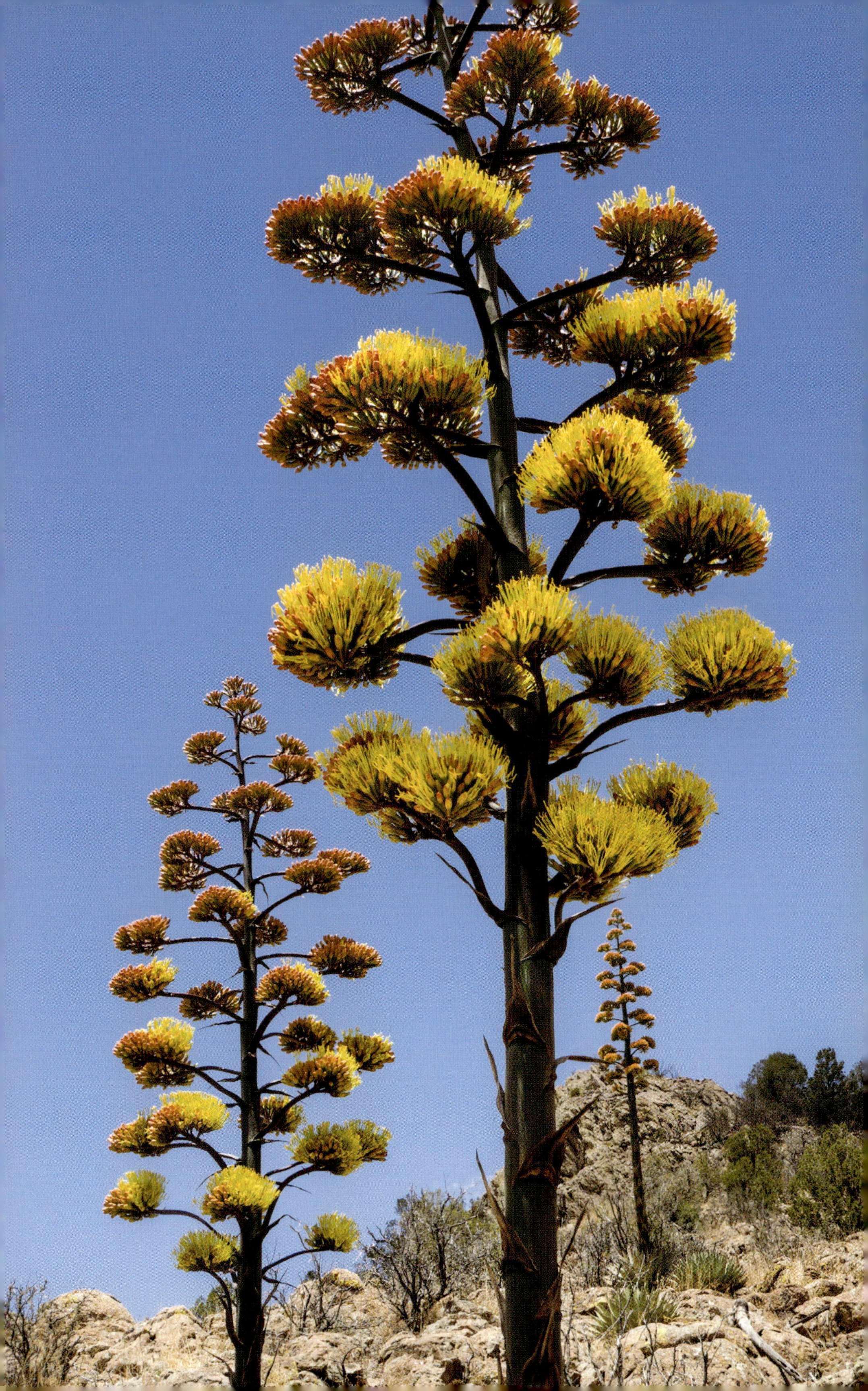

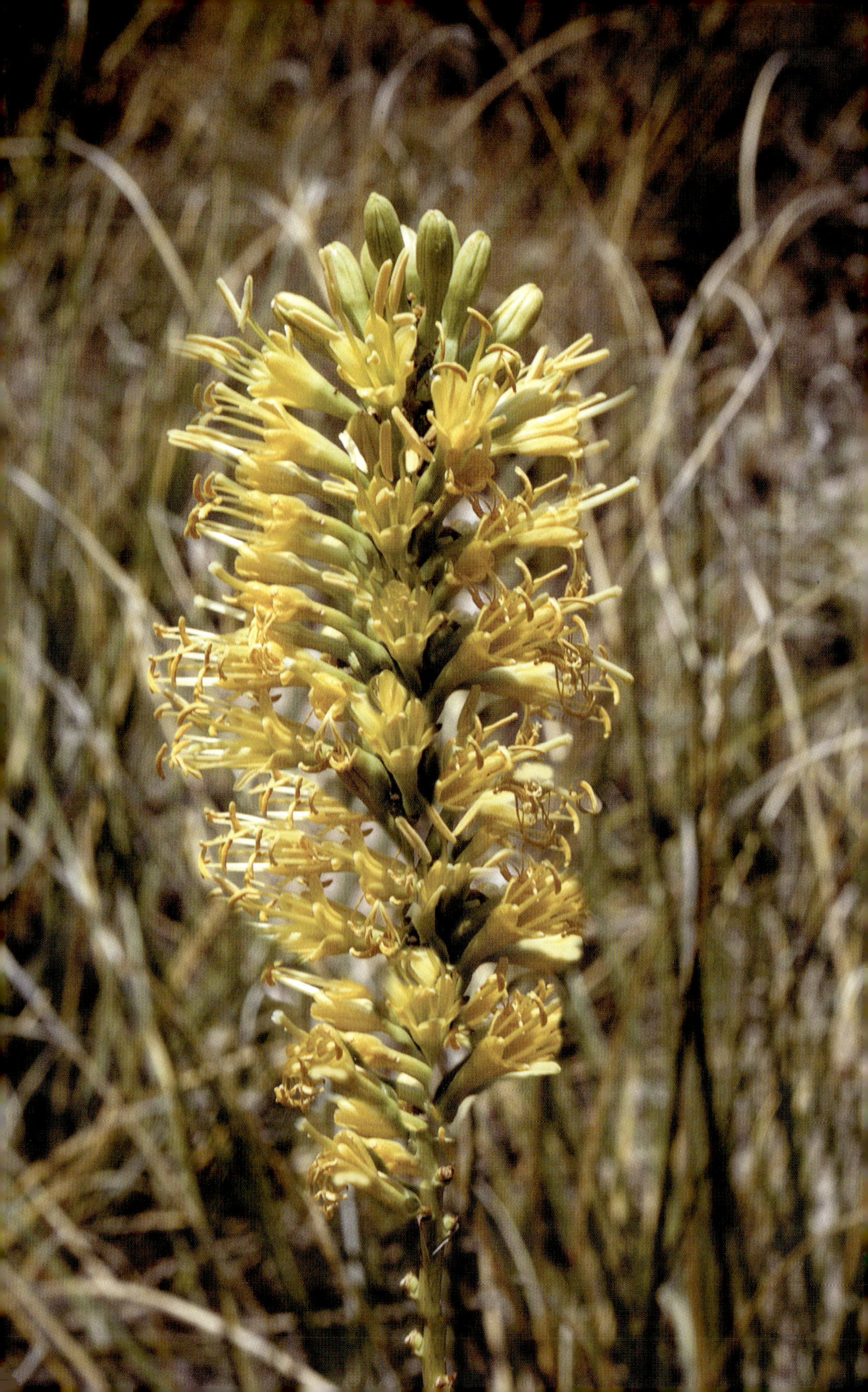

Agave schottii

Schott's Agave, Shindagger, Amole, Amolillo

Family:	Agavaceae (Asparagaceae)	**Bloom:**	May–August
Type:	Succulent	**Water use:**	Low
Size:	1–1.5' high x 1–1.5' wide, with 5–8' flower stalk	**Cold hardiness:**	To 0°F or below
		USDA zone:	7–10

Author citation: Engelmann

This delightful agave produces a tall spike of lovely butter-yellow flowers that in some areas are the primary summer nectar source for Broad-billed Hummingbirds and also of considerable importance to Violet-crowned Hummingbirds, whose arrival on their breeding grounds coincides with the bloom. Black-chinned and migrant Rufous Hummingbirds are avid visitors as well. While hummingbirds no doubt aid somewhat in pollination, the primary pollinators are probably large bees and, where they occur, nectivorous bats. Orioles and myriad insects also take nectar from the fragrant blossoms. The plant is a larval host for the Poling's giant skipper butterfly.

Schott's agave has a fairly limited geographical range, from southeast Arizona and extreme southwestern New Mexico southward into Sonora, Mexico. It can be found in a variety of habitats, including desert scrub, grama grasslands, and oak and juniper woodlands, but it is most common on rocky lower slopes and ledges of the sky island ranges at elevations of 3,000 to 6,000 feet. Colonies on the hillsides surrounding Guadalupe Canyon, on the Arizona–New Mexico border, are positively breathtaking in bloom, particularly when complemented by the flaming red spikes of southwest coral bean (*Erythrina flabelliformis*), as they are in June. The extremely narrow, yellowish green leaves are borne in a rosette, and unlike those of most agaves do not have teeth along the margins, just a sharp spine at the tip. The stout flower stalk typically forms after five or more years, after which the mother plant dies and makes way for the many offsets to mature.

Like all agaves, this one needs excellent drainage and a sunny exposure but thrives in poor soils, blistering heat, and drought. Reportedly this species may hybridize with several other agaves, including *Agave parryi*. Schott's agave makes a dramatic accent for naturalistic plantings, and can be used effectively for controlling erosion on slopes. Plants typically offset readily, often forming enormous colonies. They can be divided by gently cutting individual pups from the clump, allowing to air dry several days, and then planting in the desired location.

Agave utahensis

Utah Agave, Clark Mountain Agave, Yant

Family:	Agavaceae (Asparagaceae)	**Bloom:**	May–July
Type:	Succulent	**Water use:**	Low
Size:	To 1.5' high x 1.5' wide, with 5–15' flower stalk	**Cold hardiness:**	To -10°F
		USDA zone:	6–10

Author citation: Engelmann

ALTHOUGH THE YELLOW URN-SHAPED FLOWERS OF THIS AGAVE are most likely pollinated primarily by insects, hummingbirds probing the blossoms for both nectar and insects also aid considerably in pollination, and Costa's Hummingbirds will occasionally nest on the flower stalks. Spent stalks also are popular sentinel posts for a variety of birds. The succulent leaves host the larvae of the Mojave giant skipper butterfly.

Utah agave ranges through the Mojave and Great Basin Deserts from southeastern California through northern Arizona (including both rims of the Grand Canyon), southern Nevada, and southwestern Utah. While several varieties of the plant exist, all form broad clumps of rosettes up to several feet wide on open rocky limestone slopes, in canyons, and on foothill grasslands, generally between 3,000 and 7,500 feet in elevation. Plant communities they inhabit include piñon-juniper woodlands, Joshua tree woodlands, and creosote scrublands. The leathery, lanceolate leaves range from bluish-gray to pale gray-green and have blunt teeth on the margins and long terminal spines that are brown or white depending upon the variety. When this slow-growing plant blooms, typically when about eight to ten years old, the small flowers occur in clusters of two to eight on one-inch stems along the slender stalk.

Utah agave is among the most cold hardy of the agaves and established plants have been known to withstand temperatures well below zero. For best growth provide full sun and dry, alkaline, fast-draining soil. New plants need to be given a deep soaking once or twice a month until established and then can survive without supplemental water, although a monthly soaking will improve their appearance. The compact size makes this a terrific agave for small rock gardens and containers. Utah agave freely forms offsets, so pups can be cut from the mother plant, allowed to air dry, and planted where desired. The oval, short-beaked seeds can also be sown and reportedly germinate in one to three months at 70°F.

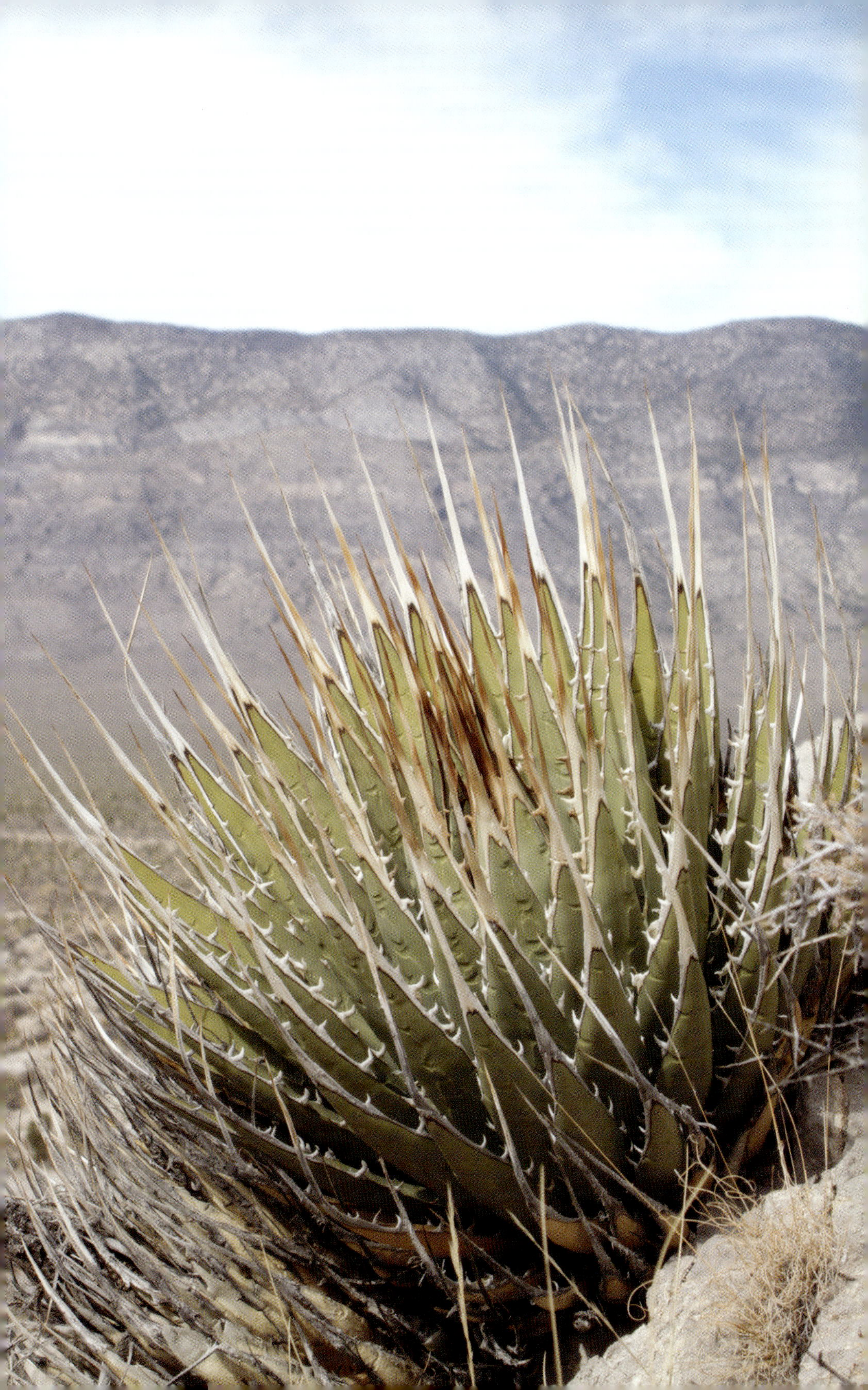

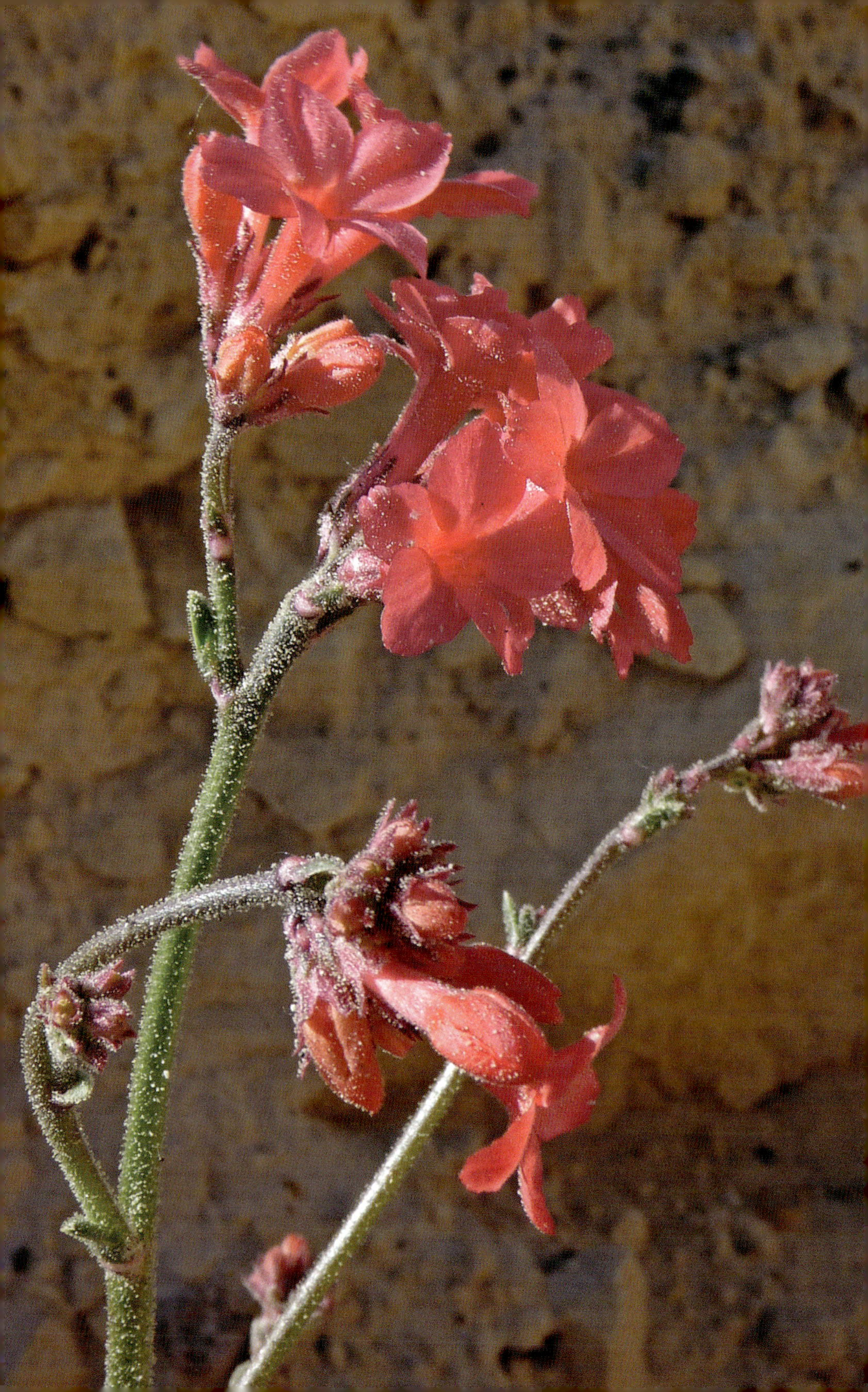

Aliciella subnuda

Coral Gilia, Carmine Gilia, Canyonlands Gilia

Family:	Polemoniaceae	**Water use:**	Low–moderate
Type:	Perennial	**Cold hardiness:**	Roots to -20°F
Size:	1.5' high x 1' wide	**USDA zone:**	5–7
Bloom:	May–August		

Author citation: (Torrey ex A. Gray) J. M. Porter
Synonym: *Gilia subnuda* Torr. ex A. Gray

THIS LITTLE CHARMER FEATURES BRILLIANT CORAL-PINK FLOWERS that are at least partially dependent upon hummingbirds for pollination. Broad-tailed Hummingbirds are known to visit the slender trumpet-shaped blooms that occur over a long season, as surely must other species moving southward in late summer. The relatively tiny blossoms seem tailor-made for the small bills of Calliope and Rufous Hummingbirds.

Coral gilia (pronounced *jee-lee-ah*, in honor of an 18th century Italian priest and naturalist, Filippo Luigi Gilii) is chiefly associated with the canyonlands of the Colorado Plateau, ranging from northern Arizona and New Mexico northward through south-central and southeastern Utah. In Utah alone it is a resident of at least four national parks or monuments: Capitol Reef, Canyonlands, Natural Bridges, and Arches. Typically occurring at elevations of 5,000 to 8,000 feet, its slender willowy form graces sandy or rocky hillsides, piñon-juniper slopes, and rock crevices in canyons. It has a basal cluster of coarsely toothed, spatula- or egg-shaped leaves, with a few small linear leaves here and there along the erect flower stem. Both the stem and foliage are covered with sticky hairs. The enchanting blossoms, borne in loose, branched clusters at stem tips from late spring through summer, have very slim half-inch corollas of deep coral and five flaring petal lobes with pointed tips that are of a paler coral pink.

This winsome perennial reportedly is not terribly fussy, preferring dry sandy or gravelly soil that is well drained, a sunny exposure, and protection from wetness during the winter dormant season. In hot lower elevation landscapes it may well require a cool microclimate. New plants will need a deep soaking at least once a week during summer dry periods until established, after which they are quite drought tolerant. Propagate by seed sown in fall. Although short-lived, plants in the wild typically reseed readily, so developing a nice swath of these striking wildflowers may not take long. Look for this dainty gilia at native plant sales or specialty nurseries. For the greatest impact and hummingbird appeal, mass plants on slopes or in raised beds to elevate the height of the flowers.

Anisacanthus andersonii
Limita, Big Honeysuckle

Family:	Acanthaceae	**Water use:**	Moderate
Type:	Semi-evergreen shrub	**Cold hardiness:**	To 25°F
Size:	2–8' high x 3–6' wide	**USDA zone:**	9b–11
Bloom:	February–April		

Author citation: T. F. Daniel

TIPTOEING EVER SO CLOSE TO THE U. S. BORDER is this standout Mexican desert-honeysuckle that provides extremely valuable nectar to both resident and migrating hummingbird species during a time when nectar sources are quite scarce. The scarlet to brick-red flowers are especially important to migrant Rufous Hummingbirds and are avidly visited by Broad-billed, Berylline, Violet-crowned, White-eared, and Broad-tailed Hummingbirds as well. Hummingbirds are undoubtedly the plant's chief pollinators, although various swallowtail butterflies likely assist them.

Limita begins appearing in northeastern Sonora just south of Sierra Vista, Arizona, and continues southward along the Sierra Madre Occidental through eastern Sonora and southwestern Chihuahua. Among its favored haunts are tropical deciduous forest, rocky stream canyons with Sonoran cottonwood and willow riparian gallery forest, oak grasslands, often associating with Emory oak (*Quercus emoryi*), gravelly slopes, arroyos, and dry desert washes, at elevations ranging from 900 to 5,500 feet. Although consistently upright in form in the wild, its stature varies widely, from a small two-foot clump poking out of a boulder crevice to an enormous eight-foot shrub in open grassland. The sometimes sparse but mostly evergreen lime-green foliage is oval- to lance-shaped and pointed at the tip, with leaves becoming progressively smaller toward branch tips. The slender two-inch flowers, each with four extravagantly long recurving petals, begin to appear in terminal clusters in midwinter and typically continue in flushes at least through early spring. Multi-chambered seedpods that are about three-fourths of an inch long form after flowering.

This handsome shrub, first described only in 1982 and well studied by Arizona-Sonora Desert Museum researchers, truly deserves a corner in any hummingbird garden where winters are mild and mostly frost-free. Full sun to light shade, moderate watering during the summer, and good drainage are recommended to keep it happiest. Some gardeners suggest cutting back older plants that have become shaggy every few years after the bloom season ends to keep them more manageable and promote increased flowering. Limita reportedly can be easily propagated by seed or semi-hardwood cuttings.

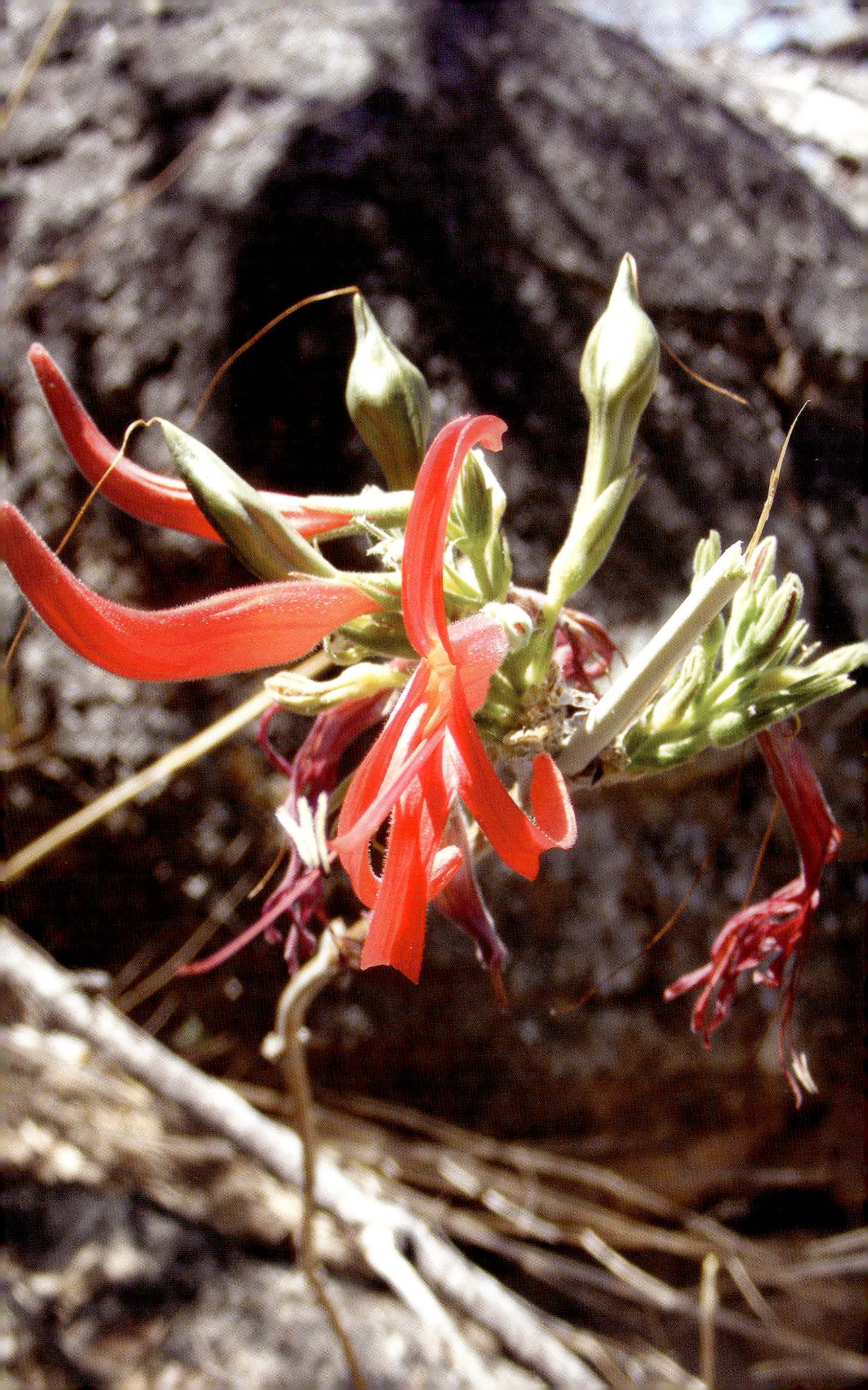

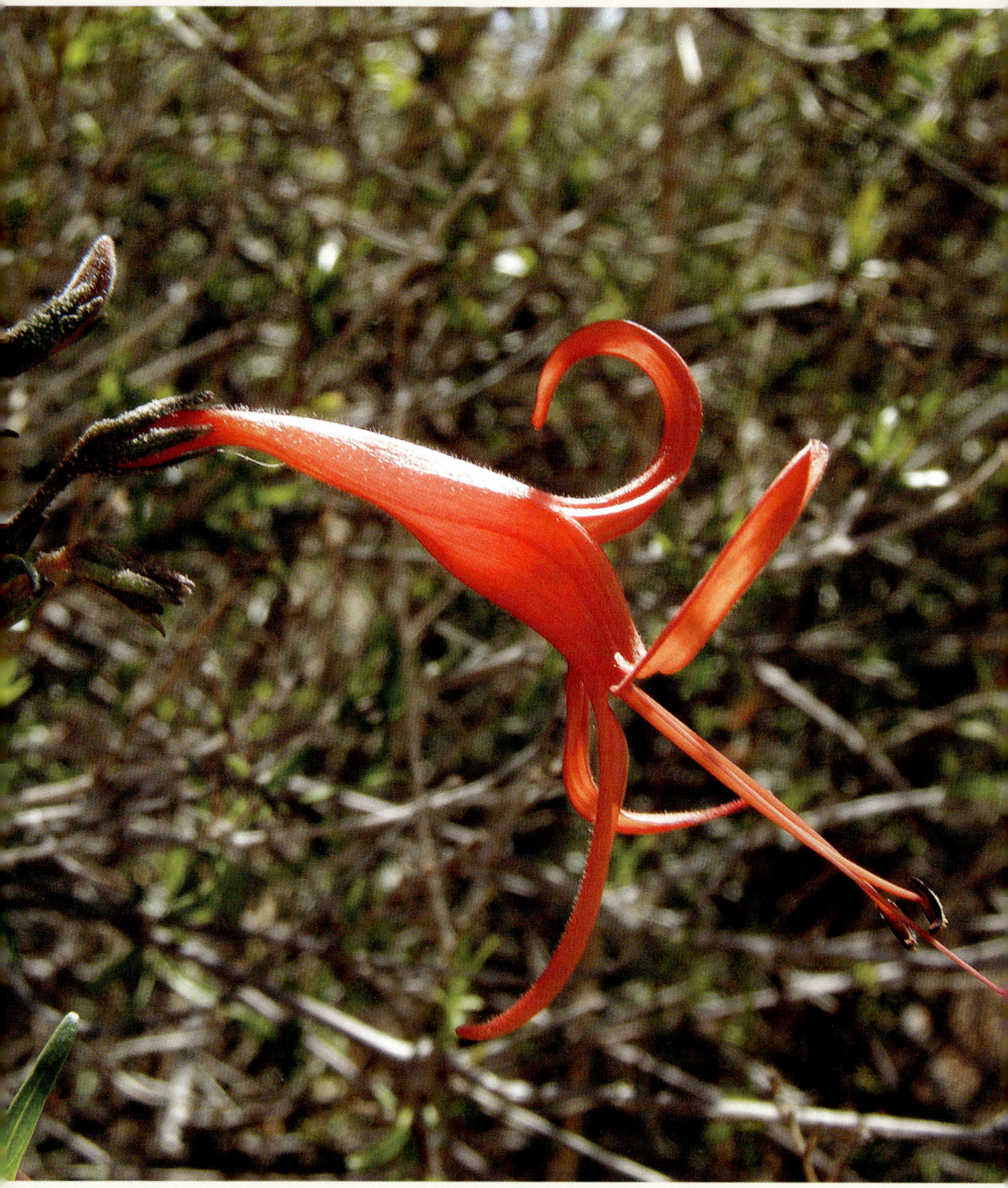

Anisacanthus linearis

Narrowleaf Desert-Honeysuckle, Dwarf Anisacanth

Family:	Acanthaceae	**Water use:**	Low–moderate
Type:	Deciduous shrub	**Cold hardiness:**	To 10°F
Size:	3' high x 3' wide	**USDA zone:**	8–10
Bloom:	July–September		

Author citation: (S. H. Hagen) Henrickson & E. J. Lott

THE FIERY ORANGE-RED FLOWERS of this Chihuahuan Desert denizen provide important late summer nectar to both Lucifer and Black-chinned Hummingbirds in the Big Bend region of west Texas. It is the primary lowland nectar source for Lucifer Hummingbirds in July and August, when males often vigorously defend stands of blooming plants. Butterflies take nectar from the flowers as well, and the plant is a host for crescentspot and Janais patch butterfly caterpillars. Hummingbirds are thought to be the primary pollinators.

Narrowleaf desert-honeysuckle has a fairly limited distribution but is fairly common within its range, occurring in west Texas from the Quitman Mountains southeast of El Paso eastward through the Big Bend region and southward into Coahuila in Mexico. Its favored haunts include dry washes, arroyos, and canyons at elevations of 3,000 to 5,000 feet. Rather carefree in form, its wiry branches bear sparse, extremely narrow leaves and are unremarkable until they burst into bloom with the summer rains. The two-inch flowers occur along the upper part of the stem and have twisted corollas, strongly decurved lobes, and lavish stamens that protrude an inch or more past the corolla.

Preferring a sandy, well-drained soil and full sun for best performance, this desert plant thrives in heat and needs little supplemental water once established, perhaps only a deep soaking once a month during prolonged periods of drought. Narrowleaf desert-honeysuckle is unfortunately not widely available in the trade, but would make a superb addition to a mixed shrub border or simulated dry wash planting. Like others in its family, it also does well in containers, but keep in mind that more frequent watering will be necessary. Plants readily self-seed, producing volunteers that transplant easily. New plants can also be grown by sowing fresh untreated seed or by taking softwood cuttings in early summer or fall and placing under intermittent mist until rooted. This is definitely a plant to seek out at native plant sales and niche nurseries, and it is particularly appropriate for Texas hummingbird gardens. Its pink-flowering cousin, pinky anisacanth (*Anisacanthus puberulus*) from Big Bend into Coahuila and southward, is also highly attractive to hummingbirds.

Anisacanthus quadrifidus

Flame Acanthus, Wright's Desert-Honeysuckle

Family:	Acanthaceae	**Water use:**	Low–moderate
Type:	Deciduous shrub	**Cold hardiness:**	Roots to -5°F
Size:	4–5' high x 4–5' wide	**USDA zone:**	7–10
Bloom:	June–November		

Author citation: (Vahl) Nees; includes *Anisacanthus quadrifidus* var. *wrightii* (Torrey) Henrickson

THIS PRETTY SHRUB IS AN OUTSTANDING PERFORMER and should be a mainstay of the summer hummingbird garden wherever it is appropriate, particularly in the southeastern portion of the area covered by this book. Its delicate tubular blooms of flaming scarlet appear from early summer until frost, providing a nonstop nectar reserve for nesting and post-breeding Lucifer and Black-chinned Hummingbirds in Texas and northern Mexico. Migrating Broad-tailed and Rufous Hummingbirds also patronize the blossoms, and both Broad-billed and Violet-crowned Hummingbirds are attracted to plantings. Several species of butterflies take nectar from the flowers, and their larvae feed upon the foliage. Hummingbirds not surprisingly serve as the chief pollinators.

Flame acanthus is native to rocky stream banks and limestone drainages of the Chihuahuan Desert, from Big Bend and south-central Texas southward into northeast Mexico, at elevations ranging from 1,000 to 5,000 feet. Its irregular arching branches arise from a woody base and bear bright green, narrow, lance-shaped leaves that turn yellow and drop in late fall. Young stems are fuzzy and greenish, while older bark is tan and shredding.

The plant is quite drought tolerant once established, only requiring a deep soaking every two to three weeks during the summer, and is fairly cold hardy as well. Full sun is usually best for optimum flowering, but plants in hot low-elevation locations may not mind some afternoon or filtered shade. Good drainage is preferred, although plants seem to be able to tolerate a wide range of soils from clay to caliche. Note that with abundant water they can get rangy. For denser growth and more blooms, cut back hard in late winter. Where rabbits can be a problem, protect young plants with a wire cage until stems are woody. Volunteer seedlings may tend to pop up in unwanted areas but happily these can be easily transplanted to desired locations. Propagation is also easy by seed or by softwood cuttings taken in early summer or fall. Use as a flowering specimen along walkways, in a container on a patio, or grouped as an informal low hedge in a wildlife garden. Wherever placed, it is certain to be discovered by hummingbirds.

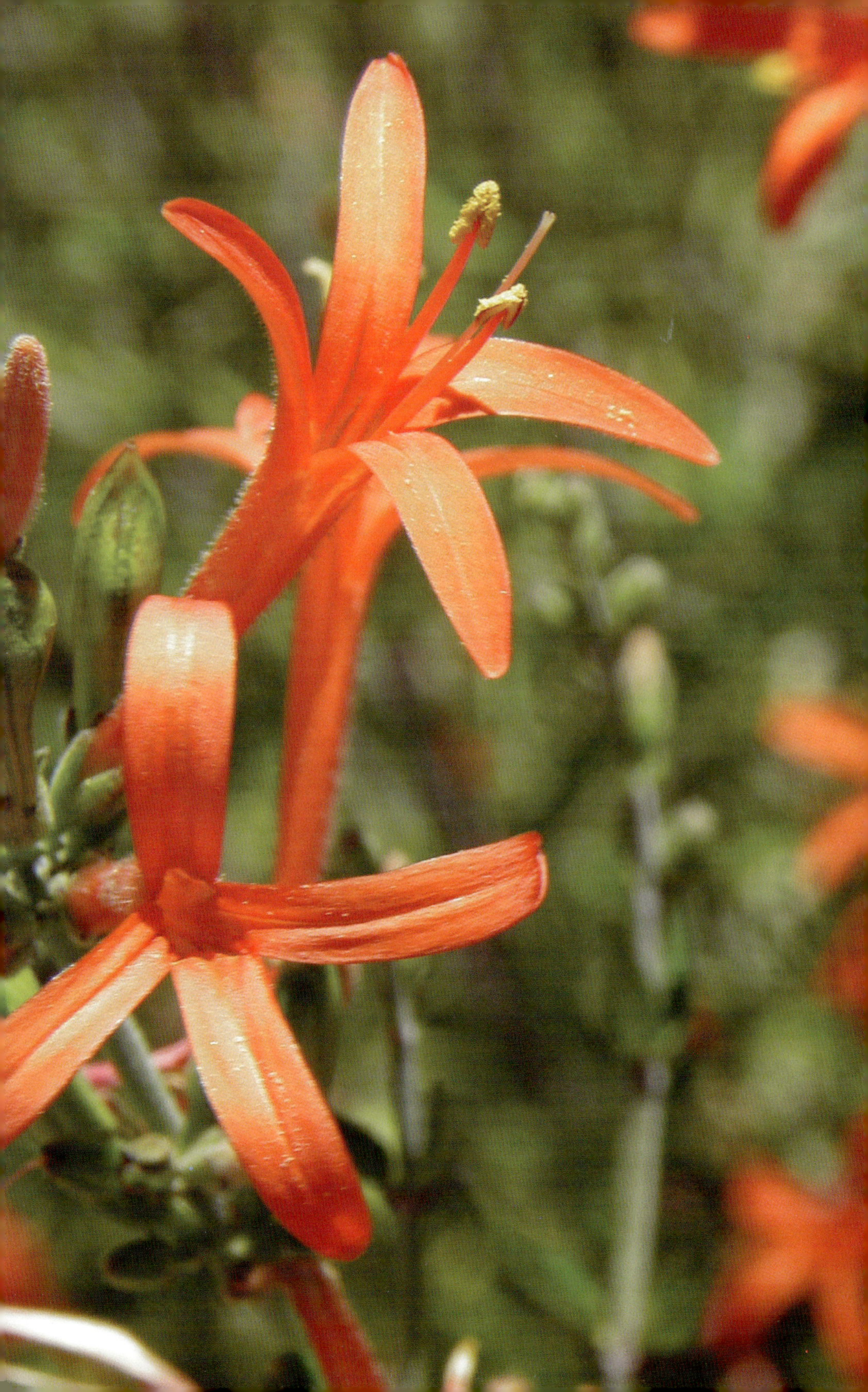

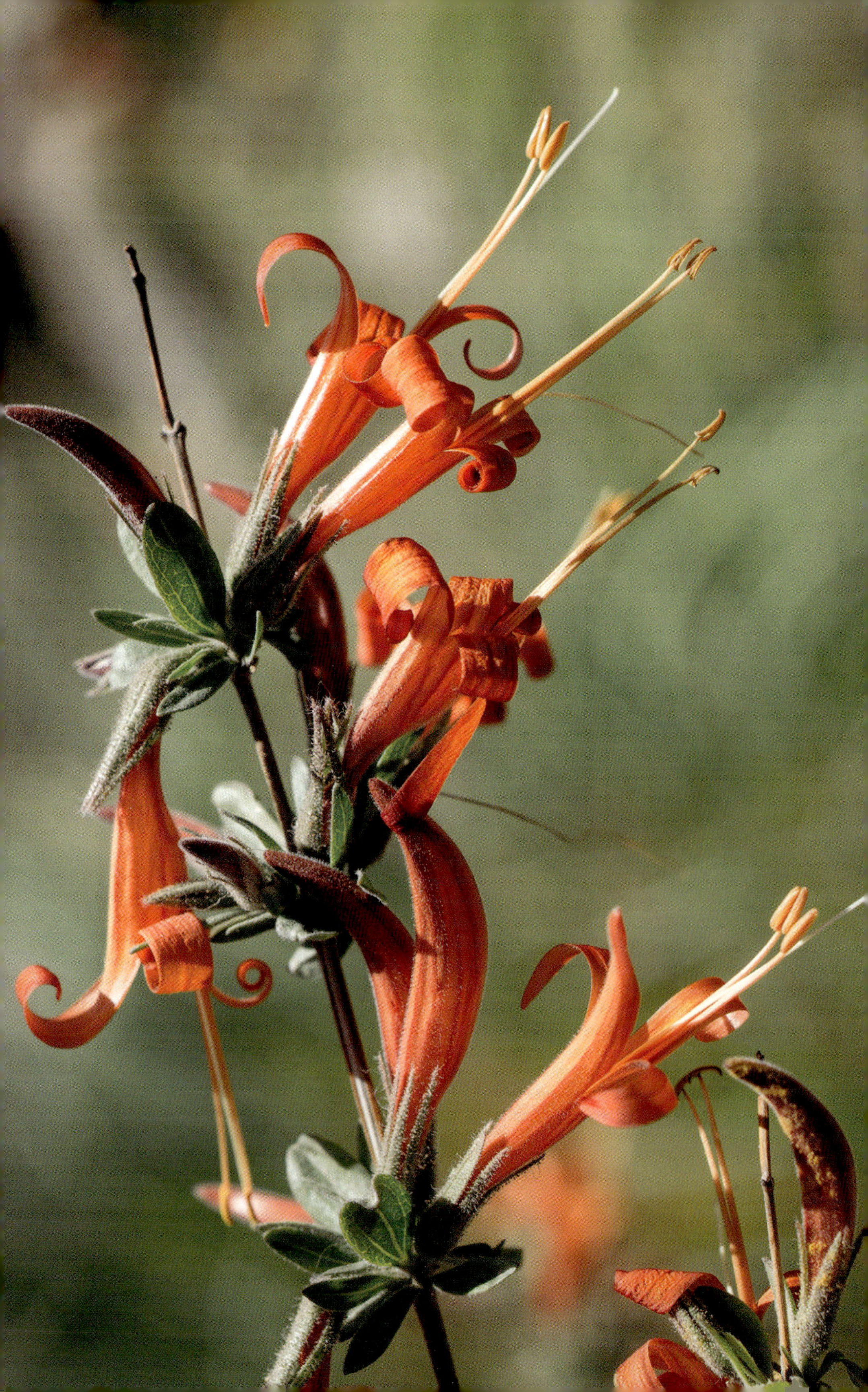

Anisacanthus thurberi

Desert-Honeysuckle, Taperosa

Family:	Acanthaceae	**Water use:**	Low–moderate
Type:	Deciduous shrub	**Cold hardiness:**	To 0°F or below
Size:	4–6' high x 3–4' wide	**USDA zone:**	7–10
Bloom:	January–April in Sonora, April–June in U. S., sporadic fall		

Author citation: (Torrey) A. Gray

THIS IS A CHARMING SHRUB FOR THE SPRING HUMMINGBIRD GARDEN, especially for difficult, hot, low-desert landscapes. The tubular blooms, in shades that range widely from golden yellow to burnt orange to nearly vermilion, provide valuable nectar for nesting Black-chinned, Costa's, and Broad-billed Hummingbirds, and are also much used by Blue-throated, Magnificent, Violet-crowned, and migrant Rufous Hummingbirds along with occasional Plain-capped Starthroats. Butterflies likewise visit the flowers, but the plant depends chiefly upon hummingbirds and bees for pollination. In some locations, blossoms may occur most any time of year.

Desert-honeysuckle dwells on rocky canyon slopes and in sandy washes and streambeds of the northeast Sonoran Desert and its transition zone into the northwest Chihuahuan Desert, from southern Arizona and southwestern New Mexico southward into Mexico. It is most often found at elevations of 2,000 to 5,500 feet. Plants are upright when young, then spreading somewhat as they mature, with many slender branches and white shredding bark. On range lands, plants are often heavily browsed by livestock. The opposite lance-shaped leaves are olive green, appearing along with the flowers in spring and dropping with the first hard freeze. The two-inch flowers have notched upper lips and three-lobed lower lips that are often curly.

Established plants are quite drought tolerant once established, requiring a deep soaking only once a month during summer dry periods. Leaf drop occurs in the mid-20s, but the top growth is hardy to about 0°F and the roots reportedly to -15°F. Desert-honeysuckle prefers to be in full sun and even tolerates reflected heat. Other than insisting upon good drainage it is not fussy about soil. Plants seem to perform best if cut back hard in late winter every few years. To propagate, collect seed capsules when nearly dried (you may need to race the finches for them) and store until they split open. Propagation is also fairly easy by rooting semi-hardwood cuttings in a perlite-vermiculite mix in late summer. Groupings can be incorporated into an informal border or seasonal hedge, and singular plants work well in patio or poolside plantings and along pathways.

Aquilegia chrysantha
Golden Columbine, Canary Columbine

Family:	Ranunculaceae	**Water use:**	Moderate
Type:	Perennial	**Cold hardiness:**	Top to 10–18°F, roots to -30°F
Size:	2–3' high x 2–3' wide		
Bloom:	April–July or longer	**USDA zone:**	4–10
Author citation:	A. Gray		

THE SUNNY YELLOW FLOWERS OF THIS LONG-BLOOMING PERENNIAL are a perfect complement to the many reds so prevalent in the typical hummingbird garden. Blue-throated, Magnificent, Black-chinned, and Broad-tailed Hummingbirds are known to take nectar from the long slender spurs, but the plants are primarily pollinated by sphinx moths and bees. Bumblebees will often punch holes at the bases of the spurs to get at the nectar.

Golden columbine, comprising several near look-alike varieties, ranges from southwestern Utah and a few spots in central Colorado, where it is rare, south through Arizona, southwestern New Mexico, and west Texas, and southward into northern Mexico in Sonora, Chihuahua, and western Coahuila. Most common in the pine belt, its favored habitats include riparian seeps, cliff faces, canyon springs, limestone crevices, and shady mountain forests over a huge elevation range, from 3,000 to over 11,000 feet. In mild winter areas, the mound of basal foliage is evergreen, with lacy, divided, pale blue-green leaves that have a soft coating of hair on the undersides. In spring, beginning in its second year, the plant sends up slender stems with multiple branches. The enchanting flowers, each with five curving spurs, are two to three inches long and are held horizontally or upright near stem tips.

Plants prefer moist, rich soil but grow well in sand, loam, limestone, or igneous soil, demanding only good drainage. Although more drought tolerant than the other columbines, plants will still require some supplemental water in the summertime, particularly in hot low desert locations. A deep soaking twice a month during summer should suffice to prevent dormancy and prolong the bloom. With more water or in cool high-elevation gardens, plants can handle full sun but generally are happiest in dappled to deep shade. Deadheading spent blooms and cutting back old stems will promote continued flowering, but eventually you will want to allow seed capsules to form so as to encourage volunteer seedlings. Plants can also be propagated by division. This long-blooming beauty is an attractive addition to perennial borders, planters, rock gardens, and desert oasis plantings. It is frequently found growing with scarlet betony (*Stachys coccinea*), a highly appealing combination whether naturally occurring or contrived.

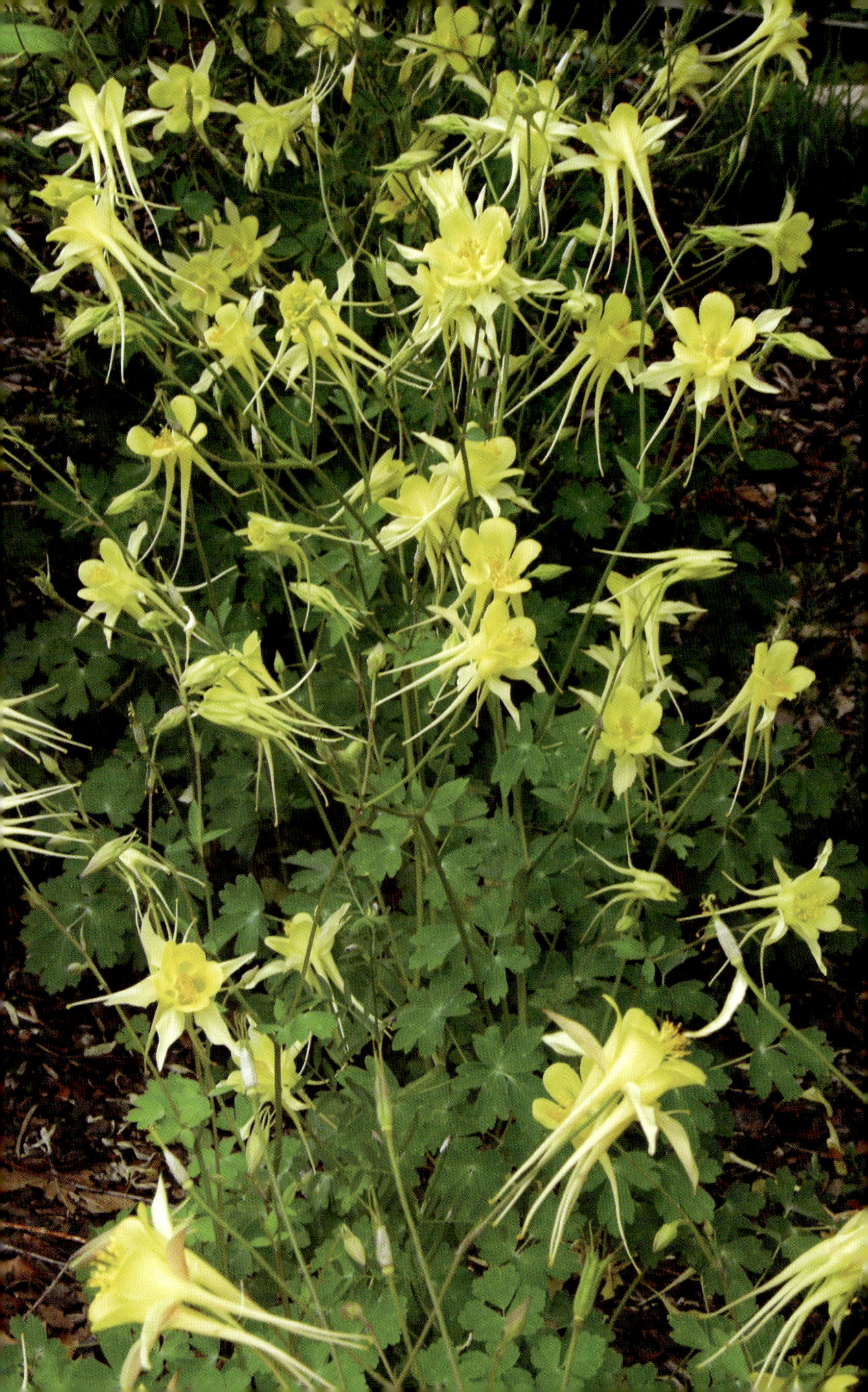

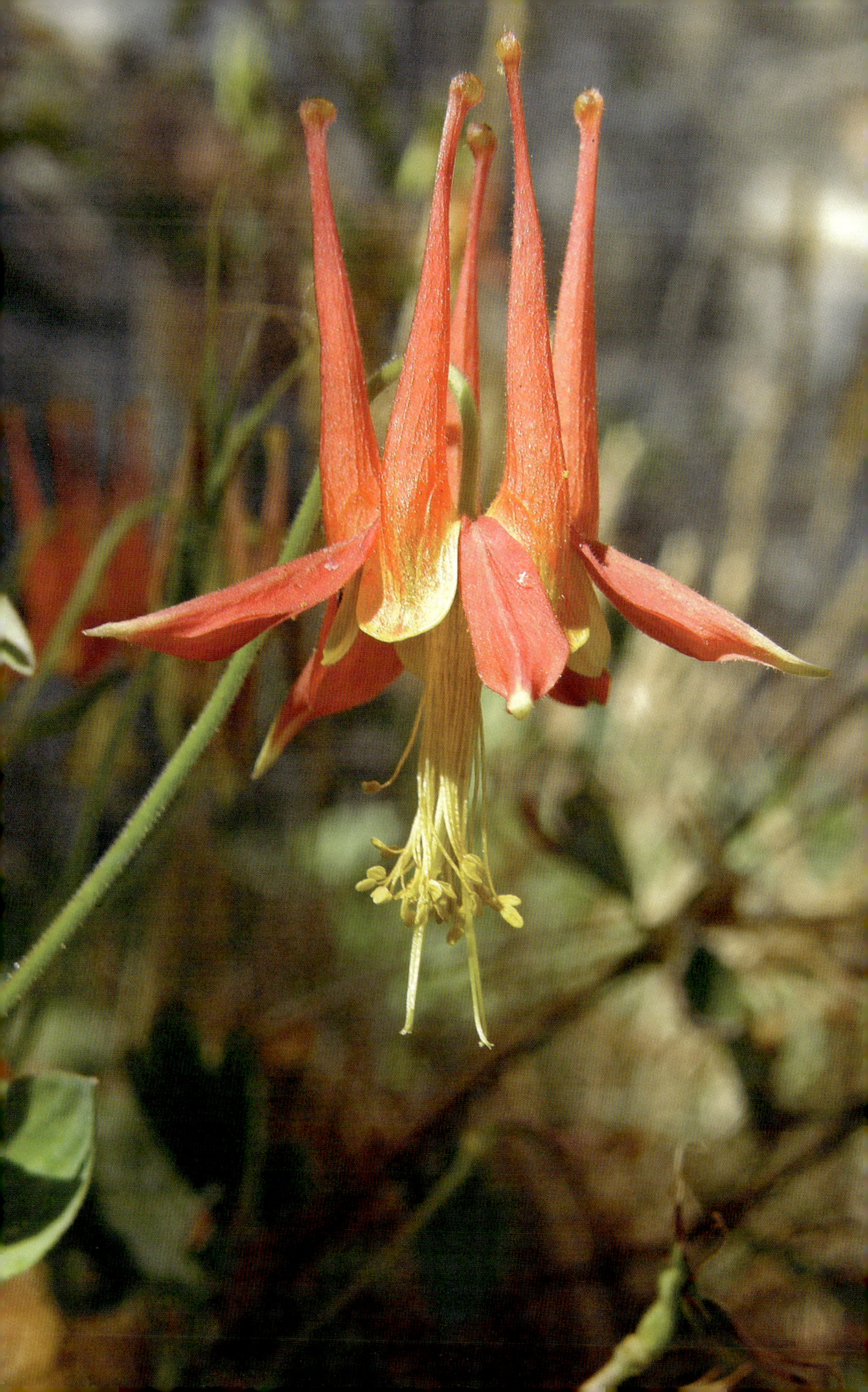

Aquilegia desertorum

Chiricahua Mountain Columbine, Desert Columbine

Family:	Ranunculaceae	**Water use:**	Moderate
Type:	Perennial	**Cold hardiness:**	Roots to -20°F
Size:	1–2' high x 1' wide	**USDA zone:**	5–9
Bloom:	May–October		

Author citation: (M. E. Jones) Cockerell ex A. Heller
Synonym: *Aquilegia triternata* Payson

THE NODDING, YELLOW-TIPPED, RED-ORANGE FLOWERS of this charming perennial provide important mid and late summer nectar for both Broad-tailed and Magnificent Hummingbirds in the mountains of Arizona and New Mexico. Migrating Rufous and Calliope Hummingbirds also partake of the sucrose-rich nectar where available. Hummingbirds serve as the plant's chief pollinators, with an assist from white-lined sphinx moths.

Controversy has abounded concerning the lineage of this plant, once considered a variety of western columbine (*A. formosa*) and until recently regarded by many as two distinct species, this one occurring only in north-central Arizona, in the Rocky Mountain conifer forests near Flagstaff and slightly eastward, and barrel columbine (*A. triternata*) which has a much broader distribution in southern and eastern Arizona and western New Mexico. Quite easy to discern, however, is that hummingbirds care nothing about the taxonomy and are avid visitors wherever populations occur. Strictly a montane plant, it is quite common in various moist niches of mixed coniferous forests, such as rock crevices near seeps or springs, typically at elevations ranging from 5,000 to 8,000 feet. Its form is airy and graceful, with slender branching stems that bear lacy, blue-green leaves that are tripinnately divided with lobed leaflets. The enchanting flowers occur at stem tips and resemble top hats, with their five slightly spreading, upwardly held spurs and "brim" of widely flaring, pointed sepals. Distinctive upright seed capsules form after flowering ceases.

Reportedly, this columbine is long-lived once established. Despite its botanical name this is not a smart choice for the intense heat of the low deserts, but if given a partly shaded exposure, protection from hot afternoon sun and drying winds, a moist, gravelly, well-drained soil, and some supplemental water during summer dry spells, this columbine would make a colorful accent for subalpine or oasis gardens, gracing a water feature or tucked into a boulder crevice. Cut back spent flower stems to encourage a second bloom, but allow some of the seed capsules to form in late summer to produce volunteer seedlings. Plants can be easily propagated by seed or by gently dividing mature clumps in early spring.

Aquilegia elegantula
Comet Columbine, Shooting Star Columbine

Family:	Ranunculaceae	**Water use:**	Moderate–high
Type:	Perennial	**Cold hardiness:**	Roots to -20°F
Size:	1–2' high x 1' wide	**USDA zone:**	5–7
Bloom:	May–August		

Author citation: Greene

THE ELEGANT SCARLET AND YELLOW FLOWERS of this columbine are an important source of nectar for breeding Calliope Hummingbirds in Utah and breeding Broad-tailed Hummingbirds in many Rocky Mountain locations, and undoubtedly southbound Rufous Hummingbirds partake of them as well. The long, typically spreading spurs stream out like the tail of a comet, and hold abundant nectar as sugary recompense to the hummingbirds that serve as the plant's chief pollinators.

Comet columbine graces a variety of upland coniferous forest habitats in northeastern Arizona, northwestern and central New Mexico, southern and eastern Utah, and southwestern Colorado. Growing singly or in small patches, this beguiling beauty is commonly found on wooded slopes, rock ledges, or cliff faces of upper foothills and mountains at elevations that range from 5,000 to 11,000 feet. Its dainty, upright, branching stems emerge from a tuft of lacy, pinnately divided leaves, each with three segments that are three-lobed, and bend gracefully at the tips from the weight of the flowers. The nodding blossoms have yellow petals, bright red-orange spurs and sepals, and very short yellow stamens. Flowers begin appearing in early spring at lower elevations and may continue all summer long near timberline. Multi-compartmented capsules, each containing numerous tiny black seeds, form after the bloom ends.

Comet columbine typically grows in partly shaded mountain niches where soil is moist, rich in humus, and fast draining. It most certainly would not tolerate the blistering heat of most desert gardens, but if protected from drying winds and mid-afternoon heat should do well in the cooler northern portions of our area. Individual plants tend to be short-lived, rarely lasting more than three to four years, but fortunately they self-seed readily. Columbines tend to hybridize quite freely, so to maintain species integrity, plant just one species in the garden or plan to pull up volunteer seedlings if others are growing nearby. This enchanting perennial is not widely available, but if seeds or nursery-grown plants can be obtained, they would make a wonderful addition to a mountain cottage garden and are certain to delight any summering Broad-tailed Hummingbirds in the vicinity.

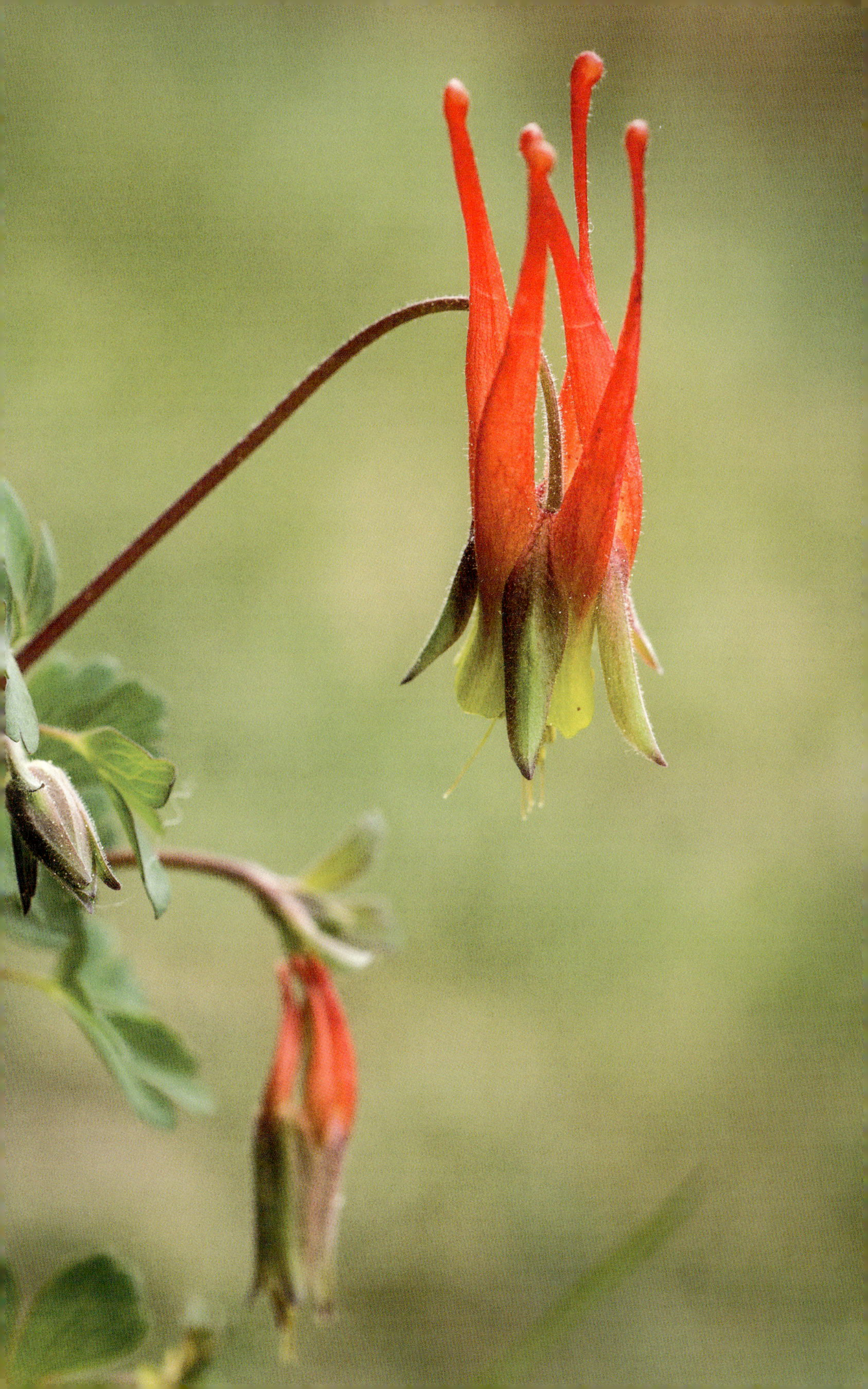

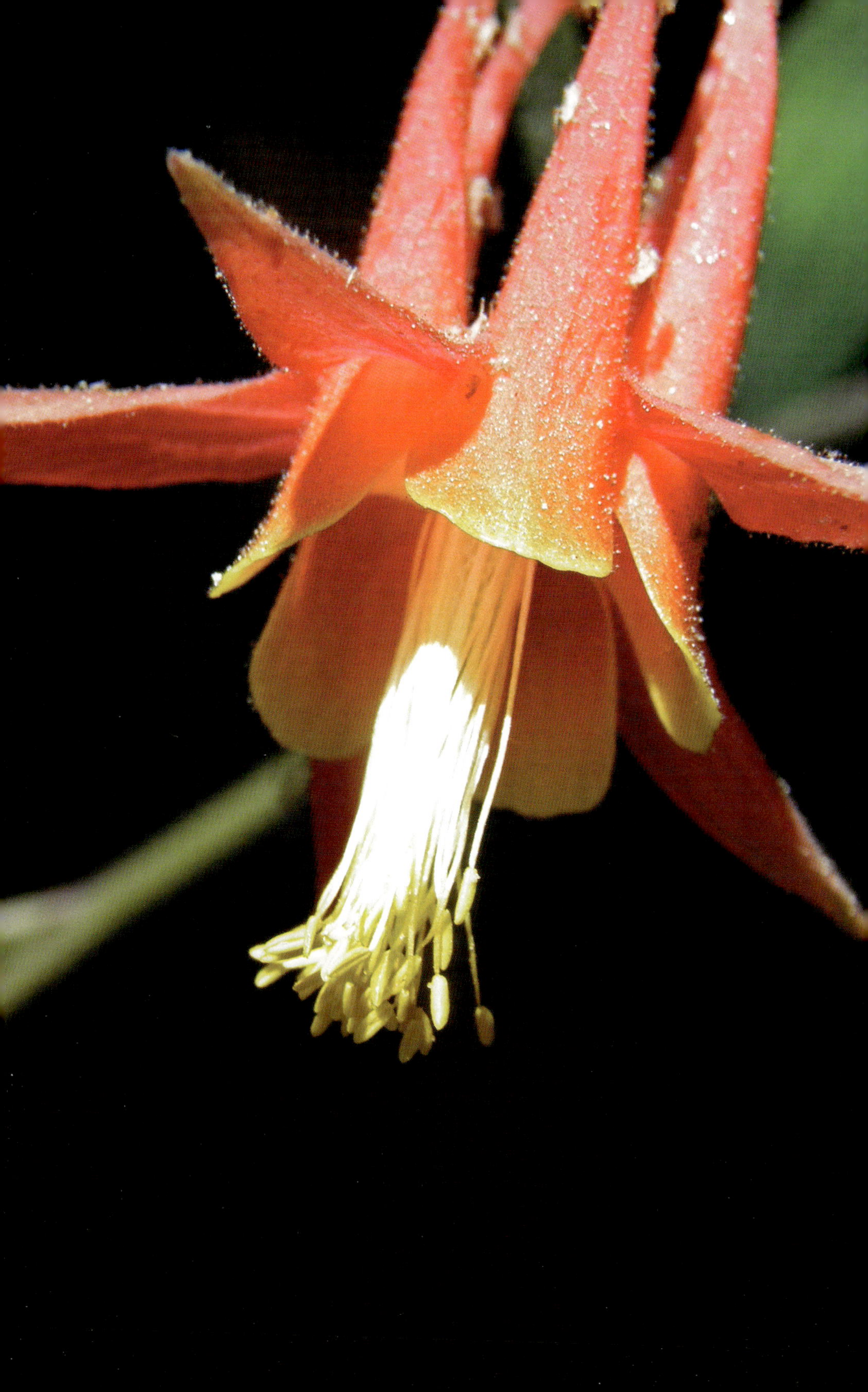

Aquilegia formosa
Western Columbine, Crimson Columbine

Family:	Ranunculaceae	**Water use:**	High
Type:	Perennial	**Cold hardiness:**	Roots to -23°F
Size:	2–4' high x 2' wide	**USDA zone:**	4–9
Bloom:	May–August (and fall with moisture)		

Author citation: Fischer ex de Candolle

This captivating perennial may appear dainty but it is a veritable nectar machine, cranking out four times the nectar of another hummingbird favorite, Indian paintbrush (*Castilleja*). Its red and yellow blooms provide valuable high-sucrose nectar to Anna's and Calliope Hummingbirds during the breeding season and to migrating Rufous and Allen's Hummingbirds in late summer. Rufous Hummingbirds may even set up temporary territories to defend stands of flowering plants. Not surprisingly, hummingbirds are the chief pollinators. The seeds are a favorite of Song Sparrows and Dark-eyed Juncos.

Western columbine enjoys a broad latitudinal range, from northern Baja California in Mexico throughout most of California, Nevada, and western Utah, and northward through Oregon, Washington, Idaho, Wyoming, western Montana, and southern Alaska. Primarily a denizen of mountains, where it is found in forested canyons, along streams, and in open woods to 11,000 feet in elevation, it also occasionally occurs in moist cachements on the brushy slopes and coastal bluffs of chaparral country. The slender, branching stems and lacy, trilobed, blue-green foliage give the plant an airy appearance. Each nearly two-inch flower has five yellow scoop-shaped petals that are framed by five red flaring sepals and extend into stout, backward-projecting, red spurs containing the nectar. The blossoms are pendant and occur near stem tips. When a hummingbird hovers beneath a flower, pollen from the fluffy yellow stamens brushes its forehead or chin.

This columbine is tolerant of most soil types as long as drainage is excellent. Morning sun and dappled afternoon shade are preferred, particularly in hot locations. Plants will grow in full sun but will need almost constant watering to prevent them from going into dormancy; otherwise a deep soaking twice a month during dry intervals in the summer should be sufficient. Cut back spent blooms to prolong flowering. When stalks turn brown, the seeds are mature and can be shaken out wherever new plants are desired. Note that where other columbines are present they will likely hybridize and colors will not remain true to species. Western columbine makes a lovely accent for shady gardens and is stunning massed as a ground cover.

Aquilegia skinneri

Mexican Columbine, Skinner's Columbine, Granny's Bonnets

Family:	Ranunculaceae	**Water use:**	Moderate–high
Type:	Perennial	**Cold hardiness:**	Roots to 0°F or below
Size:	1–2' high x 1–2' wide	**USDA zone:**	7–9
Bloom:	June–September		

Author citation: Hooker

THIS ENCHANTING MEXICAN BEAUTY beckons hummingbirds in the middle to upper elevations of the Sierra Madre Occidental in mid to late summer with its bright red spurs and petals, yellow "skirt," and shiny yellow tassels. White-eared, Blue-throated, and Magnificent Hummingbirds are likely patrons and probably important pollinators, and the flowers are visited by butterflies as well.

Although Mexican columbine ranges within one hundred miles of the U. S. border in Chihuahua and southward nearly to Mexico City, the heart of its range and where it is most common is in the Copper Canyon region and environs of southwestern Chihuahua, southeastern Sonora, and northwestern Durango. Most often found at elevations of 4,000 to 8,000 feet, it inhabits pine-oak woodlands, shady mountain canyons, rocky slopes, roadsides, wet meadows, mossy outcrops, and streamsides. Growing in a neat clump, its lacy foliage is finely divided and mostly clustered at the base of the plant. The erect, branching stems present the lovely, two-inch, nodding flowers well above the foliage for easy hummingbird access. Sometimes blooms begin to appear in late spring, but in dry years plants may not bloom at all until after late summer rains. Multi-chambered seedpods form after the flowers fade.

Best suited for cooler or higher elevation locations, Mexican columbine is said to be easy to grow in light shade and fertile well-drained soil, with regular water during the bloom season. Some gardeners suggest adding compost to enrich the planting area and mulching to keep roots cool in summer. Like all columbines, this one reseeds readily, but where multiple species are present the seeds will not come up true to type, so remove seedpods before they dry if volunteer seedlings are not desired. Otherwise, allow seeds to develop and self-sow, and they will soon fill a shady corner with color. Plants can also be propagated by division in the spring, by gently dividing clumps of roots and replanting them. The slight toxicity of the leaves and stems may be the reason that deer and rabbits reportedly do not favor it.

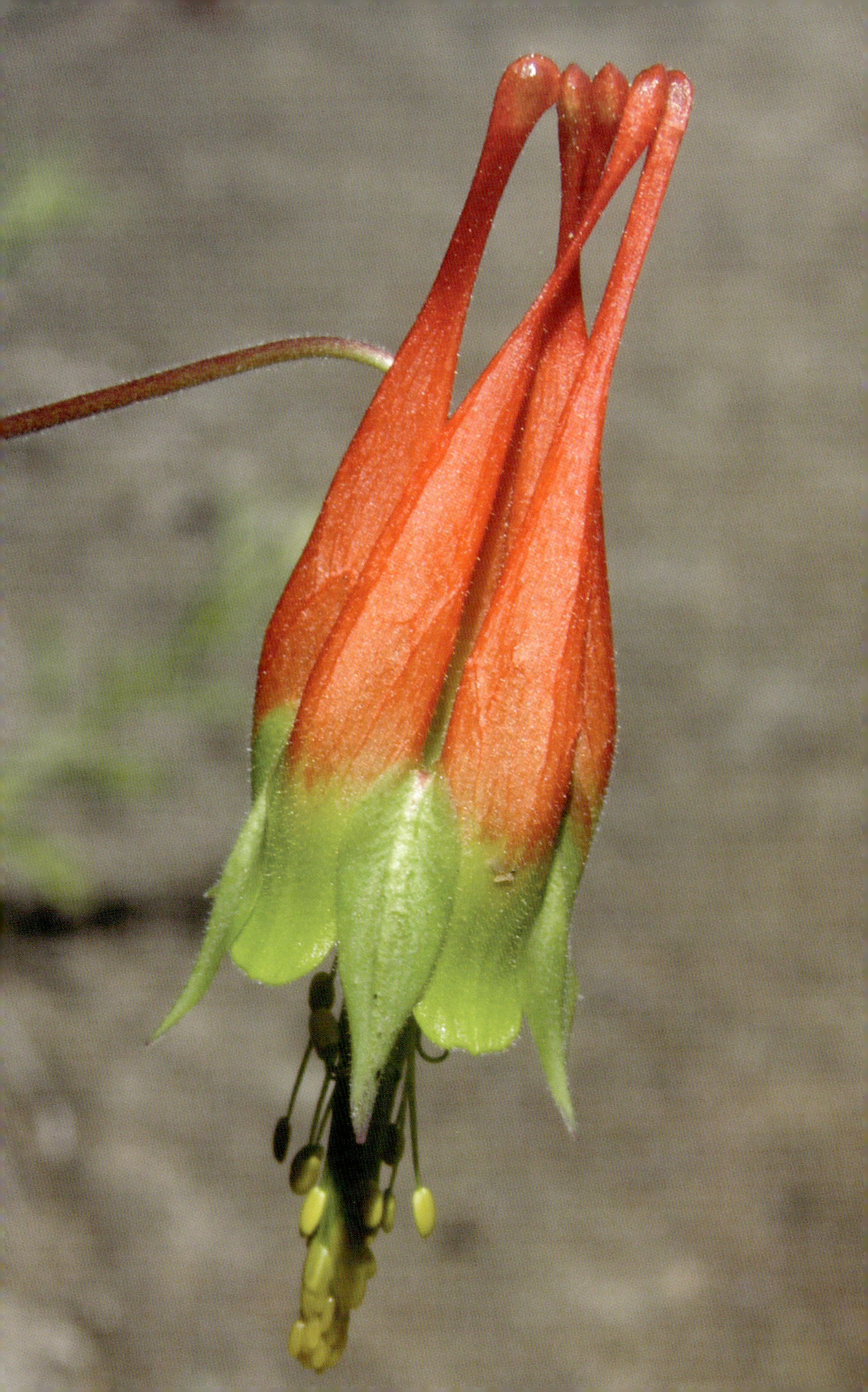

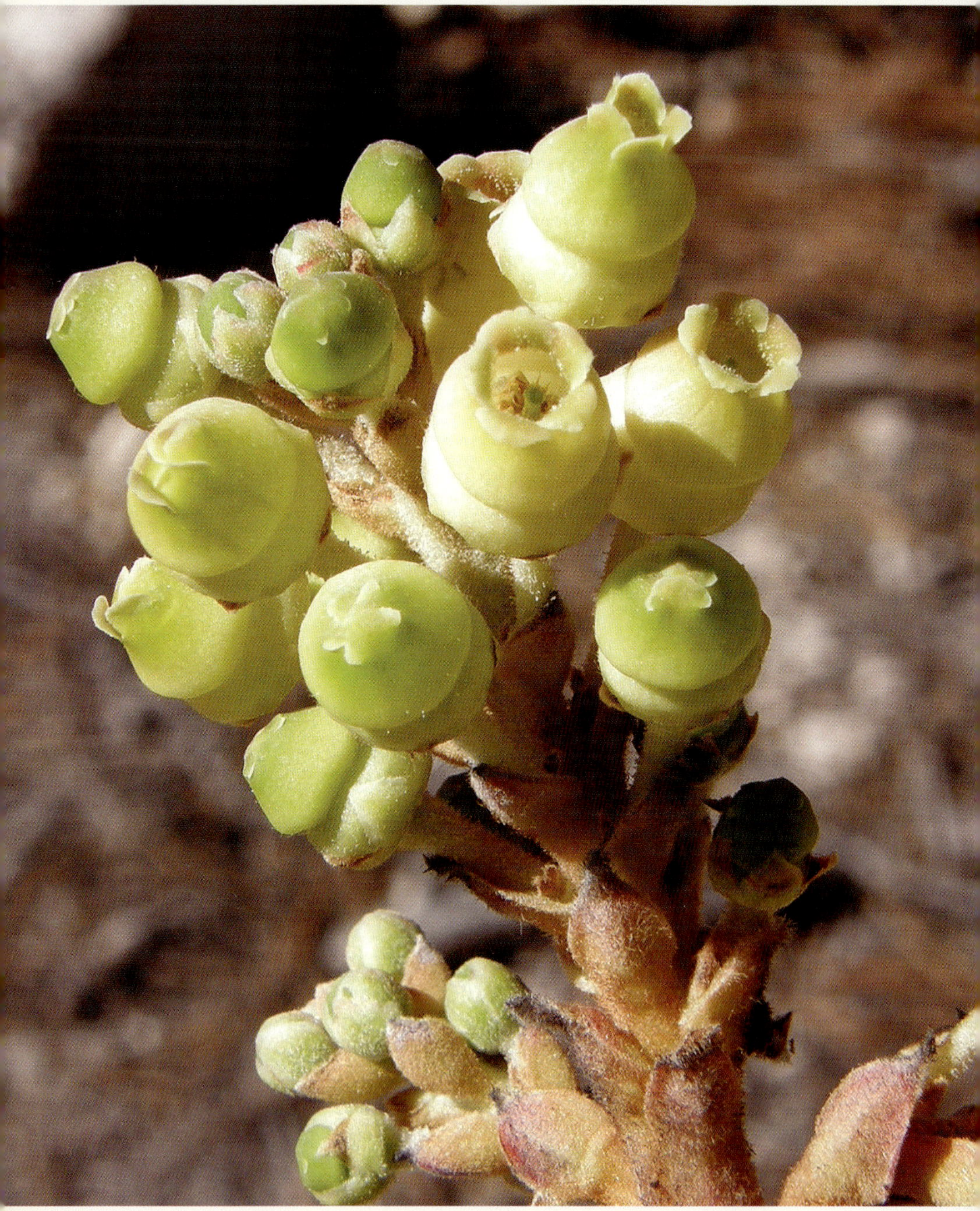

Arbutus species

Madrone, Madroño

Family:	Ericaceae		May–June (*arizonica*)
Type:	Evergreen tree	**Water use:**	Low–moderate
Size:	15–30' high x 8–10' wide	**Cold hardiness:**	To 10°F or below
Bloom:	March–April (*xalapensis*),	**USDA zone:**	8–9

Author citation: *Arbutus arizonica* (A. Gray) Sargent
Arbutus xalapensis Kunth; syn. *A. texana* Buckley

WITHIN THESE DIMINUTIVE, white to pinkish urn-like blossoms are tiny nectaries that are open for business as hummingbirds are returning to their breeding grounds. Broad-tailed, Rufous, Blue-throated, and White-eared Hummingbirds tap into this resource from late winter into spring, when other nectar sources are often in short supply. The dimpled scarlet or orange fruits are relished by a variety of birds and other wildlife.

Arizona madrone has a fairly small geographical distribution in the United States, occurring only in mountains of southeastern Arizona and extreme southwestern New Mexico, but in Mexico it ranges southward through the Sierra Madre Occidental to Jalisco. Its slightly smaller cousin, Texas madrone, makes its home in several mountain ranges of western Texas and southeastern New Mexico, also occurring eastward to the Edwards Plateau and southward through Mexico all the way to Guatemala. Both madrones are most often encountered in open spots of wooded canyons or in oak stands on rocky slopes, typically at elevations of 4,000 to 8,000 feet (though Texas madrone may occur as low as 2,000 feet). Although Texas madrone usually occurs as a multi-trunked shrub, both species have a rounded crown, gnarled twisting trunk, and leathery foliage that is glossy dark green above and paler below. They can usually be easily distinguished by their bark. Arizona madrone is gray becoming checkered on mature trees, whereas Texas madrone is red on the young branches peeling away to pink underneath. The quarter-inch flowers occur in panicles at branch tips.

Like many members of the heath family, madrones are notoriously difficult to establish. Having no hair roots makes transplanting a challenge, but once established they can be long-lived, provided their root zone is not compacted. They require a lean, medium to coarse gravelly soil with excellent drainage and are said to prefer a pH between 6.1 and 8.1. A partly sunny site with afternoon shade is best, particularly at lower elevations. New plants will need periodic deep soakings while getting settled and during periods of drought thereafter, but avoid getting water on the foliage. Plants reportedly are best propagated by seed, either planted on site in fall or cold stratified for one month before planting. These highly ornamental trees take many years to develop to maturity, and should be protected wherever they occur in the wild.

Arctostaphylos species
Manzanita

Family:	Ericaceae		February–April (*pungens*)
Type:	Evergreen shrub	**Water use:**	Low–moderate
Size:	8–12' high x 8–12' wide (*glauca*), 3–6' high x 6–10' wide (*pungens*)	**Cold hardiness:**	To 12°F (*glauca*), -20°F (*pungens*)
Bloom:	December–March (*glauca*),	**USDA zone:**	8–10 (*glauca*), 5–9 (*pungens*)

Author citation: Arctostaphylos glauca Lindley
Arctostaphylos pungens Kunth

THE TINY NODDING URN-SHAPED BLOSSOMS OF PALE PINK OR WHITE that these attractive shrubs produce in winter and early spring are neither extravagantly showy nor particularly rich in nectar, but they are a valuable food source for several hummingbird species returning to their breeding grounds when little else is in bloom. Anna's and Black-chinned Hummingbirds in California make particular use of bigberry manzanita (*Arctostaphylos glauca*), while Anna's, Broad-tailed, Blue-throated, and White-eared Hummingbirds in uplands there and elsewhere have been observed at pointleaf manzanita (*A. pungens*) blooms. Various butterflies also visit the blossoms, which are mainly pollinated by bees, bee-flies, and flies. The fruits of both manzanitas are taken by a number of birds and mammals.

Bigberry manzanita ranges from the San Francisco Bay area southward to Baja California in Mexico, where it inhabits dry rocky slopes in chaparral or in the piñon belt at elevations of 2,000 to 4,700 feet, often forming huge thickets. Its mahogany-colored bark that peels in summertime and its crooked branches make this manzanita easy to recognize. Pointleaf manzanita inhabits uplands in southern California, Nevada, Arizona, southwestern Utah, southwestern New Mexico, western Texas, and northern Mexico, at elevations of 3,000 to 8,000 feet. It too may form dense thickets in favored niches, such as rocky mesas or gravelly hillsides studded with oaks or ponderosa pines. Its twisting branches, downy gray twigs, and smooth chestnut-colored bark are distinctive, as is the foliage that gives the plant its common name. The rich green leathery leaves are narrowly oval and pointed at both tip and base, and are often held upward to conserve moisture. The flower clusters of both manzanitas and the miniature apple-like fruits that follow form at branch tips.

Manzanitas are not well known in cultivation. A sandy or gravelly soil that is well drained and low in organic content, some afternoon shade (particularly in hot locations), and regular watering as long as needed are suggested. Their extremely delicate roots make them difficult to transplant, so planting seed in place is suggested. Once settled in, they can be long-lived and are excellent for wildlife habitat gardens.

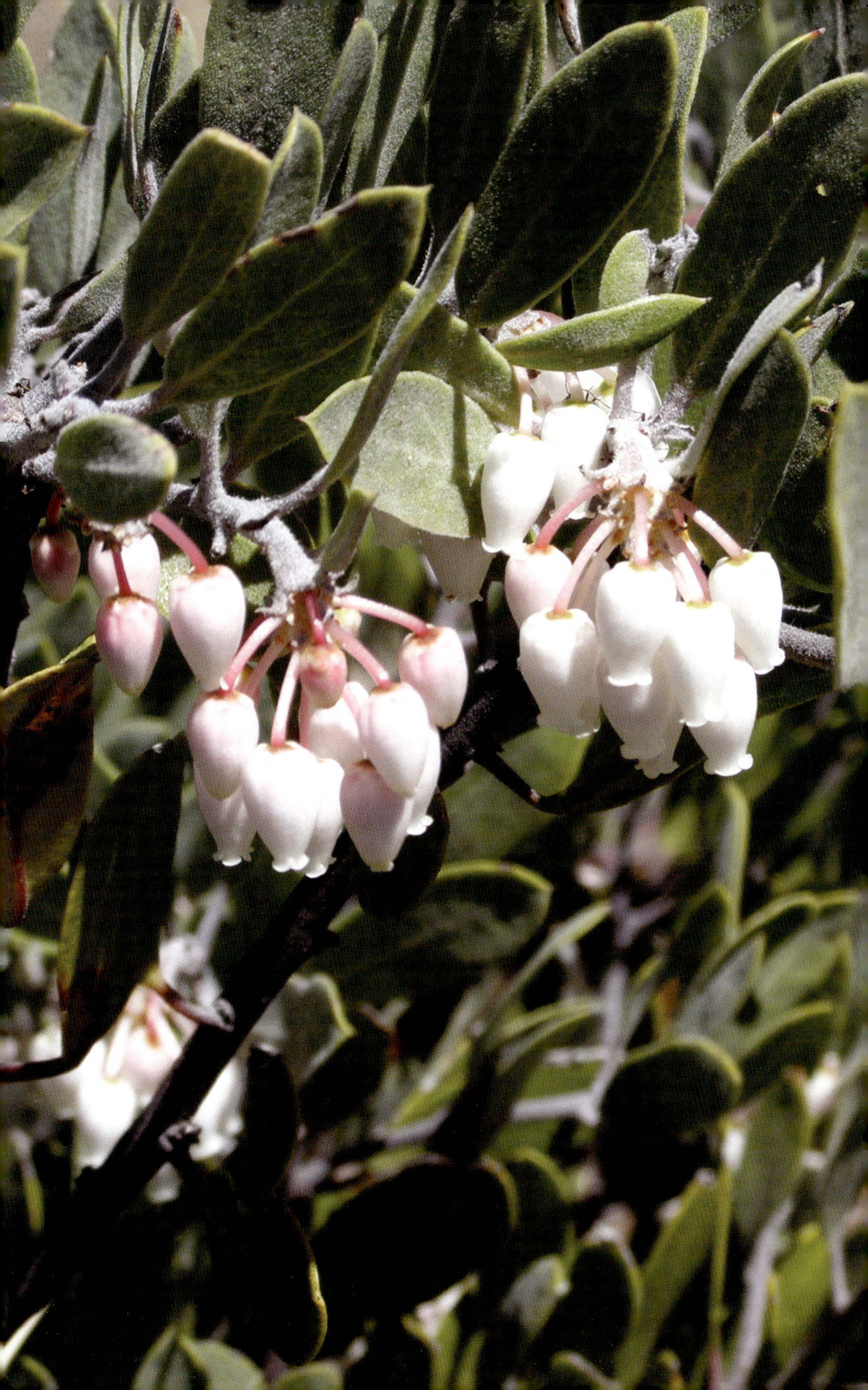

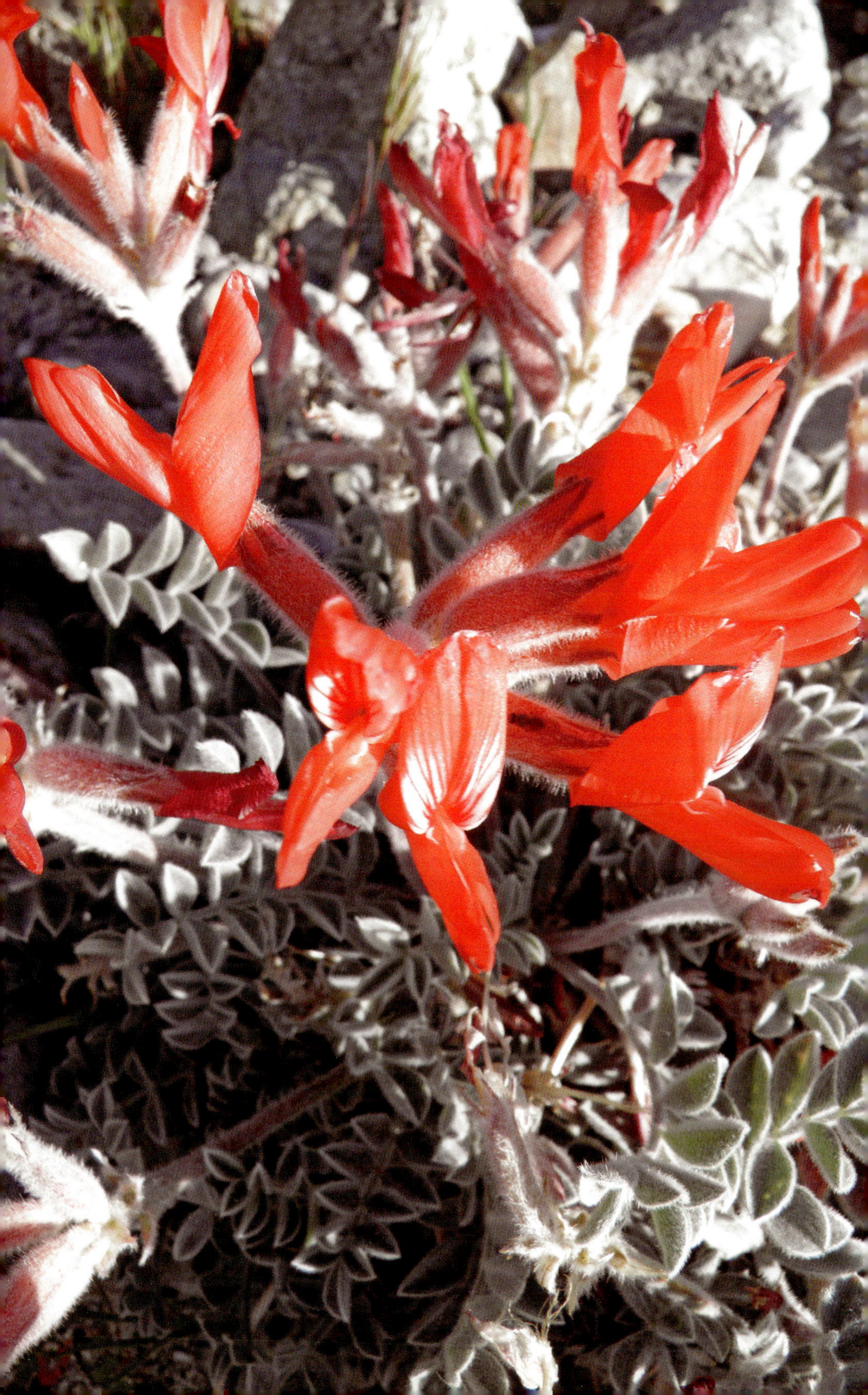

Astragalus coccineus

Scarlet Locoweed, Scarlet Milkvetch, Crimson Sheeppod

Family:	Fabaceae	**Water use:**	Low–moderate
Type:	Perennial	**Cold hardiness:**	To 30°F
Size:	4–8" high x 1' wide	**USDA zone:**	10–11
Bloom:	March–June		

Author citation: (Parry) Brandegee

THIS FETCHING LITTLE WILDFLOWER IS HIGHLY UNUSUAL FOR ITS GENUS and even the entire legume family in being pollinated to a significant extent by hummingbirds rather than bees. Its blooms of deep scarlet red attract hummingbirds during a long season when nectar resources in the desert can be quite scarce. Costa's and to a lesser extent Black-chinned Hummingbirds are likely to be important pollinators.

An uncommon denizen of the Mojave Desert, scarlet locoweed can be found in southern and southeastern California, southern Nevada, western Arizona, and northern Baja California in Mexico, at elevations ranging from about 2,000 to 7,000 feet. In California some of its haunts include Death Valley National Park, Joshua Tree National Monument, the San Bernardino Mountains, and the Peninsular Ranges. Most often occurring in sagebrush or piñon-juniper communities of desert mountains, the typically solitary plants may be found tucked between rocks, growing out of cracks in boulders, on scree slopes, on sandy banks, or on open gravelly ridges.

The silvery compound leaves, blue-gray with a dense covering of woolly white hairs and with seven to fifteen leaflets each, are arranged in a low-lying basal clump, with the striking flowers presented above and often nearly obscuring the foliage. The almost two-inch blooms feature fuzzy whitish calyces, a bent back upper petal or banner, inside which are intricate pale yellow or white flamelike markings, and two fused lower petals that form a tube to the nectar. Large, plump, fuzzy, pinkish seedpods form after flowering ceases and may cause the stems to lay down flat due to their weight.

Reportedly, scarlet locoweed is difficult to cultivate and has complex requirements. Success is probably most likely on sunny sites in frost-free areas, with sandy, gravelly, or rocky soil that provides fast drainage. New plants may need frequent watering but once established they will require much less. Once seedpods dry on the plant and are brittle, the ripe seeds can be harvested and direct sown or scarified and stored for spring planting. Seeds are also occasionally available from native plant purveyors.

Bouvardia ternifolia

Firecracker Bush, Scarlet Bouvardia, Trompetilla, Cigarrito

Family:	Rubiaceae	**Water use:**	Low–moderate
Type:	Deciduous or evergreen shrub	**Cold hardiness:**	To -10°F
Size:	2–4' high x 2–3' wide	**USDA zone:**	8–10
Bloom:	May–November, especially July–October		

Author citation: (Cavanilles) Schlechtendal
Synonym: *Bouvardia glaberrima* Engelmann

This eye-popping plant, with its showy clusters of deep scarlet red tubular blossoms, effectively snags southbound hummingbirds from the sky, and provides nectar for nesting birds over a long season as well. Magnificent, Broad-billed, Broad-tailed, and Rufous Hummingbirds especially favor firecracker bush, and Black-chinned, Lucifer, Violet-crowned, and Berylline Hummingbirds are also known to be avid patrons. The flowers are likely pollinated by both butterflies and hummingbirds.

Firecracker bush occurs in southern Arizona and extreme southwestern New Mexico, in the Eagle, Davis, Chisos, and Chinati Mountains of western Texas, and southward along both ranges of the Sierra Madre to central Mexico. Typically it is found in mountain canyons in igneous soil and in piñon-juniper woodlands, from 3,000 to as high as 9,500 feet in elevation. Its many woody-based branches are clad in whorls of smooth green narrow leaves that are not particularly distinctive, but when the plant begins to bloom, it needs no introduction. The one- to two-inch *trompetillas*—literally, "little trumpets"—are extremely narrow with four flaring lobes and are held upright in loose clusters of up to a dozen at stem tips. Shiny, tan-colored, two-lobed capsules form after flowering, eventually releasing a number of small winged seeds.

Plants will grow in sand, loam, or gravel, as long as it is well drained. In the lower elevations they prefer partial shade, especially during the hot mid-afternoon hours. A deep soaking at least once a month during the summer will keep established plants perky. Bloom is often continuous if spent blossoms are snipped regularly. If plants get leggy, prune back hard to encourage denser and more compact growth. Protect from hard freezes to prevent leaf drop. Propagate from fresh seed sown in late summer or by stem cuttings taken in the spring. When transplanting, note that the roots are rather fragile and spindly. This highly ornamental shrub, which unfortunately is not widely available in the trade, dresses up courtyards, patios, poolsides, and entryways. It also works well in containers, which can be easily moved to a protected location in winter.

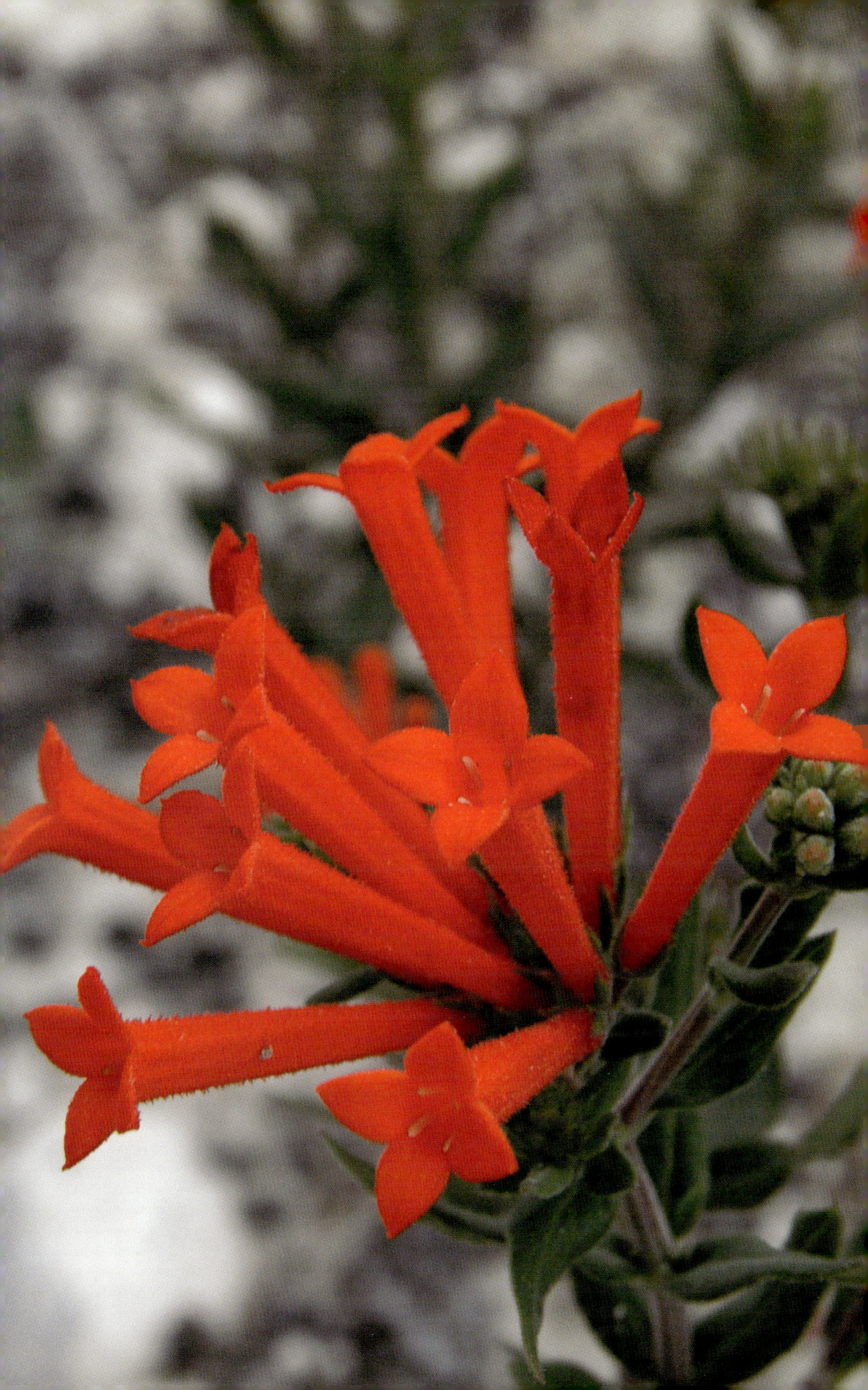

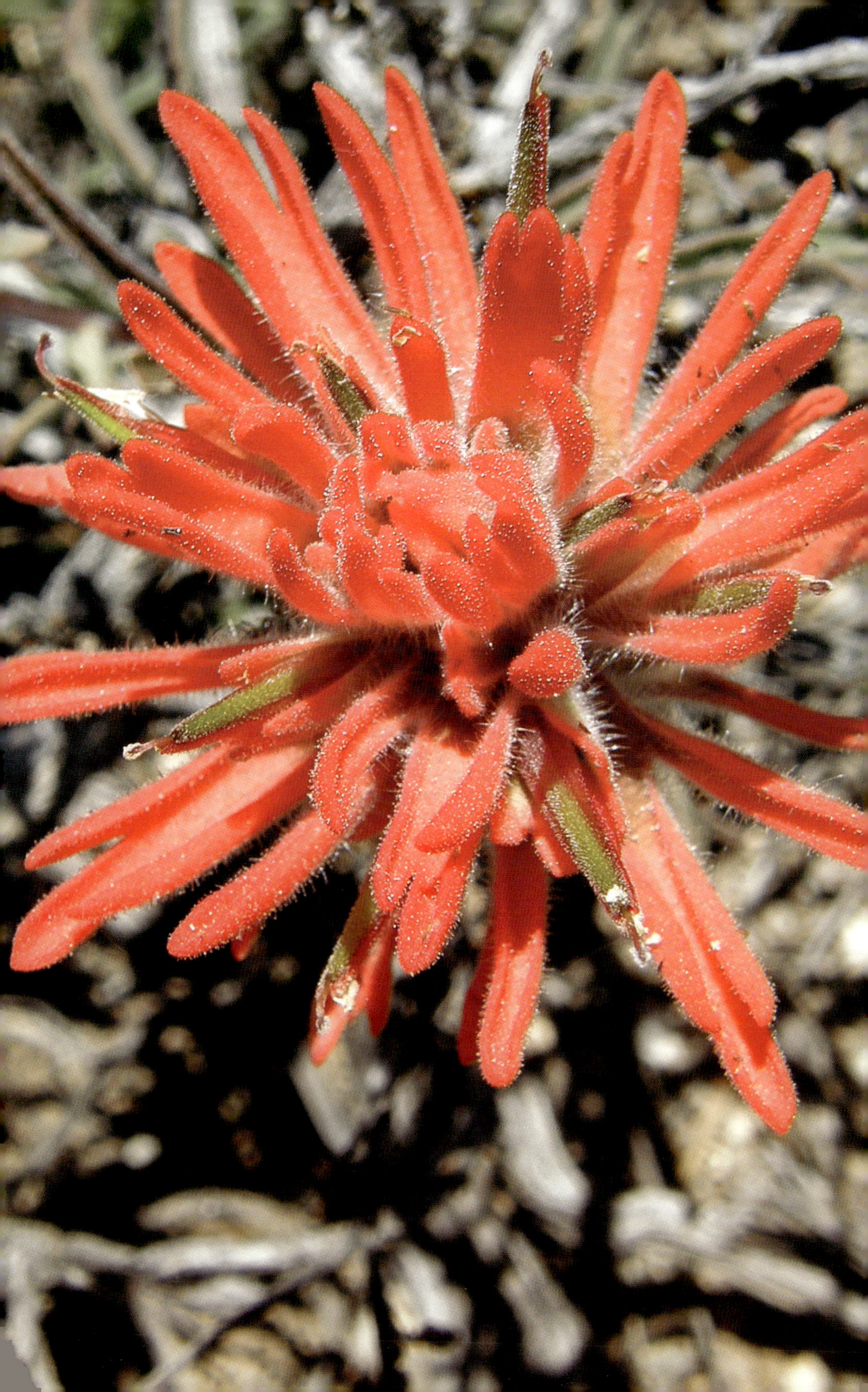

Castilleja angustifolia
Northwestern Paintbrush, Desert Paintbrush

Family: Orobanchaceae (Scrophulariaceae)
Type: Perennial
Size: 1.5' high x <1' wide
Bloom: March–June or May–September depending on elevation

Water use: Moderate
Cold hardiness: Roots to -28°F
USDA zone: 4–8

Author citation: (Nuttall) G. Don
Synonym: *Castilleja chromosa* A. Nelson

THIS SHOWY PAINTBRUSH IS ONE OF OVER THIRTY *CASTILLEJA* SPECIES THAT occur in the western United States and are specifically adapted to, and largely dependent upon, hummingbird pollination. Those selected for inclusion here are some of the most important to southwestern hummingbirds. Black-chinned and Anna's Hummingbirds are among those drawn to the red-orange bracts of this particular wide-ranging beauty, especially when stands of flowers are in peak bloom.

By virtue of some recent taxonomic shuffling that is by no means settled, northwestern paintbrush currently seems to have effectively swallowed up desert paintbrush (*C. chromosa*), which occurs in all of the western states southward as far as central Arizona and northwestern New Mexico. As might be expected, this perennial varies widely in its haunts, known from elevations ranging from near sea level to 11,000 feet. Sagebrush plains, foothill grasslands, piñon-juniper woodlands, coniferous forests of lodgepole or yellow pine or red fir, and subalpine forests are among the diverse vegetation zones where it occurs. On favored open sites it tends to form large stands. The several upright pinkish brown stems are sparsely leafed, the lower ones narrow and often wavy on the margins, and the upper with three to five distinct finger-like lobes. The one-inch flowers occur in terminal clusters, their tubular corollas clasped by richly colored, three- to five-lobed bracts. The corollas of some varieties have pointed lobes with lime green tips.

As all plants in this genus are to an unknown extent partly parasitic on roots of grasses and other plants, they are difficult at best to cultivate. Transplanting them is not only often illegal but also guaranteed to fail. The best results will be obtained by planting seed or young potted plants on a dry, open or partly shaded site that is vegetated with native grasses. Late summer or fall sowing is preferable. Plants do not tolerate salinity, most often occurring in sandy soils with a neutral to slightly alkaline pH. Where the proper conditions exist, this showy paintbrush would be sublime massed on a grassy slope and is certain to delight any hummingbirds that are about.

Castilleja applegatei
Wavy-leaf Paintbrush, Pine Paintbrush

Family:	Orobanchaceae (Scrophulariaceae)	**Bloom:**	April–July, peak May–July
		Water use:	Low–moderate
Type:	Perennial	**Cold hardiness:**	To -30°F
Size:	1–2' high x 1–2' wide	**USDA zone:**	4–9

Author citation: Fernald

Another widely distributed paintbrush that is well used by hummingbirds and likely depends significantly upon them for pollination is this showy species of the California mountains and interior West. Broad-tailed and Black-chinned Hummingbirds are presumably important pollinators. As is true of other paintbrushes, this is a fascinating example of a plant developing adapted leaves—the brightly colored bracts—to resemble red flowers in order to attract hummingbird pollinators to the otherwise inconspicuous corollas.

Wavy-leaf paintbrush can be found throughout most of California and Nevada, and northward into Oregon, Idaho, northern Utah, and western Wyoming; some botanists place it in northern Arizona as well. In southern California it occurs in Joshua Tree National Park, the San Bernardino Mountains, and the Transverse and Peninsular ranges. Occurring at elevations ranging from 1,000 to well over 10,000 feet, its varied habitats include open rocky slopes, desert mountains, sagebrush steppe, volcanic mudflows, lodgepole pine forest, and mixed coniferous forest.

Its green, relatively few stems bear striking inflorescences at their tips. The normally dark green corolla, sometimes red-tinged at the margins, may either extend beyond the bracts or be concealed within them, and the bracts, though typically red, are occasionally yellow. While highly variable across its broad range, wavy-leaf paintbrush can usually be distinguished from similar species by its characteristic combination of sticky glandular stems and foliage and wavy leaf margins. After flowering, the plants produce half-inch seed capsules that are loosely covered with a ladder-like netting.

Very little is known about this plant's cultural requirements, but they are likely complex. If seeds can be obtained from a specialty purveyor, best results will probably come from direct seeding among established grasses and forbs that are locally native, as young plants are thought to be partially parasitic on plant roots. Also recommended are a sunny exposure, with part shade advised in hot locations, a lean, fast-draining soil, and spot watering while plants are developing and during prolonged droughts thereafter. Another California paintbrush pollinated primarily by hummingbirds is coast paintbrush (*Castilleja affinis*), found along the entire California coast north to Washington.

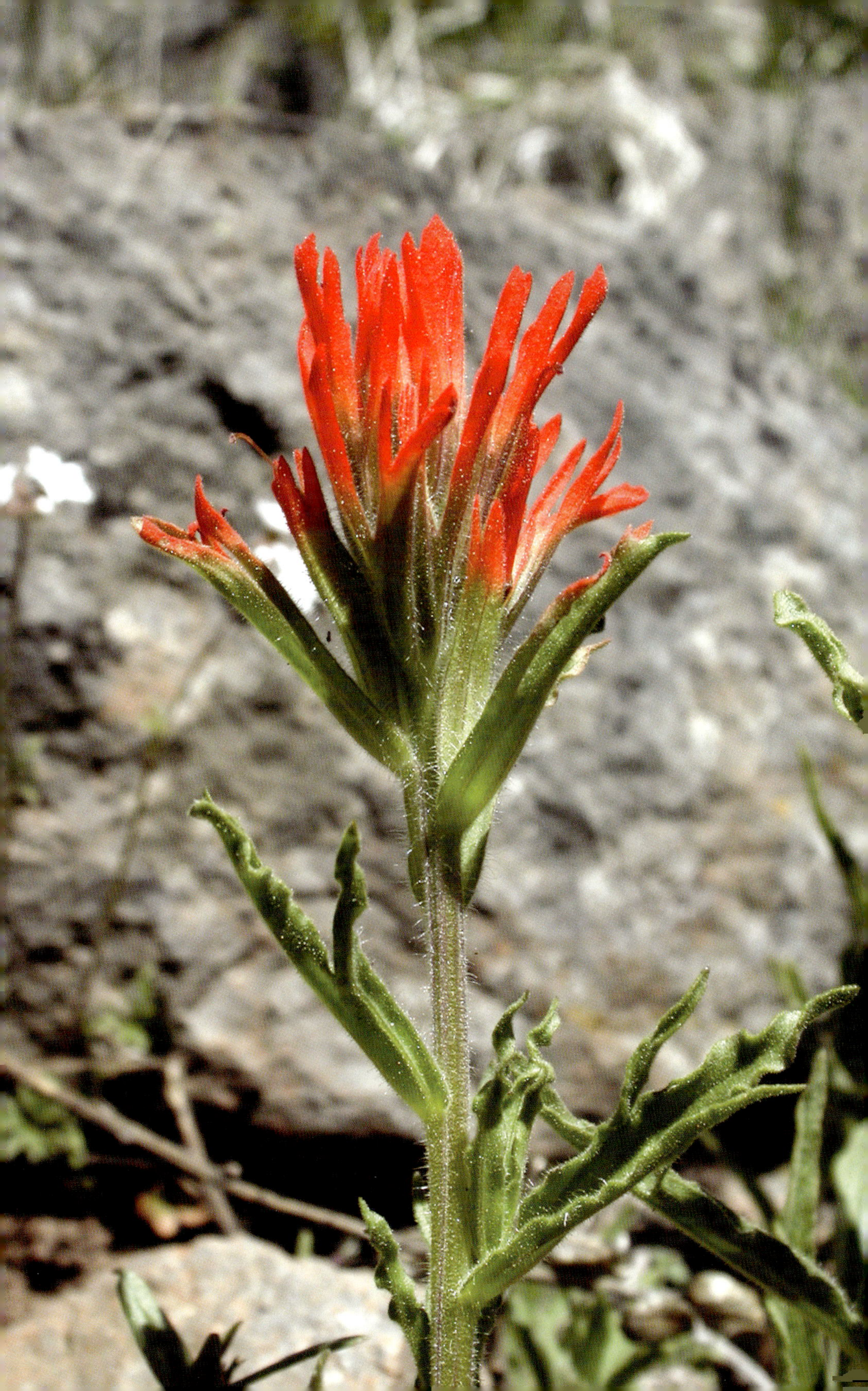

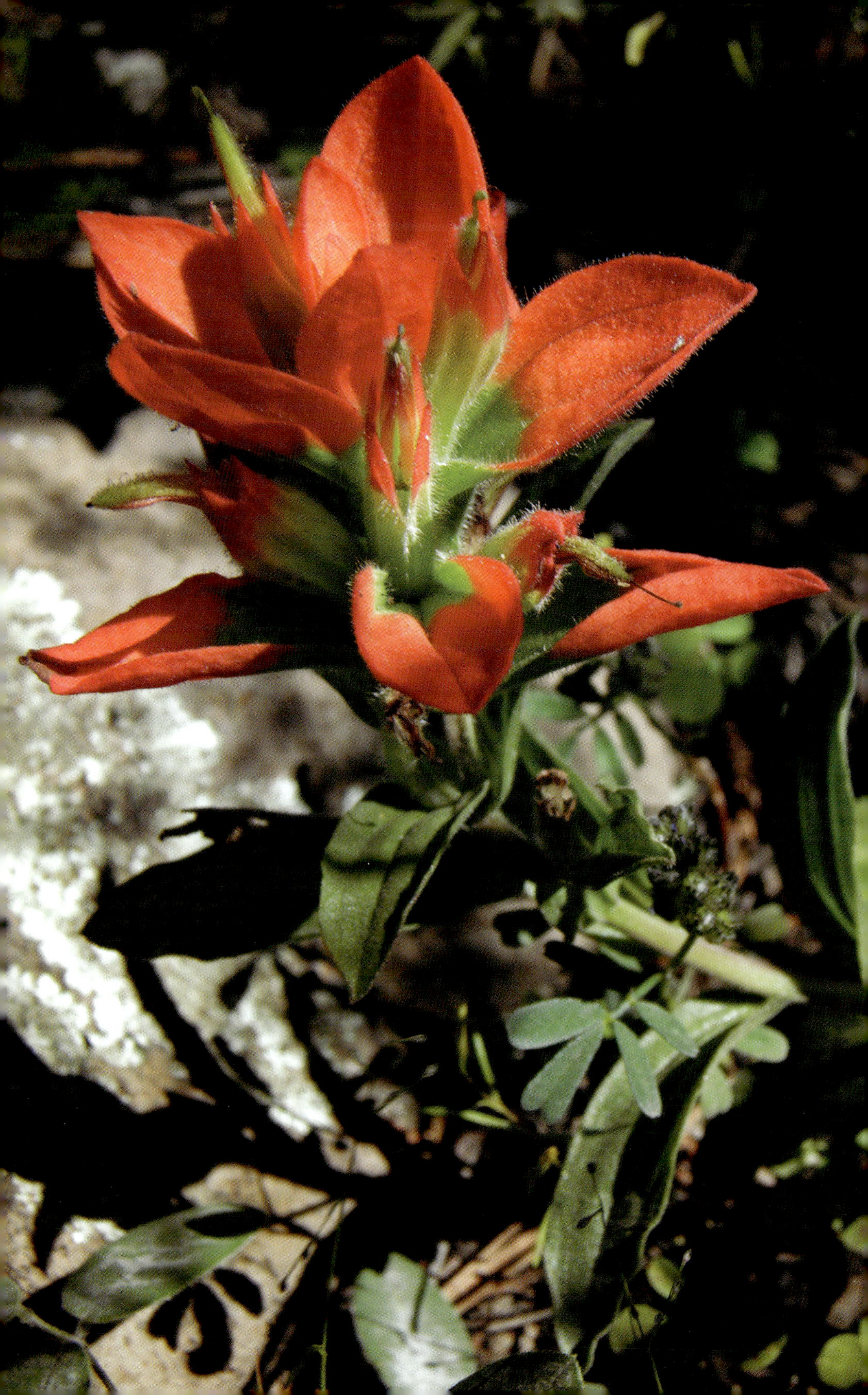

Castilleja austromontana

Rincon Mountain Paintbrush, Arizona Paintbrush

Family:	Orobanchaceae (Scrophulariaceae)	**Bloom:**	May–August
		Water use:	Moderate
Type:	Perennial	**Cold hardiness:**	Roots to -10°F
Size:	1–3' high x <1' wide	**USDA zone:**	6–8
Author citation:	Standley & Blumer		

This high-elevation paintbrush is a valuable nectar source for breeding hummingbirds, particularly the Broad-tailed Hummingbird, and is much visited by southbound migrants as well. Both Calliope and Rufous Hummingbirds seek out the flowers, with their flamboyant clusters of scarlet bracts, as they mountain-hop through the Southwest in July and August. Like most of the red-flowering paintbrushes, the plants rely almost totally upon hummingbirds for pollination. The foliage hosts the larvae of several species of checkerspot butterflies.

Rincon Mountain paintbrush occurs in Arizona from the Grand Canyon and southward, parts of western and southern New Mexico, and northern Mexico in the Sierra Madre Occidental of Sonora. It is strictly a montane plant, favoring moist high mountain slopes of ponderosa pine and Douglas-fir at elevations of about 6,300 to 10,000 feet. On open sites it often grows in the company of Parry's agave (*Agave parryi*) and may benefit from the association. Its erect stems are yellowish with tiny spreading hairs and bear alternating, yellow-green, lance-shaped leaves that have long, fine hairs on the lower surfaces. The showy flower heads are composed of bracts that are bright green at the base and scarlet on the outer parts; some have pointed tips and some have three lobes. The less conspicuous tubular calyx is bright green with a scarlet tip and averages about an inch long.

While not suitable for most southwestern landscapes, at upland locations within its natural range this paintbrush is perhaps worthy of consideration. If seeds can be obtained and the proper habitat exists for it, such as a mountain meadow or grassy hillside, Rincon Mountain paintbrush would make a splashy advertisement for prime nectar to the myriad hummingbirds traveling southward toward Mexico in late summer. To flourish, it will need a sunny to partly shaded exposure, with moist, well-drained, sandy or gravelly soil, and more than a small measure of luck. Plant fresh seeds in fall, or purchase plants potted with regionally native grasses if available. Check native plant and seed suppliers in the region.

Castilleja integra

Southwestern Paintbrush, Brocha India, Wholeleaf Paintbrush

Family:	Orobanchaceae (Scrophulariaceae)	**Bloom:**	March–October, especially late spring
Type:	Perennial	**Water use:**	Low–moderate
Size:	1.5' high x 1' wide	**Cold hardiness:**	Roots to -30°F
		USDA zone:	4–9
Author citation:	A. Gray		

THIS PARAGON OF PAINTBRUSHES IS A MAJOR FORAGE PLANT for many southwestern hummingbirds and depends almost entirely upon them for pollination. The Black-chinned Hummingbird is thought to be its most important pollinator, but Broad-tailed, Lucifer, Broad-billed, Magnificent, White-eared, Calliope, and Rufous Hummingbirds also visit the dazzling red-orange blossoms and share pollination duties. The plant is both a nectar source and larval host for the buckeye butterfly.

The fairly large native range of southwestern paintbrush extends throughout most of Arizona, much of New Mexico, parts of central and west Texas, and northward well into Colorado. The plants typically grow in drifts in grasslands, among piñon-juniper stands on foothill slopes, or in ponderosa woodland openings over a broad elevation range, from 4,500 to 10,000 feet. They have several stout brown stems emerging from a woody root that bear narrow, hairy, sage-green leaves whose edges roll inward. The showy flowers are clustered atop short stalks, consisting of small tubular calyces with pointed lobes nestled in bundles of leafy, round-lobed bracts.

These paintbrushes are thought to be partly parasitic on plant roots as seedlings and ideally should be grown alongside grama grasses (*Bouteloua* spp.), sagebrush (*Artemisia* spp.), or oaks (*Quercus* spp.) native to the vicinity. Choose a spot for them to colonize that has well-drained soil and full sun. Deep water established plants once or twice a month during the growing season to keep them vigorous. At lower elevations plants may do better with part or filtered shade in the afternoon. Like all paintbrushes this plant is next to impossible to transplant from the wild, so please resist the temptation. Either buy seedlings sold in pots with native grasses, or try seeding it in where it is to grow. Cold stratifying the seeds for two months reportedly improves the typically dismal germination rates. Of the many species of *Castilleja* adapted to hummingbird pollination, southwestern paintbrush is the most suitable for desert gardens, and once beyond the often challenging process of establishment works nicely in beds or borders with clumping grasses and succulents or naturalized in meadows.

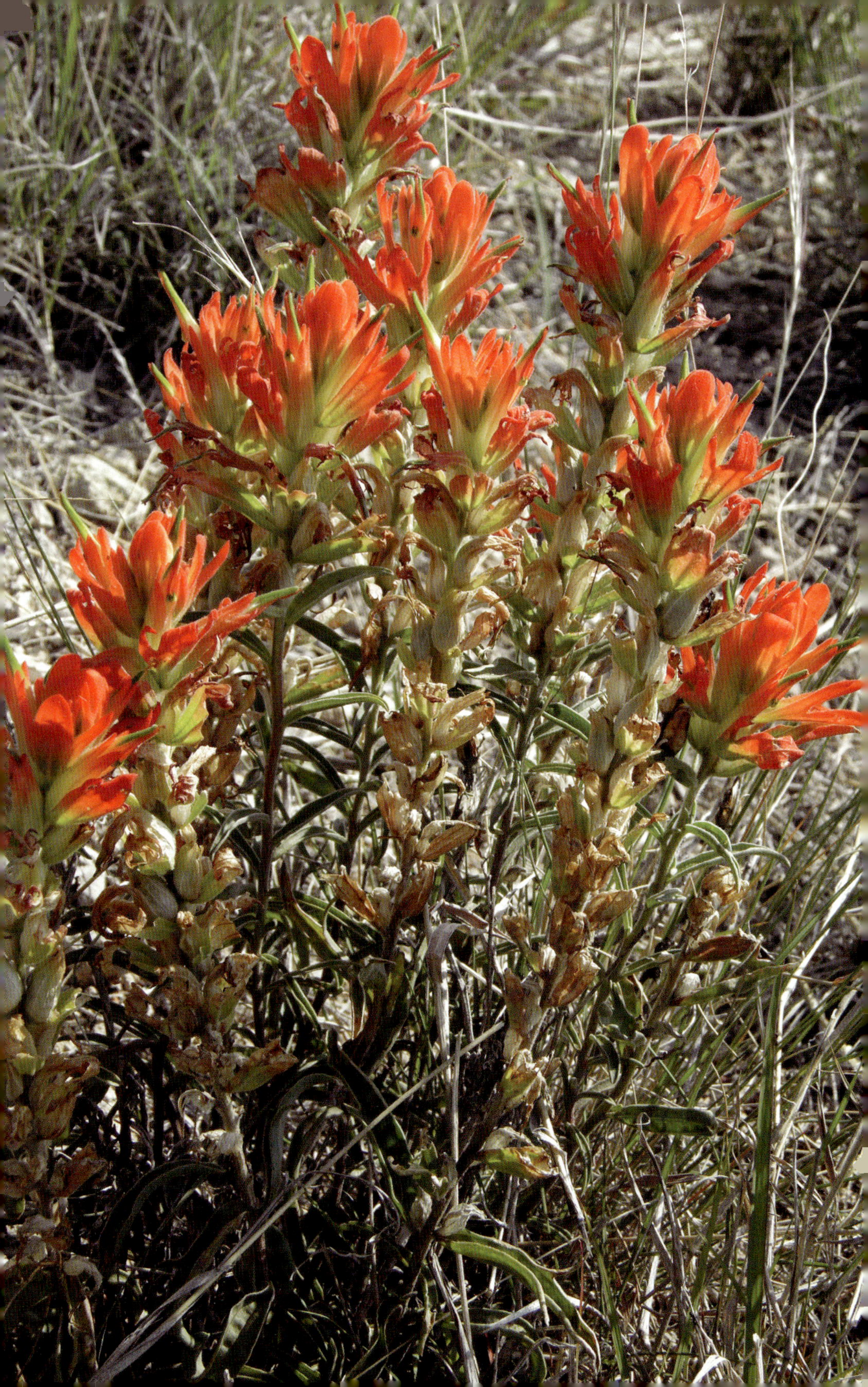

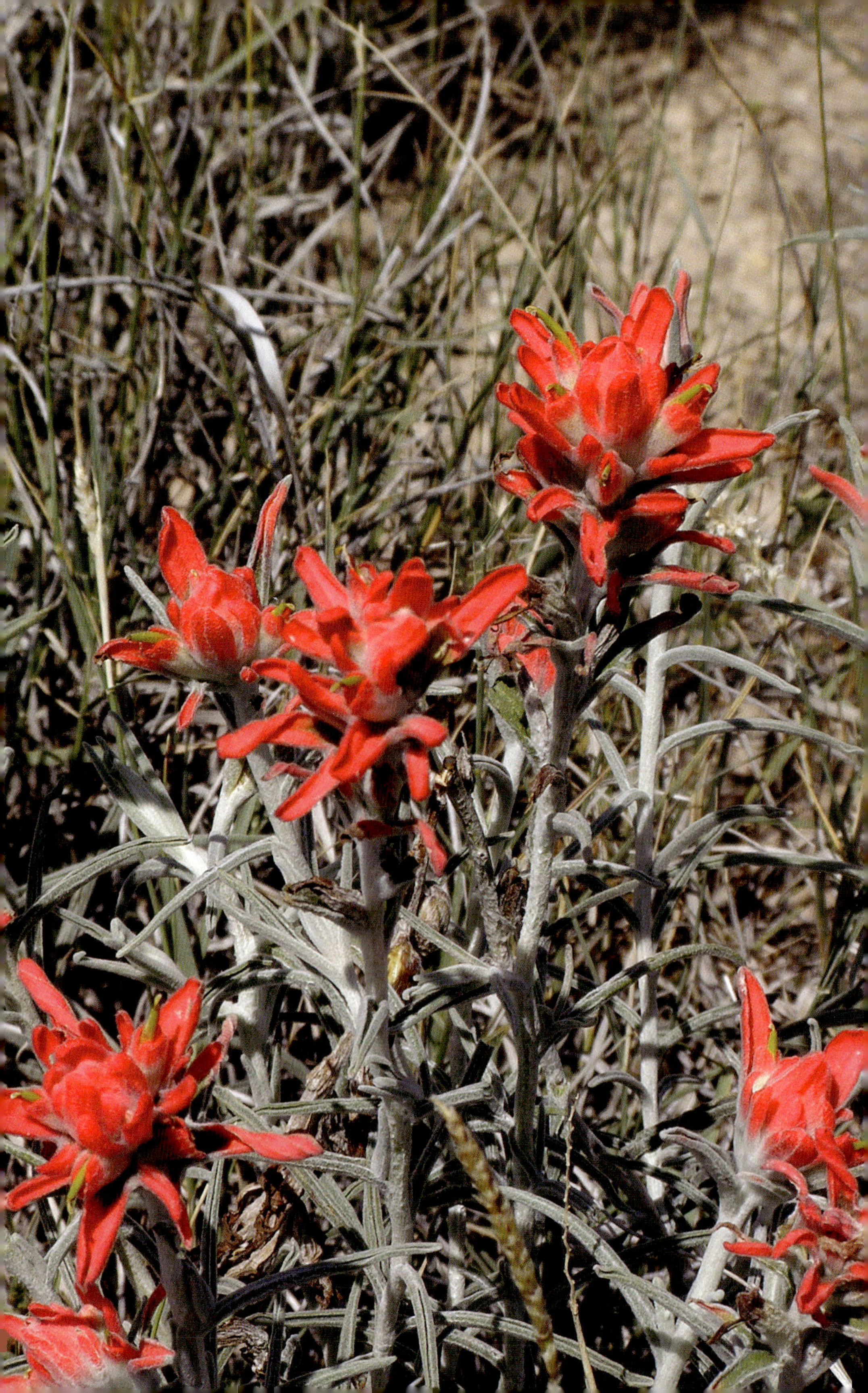

Castilleja lanata

White-Woolly Paintbrush, Sierra Woolly Indian Paintbrush

Family:	Orobanchaceae (Scrophulariaceae)	**Bloom:**	March–August, peak in spring
Type:	Perennial	**Water use:**	Low–moderate
Size:	1–2' high x 1' wide	**Cold hardiness:**	Roots to 10°F
		USDA zone:	8–10

Author citation: A. Gray

The fetching flowers of this colorful paintbrush are extremely important to breeding Lucifer Hummingbirds in the Big Bend region of west Texas, and are likely to be widely used by Black-chinned Hummingbirds as well. A subspecies of this plant, *hololeuca*, is equally valuable to Allen's Hummingbirds on the California coast. The plants positively ooze with high-sucrose nectar that biologists have measured at concentrations of nearly 38 percent sugar. Hummingbirds are undoubtedly the chief pollinators. This paintbrush is a larval host for the fulvia checkerspot butterfly.

White-woolly paintbrush occurs in a fairly narrow band across southern Arizona, southern New Mexico, and west Texas, typically colonizing limestone or granitic foothills and desert grasslands at elevations ranging from 2,500 to about 7,000 feet. The subspecies *hololeuca*, known as whitefelt Indian paintbrush, is found only on the Channel Islands off of southern California. Either is easily recognized, with stems and leaves that are bright green and densely cloaked with white woolly hairs. The lower leaves are narrow and linear, the upper deeply cleft. The two-tone flower bracts that surround the calyx each have three lobes and in white-woolly paintbrush they are green on the inner half and red on the outer half, resembling miniature parfaits; the flowers of whitefelt Indian paintbrush are entirely butter yellow. The initial burst of bloom is in the springtime, but plants continue to put out sporadic blooms through summer and in some locales seem to flower nearly year-round.

White-woolly paintbrush is believed to be partly parasitic on the roots of other plants, most often grasses, and prefers a coarse, well-drained, limestone soil. Avoid the temptation to dig wild plants, as they are next to impossible to transplant. Germination of seeds is said to be extremely difficult, but reportedly the best results come from sowing on site in fall. One can also check local native plant sales and niche nurseries for potted seedlings. This is a tough, drought-tolerant, heat-loving plant that if it can be successfully established would make an excellent addition to a high-desert hummingbird garden.

Castilleja linariifolia

Wyoming Paintbrush, Narrowleaf Paintbrush

Family:	Orobanchaceae (Scrophulariaceae)	**Bloom:**	May–September
Type:	Perennial	**Water use:**	Moderate
Size:	1–3' high x 1–2' wide	**Cold hardiness:**	Roots to -30°F
		USDA zone:	4–7

Author citation: Bentham

Several of the Indian paintbrushes important to hummingbirds have very large ranges of which the Southwest is only a part; this species is one of them. Wyoming's showy scarlet and yellow state flower is a summer staple of breeding Calliope Hummingbirds and is known to be much visited by Rufous, Broad-tailed, and Allen's Hummingbirds as well. This species, like other red-bracted paintbrushes, depends almost entirely upon hummingbirds for pollination.

In addition to its namesake state, Wyoming paintbrush occurs across a broad geographical area that dips southward into eastern and some south-coastal areas of California, parts of Utah, the western two-thirds of Colorado, northern and eastern Arizona, mostly northern New Mexico, and extends northward into central and southern Oregon, Idaho, and southern Montana. Its favored mountain haunts include dry open woods, brushy sagebrush meadows, rocky hillsides, aspen clearings, and coniferous forest edges, at elevations ranging from 3,200 to 12,000 feet. Sometimes it finds sufficient purchase to grow in surprisingly tiny crevices in otherwise solid rock. Typically fairly tall for a paintbrush, it has several upright, branched, sometimes purple-tinged stems bearing alternate, pale green, linear leaves that are two to four inches in length and roll inward. The upper leaves are three-parted. The flower clusters, occurring over a long bloom season, are composed of widely spaced yellow-green tubular corollas that are framed by bright red, deeply trilobed bracts and extend straight outward from the stem when fully developed.

This is strictly a plant for upper elevation gardens and is not even remotely suitable for desert landscapes. However, given a spot in coarse well-drained soil, with morning sun and an occasional deep soaking during extended summer droughts, Wyoming paintbrush would make a wonderful addition to a mountain meadow garden. Look for seeds from native seed suppliers, or plant seedlings that are potted with native grasses. This paintbrush commonly associates with and may be parasitic on the roots of sagebrush (*Artemisia* spp.) when young. Propagation is at your own risk, although some experts recommend sowing seed in fall to mimic nature.

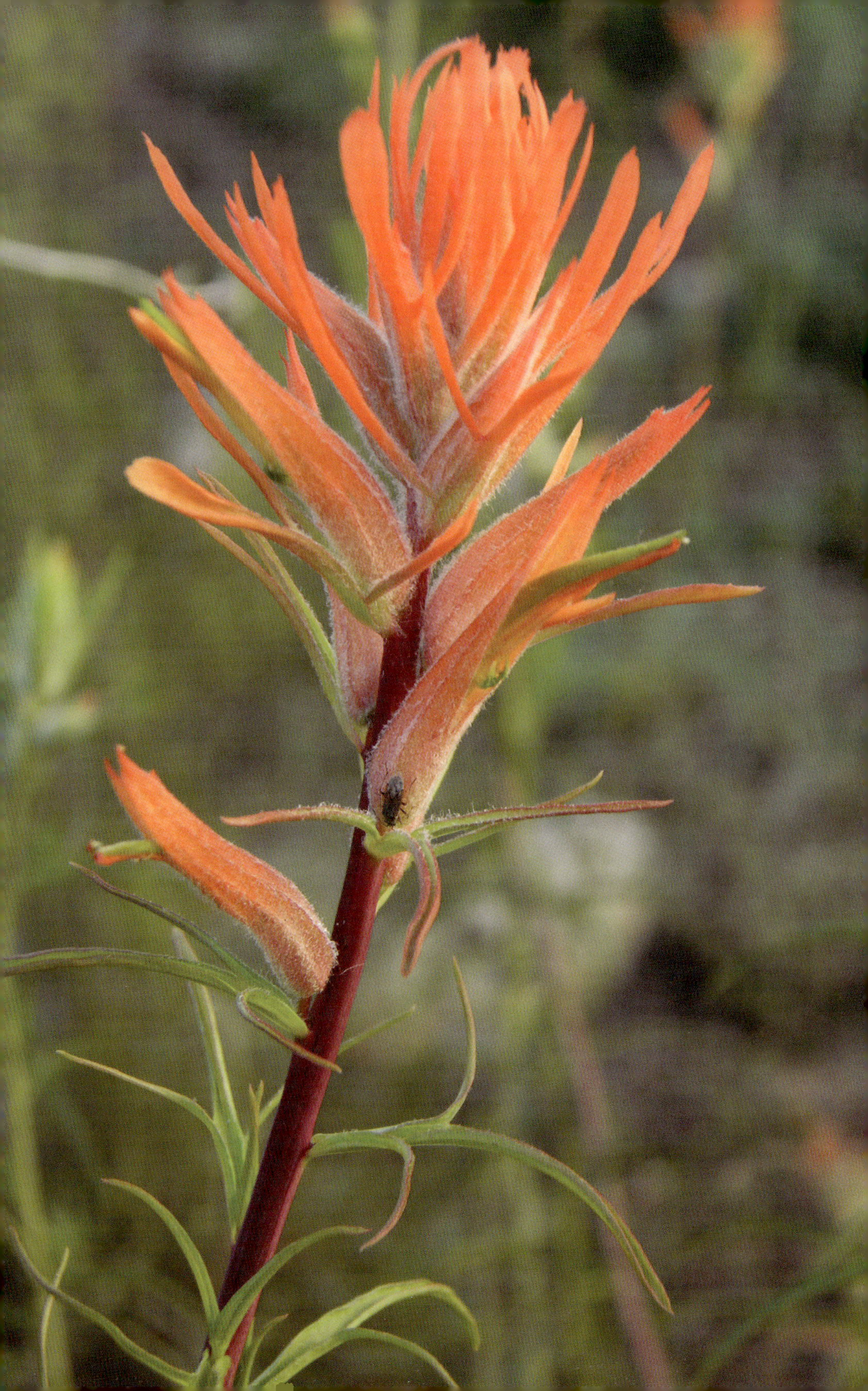

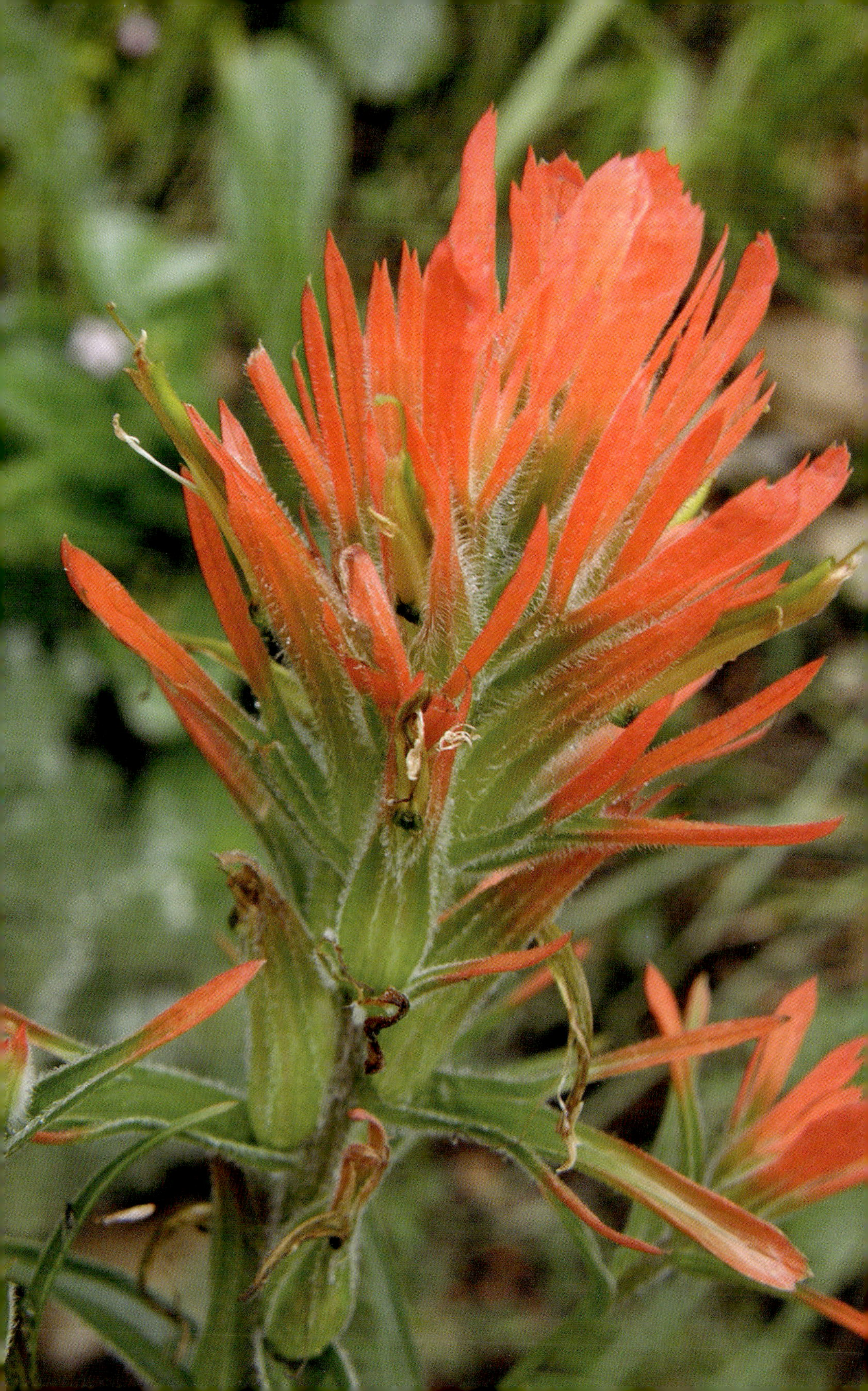

Castilleja miniata

Giant Red Paintbrush, Meadow Paintbrush

Family:	Orobanchaceae (Scrophulariaceae)	**Bloom:**	June–October
		Water use:	Moderate
Type:	Perennial	**Cold hardiness:**	Roots to -30°F
Size:	1–3' high x 1–2' wide	**USDA zone:**	4–8

Author citation: Douglas ex Hooker

THE VIVID RED BRACTS OF THIS SUMMER-BLOOMING PAINTBRUSH are justifiably extravagant advertisement for the wellspring of nectar within, of tremendous importance in particular to Broad-tailed, Calliope, Rufous, and to a lesser extent Allen's Hummingbirds over a broad geographical area. Broad-tailed and Calliope Hummingbirds rely heavily on the blooms early in the nesting season, and Rufous Hummingbirds are known to defend stands of blooming plants while moving southward in late summer. Hummingbirds are considered to be the primary pollinators. Deer relish the foliage for browse.

Giant red paintbrush ranges over the entire western United States, in our region occurring in California, Nevada, Utah, western and central Colorado, northern Arizona, and northern and central New Mexico. It is strictly a montane plant, occurring in wet mountain meadows and bogs, on streambanks, in coniferous forest openings, in aspen groves, and on piñon-juniper slopes, at elevations of 4,500 to 11,000 feet. The pinkish stems are usually unbranched and are garbed in two- to four-inch light green to deep purple lance-shaped leaves with pointed tips. The flower clusters consist of whorls of showy three-pointed bracts that range in color from vivid scarlet to rose red and a four-pointed tubular calyx that encases the barely noticeable green corolla.

Like other paintbrushes it is notoriously difficult to cultivate, but if seeds can be obtained the optimal planting site would be on moist well-drained soil, in full sun to filtered afternoon shade, with locally native grasses present. New plants should be deep watered at least weekly during their first summer. Propagate by seed sown on site in autumn and cross your fingers, or buy seedlings started in pots with native grasses. As is true of other paintbrushes, transplanting from the wild is just a roundabout way to kill plants. Giant red paintbrush absolutely cannot endure the extremes of drought and intense heat of lower elevations, but with proper placement and more than a bit of luck it would make a striking accent for a mountain cottage garden and is sure to be enthusiastically received by any summering Broad-tailed Hummingbirds and a bevy of southbound migrants.

Castilleja patriotica

Huachuca Mountain Paintbrush, Periquito, Hierba de Sapo

Family:	Orobanchaceae (Scrophulariaceae)	**Bloom:**	July–September
Type:	Perennial	**Water use:**	Moderate
Size:	1–2' high x <1' wide	**Cold hardiness:** Roots to -10°F	
		USDA zone:	6–8

Author citation: Fernald

This spectacular mountain paintbrush begins blooming on or about the Fourth of July, which leads one to wonder if that may be the derivation of its species name. Regardless, it picks up steam at about the time its cousin, Rincon Mountain paintbrush (*Castilleja austromontana*), starts to taper off, and continues to offer blooms throughout the peak of hummingbird migration. Broad-tailed, Rufous, Magnificent, Violet-crowned, White-eared, and Black-chinned Hummingbirds are all avid patrons of the high-sucrose nectar and probably are the most significant pollinators.

In the United States, Huachuca Mountain paintbrush occurs only in the Huachuca and Chiricahua mountains of southeast Arizona and in the Animas Mountains of southwestern New Mexico, but in Mexico it ranges over a broad area of the Sierra Madre Occidental in Sonora, Chihuahua, and southward to Sinaloa and Durango. While its common name would suggest otherwise, in the United States it seems to be most often encountered in the Chiricahuas, from the lower canyons up to and especially the highest peaks. At elevations of about 4,800 to over 9,000 feet and most commonly above 6,000 feet, it may form dense colonies in moist montane meadows and mixed coniferous forest openings and on rocky slopes with Apache and ponderosa pines. It is fairly easy to distinguish from other paintbrushes by its yellowish-green deeply divided stem leaves, with four pointed leaflets branching off of the main lance-shaped leaf. The flower heads are quite similar to those of Wyoming paintbrush (*C. linariifolia*), with showy scarlet to carmine-red three-lobed bracts at the base of each yellow flower, but the corollas of Huachuca Mountain paintbrush are noticeably longer.

This is a plant to be cherished and protected in natural areas, and is not suitable even to contemplate for the desert garden. However, on a grassy slope in a cool upland habitat, Huachuca Mountain paintbrush would put out a breathtaking welcome mat for the waves of migrant hummingbirds passing through in late summer. To improve the reputedly paltry odds of success, plant seeds or potted seedling starts among native grasses on a sunny, well-draining slope that receives moderate natural rainfall.

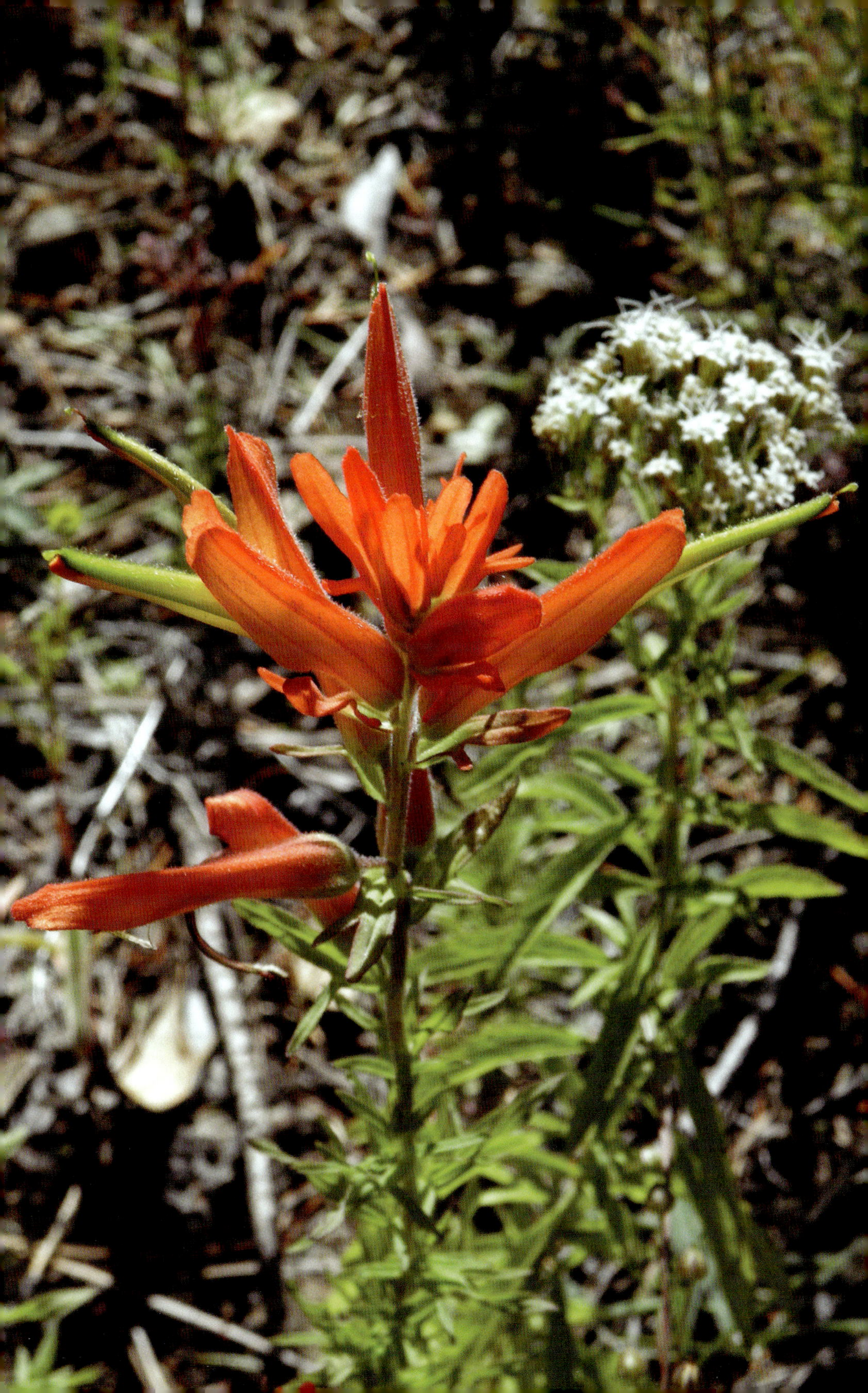

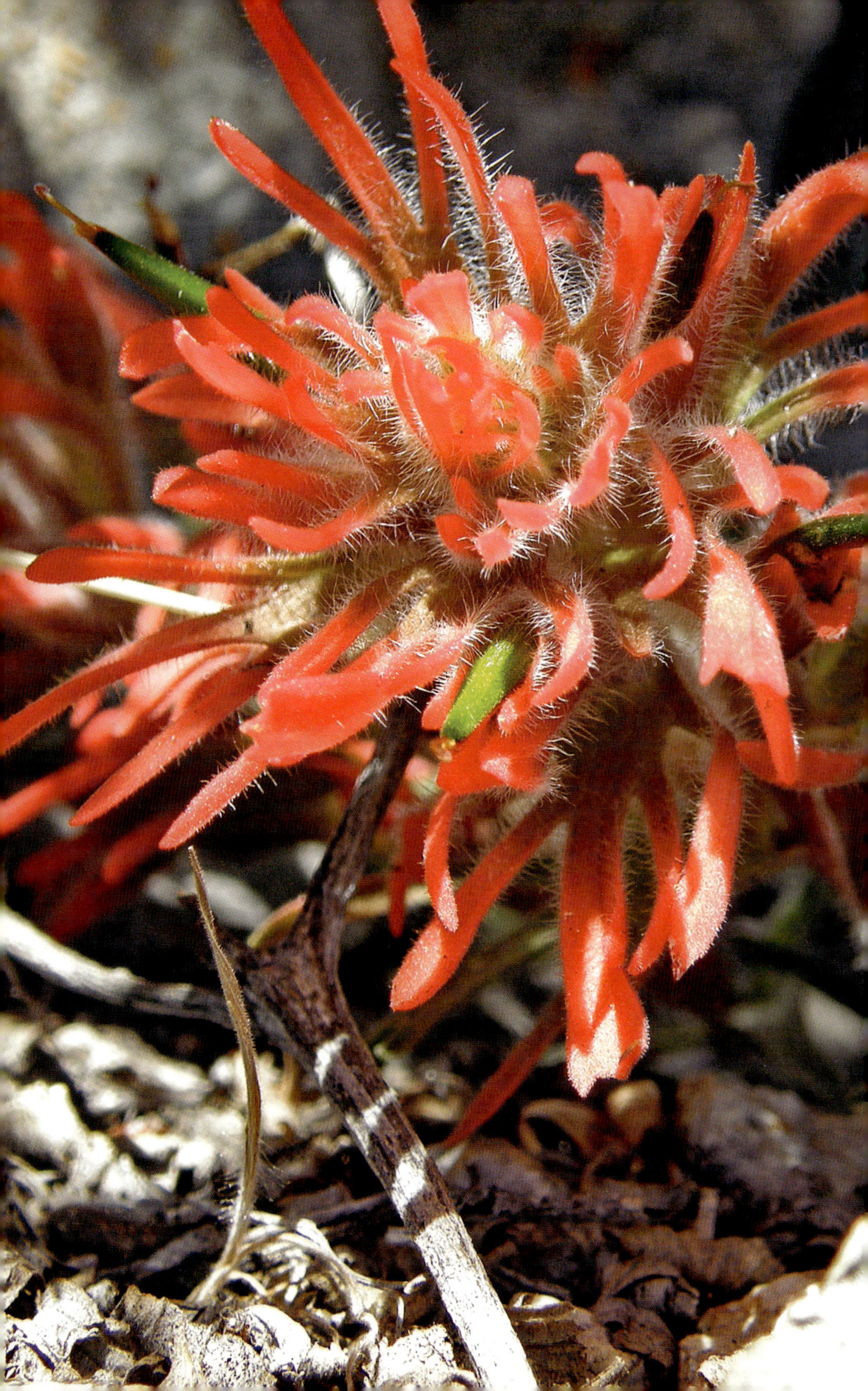

Castilleja scabrida

Rough Paintbrush, Zion Paintbrush, Eastwood's Paintbrush

Family:	Orobanchaceae (Scrophulariaceae)	**Bloom:**	May–July or longer
		Water use:	Low–moderate
Type:	Perennial	**Cold hardiness:**	Roots to -30°F
Size:	4–8" high x 1' wide	**USDA zone:**	4–8

Author citation: Eastwood

THIS TINY CHARMER MAKES A BIG SPLASH when in bloom, its fire-engine-red bracts advertising valuable nectar for the taking during most of the hummingbird nesting season from late spring through midsummer. Broad-tailed and Black-chinned Hummingbirds are likely to be its most important pollinators, and southbound Rufous and Calliope Hummingbirds may lend some assistance as well.

Although its stronghold is in the Four Corners region, where Utah, Colorado, New Mexico, and Arizona meet, rough paintbrush has populations as far westward as eastern Nevada and as far eastward as central Colorado. Known from only one county in Arizona and with few records from New Mexico, most observations are from the canyonlands of Utah and the middle elevations of the Colorado Rockies. Here it graces Arches, Canyonlands, Capitol Reef, and Zion national parks and Colorado, Dinosaur, Hovenweep, Natural Bridges, and Pipe Spring national monuments. Its neat little clumps tucked into rocks at elevations ranging from 3,300 to nearly 9,000 feet, this colorful perennial inhabits piñon-juniper woodlands, foothill grasslands, canyons, ridgetops, sandstone mesas, gravelly slopes, crevices in slickrock, niches in cliffs, and sagebrush steppe.

Its usually purplish stems bear dense grayish-green foliage near the base, the fleshy linear leaves up to three inches long and covered in short rigid hairs that give the plant its characteristic rough texture. Especially when laden with flowers the stems often trail along the ground. The blooms consist of lavish bright red bracts that encircle the relatively inconspicuous yellowish-green tubular corollas containing the nectar.

Like other paintbrushes, this beauty is difficult to cultivate and not for the casual gardener to attempt, but if seeds can be obtained the best results will likely come from direct sowing seed amongst grasses native to the area, especially grama (*Bouteloua* spp.) and/or sagebrush (*Artemisia tridentata*), as paintbrush is thought to be partly parasitic on their roots. A sunny exposure, a lean fast-draining sandy or gravelly soil, and moderate water until established and as needed thereafter are also recommended—along with a healthy dose of patience.

Castilleja tenuiflora

Santa Catalina Paintbrush, Periquito, Perico

Family:	Orobanchaceae (Scrophulariaceae)	**Bloom:**	March–October
		Water use:	Low–moderate
Type:	Perennial	**Cold hardiness:**	Roots to 0°F
Size:	1–3' high x 1' wide	**USDA zone:**	7–9

Author citation: Bentham
Synonym: *Castilleja laxa* A. Gray

Last but certainly not least on the honor roll of important southwestern paintbrushes that are pollinated in large part by hummingbirds is this colorful wildflower, whose unusually long bloom season—spanning spring through fall depending upon location—makes it an especially valuable nectar source. Although White-eared and Magnificent Hummingbirds are the only hummingbird visitors specifically mentioned in the literature, likely Broad-tailed, Blue-throated, and migrating Rufous and Calliope Hummingbirds help to pollinate the slender scarlet-bracted yellow flowers as well.

Rather uncommon in the United States, Santa Catalina paintbrush occurs only in southern Arizona—including its namesake mountains outside of Tucson—and more rarely in parts of western and southern New Mexico, but in Mexico it is much more common and ranges widely, from Sonora eastward to Nuevo Leon and southward to Oaxaca. Favored habitats include oak woodlands, pine-oak forest, tropical deciduous forest, brushy chaparral, rock outcroppings, canyon bottoms, and desert grasslands, at elevations ranging from 4,000 to almost 9,000 feet. Its green to purplish, erect, branching stems bear long, narrow, sage-green leaves and, unlike many other paintbrushes, comparatively conspicuous yellow tubular flowers that usually protrude well beyond the showy red to red-orange bracts. The entire plant is covered with fine white hairs. Soon after flowering, the seedpods begin to develop and may be present along with the flowers for much of the blooming season.

This is mostly a plant to enjoy in wild places, for like other paintbrushes it has complex requirements and is challenging to cultivate even in upland gardens. If seeds can be obtained from a specialty purveyor, sowing directly on site alongside established plants such as grama grasses (*Bouteloua curtipendula* and others) or native perennial forbs should yield the best results, for young paintbrushes may be partially parasitic on their roots. A fairly open exposure in full sun to part shade, sandy or gravelly soil, good drainage, and moderate water until established and as needed afterward are also suggested; luck and patience are wise to have on hand as well.

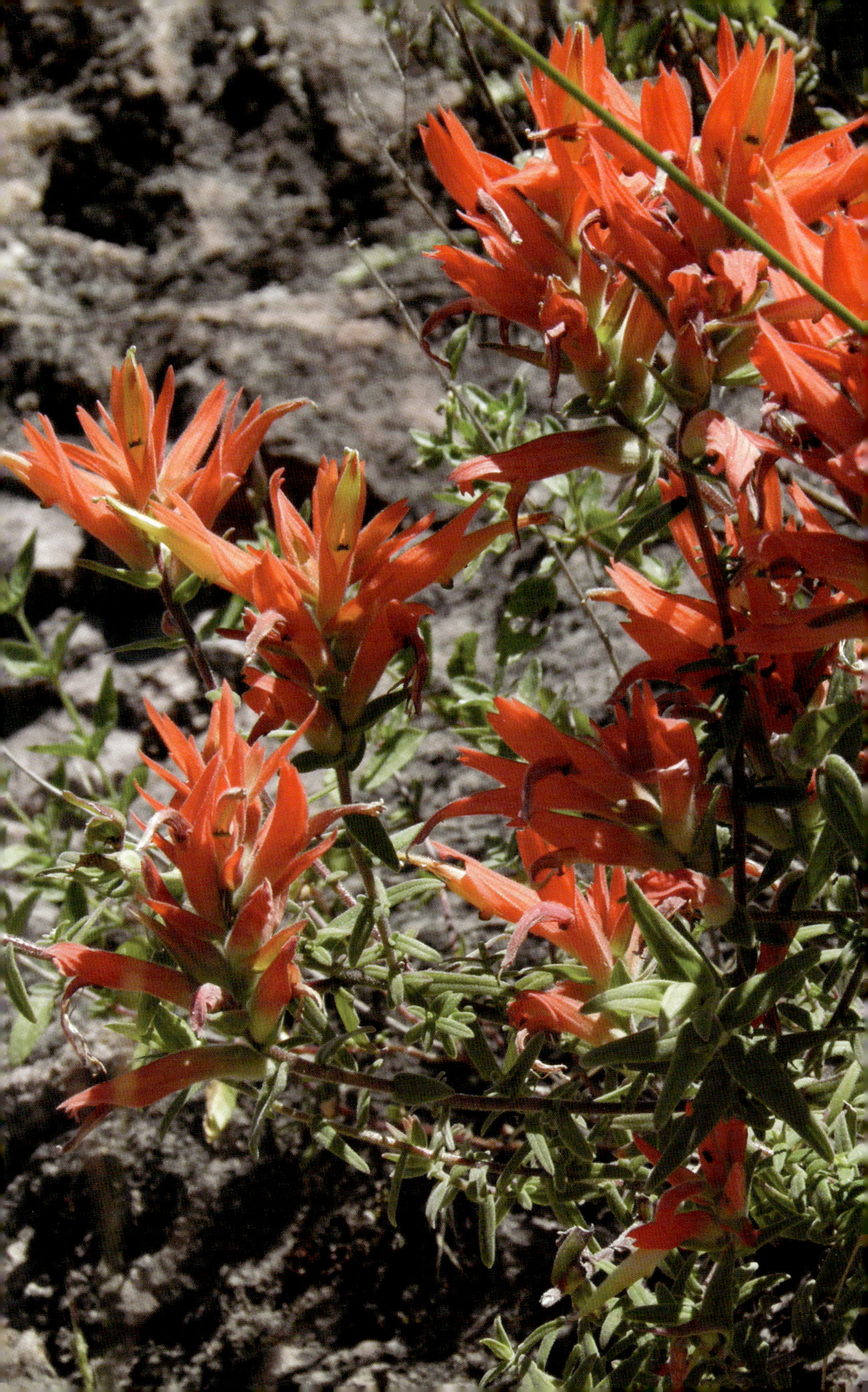

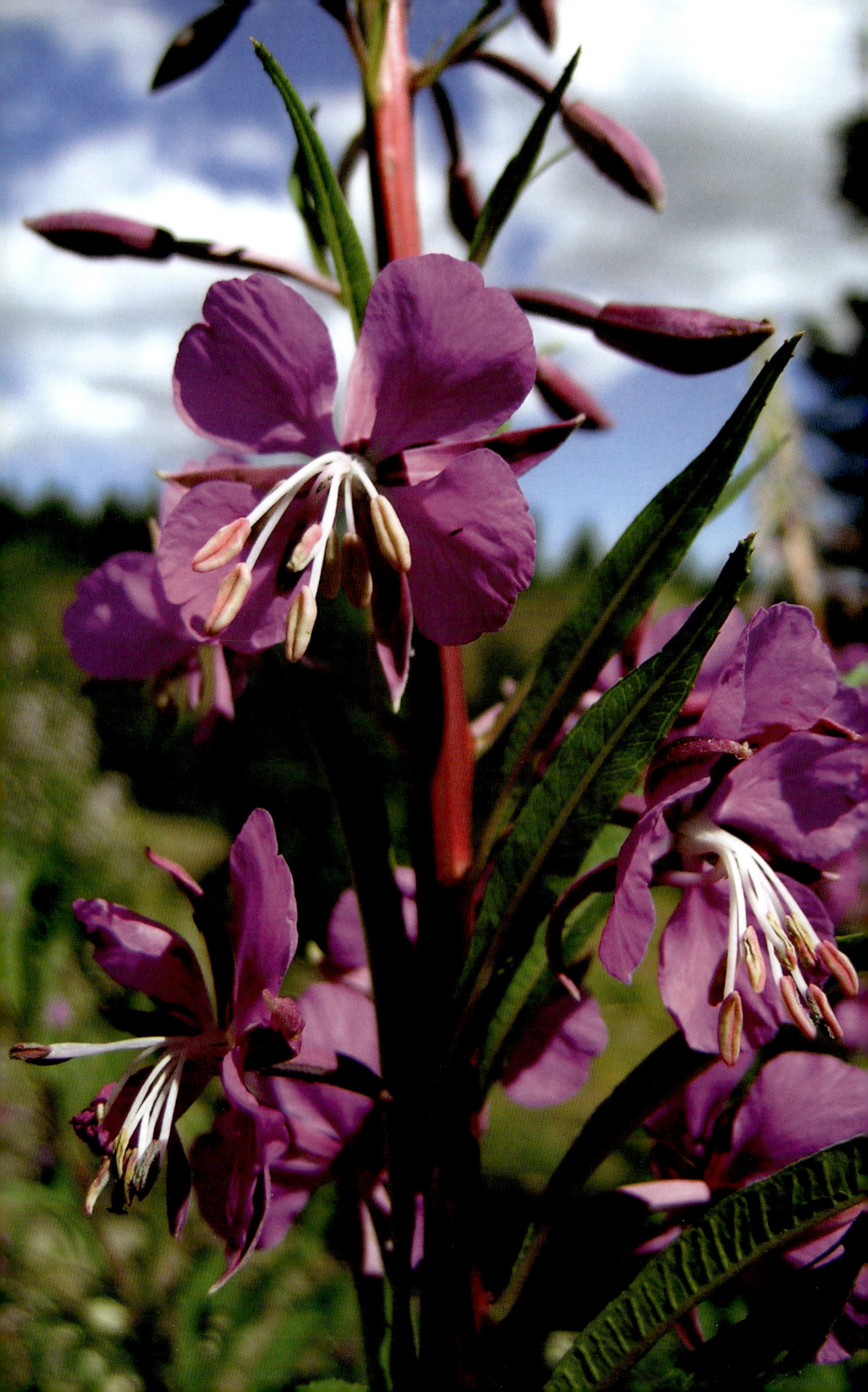

Chamerion angustifolium

Fireweed, Narrowleaf Fireweed, Rosebay Willow-herb

Family:	Onagraceae	**Water use:**	High
Type:	Perennial	**Cold hardiness:**	Roots to -30°F
Size:	2–6' high x 2–3' wide	**USDA zone:**	2–9
Bloom:	July–September		

Author citation: (L.) Holub
Synonyms: *Epilobium angustifolium* Linnaeus; *Chamaenerion angustifolium* (L.) Scopoli

The rosy purple blooms of this showy wildflower are enthusiastically visited by both Rufous and Broad-tailed Hummingbirds as they mountain-hop southward after the breeding season. Attracting butterflies as well, particularly swallowtails, the flowers rely largely on bees for pollination and are considered valuable for honey production. The foliage provides excellent forage for deer, elk, and livestock.

Fireweed enjoys a huge natural range, extending from northern and eastern California, northern and eastern Arizona, and western and central New Mexico, northward to Alaska and eastward to Maine, occurring at widely ranging elevations from foothills to subalpine zones. In the Southwest it associates with a diverse array of mixed coniferous, oak, and aspen communities. Typically cropping up in moist, disturbed soils, especially after forest fires or logging, it spreads quickly by rhizomes to colonize an area and may form impressive stands, in some situations becoming invasive.

Its tall erect reddish stems are generously clothed in narrow willow-like leaves that are four to ten inches long, with veins that converge in loops at the edges. Botanists have recently played hot potato with the classification of this plant, assigning it three different genera in the space of a few years, but hummingbirds value the nectar produced by its blooms regardless of whatever moniker it is currently given. The spreading, four-petaled flowers have numerous threadlike stamens and protruding four-parted stigmas and are loosely clustered along a terminal spike, those at the bottom opening first. After flowering, slender pods of two or three inches form, held horizontally from the stem, containing hundreds of tiny seeds that are adorned with long silky white hairs to propel them aloft.

This attractive but rampant perennial prefers a moist, rich, well-drained soil and in most upland locations will grow in full sun to full shade. Propagate by root division in spring or by seed that has been cold stratified for at least one month. This is a cool-weather plant and not at all suitable for lower elevations, but in the proper habitat it makes a colorful addition to a woodland edge or mountain meadow planting.

Chilopsis linearis

Desert-willow, Mimbre, Willowleaf Catalpa, Wash Willow

Family:	Bignoniaceae	**Bloom:**	May–June, intermittent in summer with water/rains
Type:	Deciduous tree		
Size:	20' high x 20' wide, to 30' x 30' in cultivation	**Water use:**	Low–moderate
		Cold hardiness:	To 0°F or below
		USDA zone:	7–10

Author citation: (Cavanilles) Sweet

This graceful tree provides both excellent perching sites for hummingbirds and ruffled, orchid-like, pale pink to rich burgundy (or occasionally white) flowers that peak in springtime but often continue intermittently throughout the summer. Although primarily pollinated by black carpenter bees, the blooms are avidly visited by nesting Broad-billed, Lucifer, Black-chinned, and Costa's Hummingbirds, and occasionally by Anna's, Broad-tailed, and Calliope Hummingbirds after the breeding season. Verdins, orioles, tanagers, and butterflies also take nectar from the blossoms, and White-winged Doves and Lesser Goldfinches feed upon the fringed seeds. Costa's Hummingbirds are among the many birds that may nest in the branches.

Desert-willow has an enormous natural range, occurring along dry washes and stream beds in all of our southwest deserts, from southeastern California east through southern Nevada and Utah, Arizona, central and southern New Mexico, and western Texas and southward into northern Mexico, from 1,500 to 6,000 feet in elevation. It normally has multiple trunks and an open, lacy, irregular crown. Mature trees have shaggy black bark, a twisting trunk, and roots that may extend out fifty feet or more. Fast-growing when young, irrigated plants can shoot up as much as three feet in a single season. The light green, slender, willow-like leaves that give the plant its common name have a waxy coating on the foliage that helps conserve moisture during hot dry periods. The flaring trumpet-shaped flowers occur in showy clusters at branch tips. Persistent tan seedpods provide interesting winter character that tidy-prone gardeners may consider shaggy.

Desert-willow tolerates most any soil and it is quite drought tolerant as well, although supplemental water once or twice a month during the summer will prolong flowering and prevent the foliage from dropping from drought stress. It blooms best in full sun and stands up to reflected heat well. Propagate by fresh-sown seed in late summer or by semi-hardwood cuttings in late spring or early summer. Very young volunteer seedlings can often be easily transplanted as well. This tough performer lends charm to whatever spot it is given, and can be used to shade walls, as an accent in the garden, and for erosion control in arroyos.

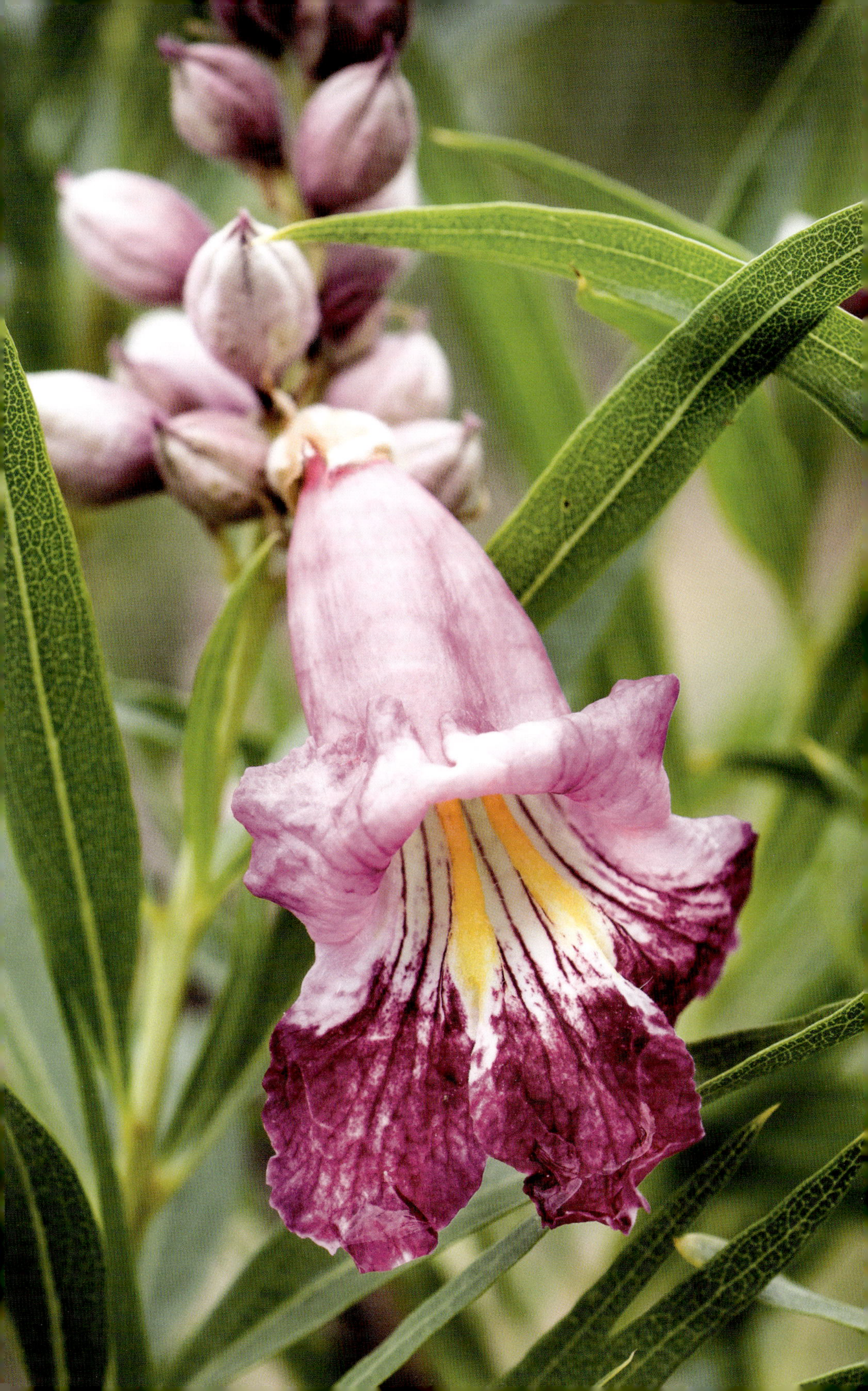

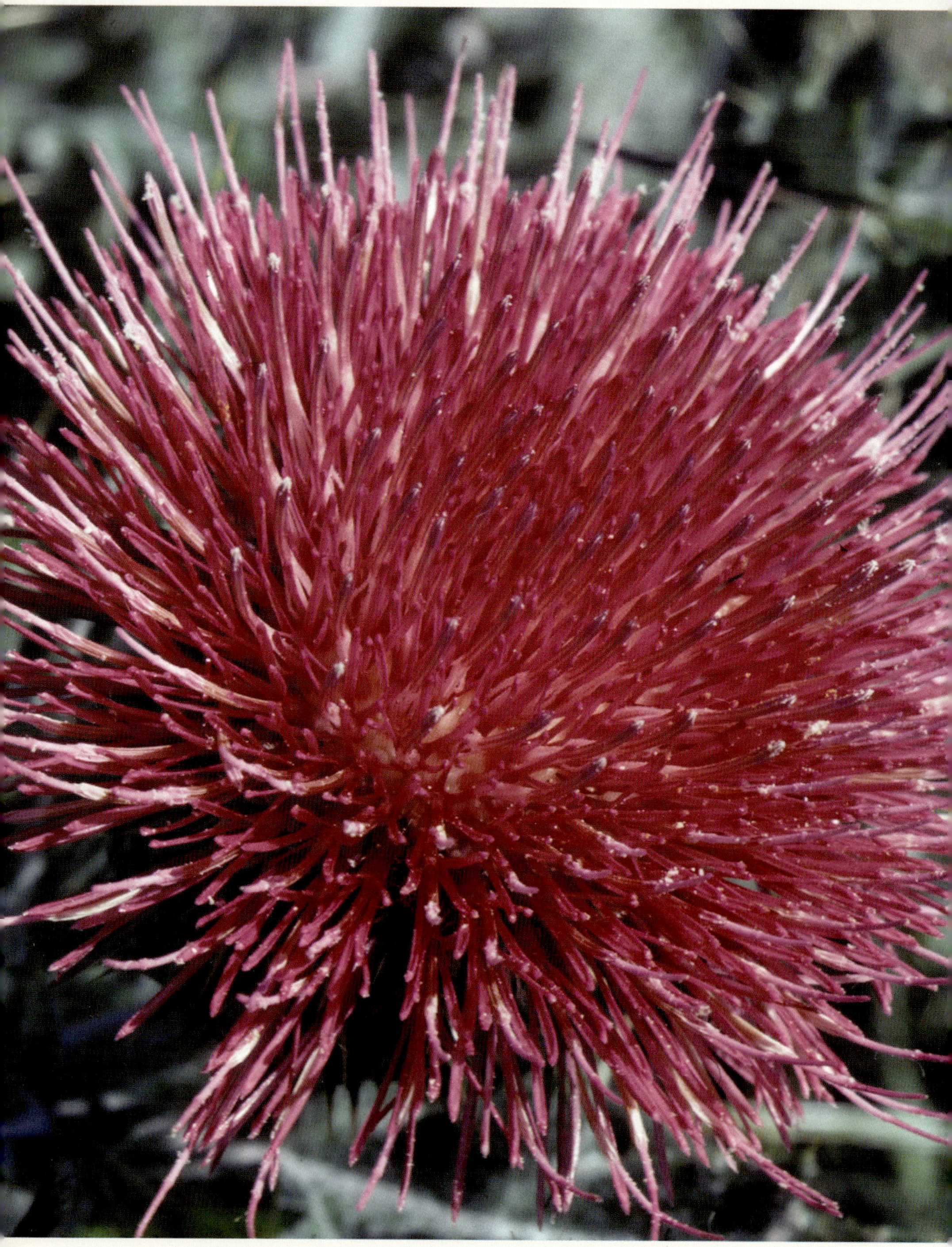

Cirsium arizonicum
Arizona Thistle

Family:	Asteraceae (Compositae)	**Water use:**	Low–moderate
Type:	Biennial/perennial	**Cold hardiness:**	To -20°F
Size:	3–4' high x 2–3' wide	**USDA zone:**	5–8
Bloom:	May–October		

Author citation: (A. Gray) Petrak

THISTLES ARE KNOWN TO BE SUPERB BUTTERFLY PLANTS, but some of them are particularly significant to various species of hummingbirds as well. The bright reddish-pink flowers of this one provide important nectar to summering Blue-throated Hummingbirds, and are known to be visited by Magnificent, Violet-crowned, Berylline, White-eared, Lucifer, Black-chinned, Broad-billed, Anna's, and Rufous Hummingbirds as well. While a wide variety of insects are attracted to the blooms, butterflies are the primary pollinators. Finches and doves are fond of the shiny brown seeds, and Lesser Goldfinches line their nests with the soft down.

Arizona thistle is native not only to much of Arizona, from the Coronado National Forest in the southeastern corner to the Grand Canyon in the northwest, but it also occurs in east-central California, southern Nevada, southern Utah, western Colorado, and western New Mexico. It is typically found along roadsides, in sagebrush scrub, on chaparral-studded slopes, or in open pine-oak woodlands, at elevations ranging from 3,500 to over 11,000 feet.

Its normally single erect stem with sparse branching rises from a woody taproot, bearing large lobed and toothed leaves that are hairy and spiny and range from a couple of inches long on upper stems to over a foot long at the base. The silvery foliage provides a striking contrast to the brilliantly colored one- to two-inch flower heads, which are cylindrical in shape and consist of many tubular disk flowers nestled in a cup of pointed bracts.

This plant is not at all fussy, requiring only a well-drained soil and full sun or light shade, and is not invasive like some alien species. A deep soaking once a month during extended periods of drought will maintain the best appearance. Plants reportedly grow easily from seed. Arizona thistle makes a handsome accent for a naturalistic garden or can be massed for an informal hedgerow. While this and the following thistle species are mentioned most often in the scientific literature about hummingbirds, virtually all thistles are valuable nectar sources for hummingbirds and especially butterflies.

Cirsium neomexicanum

New Mexico Thistle, Desert Thistle, Lavender Thistle, Cardo

Family:	Asteraceae (Compositae)	**Water use:**	Low–moderate
Type:	Biennial/perennial	**Cold hardiness:**	To -20°F
Size:	3–6' high x 1–2' wide	**USDA zone:**	5–9
Bloom:	March–May, sporadic through September		

Author citation: A. Gray

This wide-ranging desert thistle, occurring in showy clumps on favored terrain, has large, fluffy, bright lavender to pale pink flower heads that provide important nectar to both Black-chinned and Broad-billed Hummingbirds during the nesting season. Costa's, Broad-tailed, Blue-throated, Berylline, Lucifer, and Rufous Hummingbirds are also known to visit the blooms, which are pollinated chiefly by butterflies. The painted lady, black swallowtail, and gulf fritillary butterflies take nectar, and the plant is a larval host for the painted lady. Lesser Goldfinches are especially fond of the tiny dark brown seeds and use the thistle down for lining their nests.

New Mexico thistle occurs on deserts and grasslands in the western two-thirds of its namesake state as well as in much of Arizona, eastern California, southern and eastern Nevada, much of Utah, southwestern Colorado, and well southward into Sonora, Mexico. Its many diverse habitats include rocky slopes, gravelly washes, canyons, mesas, dry plains, piñon-juniper woodlands, alkaline seeps, and roadsides, from 1,000 to 7,000 feet in elevation.

Its typically single stem is woolly white with few ascending branches, and bears long strap-like gray-green foliage that is coarsely divided with spreading lobes and short spines. The sumptuous two-inch-diameter flower heads are rounded and occur at stem tips during the plant's second calendar year. They consist of numerous tube-like flowers clutched by woolly, spine-tipped bracts. The lavishly tufted seeds develop soon after flowering and those that are not quickly consumed by birds or other animals are soon dispersed by the wind.

While considered weedy in areas that receive ample water, this plant is reportedly much better behaved in more xeric gardens where it self-seeds but less enthusiastically. It needs only well-drained soil, full sun, and a deep soaking once a month during the growing season to thrive. Seed sown shallowly on site in late summer will usually bloom and set seed the following year. Germination rates depend on moisture and whether the seeds are discovered and pilfered by birds or rodents. Give this thistle a wild corner to command and the comings and goings of butterflies and hummingbirds will more than compensate for any lack of tidiness.

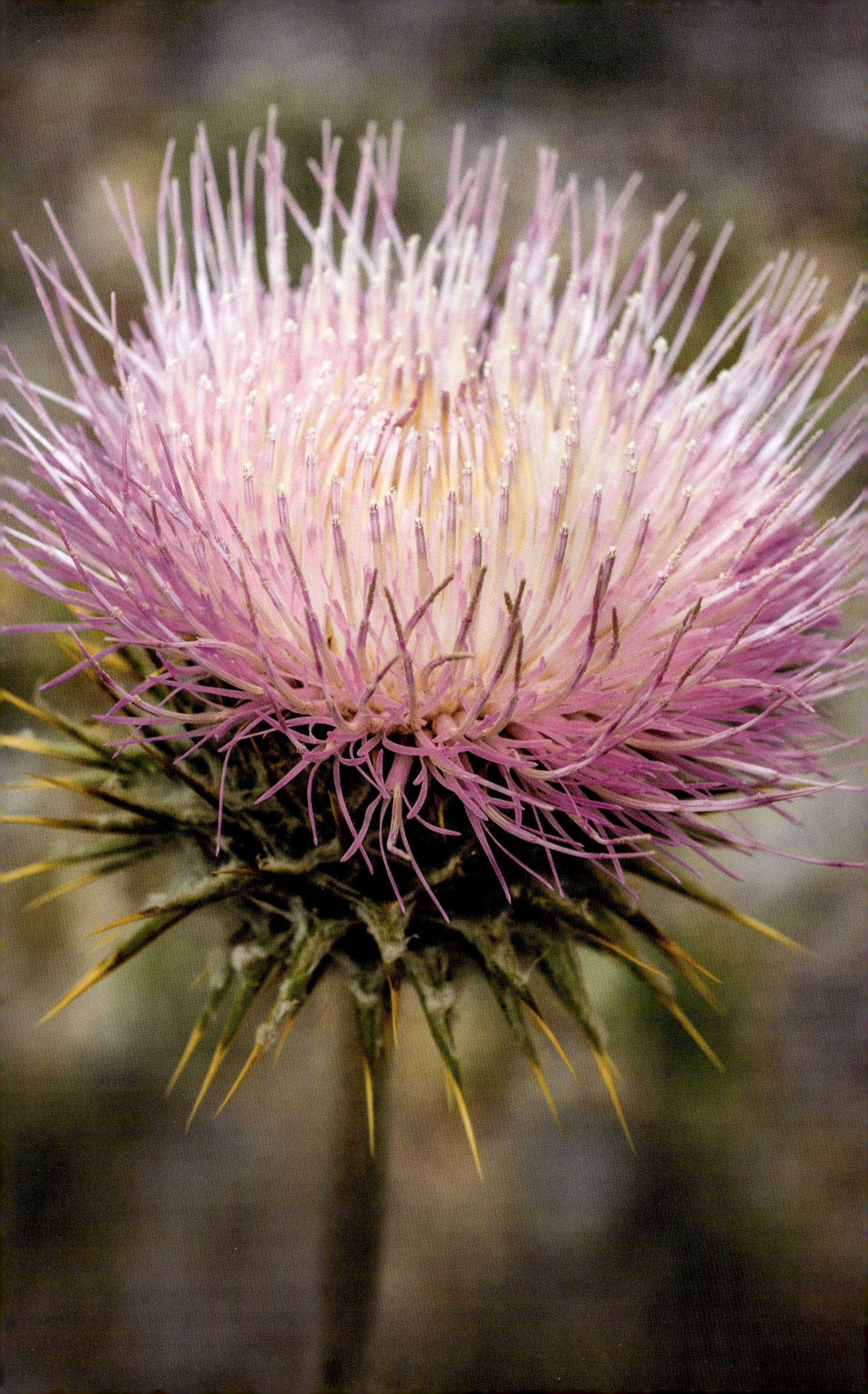

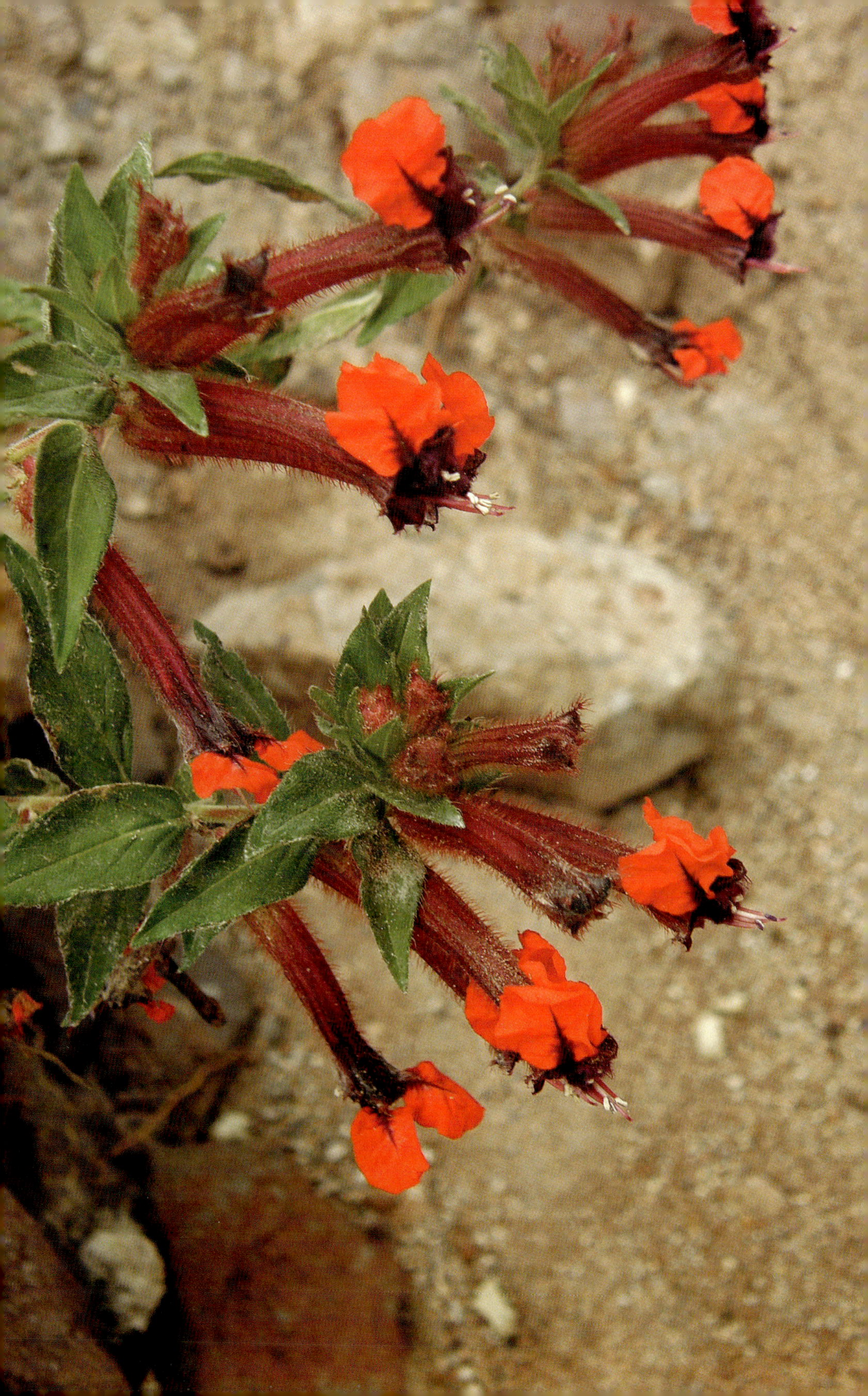

Cuphea llavea

Bat-faced Cuphea, Bat-faced Monkeyflower

Family:	Lythraceae	**Water use:**	Moderate–high
Type:	Perennial	**Cold hardiness:**	Roots to 20°F
Size:	1–2' high x 2–3' wide	**USDA zone:**	9–11
Bloom:	July–September or longer		

Author citation: Lexarza
Synonym: *Cuphea llavea* Lindley

This colorful Mexican species, unquestionably one of the most unique-looking hummingbird flowers, offers up nectar as early as June and as late as November depending upon location. Berylline and Violet-crowned Hummingbirds have been observed nectaring at the interesting blooms, with their deep crimson-red petals and purple centers that bear a striking resemblance to bat faces. Doubtless other hummingbirds partake of the nectar as well and aid in pollination, and butterflies also reportedly visit the flowers.

Widely scattered along the Sierra Madre Occidental, bat-faced cuphea is most common in Sonora but is also found in western Chihuahua, especially in the Copper Canyon region, and southward through Sinaloa, Nayarit, Jalisco, and Michoacán. Nearly always found near springs or seeps, its favored haunts include oak or pine-oak woodlands, tropical deciduous forests, riparian gallery forests, cliff faces, steep slopes, canyons, and grassy hillsides, at elevations ranging from about 2,000 to over 6,000 feet. Its mounding form, brittle hairy stems, and pointed dark green leaves are unremarkable until flowering commences. The one-inch tubular flowers, sporting the extravagant "bat faces" at their mouths, appear in the leaf axils near stem tips and beckon pollinators far and wide.

In the garden this striking plant handles blistering heat with ease if regularly watered but it is decidedly less tolerant of cold, dying back to the ground after hard freezes but usually recovering unless temperatures linger in the teens. Otherwise fairly sturdy, it can even become aggressive in well-watered gardens and should be pinched back if it gets too leggy. Full sun to light shade, fast drainage, and moderate to regular irrigation in summer will generally keep plants looking their best. They also perform beautifully in hanging baskets or other containers, providing saturated color over a long period of time, but will need more water than plants in the ground. This intriguing perennial can be propagated by seed sown in early spring, stem cuttings of new emerging growth taken in late spring, or root division; it may self-sow in optimal situations.

Delphinium cardinale

Scarlet Larkspur, Cardinal Larkspur

Family:	Ranunculaceae	**Water use:**	Moderate
Type:	Perennial	**Cold hardiness:**	To –15°F
Size:	3–6' high x 2' wide	**USDA zone:**	8–9
Bloom:	April–July		

Author citation: Hooker

THIS CALIFORNIA BEAUTY BECKONS EVERY HUMMINGBIRD WITHIN VIEW when its scarlet and yellow flowers are in bloom in spring and early summer. Anna's, Allen's, Costa's, and Black-chinned Hummingbirds take nectar from the spectacular blossoms and serve as the plant's principal pollinators. Costa's Hummingbirds in particular may actively defend large stands of flowering plants.

Scarlet larkspur is native to west-central and southern California and northern Baja California in Mexico, occurring from the South Coast Ranges south of Monterey through the Transverse and Peninsular ranges and eastward to the western edge of the Sonoran Desert. Its characteristic haunts include rocky foothills, rock-strewn washes, talus slopes, and sage scrub outwash plains, typically at elevations below 4,500 feet.

Its basal rosette forms from a thick woody root crown after winter rains, and in spring sends up one or more erect grayish stalks bearing twisted, narrowly divided, toothed leaves. The single-spurred flowers, rich scarlet with yellow upper petals, are held horizontally and are loosely staggered at the tops of the stems. All of the flowers on a particular stalk open simultaneously and mature at the same rate, and as they are pollinated and begin to fade, another stalk's flowers begin producing nectar. As a hummingbird hovers in front of a flower to sip from the slender spur, its chin is dusted with pollen from the stamens just within, to be deposited at the next blossom visited. During the summer dry season the plant goes dormant.

Plants under cultivation, however, reportedly look best with a deep soaking once or twice a month during dry periods. Scarlet larkspur needs a well-drained, somewhat alkaline soil, and will grow in full sun or partial shade. It makes an excellent addition to perennial borders, desert oasis gardens, and rock gardens. Plants are said to be easy to grow from seed. Sow in a light soil mix in early summer under shade cloth and transplant seedlings to the desired location in early fall. Guard against snails and slugs, which can quickly decimate the foliage.

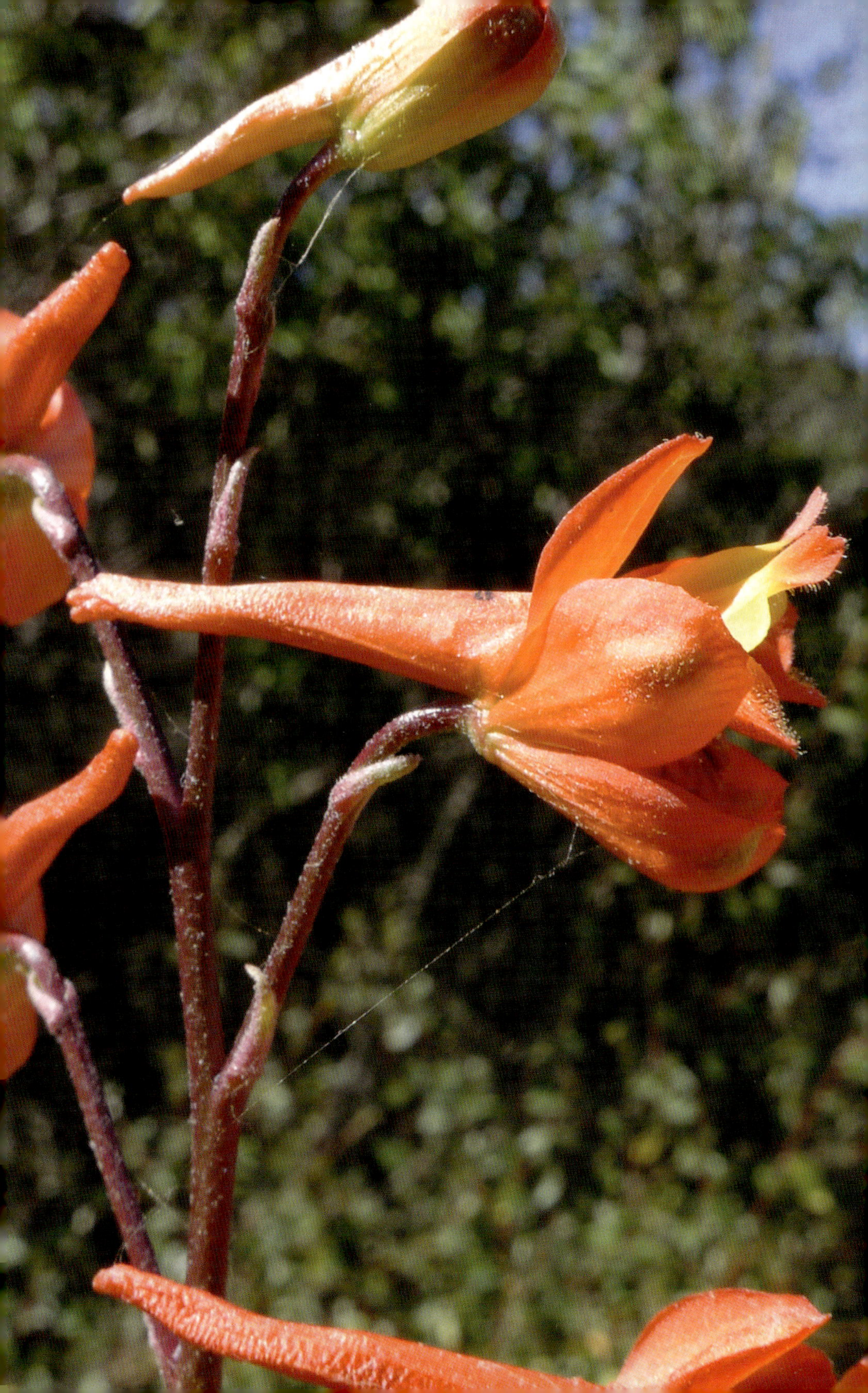

Family:	Ranunculaceae	**Water use:**	Moderate–high
Type:	Perennial	**Cold hardiness:**	Hardy to -10°F, some to -25°F or below
Size:	4–6' high x 2' wide (*barbeyi*), 1–3' high x 1' wide (others)	**USDA zone:**	5–7 (*scopulorum*), 4–7 (others)
Bloom:	April–July (*nuttallianum*), July–September (others)		

Author citation: *Delphinium barbeyi* (Huth) Huth
Delphinium nuttallianum Pritzel ex Walpers; syn. *D. nelsoni* Greene; syn. *D. sonnei* Greene
Delphinium scopulorum A. Gray; syn. *D. macrophyllum* Wooton

Delphinium species
Larkspur, Delphinium

THE RICHLY COLORED BLUISH-PURPLE FLOWERS of these showy perennials offer nectar that can be astonishingly sweet, at up to 45 percent pure sucrose. While the plants depend more upon bumblebees than hummingbirds for pollination, both breeding and migrating hummingbirds make good use of this high-energy nectar source whenever it is in bloom. Two-lobe larkspur (*Delphinium nuttallianum*) is the primary nectar source of Broad-tailed Hummingbirds early in the nesting season in some locations and is visited by Calliope Hummingbirds as well. Broad-tailed, Calliope, and Rufous Hummingbirds are all strongly attracted to the vivid blooms of both subalpine larkspur (*D. barbeyi*) and Rocky Mountain larkspur (*D. scopulorum*) as they mountain-hop southward through the Southern Rocky Mountains in late summer.

Subalpine larkspur occurs from northern New Mexico northward through west-central Colorado and south-central Wyoming, with scattered populations in eastern Arizona and central and southern Utah. Found at elevations of 7,500 feet to past timberline, this high mountain beauty prefers damp meadows and thickets, shady stream banks, springs and seeps, moist aspen woods, and coniferous forest edges, and it is most commonly encountered where snowpack persists. Two-lobe larkspur inhabits all of the western states east to New Mexico, Colorado, Nebraska, and South Dakota, where its varied habitats include dry meadows, sagebrush scrub, chaparral, foothill grasslands, piñon-juniper woodlands, ponderosa pine forests, aspen woods, and spruce-fir forests, at elevations of 3,000 to over 10,000 feet. Rocky Mountain larkspur, with a comparably limited range in southern and eastern Arizona and western New Mexico, is fairly common within that range and most often encountered between 5,500 and 8,500 feet in elevation. Typical haunts include ravines, stream banks, moist meadows, and valleys, frequently in the company of oaks and Arizona sycamores.

What these larkspurs need most are cool temperatures, thin air, and moist feet—conditions profoundly lacking in a desert garden. But at higher elevations and in a moist, shady niche, any of these species would make a splendid planting for a hummingbird oasis or pollinator garden. Plants will do best in a well-drained, deep, loamy soil where there is moderate to ample moisture either from natural precipitation or supplemental irrigation. Propagate either by seeds sown in fall or winter (for natural cold stratification) or by cuttings taken in spring.

Diplacus species
Bush Monkeyflower, Sticky Monkeyflower

Family:	Phrymaceae (Scrophulariaceae)	**Water use:**	Low–moderate
Type:	Perennial subshrub	**Cold hardiness:**	To 20°F (*puniceus*), 10°F (others)
Size:	2–4' high x 2–4' wide		
Bloom:	January–June (*longiflorus*), March–July (others)	**USDA zone:**	9–10 (*puniceus*), 7–10 (others)

Author citation: *Diplacus aurantiacus* (W. Curtis) Jepson; syn. *Mimulus aurantiacus* W. Curtis
Dipacus longiflorus Nuttall; syn. *Mimulus longiflorus* (Nutt.) A. L. Grant
Diplacus puniceus Nuttall; syn. *Mimulus puniceus* (Nutt.) Steudel

This trio of long-bloomers just radiates California sunshine, serving up both human smiles and valuable hummingbird nectar wherever they occur. Biologists have noted that the range of the nonmigratory population of Allen's Hummingbirds closely parallels that of orange bush monkeyflower (*Diplacus aurantiacus*), whose pale buff to rich orange blooms are an important summer food source for them and are pollinated by Anna's and Costa's Hummingbirds as well. Southern bush monkeyflower (*D. longiflorus*) begins blooming in midwinter at low elevations and finishes up in summer in upland locales. Anna's Hummingbirds in particular rely on the nectar produced by the creamy apricot flowers in early spring, and Black-chinned, Costa's, and Allen's Hummingbirds, along with long-tongued cyrtid flies, butterflies, and bees, also help pollinate the blossoms. Red bush monkeyflower (*D. puniceus*), with its luscious crimson to orange-red blossoms, supplies high-sucrose nectar to Anna's and Costa's Hummingbirds through midsummer.

While taxonomists continue to debate the proper classification of these bush monkeyflowers, hummingbirds care only about the vital nectar they provide and avidly visit them all. Orange bush monkeyflower, occurring along the entire coast of California and well inland, in extreme southwestern Oregon, and in Baja California in Mexico, is usually found below 5,000 feet in elevation with brushy chaparral on coastal bluffs and rocky foothill slopes. Southern bush monkeyflower ranges from Monterey southward through the Southern Coast Ranges to northern Baja California, also occurring on the Channel Islands. Occasionally found as high as 7,500 feet, it is more common in the lower elevations, on rocky slopes with sage scrub or in foothill woodlands. Red bush monkeyflower inhabits the southern California coast and inland, from Santa Barbara southward to Point Loma, and Baja California in Mexico. Favoring lower elevations than its cousins, typically below 2,500 feet, it grows among the chaparral on dry slopes, mesas, and inland foothills and often in the shade of live oaks.

In the wild, plants may drop leaves during summer drought but under cultivation a monthly deep soaking can prevent this. For best results, provide part or dappled shade, a well-drained sandy or gravelly soil, and restraint with supplemental water after plants are established. Occasional pruning of brittle older stems will encourage denser growth. Propagate by sowing fresh seed in fall or by rooting leafy stem cuttings in moist sand before plants go dormant.

Family:	Cactaceae	**Water use:**	Low
Type:	Succulent	**Cold hardiness:**	To -0°F
Size:	1' high x 1–2' wide or more	**USDA zone:**	7–10
Bloom:	April–June, depending upon elevation		

Author citation: *Echinocereus arizonicus* Rose ex Orcutt; syn. *E. coccineus* Engelm. var. *arizonicus* (Rose ex Orcutt) D. J. Ferguson
Echinocereus coccineus Engelmann
Echinocereus polyacanthus Engelmann; syn. *E. triglochidiatus* var. *polyacanthus* (Engelm.) L. D. Benson
Echinocereus triglochidiatus Engelmann; syn. *E. triglochidiatus* var. *mojavensis* (Engelm. & J. M. Bigelow) L. D. Benson

Echinocereus species
Claretcup Cactus

THE PROPER CLASSIFICATION OF THESE SPECTACULAR CACTI has long been a prickly issue among taxonomists, but one certainty is that hummingbirds, caring naught about nomenclature, visit all of them wherever they are in bloom. Differing from most of their kin in being adapted to hummingbird pollination, the large scarlet to crimson red flowers remain open for several days and literally gush nectar, each producing thirty milligrams of sugar per day or about ten times that of most typical hummingbird flowers. Broad-tailed, Magnificent, Blue-throated, and Black-chinned Hummingbirds are all patrons of the wellspring, along with Scott's Orioles, many bees, and several species of butterflies.

Most of us will likely have difficulty distinguishing these species, particularly where their ranges overlap. The most northerly is *Echinocereus triglochidiatus*, ranging from the Mojave Desert in southeastern California eastward through southern and eastern Nevada, southern Utah, and southwestern Colorado southward through northern Arizona and northwestern and central New Mexico. *Echinocereus coccineus* ranges mostly south and east of its cousin, occurring from primarily southern Arizona eastward through southwestern and central New Mexico, northward into south-central Colorado, and southward into western Texas and the Mexican border states of Coahuila, Chihuahua, and Sonora. *Echinocereus arizonicus* has a comparatively tiny range in southeastern Arizona and extreme southwestern New Mexico and *Echinocereus polyacanthus*, with its noticeably elongated stems, is found only in northern Mexico. All have spiny, spreading mounds of cylindrical stems that can be found in a wide variety of habitats, including gravelly desert slopes, ledges, canyons, grasslands, piñon-juniper-oak woodlands, and ponderosa pine forest openings, from about 3,500 to over 8,000 feet in elevation.

In the wild, claretcups occur on varying soil types—some preferring sand, others gravel, some limestone, and others igneous—but all require excellent drainage and are susceptible to fungal infection with too much water. Plants typically do best in sunny or lightly shaded exposures but in extremely hot locations prefer mid-afternoon shade. Like most cacti, they perform beautifully in containers. Once established, they require little supplemental water, and will slowly grow to a nice-sized clump of virtual hummingbird magnets. These distinctive cacti are too frequently yanked from the wild, often illegally, and such practices are decimating native populations in some locations, so purchase only plants that have been seed-grown or legitimately salvaged. Plants may be propagated by seed or careful division.

Epilobium canum

Hummingbird Trumpet, California Fuchsia

Family:	Onagraceae		hard frost
Type:	Shrubby perennial	**Water use:**	Low–moderate
Size:	1–2' high x 2–4' wide	**Cold hardiness:**	Top to 20°F, roots to 0°F
Bloom:	July–October, or until first	**USDA zone:**	7–10

Author citation: (Greene) P. H. Raven
Synonyms: *Zauschneria californica* K. Presl; *Z. cana* Greene

HUMMINGBIRD TRUMPET MAY NOT BE THE TIDIEST PLANT and its brilliant scarlet flowers can sometimes seem almost garish, but the myriad hummingbirds that pollinate it do not seem to mind. It is an important nectar source for both Anna's and Allen's hummingbirds and is avidly visited by Rufous, Calliope, Black-chinned, and Broad-billed Hummingbirds as well. Verdins and several species of butterflies also take nectar from the blossoms, as do carpenter bees that slit the corollas to access the nectar. Goldfinches are reportedly fond of the seeds.

The plant's several subspecies collectively have a range that extends from California and southern Oregon east through southern Nevada, southern and western Utah, and western Wyoming, and southward through Arizona, extreme southwestern New Mexico, and northern Mexico in Baja California and Sonora. The subspecies *latifolium* has the widest distribution and is the most commonly available in the nursery trade, occurring on rocky slopes, in canyons, along dry washes, and in riparian areas at elevations of 2,500 to 7,500 feet. Its brittle arching stems break easily and give the plant a twiggy look in the wintertime. The leaves, evergreen in mild climates, are narrowly lance-shaped and a velvety grayish green. The tubular blossoms, with four flaring, notched lobes and long exserted stamens, appear in loose clusters on short spikes above the leaves and typically all point in the same direction. Four-segmented capsules containing the fluff-tailed seeds develop after the flowers.

The plant needs a light, well-drained, sandy or rocky soil that is neutral to alkaline and a deep soaking at least twice a month in summer. New plants may also need to be watered during dry winters until established. This tough perennial usually handles heat extremes well but in the lower deserts does best in part or filtered shade. Leggy plants may be cut back hard in early spring to promote density. Hummingbird trumpet both reseeds itself and spreads by underground rootstocks, so it may pop up in areas of the garden where not intended. Propagate by seed, root division, or stem cuttings. This fast-growing plant works well along pathways, in rock gardens, as a ground cover, to control erosion on hillsides, in wildflower meadows, and in large containers.

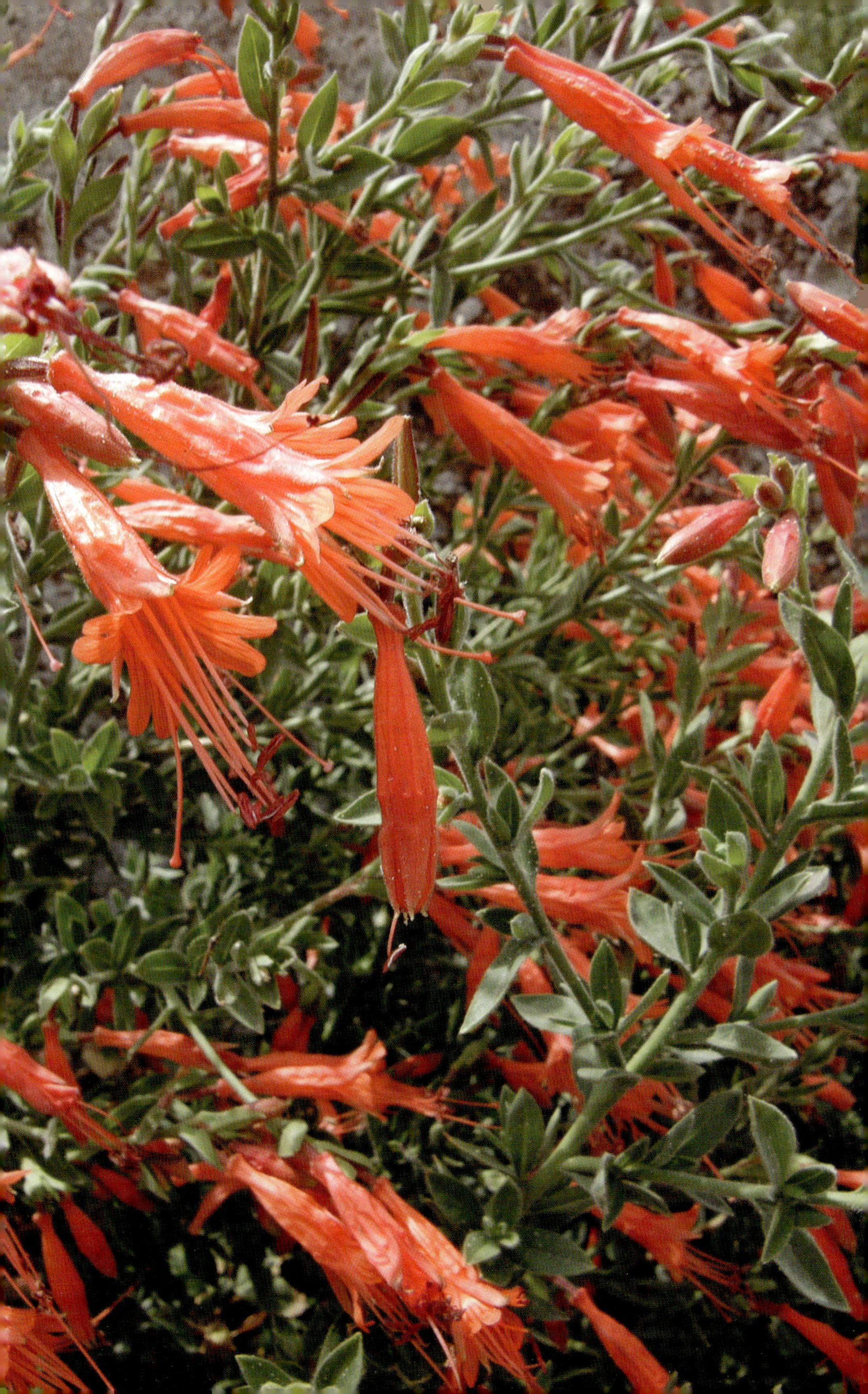

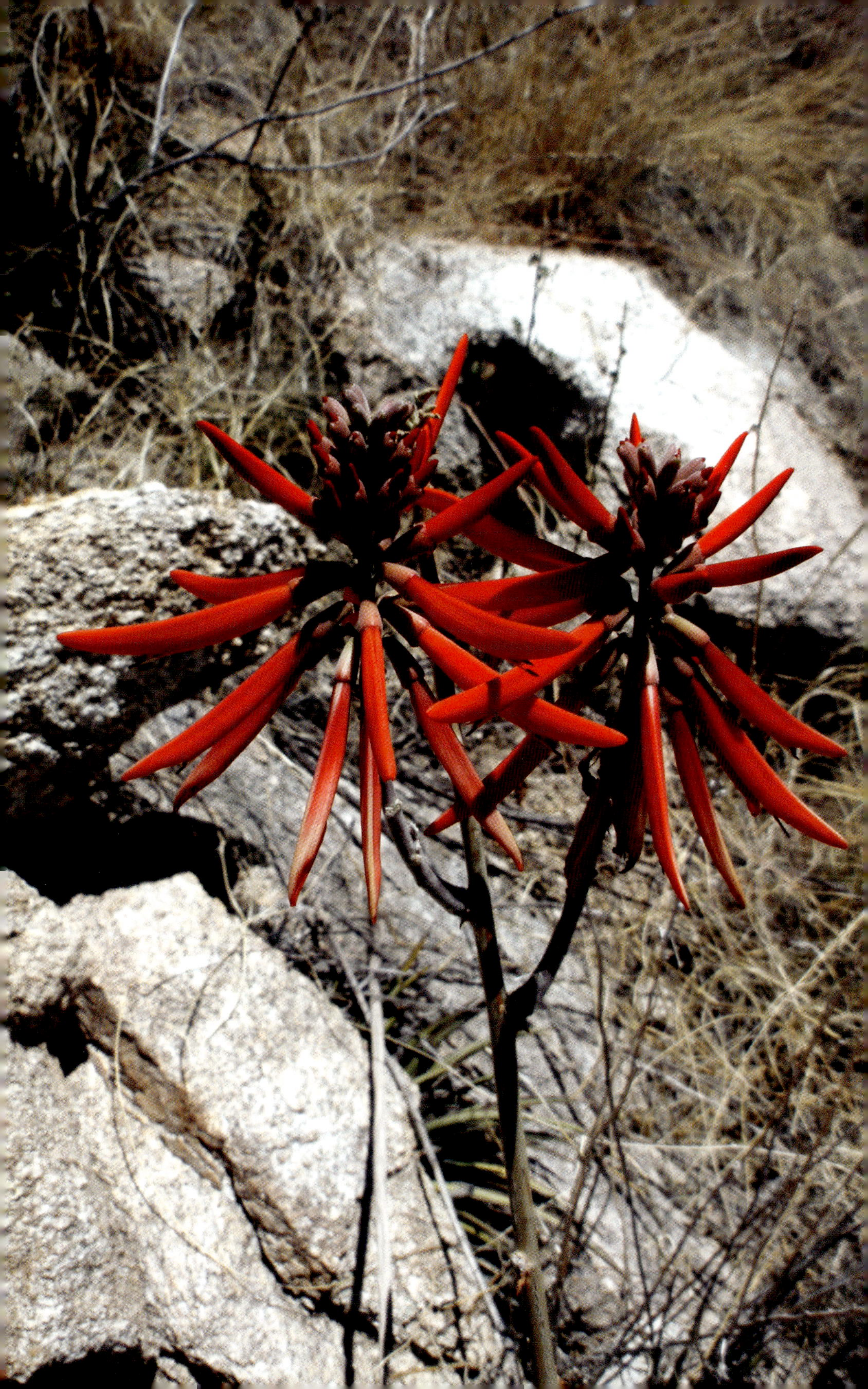

Erythrina flabelliformis

Southwest Coral Bean, Chilicote, Coralina, Zampantla

Family:	Fabaceae	**Water use:**	Low–moderate
Type:	Deciduous shrub or tree	**Cold hardiness:**	Top to 28°F
Size:	4–6' high x 4–6' wide, to 20' in frost-free areas	**USDA zone:**	9–11
Bloom:	June–July, occasionally after summer rains		

Author citation: Kearney

THIS DISTINCTIVE PLANT'S TIME TO SHINE IS IN LATE SPRING, when its spectacular terminal spikes of bright coral-red flowers provide valuable nectar for breeding hummingbirds. Among the enthusiastic takers are Costa's, Broad-billed, Violet-crowned, and Black-chinned Hummingbirds, together responsible for the bulk of pollination.

Southwest coral bean has a restricted range in the United States, occurring only in southeastern Arizona and southern New Mexico, but in Mexico can be found in Baja California, Sonora, Chihuahua, and southward to Michoacán. Look for it growing among boulders on rocky hillsides and canyon slopes, in pine-oak woodlands, or along washes, at elevations of 3,000 to 5,500 feet.

In frost-free areas, plants can get tree-sized, but in most gardens they are shrubby in form. The tan, cork-like stems bear tiny hooked spines and will die back to the ground with a prolonged hard freeze, the huge root system sustaining the plant until regrowth. The bright green compound leaves each have three triangle-shaped leaflets and a downward-curved spine just below the base. The foliage is also frost tender and typically quite late arriving on the scene, often not appearing until late spring or early summer and then turning a bright golden yellow in autumn. The tubular-appearing flowers, lacking lips that would offer a foothold to insects, sport a long, narrowly rolled banner up to two inches long. Summer rains or supplemental irrigation may bring on a second bloom. After flowering, eight-inch lumpy pods form, containing the large scarlet-red seeds that give the plant its common name and are highly poisonous.

Southwest coral bean needs a well-drained soil, full sun, and protection from frost for best performance, and thus is suitable for only the mildest winter areas such as Phoenix or southern California. Locate it against a west- or south-facing wall, among boulders, or within a courtyard for winter warmth. The lush foliage gives the plant a tropical appearance that will dress up courtyards, poolsides, and patio gardens. Plants bloom on the previous year's growth, so wait to prune any frost damage until after flowering. Propagate by scarified seed in spring or semi-hardwood cuttings taken in summer and misted.

Fouquieria macdougalii

Tree Ocotillo, Chunari, Ocotillo Macho, Jaboncillo, Torote Verde

Family:	Fouquieriaceae	**Water use:**	Low–moderate
Type:	Deciduous shrub or tree	**Cold hardiness:**	To at least 20°F
Size:	6–20' high x 4–15' wide	**USDA zone:**	9–11
Bloom:	February–March, July–October		

Author citation: Nash

THIS HANDSOME PLANT MAY HAVE LIMITED APPLICATIONS in the southwestern United States, but in areas where it is hardy it is a veritable hummingbird magnet. Its deep red tubular flowers offer nectar that is prized by Costa's, Anna's, Broad-billed, Violet-crowned, and Rufous Hummingbirds at various times of the year, in many cases on their wintering grounds or in migration. Hummingbirds are thought to be the chief pollinators.

Tree ocotillo occurs solely in Mexico in central and southern Sonora, southern Chihuahua, and northern Sinaloa, gracing rocky slopes and sandy flats in Sonoran Desert scrublands, tropical deciduous forests of Sierra Madrean foothills, and tropical thornscrub at elevations ranging from sea level to about 4,500 feet. In woodlands it tends to grow as a tree, while in other habitats it is usually a multi-trunked shrub, growing to twenty feet or more in height in frost-free areas. It has a stocky, yellowish-green trunk up to a foot in diameter and many diverging branches with peeling bronze bark and half-inch gray spines. The lance-shaped leaves are light gray and one-and-a-half inches long, appearing after heavy rains and then dropping during drought to conserve water. The narrow one-inch tubular flowers are presented in open sprays at the pendulous stem tips and bloom in response to rainfall, typically in summer but occasionally also at other times of the year.

This striking ocotillo prefers a lean, well-drained soil, full sun to part shade, protection from hard freezes, and a deep soaking every two to three weeks during the summer. In marginal climates, try planting it against a south wall for winter warmth. In a suitable climate such as Phoenix or the proper microhabitat in cooler areas, tree ocotillo would make a dramatic specimen for a courtyard or patio, and also works very well in a large container. Propagate from softwood cuttings taken during the growing season. Reportedly even cut branches stuck in the ground will take root. A close cousin of this plant, palo adán (*Fouquieria diguetii*), occurs in Sonora and Baja California in Mexico, where it provides valuable nectar for breeding Costa's Hummingbirds.

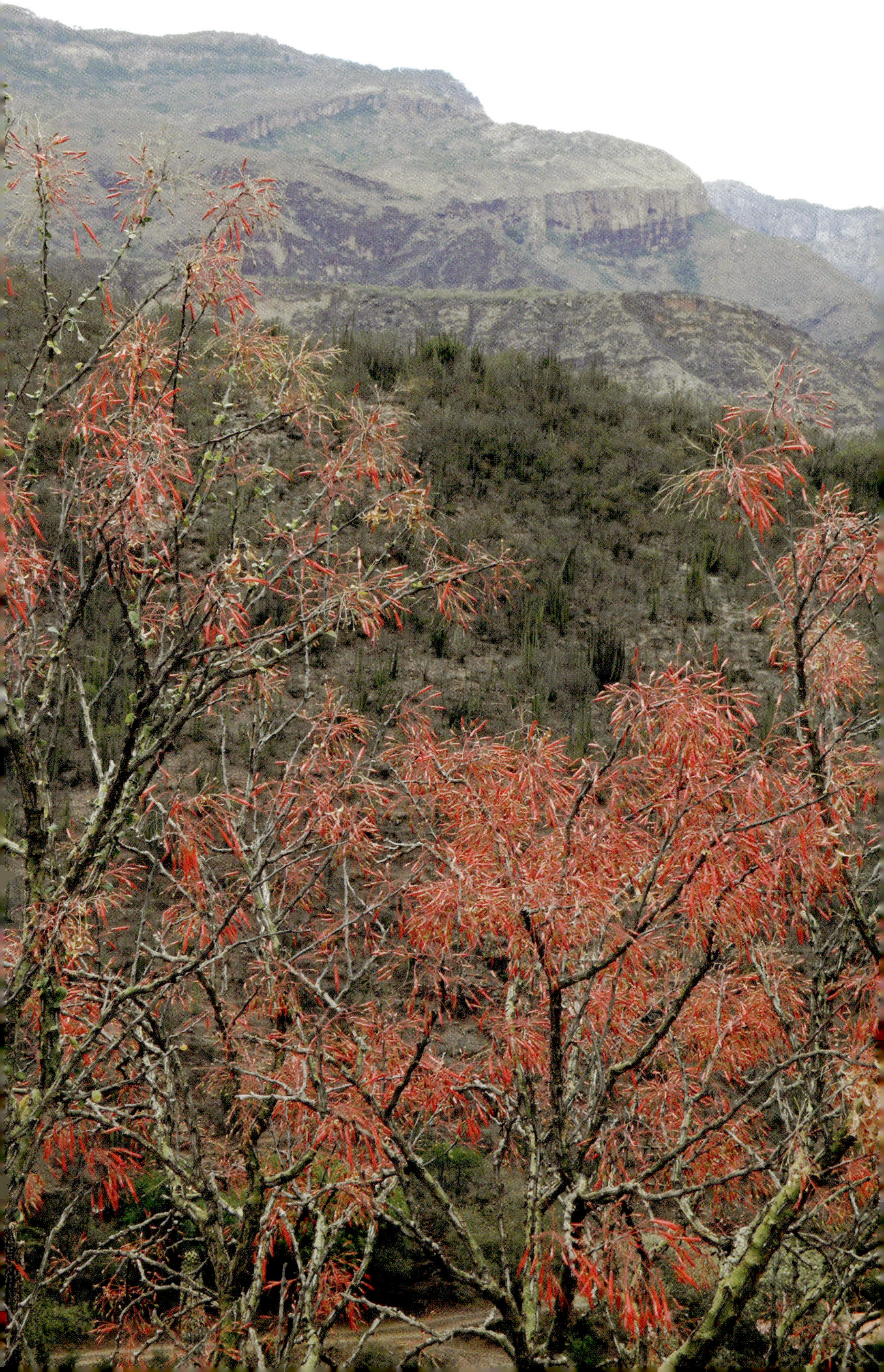

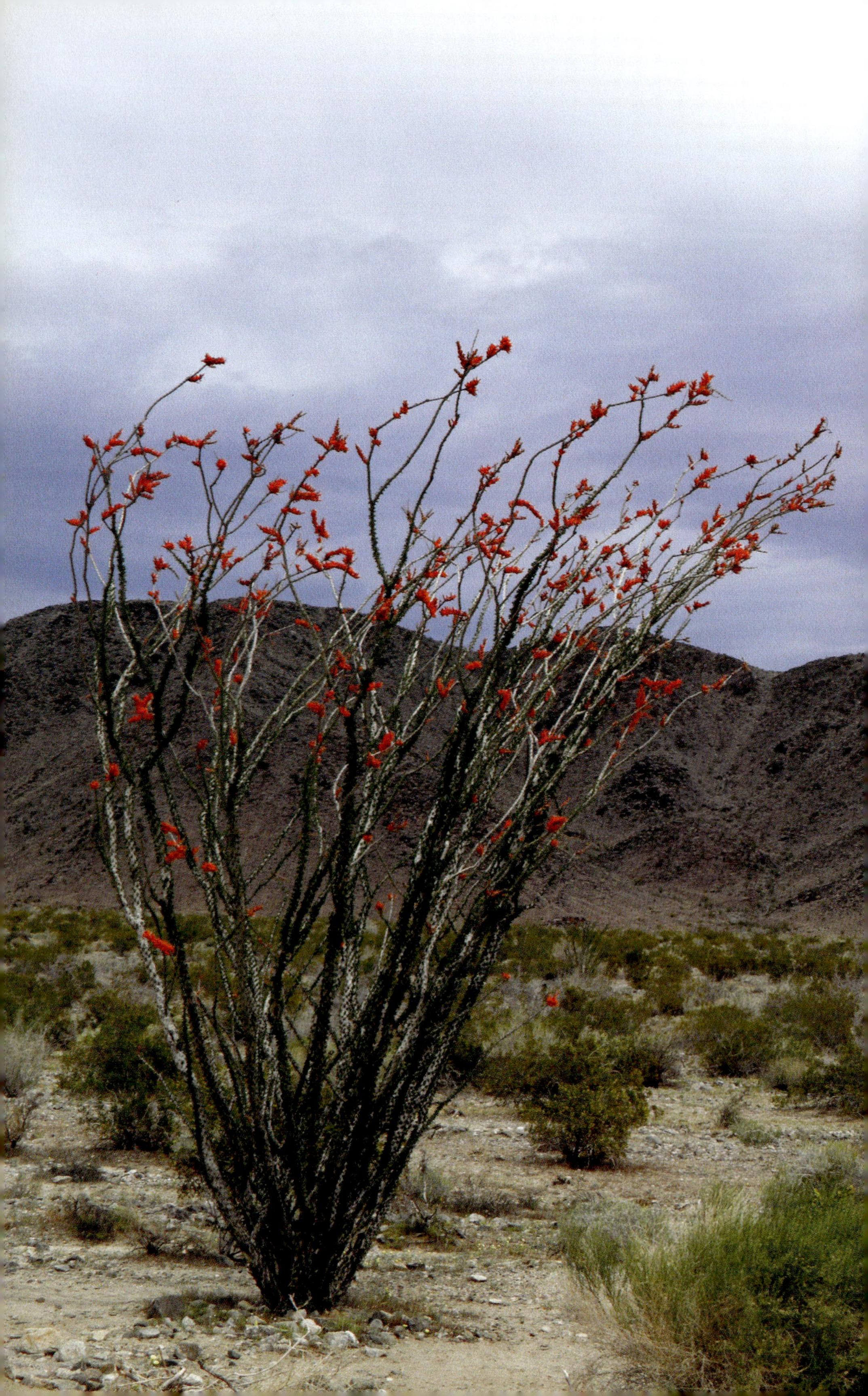

Fouquieria splendens
Ocotillo, Devil's Coachwhip, Albarda

Family:	Fouquieriaceae		elevation and latitude
Type:	Deciduous shrub	**Water use:**	Low–moderate
Size:	8–12' high x 6–10' wide	**Cold hardiness:**	To 0–5°F
Bloom:	March–June, depending on	**USDA zone:**	7–10

Author citation: Engelmann

HILLSIDES OF THIS SHOWY PLANT IN THE SPRINGTIME SERVE AS NECTAR and insect cafeterias for migrating and nesting hummingbirds, which along with carpenter bees are the main pollinators. The clusters of fiery orange-red tubular flowers, with sumptuous tufts of long yellow stamens, appear at the tips of the whip-like stems and attract Black-chinned, Lucifer, Costa's, Anna's, Broad-billed, Violet-crowned, Broad-tailed, and Rufous Hummingbirds. Among the many other nectar customers are orioles, tanagers, warblers, finches, hoverflies, and butterflies. Lucifer and Costa's Hummingbirds often nest on the leafy stems, and many birds use them as sentinel posts.

Ocotillo occurs in all of our southwestern deserts from sea level to 5,000 feet, in southeastern California, southern Nevada, most of Arizona, southern New Mexico, west Texas, and southward into Mexico from Coahuila west to Baja California. Its yellowish-green vase-shaped clumps favor gravelly lower slopes and mesas or sandy washes, in limestone or igneous soils. The scaly stems are stoutly armed with thorns and rise from a bulbous base and a root system that is shallow but quite broad, extending outward up to twenty feet. The small, oval, fleshy, bright green leaves appear a few days after rains and drop when the soil dries, often cycling several times a season.

This is an extremely slow grower that can be tricky to establish but when happy is long-lived. Ocotillos prefer full sun and take reflected heat well. They demand excellent drainage and will rot with too much water; a deep soaking once or twice a month during summer droughts should be sufficient to prevent leaf drop. This is a fine accent plant for courtyards, rock gardens, and naturalistic plantings. Its thorny branches make it unsuitable for walkways but perfect for barriers. Living fences can be erected by planting stem cuttings and weaving them together with wire as early settlers did. Ocotillos are not widely propagated because of their slow growth, so plants for sale are commonly dug from the wild, often illegally. Buy seed-grown plants if available, and purchase only bare-root plants that have been legitimately salvaged from development operations. Those with patience can also grow plants by seed or try rooting stems cut at the base in one-gallon containers of perlite and watering every two weeks during the growing season.

Gambelia speciosa
Island Bush Snapdragon, Showy Greenbright

Family:	Plantaginaceae (Scrophulariaceae)	**Bloom:**	February–May, and intermittent all year
Type:	Evergreen shrub	**Water use:**	Low–moderate
Size:	3' high x 5' wide, or to 10' when climbing	**Cold hardiness:**	Roots to -20°F
		USDA zone:	9–11

Author citation: Nuttall
Synonym: *Galvezia speciosa* (Nutt.) A. Gray

Channel Island endemics are certainly not the prime focus of this book, but this plant is simply stunning in bloom and is fairly adaptable to many inland locations. Its bright red tubular flowers are an extremely important source of sucrose-rich nectar for Allen's Hummingbirds and depend upon the birds significantly for pollination. Butterflies are also attracted to the showy blossoms and probably play a role in pollinating as well.

This cousin of the snapdragons is found only on the islands off the coast of southern California and northern Baja California in Mexico. It is quite rare in the wild, occurring on sea bluffs or in rocky canyons below 3,000 feet in elevation, where it is either mounding in form or sprawling, frequently rambling over surrounding shrubs. Its long, arching, woody stems bear thick, one-inch narrow oval bright green leaves in whorls. The one-inch snapdragon-like flowers occur in clusters near the tips of branches and are nearly continuous throughout the bloom season.

Island bush snapdragon favors a lean well-drained soil and full sun, although in warmer inland locations it may do better in filtered sun or afternoon shade; in the hottest deserts it may languish regardless. In most instances, plants need little supplemental water once established. They will not survive a prolonged hard freeze but if well mulched will usually bounce back from light frosts. Prune in late winter for density. This attractive shrub makes a striking specimen whether freestanding or trained onto a trellis or fence, or it can be massed for effective erosion control on banks or used as a ground cover under established trees. Propagate by stem cuttings or by seed. A selection of this plant, 'Firecracker', is reportedly more compact and more drought-tolerant than the species. Baja bush snapdragon (*Gambelia juncea*; syns. *Galvezia juncea, Saccularia juncea*), a frost-tender relative from Baja California in Mexico, blooms in winter and is also quite popular with and largely pollinated by hummingbirds. Reportedly, it is better able to handle the intense heat of the low deserts.

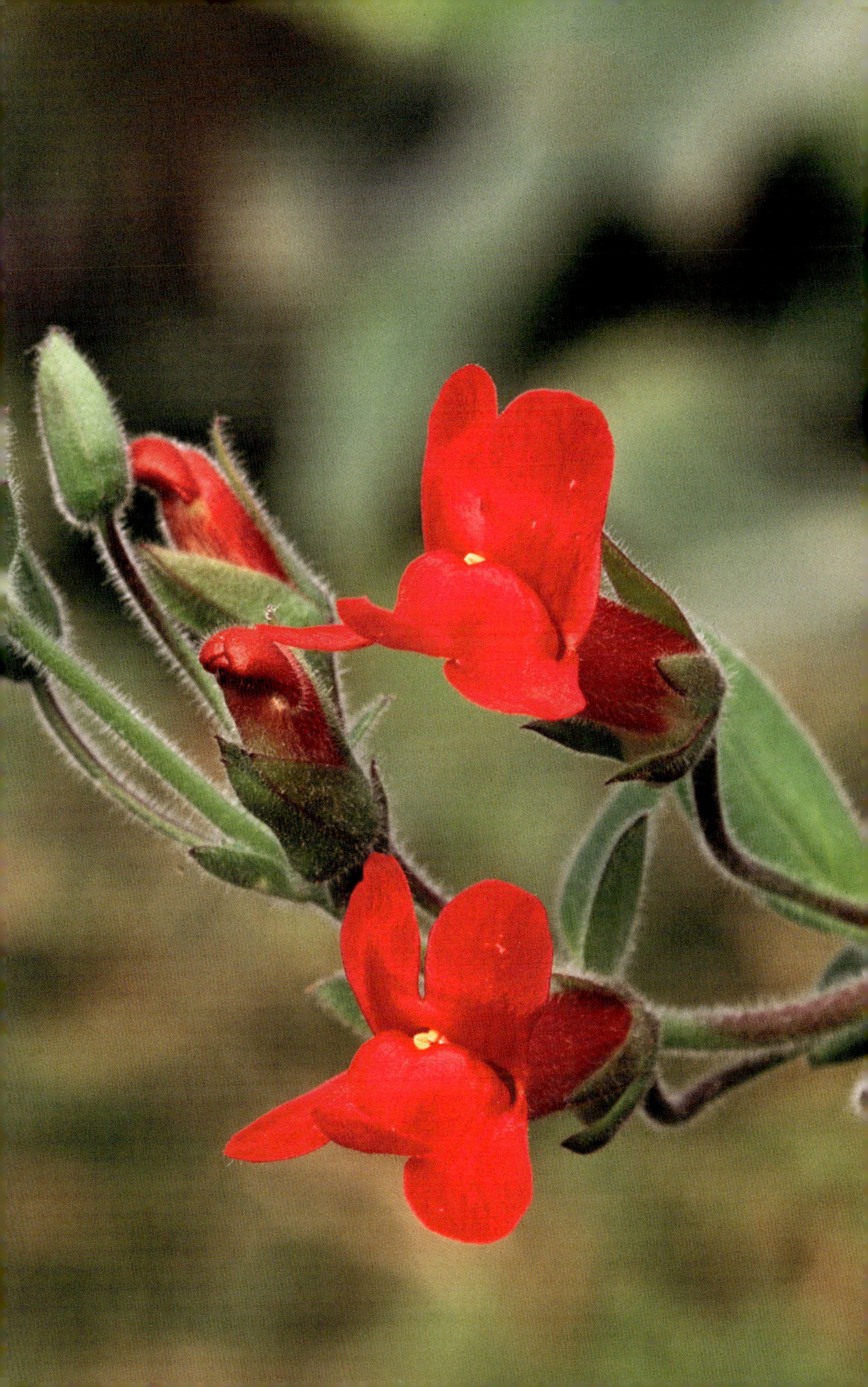

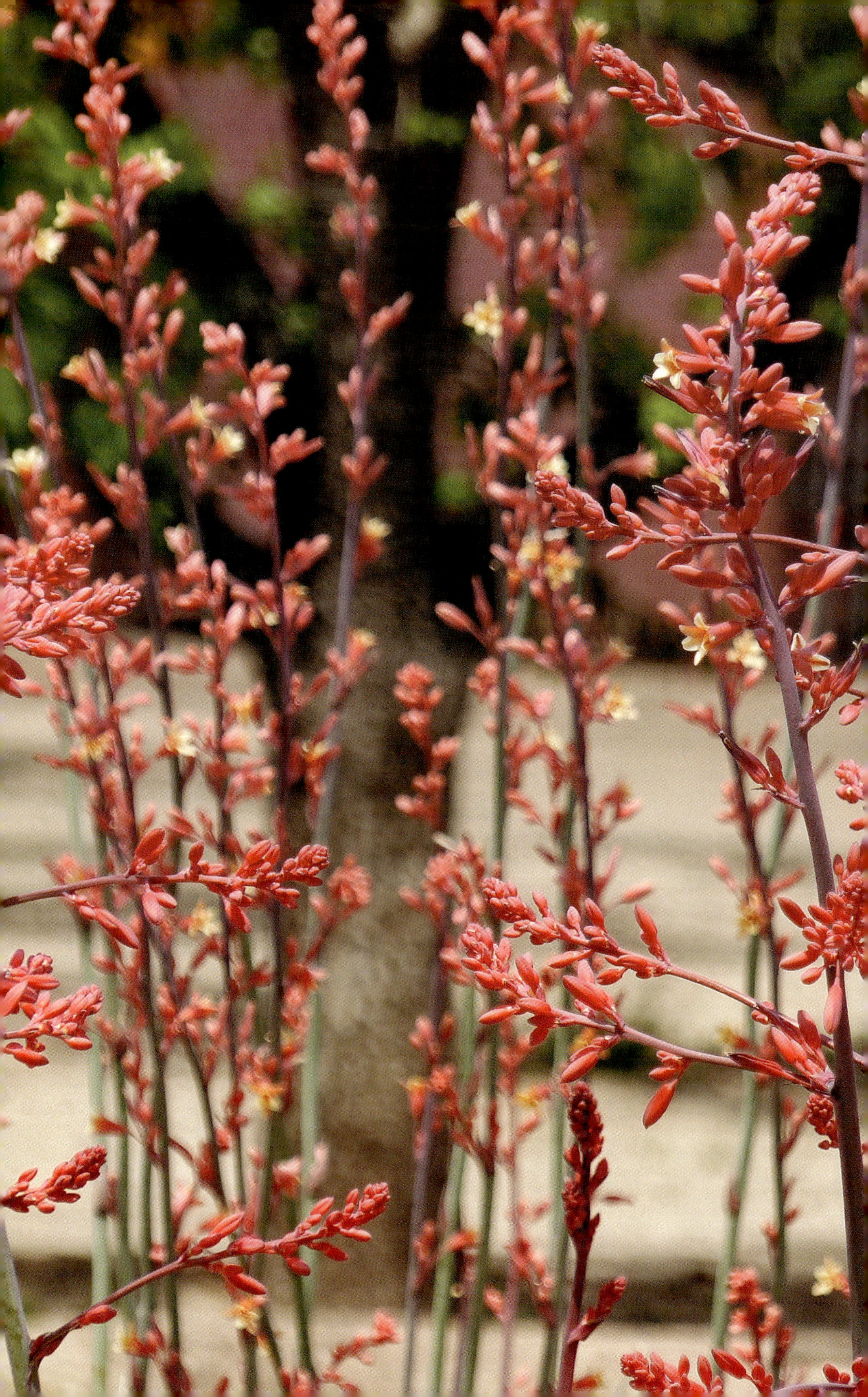

Hesperaloe parviflora
Red Yucca, Redflower False Yucca, Semandoque

Family:	Agavaceae (Asparagaceae)	**Bloom:**	May–September, into fall if pods removed
Type:	Succulent		
Size:	3' high x 3' wide, with 4–6' flower stalks	**Water use:**	Low–moderate
		Cold hardiness:	Top to 0°F, roots to -15°F
		USDA zone:	5–10

Author citation: (Torrey) J. M. Coulter

THIS YEOMAN OF THE SPRING AND SUMMER HUMMINGBIRD GARDEN IS neither red (though plants may become purple-tinged in winter) nor a yucca, but its less-than-accurate common name makes little difference to Black-chinned Hummingbirds, who take nectar from the coral-pink flowers throughout the nesting season and often use the tall flower stalks for lookout perches. Migrating Rufous and Broad-tailed Hummingbirds also visit the blooms, as will Broad-billed Hummingbirds at garden plantings. Hummingbirds are thought to be the primary pollinators. Deer and rabbits occasionally browse the foliage, and aphids may colonize flower stems.

Red yucca is not common in the wild. Its native habitat is limestone hills, arroyos, and mesquite groves of the Llano Basin in the Hill Country of central Texas and the eastern edge of the Chihuahuan Desert in southwestern Texas and northern Coahuila in Mexico. Its stiff, blue-green, swordlike leaves have fibrous threads along the margins and form an arching grass-like clump. The flaring tubular flowers, with toothed openings and yellow or white centers, appear along the tops of the arching flower stalks and bloom from the bottom up.

This sturdy succulent is both drought tolerant and heat loving, preferring full sun and withstanding reflected heat quite well. It tolerates a variety of soils, demanding only fast drainage, and is hardy well north of its natural range, handling freezing temperatures for prolonged periods. In extremely hot locations, a deep soaking once or twice a month in the summer will improve its appearance; in very wet areas the plant is likely to rot. Bloom time can be lengthened considerably by removing developing seedpods. This low-maintenance evergreen is widely available and works beautifully as an accent for courtyards, poolsides, and patios, along walkways, in rock gardens, or massed as a tall ground cover. It also makes an excellent container plant. Propagation is easy by division in late winter, but allow the cut to dry before planting. Alternatively, collect seeds from the woody seedpods and plant. If seeds are not to be harvested, spent flower stalks can be cut back or left to stand as sentinel perches. A yellow form of this plant that also appeals to hummingbirds has pale butter-yellow blossoms on shorter stalks.

Heuchera sanguinea
Coral Bells, Blood Alum Root

Family:	Saxifragaceae	**Water use:**	Moderate
Type:	Perennial	**Cold hardiness:**	Roots to at least -25°F
Size:	1.5' high x 1.5' wide	**USDA zone:**	4–9
Bloom:	March–June, sporadic through September		

Author citation: Engelmann

This pretty little perennial looks nice year-round, and with its long bloom season is a terrific addition to a hummingbird garden. The nodding, pubescent, bell-like flowers, in shades ranging from coral pink to bright crimson, are said to be not particularly rich in nectar but are avidly visited by Costa's, Anna's, Blue-throated, Berylline, Black-chinned, Calliope, and Rufous Hummingbirds nonetheless.

In the wild, coral bells colonizes moist hillsides and seeps in shady mountain habitats from 4,000 to 8,500 feet in elevation, in south-central and southeastern Arizona, extreme southwestern New Mexico, and northeastern Sonora and western Chihuahua in Mexico. The basal cluster of large medium-green leaves, each with several ruffled lobes, is evergreen in mild climates. Often the toothed margins are tipped with bristles. Individual plants are compact in form but frequently spread to form large clumps. In the early spring, several slender, wiry, hairy stems shoot up above the foliage, bearing loose clusters of tiny flowers that bloom over a long period, particularly if faded stalks are removed.

Plants prefer a light, well-drained, moist soil that is rich in organic matter but certainly will make do with leaner soil. In warmer locations they perform the best with filtered or partial shade, particularly during hot summer afternoons. They are not reliably drought tolerant and may languish in hot, arid low-desert areas; they can also be susceptible to rot if overwatered, as is possible during the monsoon season. Given the right niche, however, they are well behaved and long-lived, and work wonderfully along walkways, at the front of perennial borders, under trees, next to water features, and in the shade of boulders in rock gardens. They also do well in containers, which elevates the flowers and makes them more appealing to hummingbirds. New plants can be propagated by division every few years in spring or fall; plant the crowns right at the soil surface. Plants are also easy to propagate from seed sown in spring or by cuttings of a leaf along with a short segment of stem taken in midsummer and rooted in moist sand or a light mix of potting soil and vermiculite.

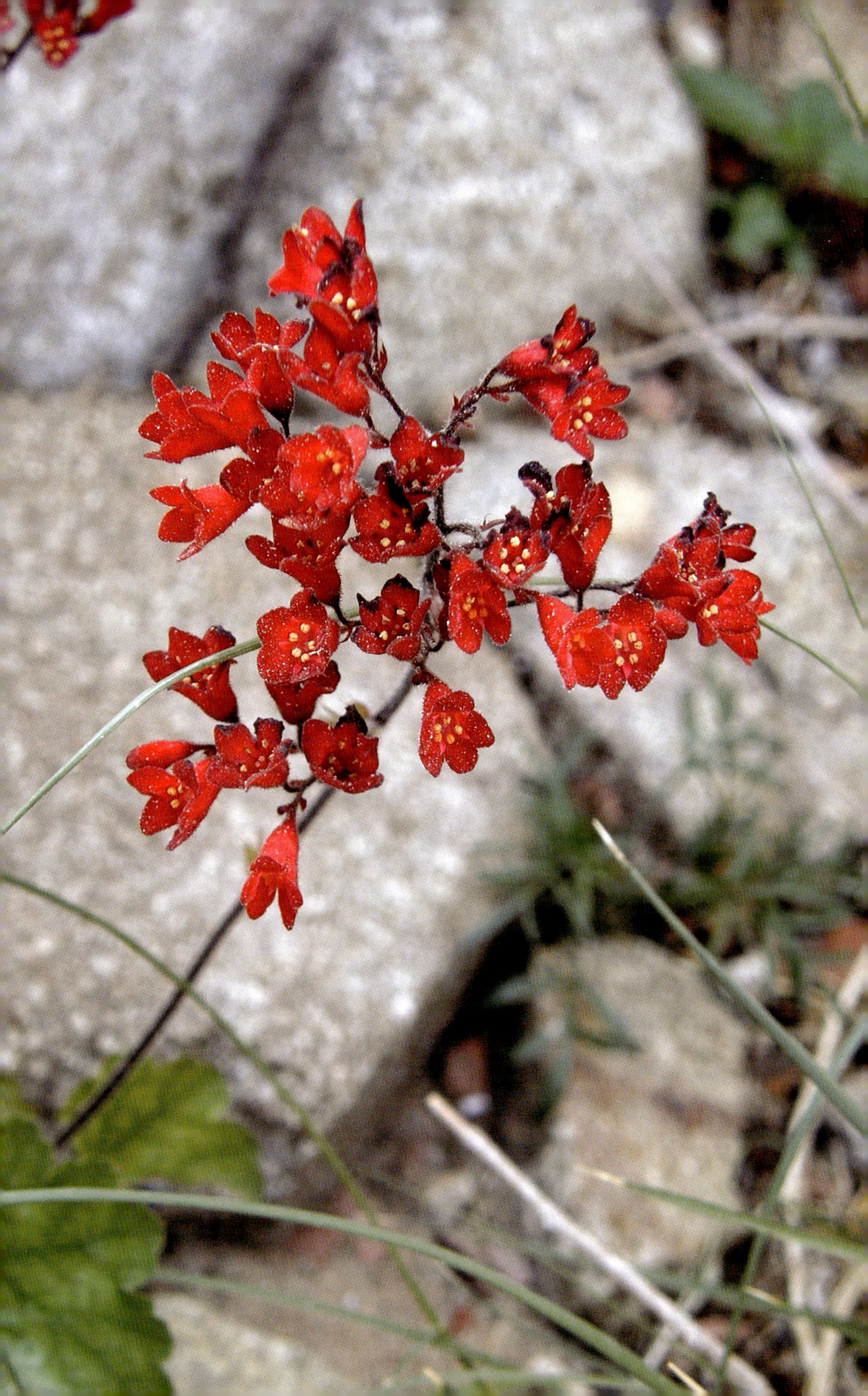

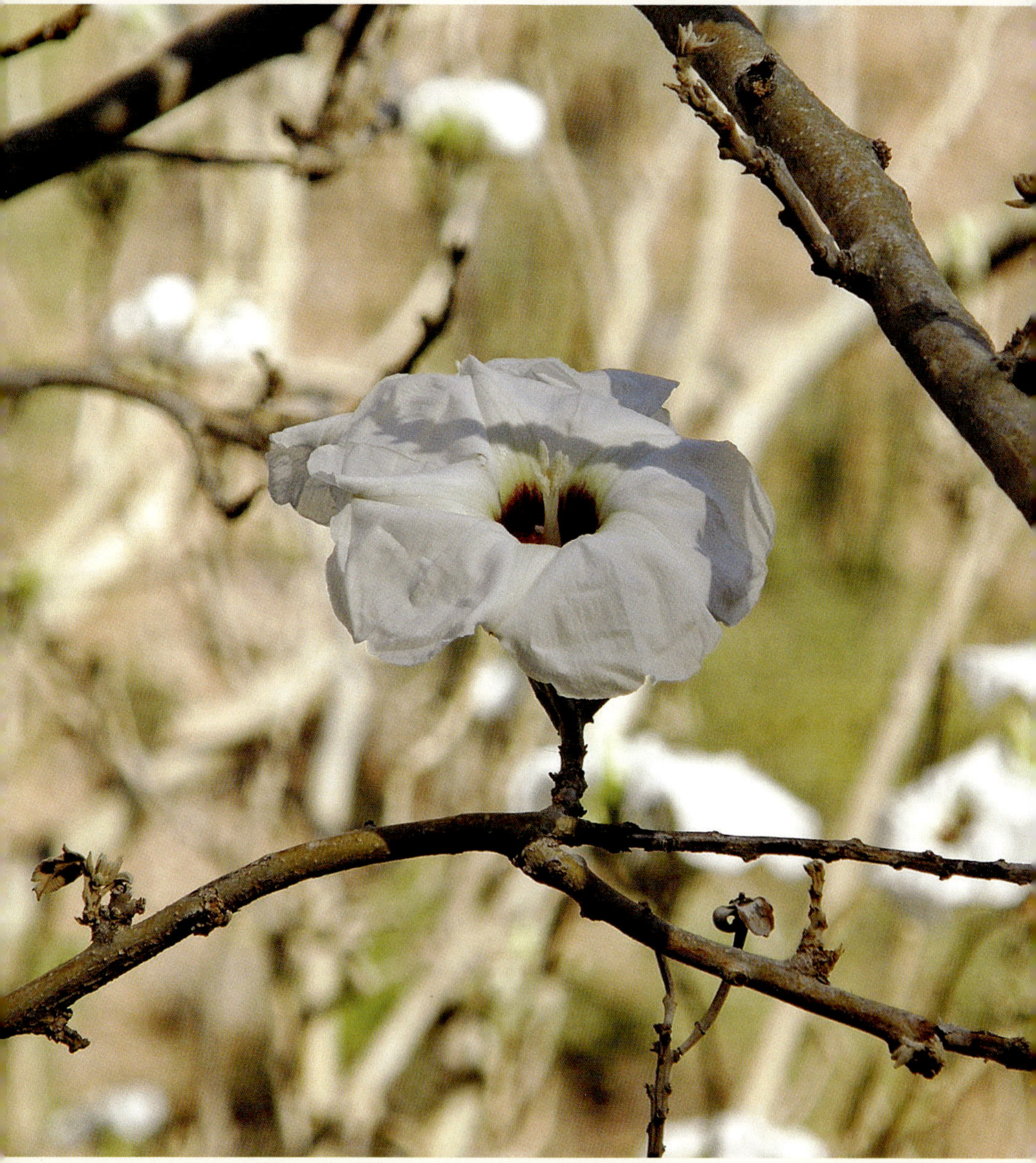

Ipomoea arborescens
Tree Morning Glory, Palo Blanco, Palo Santo, Jútuguo

Family:	Convolvulaceae		sometimes longer
Type:	Deciduous tree	**Water use:**	Moderate
Size:	20–30' high x 15–20' wide	**Cold hardiness:**	To 25°F
Bloom:	November–March,	**USDA zone:**	9b–11

Author citation: (Humboldt & Bonpland ex Willdenow) G. Don
Synonym: *Ipomoea arborescens* Sweet

Because of its abundance, bloom time, and copious nectar, this lovely tree is one of the most important sources of nectar for hummingbirds in northern Mexico in late winter and early spring. Although the huge white flowers are primarily pollinated by long-nosed bats, they provide vital nectar for Costa's Hummingbirds wintering in Sinaloa and for many other species migrating northward from central Mexico along the Sierra Madre Occidental and Sonoran coast. Anna's, Broad-billed, Violet-crowned, Beryl-line, White-eared, and Rufous Hummingbirds and Plain-capped Starthroats have all been observed visiting the enchanting blooms.

Tree morning glory enjoys a wide distribution in Mexico, occurring nearly to the U. S. border in the Rio Yaqui drainages of northern Sonora and Chihuahua and southward through the western barrancas at least to Guerrero. Favorite haunts include tropical deciduous forests and oak woodlands on lower slopes and benches above major rivers, barranca bottoms, and thornscrub in desert ranges and along the coast. Growing at elevations ranging from about 300 to 3,000 feet, its smooth gray bark and leafless habit during flowering are distinctive, and can separate it from a close cousin, *Ipomoea chilopsidis*, which has nearly identical flowers (also well used by hummingbirds) but is shrubby, only six to ten feet tall, tends to occur at higher elevations, blooms earlier and longer than tree morning glory, and has long, narrow, willow-like leaves during flowering. The leaves of tree morning glory typically appear only after summer rains and are large (up to six inches long), heart-shaped at the base, prominently veined, and lime green in color, turning bright yellow in the fall. The three- to five-inch-long funnel-shaped flowers are creamy white with raspberry-red centers and are followed by small oval reddish-brown capsules, each containing four black seeds fringed with pale silky hairs.

Because of its sensitivity to frost, this pretty tree's suitability for most southwestern landscapes is quite limited, but in locations where winter temperatures remain consistently above freezing, such as southern California, it thrives in full sun with low to moderate irrigation in the winter and regular watering during summer, and would make an excellent anchor for a winter hummingbird garden. Plants can reportedly be propagated by either seed or semi-hardwood cuttings.

Ipomoea bracteata

Wild Jícama, Bejuco Blanco, Tosa Huira, Flor de la Candelaria

Family:	Convolvulaceae	Water use:	Low–moderate
Type:	Woody perennial vine	Cold hardiness:	To 30°F
Size:	10–20' high	USDA zone:	10–11
Bloom:	January–May		

Author citation: Cavanilles
Synonyms: *Ipomoea bracteata* Wight; *Exogonium bracteatum* (Cav.) Choisy ex G. Don

THE SHOWY DEEP PINK TO PURPLE BRACTS of this long bloomer from Mexico resemble those of *Bougainvillea* and advertise vital nectar for the taking to Rufous, Broad-tailed, Broad-billed, Violet-crowned, Berylline, and Costa's Hummingbirds and Plain-capped Starthroats from midwinter through early spring, a critical time when most hummingbird-pollinated plants are in extremely short supply. The blooms are said to be especially important to Rufous Hummingbirds as they move northward from their southern Mexico wintering grounds each spring. Doubtless hummingbirds must play at least a minor role in pollination.

Decorating winter landscapes from Sonora and southwest Chihuahua southward along the Pacific slope of the Sierra Madre Occidental through Sinaloa, Nayarit, Jalisco, and Michoacán to Guerrero and Puebla, wild jícama can be found at elevations ranging from sea level to nearly 4,500 feet.

Its slender gray stems arise from a large tuberous root and woody base, twining around shrubs and climbing trees in foothills thornscrub, tropical deciduous forest, oak woodlands, rocky canyonsides, lowland river valleys, desert washes, and sandy flats. The unique flowers, with narrow tubular corollas surrounded by colorful papery bracts, typically bloom on leafless stems until moisture later in the season brings forth the sage-green compound leaves, with five lance-shaped or oblong leaflets each. As leaves begin to emerge the flowers disappear for the remainder of the rainy season. Throughout the long bloom period, the plants produce smooth half-inch conical seed capsules each containing four elongated hairy seeds.

This intriguing plant is suited for only the balmiest of climates, as it absolutely cannot tolerate freezing temperatures. Given a warm location, a coarse, gravelly, well-drained soil, and a trellis or other structure to climb, however, it should thrive in full sun to part shade with moderate watering until established and as needed afterward. Allow seed heads to dry on the plant, then collect and store or sow. Plants can also be propagated by semi-hardwood cuttings. The fleshy roots, said to be the size of a turnip, are reportedly gathered by native people and eaten raw or cooked.

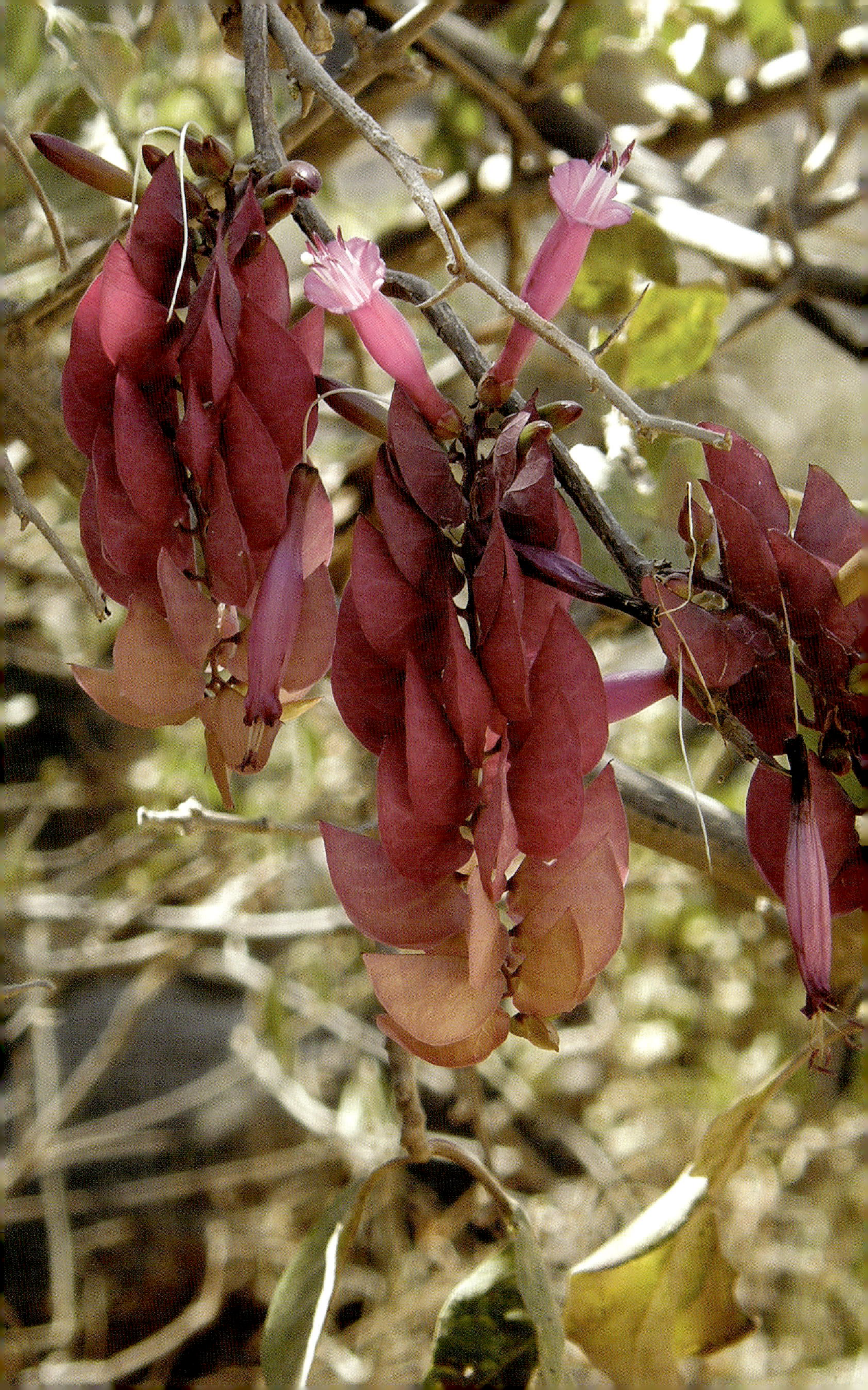

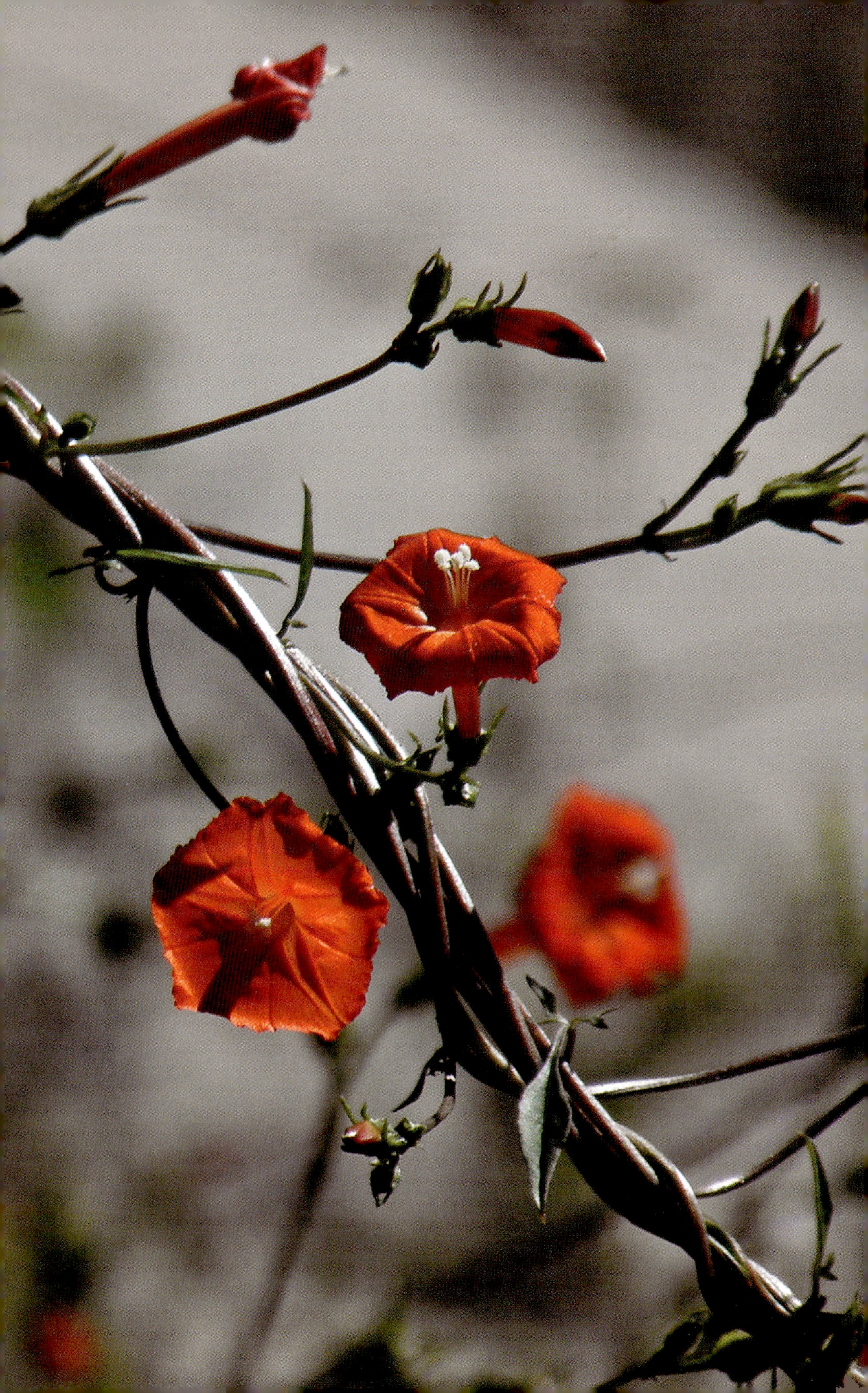

Ipomoea cristulata

Scarlet Creeper, Trans Pecos Morning Glory, Star Glory

Family:	Convolvulaceae	**Water use:**	Low–moderate
Type:	Annual vine	**Cold hardiness:**	To -20°F
Size:	3–6' high	**USDA zone:**	5–10
Bloom:	May–October		

Author citation: Hallier f.

THIS CHARMING LITTLE VINE BECKONS HUMMINGBIRDS far and wide when its bright red tubular flowers are in bloom, which happens from late spring until frost with sufficient water. Black-chinned and Rufous Hummingbirds avidly take the reportedly rich nectar from the blossoms and are probably important pollinators. The seeds are readily consumed by Scaled, Gambel's, and Montezuma Quail.

Scarlet creeper inhabits gravelly slopes and drainages of deserts, grasslands, and open woodlands in Arizona, much of New Mexico, parts of western Texas (including the Davis and Chisos mountains), and southward through Mexico to Central America, typically occurring at elevations of 4,500 to 6,500 feet but occasionally as high as 9,000 feet. It is customarily found twining around and through low shrubs, on rocky slopes and brushy hillsides, and in canyons, swales, and dry creek beds. Plant communities that it frequently associates with include netleaf hackberry, Arizona sycamore, various oaks, alligator juniper, piñon, and ponderosa pine. Its slender, pinkish, branching stems hold fleshy, deeply trilobed, bright green leaves. The one- to one-and-a-half-inch-long flowers have extremely narrow corolla tubes with five widely flaring pointed lobes and are vivid scarlet with yellow throats and prominent stamens. They appear quickly by late spring and continue to bloom as long as water is available.

Plants prefer a lean well-drained soil and full sun for best performance, and regular watering during the summer months will maximize bloom time. They can be trained to grow on a support such as a trellis, fence, or mailbox post, draped over a rock wall, or allowed to weave in and out of a shrub or small tree. Seeds germinate fairly easily in up to two inches of soil; sow scarified seed in early spring for blooms before summer. Red morning glory (*Ipomoea coccinea*; syn. *I. rubriflora*) is a closely related cousin that is native to tropical America and has naturalized in the southeastern United States west to eastern Texas. Note that both species are considered noxious weeds in agricultural areas and are currently prohibited by the state of Arizona.

Ipomopsis aggregata

Scarlet Gilia, Desert Skyrocket, Desert Trumpet

Family:	Polemoniaceae		June–September
Type:	Biennial/perennial	**Water use:**	Low–moderate
Size:	1–3' high x <1' wide	**Cold hardiness:**	Roots to at least -18°F
Bloom:	May–October, especially	**USDA zone:**	3–8

Author citation: (Pursh) V. E. Grant
Synonym: *Gilia aggregata* (Pursh) Sprengel

SCARLET GILIA SPENDS THE FIRST SEASON OF ITS LIFE AS A LACY BASAL rosette of foliage, then rolls out the red carpet for hummingbirds during its second year, sending up a slender stalk laden with scarlet flowers that are a vital source of nectar for Black-chinned, Broad-tailed, Calliope, Rufous, and Blue-throated Hummingbirds. Calliope Hummingbirds in particular are so closely associated with this plant that some biologists believe they may have coevolved. The nectar yield is reportedly low, so if juicier hummingbird flowers happen to be in bloom scarlet gilia may be ignored. Not surprisingly, hummingbirds, along with sphinx moths, are the plant's primary pollinators. Carpenter bees often rob the nectar by slitting open the corolla at the base.

This montane beauty occurs throughout the western United States, on dry slopes, sagebrush flats, and piñon-juniper or ponderosa pine meadows from 5,000 to over 10,000 feet in elevation. The finely divided foliage has a skunky smell when bruised that can be forgiven once the flowers appear, sometimes the first summer but more often the next. The one- to one-and-a-half-inch tubular blooms occur in clusters along the sticky, upright flower stalk. Each is bright scarlet with stripes of white or yellow down the centers of the five spreading, pointed lobes. Interestingly, as the season progresses and hummingbirds become less abundant, the flower color may gradually fade in hue to attract its other pollinators, the nocturnal sphinx moths.

Gardeners report that plants insist upon excellent drainage and seem happiest in slightly alkaline sandy or gravelly soils. Full sun is normally preferred, but this plant will definitely wither at low elevations without extra water and part shade. Scarlet gilia is most effective when massed for a splash of color, particularly in a wild corner of the garden where it can be left to its biennial cycle undisturbed. Take a cue from Broad-tailed Hummingbirds that seek out taller plants and plant on a slope or raised bed to elevate the height of the flowers. Stratify seeds in moist perlite for one month and sow in spring for bloom the following summer. For flowers every year, plant seeds two years in a row and allow plants to reseed. Deer will browse the stems but reportedly that sometimes can encourage more prolific flowering.

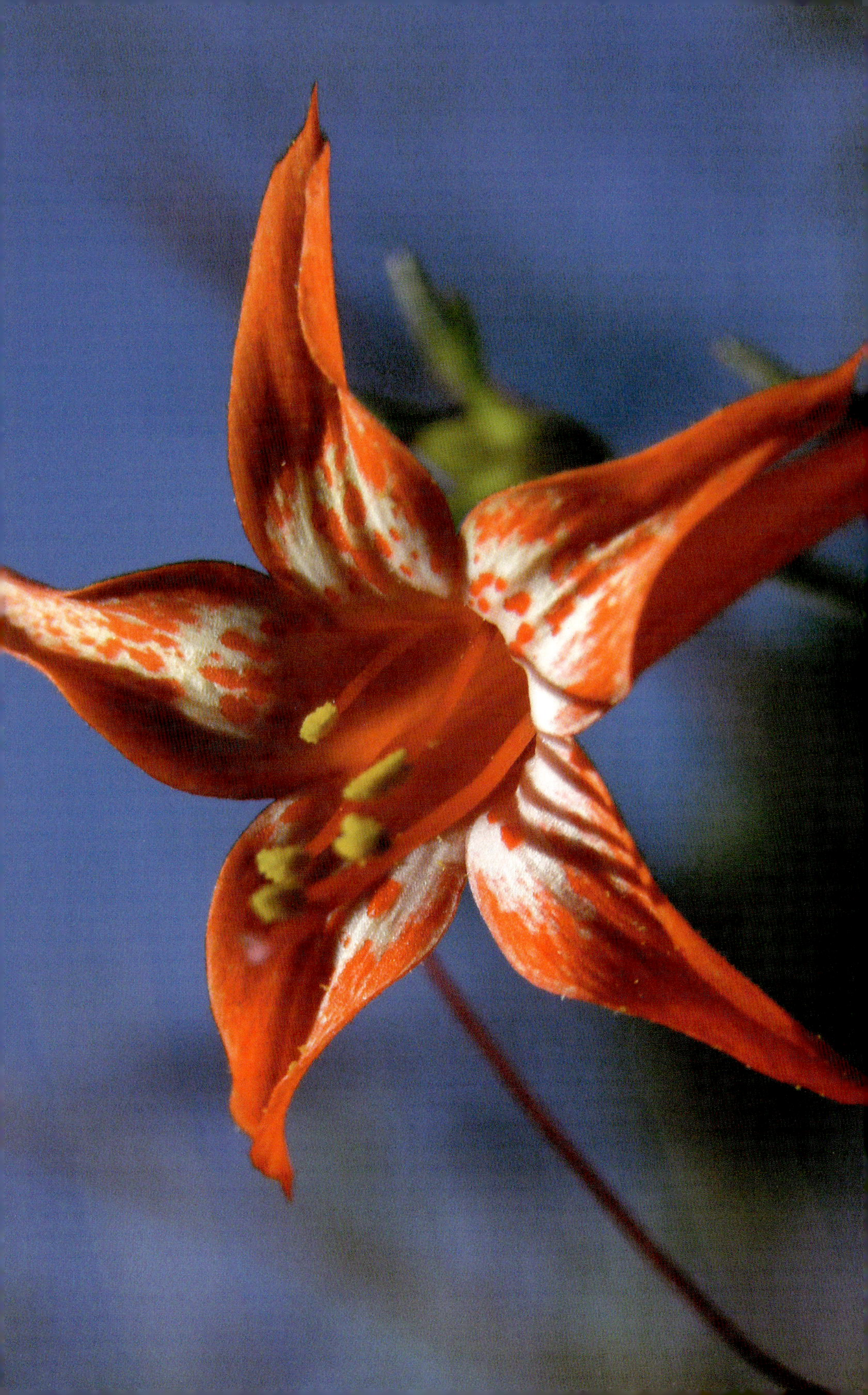

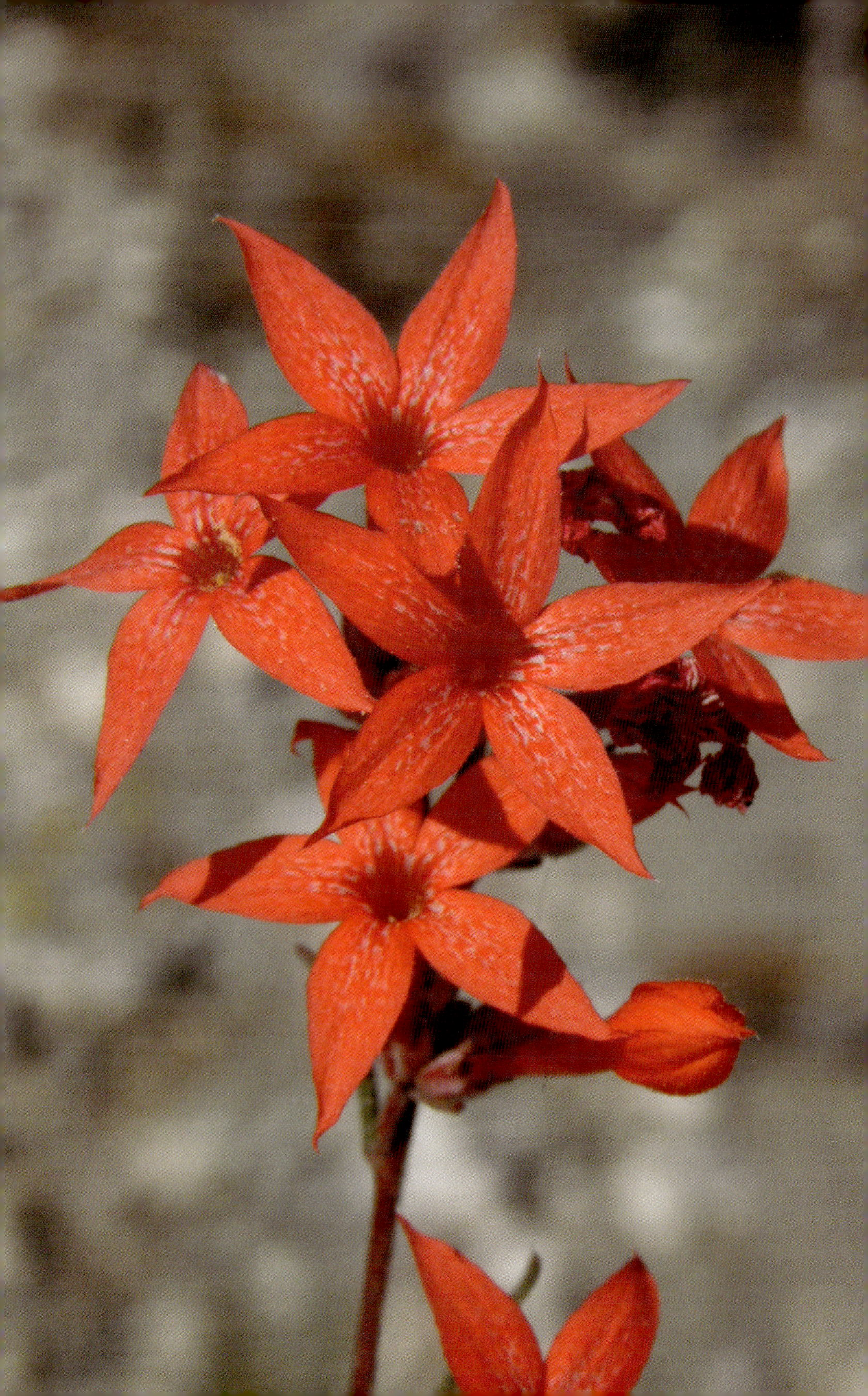

Ipomopsis arizonica

Arizona Gilia, Arizona Skyrocket

Family:	Polemoniaceae	**Water use:**	Low–moderate
Type:	Biennial	**Cold hardiness:**	To -20°F
Size:	1–2' high x 1' wide	**USDA zone:**	5–9
Bloom:	June–September		

Author citation: (Greene) Wherry
Synonym: *Ipomopsis aggregata* ssp. *arizonica* (Greene) V. E. Grant & A. D. Grant

THIS DELIGHTFUL BIENNIAL IS ANOTHER GILIA that is specifically adapted to hummingbirds. The flared to reflexed lobes of its rich scarlet flowers are designed to deter would-be nectar robbers from accessing the corolla tube, saving the nectar for the Broad-tailed and Rufous Hummingbirds that are the principal pollinators.

Arizona gilia occurs in open areas of desert mountains and cinder hills in northern Arizona, southwestern Utah, southern Nevada, and southeastern California, primarily in San Bernardino County. It is typically found in rocky canyons, dry washes, or clearings in ponderosa pine or piñon-juniper woodlands at elevations ranging from 5,000 to over 10,000 feet. Usually shorter-stemmed and a bit bushier than its cousin, scarlet gilia (*Ipomopsis aggregata*), this one is garbed with basal leaves that are even more finely divided, with seven to eleven leaflets. In its second year the plant sends up erect, somewhat hairy stems that bear dark-green pine-needle-like foliage and loose clusters of one-inch tubular flowers near the tips that summon every hummingbird within view.

In the garden, Arizona gilia prefers a sandy or gravelly soil that is well drained. A sunny exposure is best, but in hot lower elevation locations some afternoon shade is probably warranted. It is native to regions of summer rain and may need an occasional deep soaking during extended summertime drought, but the remainder of the year requires little water. This petite charmer would make a fine accent for an upland summer hummingbird garden and should be sought out at native plant sales in its home region. Seeds are said to germinate readily; plant in early spring for bloom the following summer. As with scarlet gilia, deer are known to browse this plant, but according to biologists the plant compensates for browsing by producing more stems. Although Arizona gilia often occurs alongside scarlet gilia and the two are pollinated by the same hummingbird species (at times by the same individuals), the two do not appear to hybridize.

Ipomopsis tenuifolia
Slenderleaf Skyrocket

Family:	Polemoniaceae	**Water use:**	Low–moderate
Type:	Perennial	**Cold hardiness:**	To 30°F
Size:	1' high x 1' wide	**USDA zone:**	10–11
Bloom:	March–May		

Author citation: (A. Gray) V. E. Grant
Synonym: *Loeselia tenuifolia* A. Gray

THIS CLASSIC SCARLET-RED HUMMINGBIRD FLOWER may have a rather small geographic range, but where it occurs it offers valuable spring nectar to both resident hummingbirds and those migrating northward up the California coast and likely depends significantly upon them for pollination services. Anna's, Costa's, Black-chinned, and Rufous Hummingbirds are probable nectar patrons.

Slenderleaf skyrocket hails from the Sonoran Desert and southeastern Peninsular Ranges of southern California (where it is considered endangered by the California Native Plant Society) and northern Baja California in Mexico (where fortunately it is more common). Found at elevations ranging from 300 to over 6,000 feet, it graces dry rocky slopes, canyon bottoms, sandy washes, creosote scrublands, chaparral habitats with sugarbush (*Rhus ovata*) and white sage (*Salvia apiana*), and piñon-juniper woodlands. Often associating with large boulders and sometimes even growing from rocky crevices within them, this charming perennial may be meager in stature, but its fire-engine-red blooms more than compensate. Typically growing as a solitary clump of slender, erect, multi-branched stems, the plants bear narrow threadlike leaves along the branches and present their winsome flowers at the tips, each cluster composed of one to seven narrow tubular blooms with five toothed lobes. Both the five stamens with their purple-tinged anthers and the style with its white stigmas protrude well beyond the mouth of the flower.

In the garden this petite but showy skyrocket likely prefers a light, well-drained, sandy or gravelly soil and full sun to part shade, the latter advised in particularly hot and exposed locations. Mulching to keep roots cool in summer and warm during winter is recommended; decomposed granite would be ideal for this purpose. Allow established plants to dry out a little between waterings and protect from hard freezes. Seeds of this uncommon beauty are occasionally available locally from native plant purveyors. Tucked among boulders in a southern California rock garden to mimic its natural habitat, slenderleaf skyrocket would provide a splash of vibrant color and welcome spring nectar to a bevy of hummingbirds.

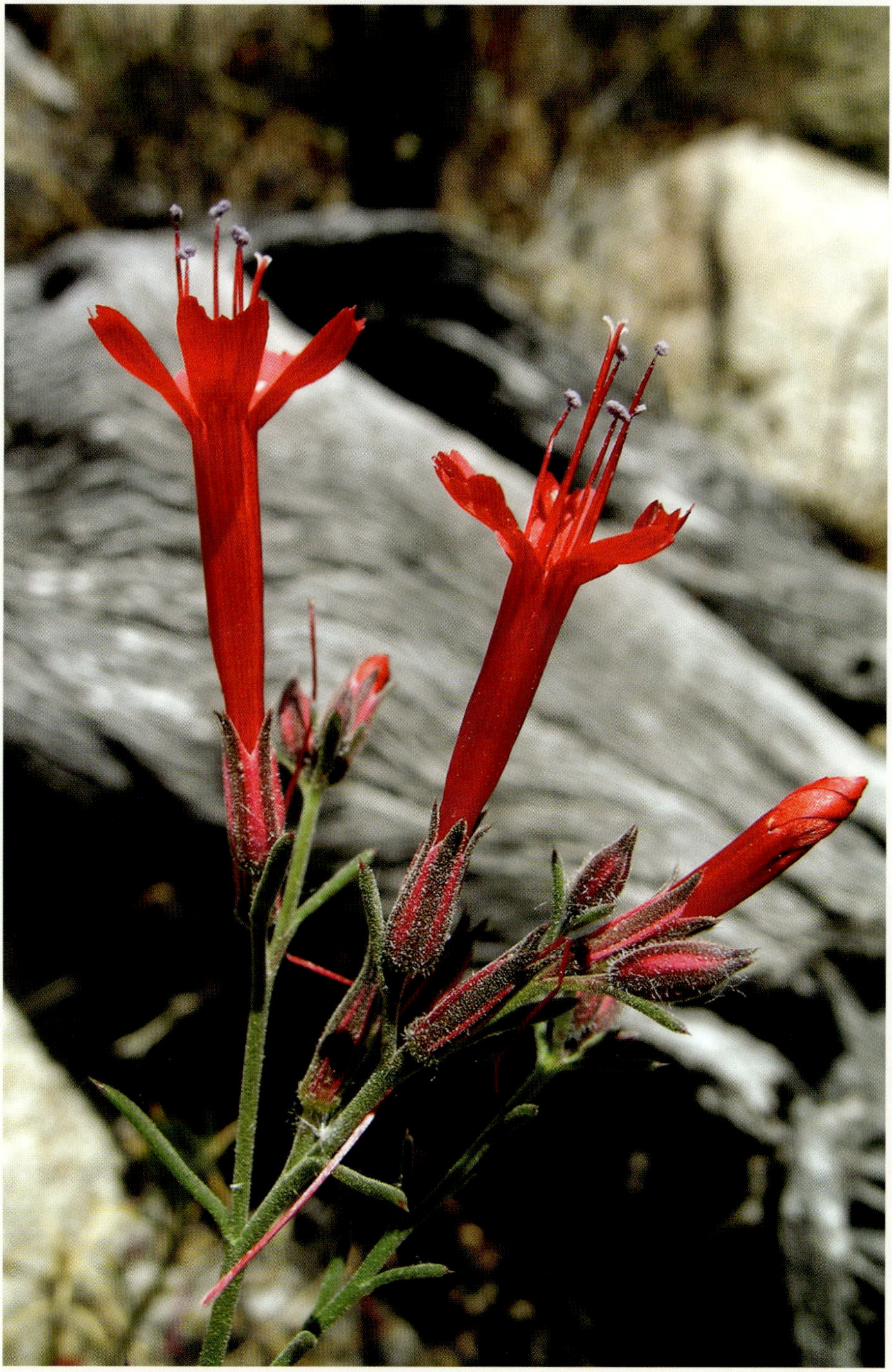

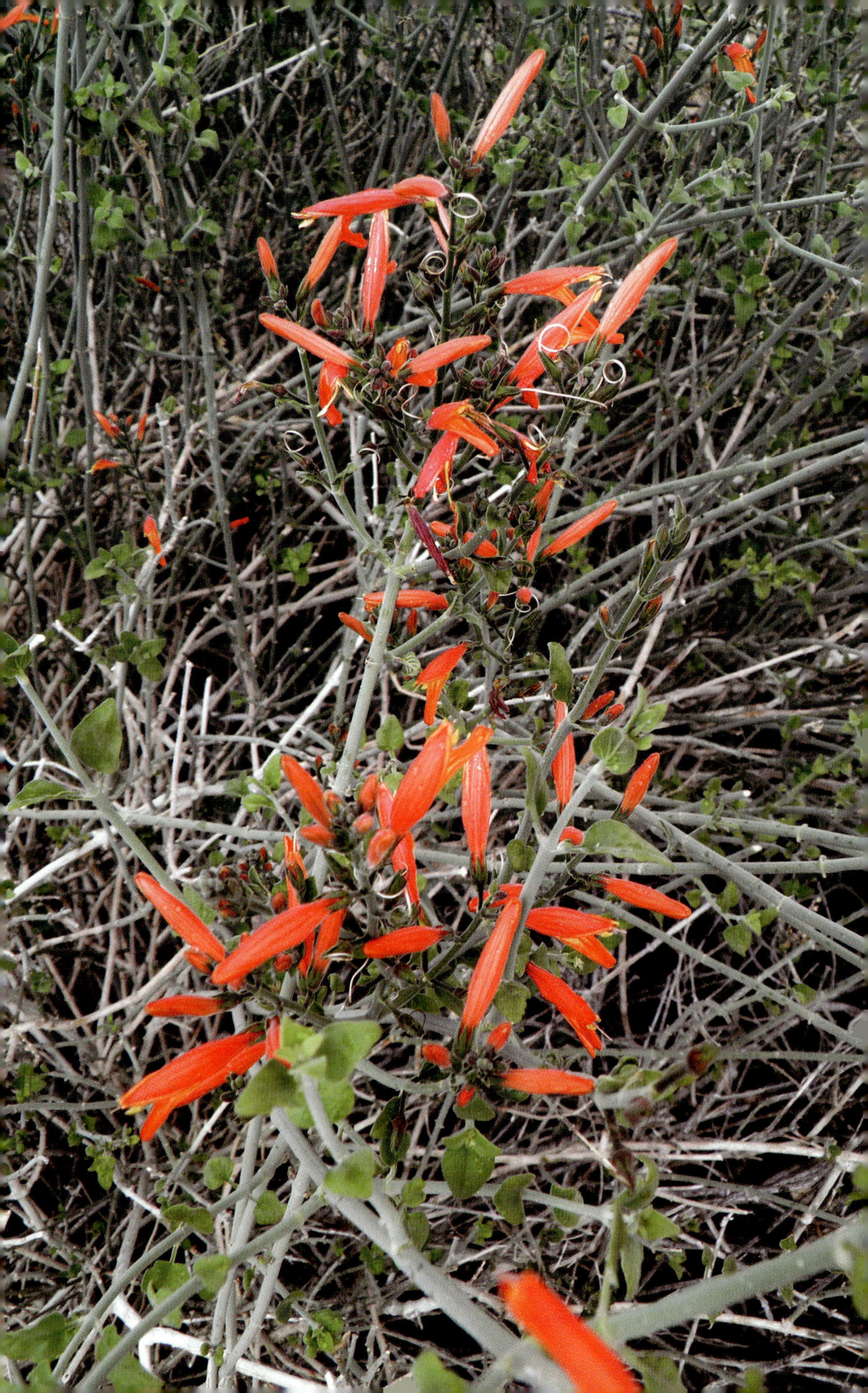

Justicia californica
Chuparosa, California Beloperone

Family:	Acanthaceae	**Water use:**	Low–moderate
Type:	Semi-evergreen shrub	**Cold hardiness:**	Top to 25°F, roots to below 20°F
Size:	4–5' high x 5–6' wide		
Bloom:	October–June in frost-free areas, February–March peak	**USDA zone:**	8b–10

Author citation: (Bentham) D. N. Gibson
Synonym: *Beloperone californica* Bentham

THE NAME CHUPAROSA, which in Spanish means hummingbird, honors the star pollinator of this long-blooming shrub. Its bright scarlet to dark red tubular blossoms are an extremely important source of nectar for wintering Costa's Hummingbirds as well as for migrating Black-chinned, Broad-billed, Allen's, Rufous, and Calliope Hummingbirds in the early spring. Anna's and Broad-tailed Hummingbirds often visit the blossoms in the fall. Nectar is also taken by orioles, warblers, goldfinches, honeybees, and some butterflies. House Finches and White-crowned Sparrows bite the bases of the blooms to get at the nectar; finches and quail gobble up the seeds. The plant is also a larval host to checkerspot butterflies.

Chuparosa has a limited geographical range within the Upper Sonoran and Colorado deserts, from southeastern California to southwestern Arizona and southward into Mexico in Baja California, Sonora, and northern Sinaloa. It occurs from sea level to 2,500 feet in sandy washes and arroyos and on low rocky slopes, where its densely branched, twiggy, mounding form is distinctive. Both the stems and the tiny oval to heart-shaped leaves are a pale sage green, the stems gathering chlorophyll during periods when the shrub is leafless during cold (28°F) or drought. The bloom peaks about March, when the plant is blanketed with clusters of bright red blooms.

Chuparosa will grow in a variety of sandy or rocky soils but excellent drainage is essential and it absolutely will not tolerate humidity. For best appearance, give plants a deep soaking once or twice a month during summer, and then harden them off by reducing water in the fall. In areas prone to frost, plant in a protected location to maximize the season of bloom. Any frost damage should be pruned back in spring after frost danger has passed. Plant this iconic hummingbird magnet in full sun or light shade in courtyards, foundation plantings, public parks, and desert gardens. Chuparosa also works beautifully in a large pot, provided drainage is good. Propagate by seeds, which pop as soon as they are mature, or softwood cuttings. Rabbits usually do not bother mature plants, but young plants should be protected with a cage.

Justicia candicans

Red Justicia, Rama del Toro, Arizona Water-willow

Family:	Acanthaceae	**Water use:**	Moderate–high
Type:	Evergreen shrub	**Cold hardiness:**	Top to mid-20s°F, roots to 10°F
Size:	3–5' high x 3' wide		
Bloom:	January–May and October–December	**USDA zone:**	9–10

Author citation: (Nees) L. D. Benson
Synonym: *Jacobinia ovata* A. Gray

This handsome hummingbird plant is a real workhorse, cranking out blooms much of the year in frost-free regions. Its carmine-red tubular flowers, with distinctive three-lobed lower lips, are extremely valuable for wintering hummingbirds, such as Anna's and Costa's Hummingbirds, when other potential nectar sources are typically scarce. Costa's, Broad-billed, and White-eared Hummingbirds have all been observed feeding at the blossoms in late winter and early spring in Sonora, Mexico. As with many other justicias, hummingbirds are the plant's most significant pollinators.

Red justicia is a Sonoran Desert native found in sandy washes and rocky canyon bottoms at elevations of 1,500 to 3,500 feet, in Mariposa, Pima, and Santa Cruz counties in southern Arizona and in Sonora, western Chihuahua, Sinaloa, and Durango in Mexico. It has a graceful upright to somewhat spreading form and numerous downy brownish-gray stems that are clad in bright-green heart-shaped leaves, which are evergreen unless temperatures persist in the low 20s. The flowering period begins in earnest in autumn, when clusters of buds appear at branch tips, but even then blossoms can be sparse. The astonishingly long bloom period more than makes up for any lack in volume.

This fast-growing shrub likes well-drained fertile soil, part to filtered sun depending upon the elevation, and protection from frost. A deep layer of mulch will conserve moisture and help keep roots cool in summer and warm in winter. Prune back any damage in early spring and plants will usually recover quickly. Give the plants a deep soaking once a week during the hot summer months to keep them in fine form and to encourage continuous flowering. Unlike other justicias, this one is not at all drought tolerant, so place it in oasis environments along pathways, in courtyards, or in simulated wash plantings. It will also do beautifully in a large container but naturally will require more frequent watering. Propagate by seeds or softwood cuttings. 'Sonoran Red' is a named variety of red justicia that is reported to be hardy to USDA Zone 8.

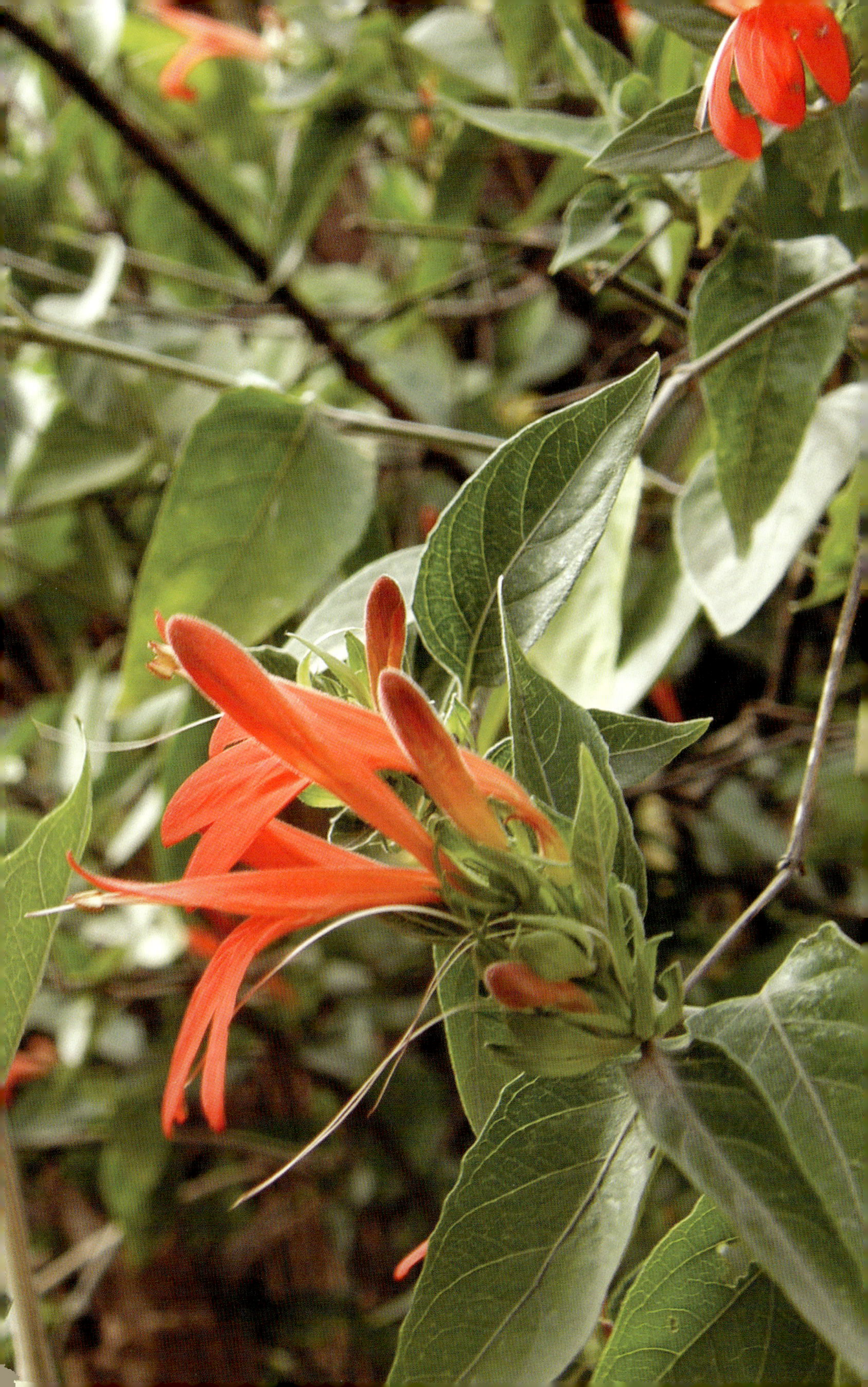

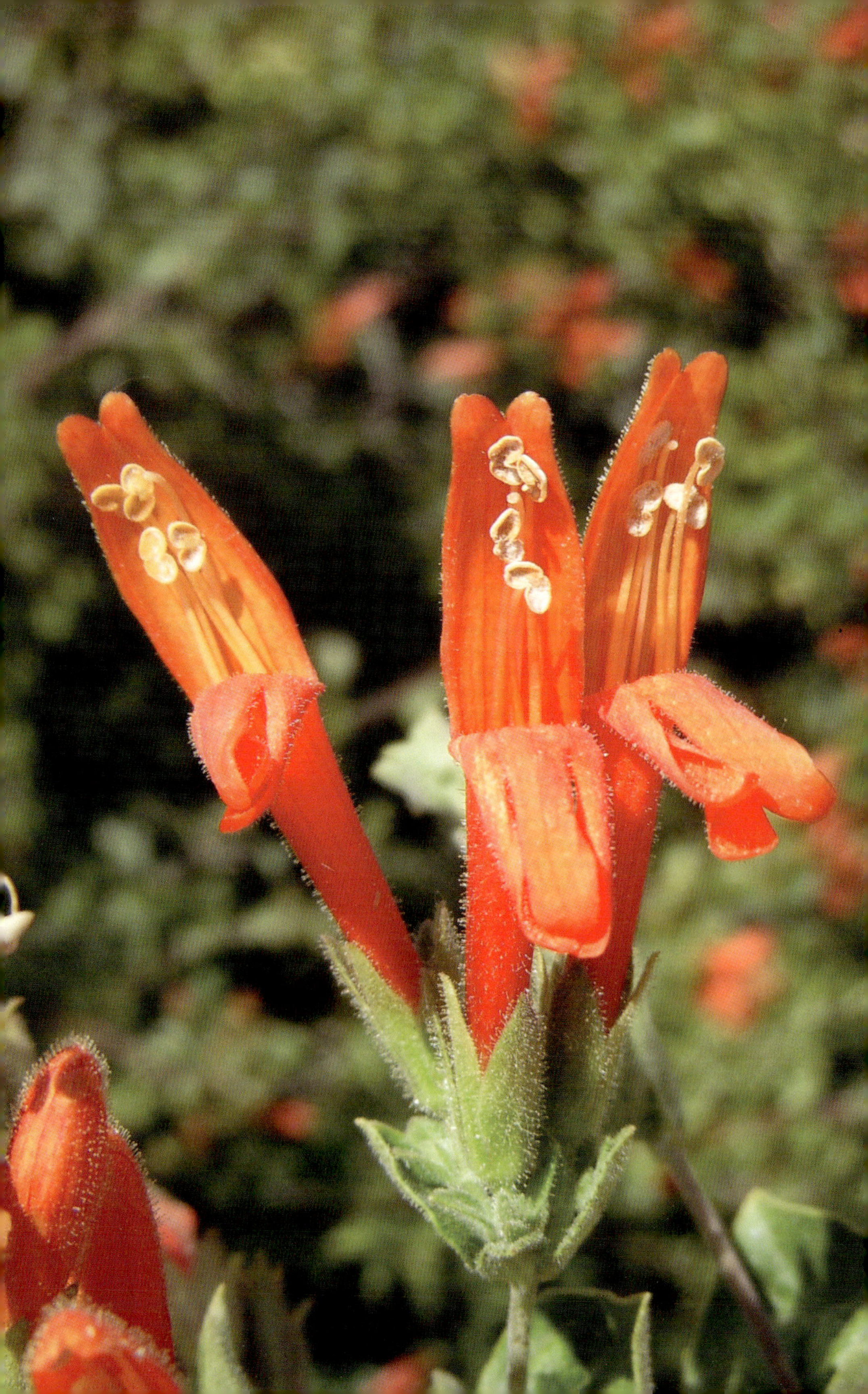

Keckiella cordifolia

Heartleaf Keckiella, Red Bush Penstemon, Climbing Penstemon

Family:	Plantaginaceae (Scrophulariaceae)	**Bloom:**	May–August
		Water use:	Low–moderate
Type:	Evergreen or deciduous shrub	**Cold hardiness:**	Top to -20°F
Size:	3–5' high x 5–8' wide	**USDA zone:**	8b–10

Author citation: (Bentham) Straw
Synonym: *Penstemon cordifolius* Bentham

This captivating cousin of the penstemons is an extremely valuable late spring and early summer food source for nesting Anna's, Costa's, and to a lesser extent Allen's Hummingbirds. Its deep red tubular blooms yield abundant nectar, a whopping 26–50 microliters per flower per day, and not surprisingly are primarily pollinated by hummingbirds. The tiny seeds are snapped up by a number of birds.

Heartleaf keckiella is a member of the coast sage community, occurring at elevations below 4,000 feet in coastal and inland foothills and canyons from central California southward into northern Baja California in Mexico. It is mounding in form, with twining stems that often trail up taller neighboring shrubs. The glossy, green paired leaves are heart-shaped with pointed tips and clasp the stem at the base. In fall the leaves turn from green to yellow to crimson red, providing interest year-round. The rather fuzzy one- to two-inch blossoms are two-lipped, the upper forming a hood over the corolla and the lower trilobed and reflexed backward.

This vine-like penstemon's chief requirement is perfect drainage. It will grow in full sun or part shade, usually requiring little water, but supplemental water during the hot summer months will keep it from dropping its pretty leaves and will prolong flowering. In extreme heat plants do best in semi-shade or with eastern exposures. Leggy older plants may be cut back hard to rejuvenate. This is a great plant for naturalizing on slopes or banks or draping over other shrubs. It also does well growing in the shade of trees, especially native oaks, and is a must for southern California hummingbird gardens. Propagation is said to be easy by seed or semi-hardwood cuttings. Yellow penstemon (*Keckiella antirrhinoides*) is a cousin that ranges eastward to central Arizona but in southern California shares some of the same habitats, and the two may hybridize where they occur together and create offspring with red and yellow flowers. It is also quite popular with hummingbirds, but if the true red flowers of heartleaf keckiella are desired, do not plant them both in the same garden.

Keckiella ternata

Scarlet Keckiella, Wand Penstemon, Whorl-leaf Penstemon

Family:	Plantaginaceae (Scrophulariaceae)	**Bloom:**	July–October
		Water use:	Low–moderate
Type:	Perennial subshrub	**Cold hardiness:**	To -20°F
Size:	4–6' high x 2' wide	**USDA zone:**	8b–10

Author citation: (Torrey ex A. Gray) Straw
Synonym: *Penstemon ternatus* Torr. ex A. Gray

THE SHOWY BRIGHT-RED TUBULAR BLOSSOMS OF THIS WISPY PLANT offer valuable nectar to Anna's Hummingbirds beginning in midsummer, when many California plants go dormant to conserve water and few other nectar-producing flowers are in bloom. Migrating Rufous and Allen's Hummingbirds also take nectar from this mostly hummingbird-pollinated subshrub.

Scarlet keckiella is native to a fairly small geographic area, occurring primarily in the Lower Coast Ranges of southern California and adjacent Mexico in northern Baja California. Typically it is found on dry slopes or in canyons, in chaparral scrub, piñon-juniper woodlands, or openings in ponderosa pine forests, at elevations ranging from nearly sea level to 6,000 feet. Its form can be either erect or spreading, with the young stems slender and wand-like and often growing in and out of neighboring shrubs. Some populations have strikingly bluish stems that set off and nicely contrast with the foliage. The light green, linear or lance-shaped leaves have finely toothed margins and usually occur in whorls of three about the stem, giving rise to the species name of *ternata*. Often they are folded or curled lengthwise. Flowers are presented in clusters at stem tips, and may or may not be sticky depending upon the subspecies. The narrow corolla tubes are about one-inch long and are framed by spreading ovate lobes. The staminode, or sterile stamen, is densely bearded as it is in many penstemons.

This charmer needs a fast-draining soil and once established is quite drought tolerant, blooming as it does during the summer dry season in California. New plants should be given regular water until established, and then a deep soaking once a month in the summertime will be all they need. They will grow in full sun to part shade, but will tend to be rather leggy in heavy shade. This appealing plant would make a handsome and useful addition to the summer hummingbird garden, in a perennial bed or informal mixed border where it can be permitted to ramble and twine through surrounding shrubs. Propagate by seed as with the true penstemons. Wait for seedpods to dry, pop them open where new plants are desired, and scratch in slightly.

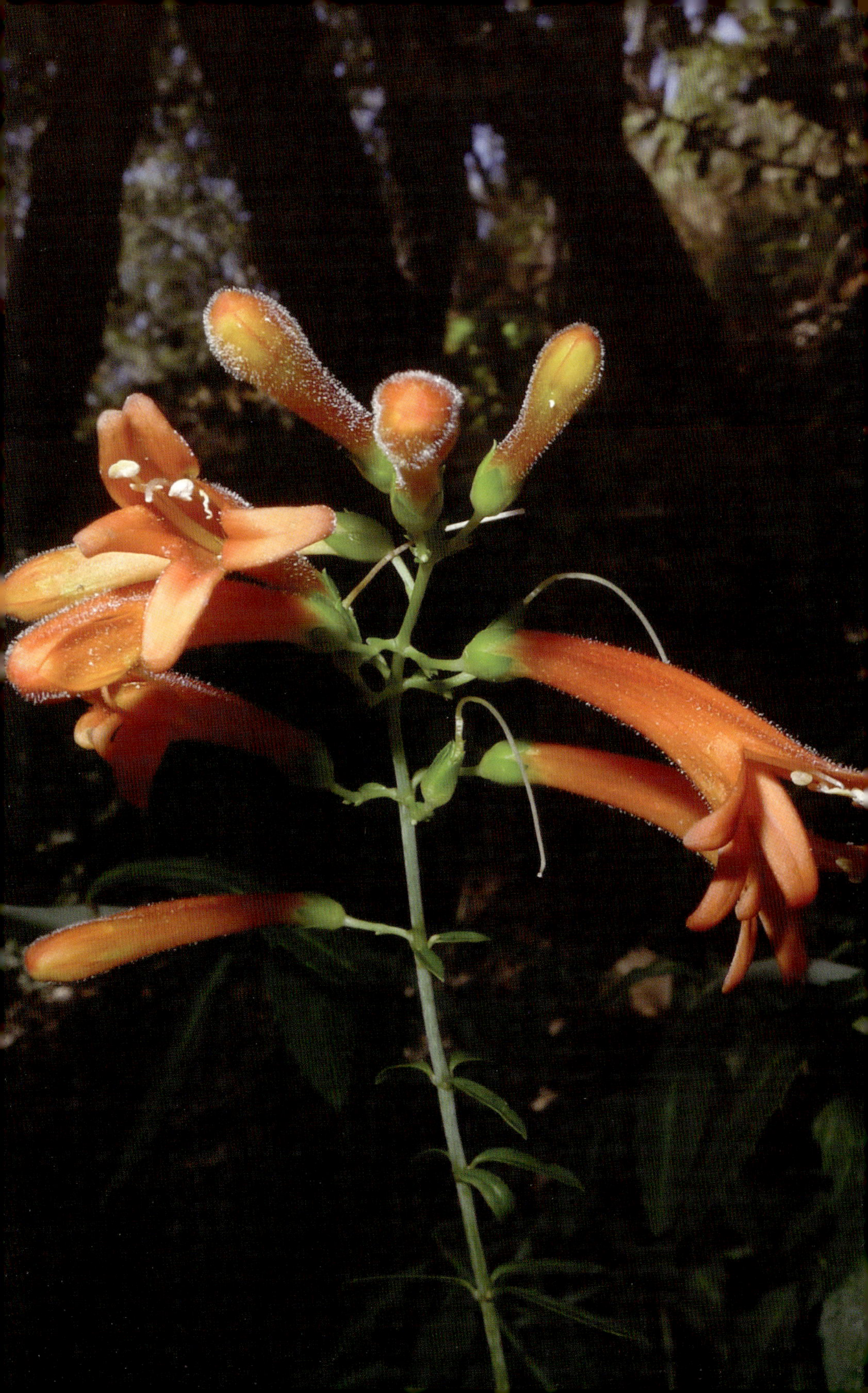

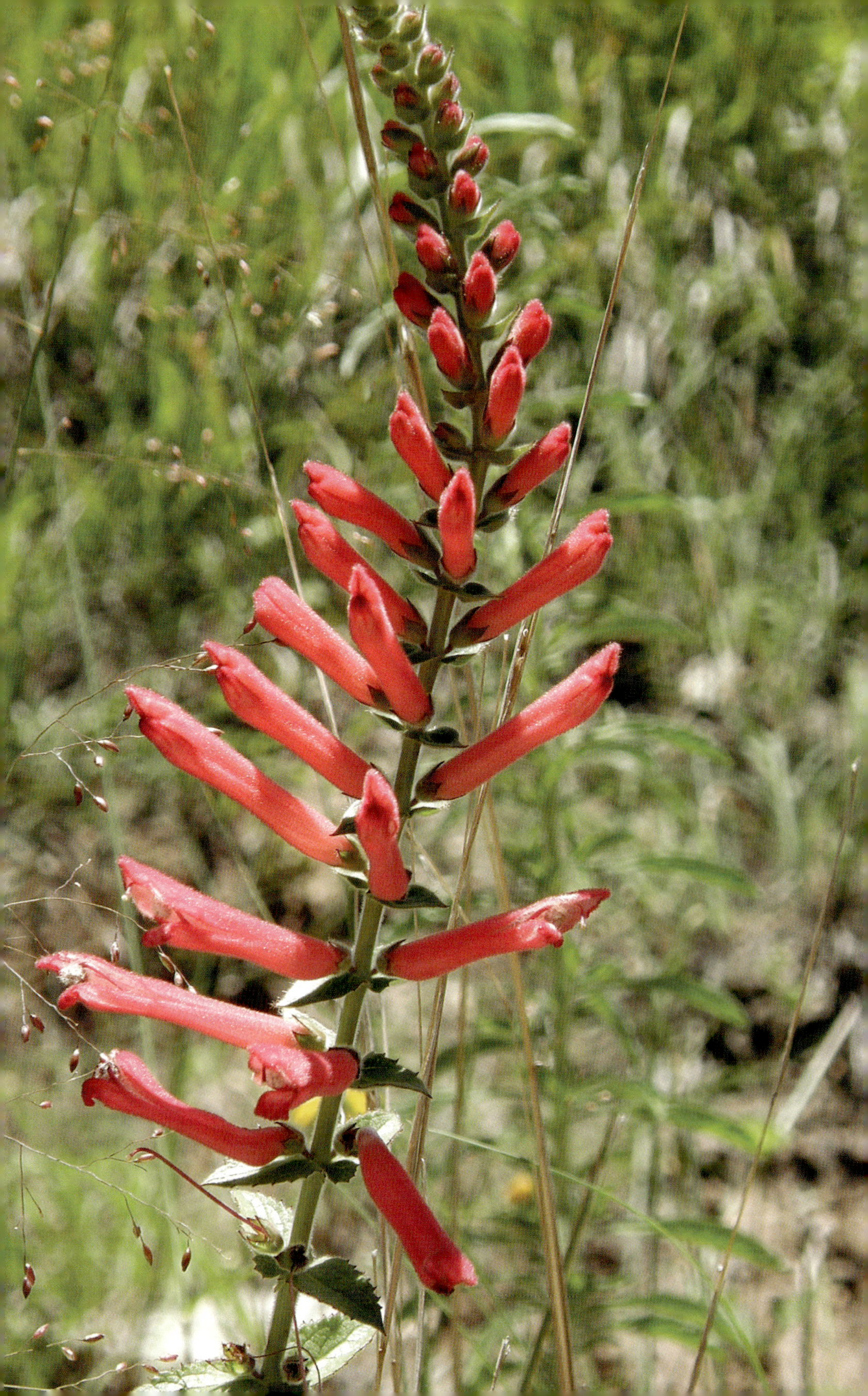

Lamourouxia viscosa

Najicoli, Chupamiel

Family:	Orobanchaceae (Scrophulariaceae)	**Bloom:**	Peak September–December, blooms most of year
Type:	Perennial	**Water use:**	Moderate
Size:	3–6' high x 2' wide	**Cold hardiness:**	To 20°F
		USDA zone:	9–11

Author citation: Kunth
Synonym: *Lamourouxia coccinea* A. Gray

This sumptuous, long-blooming beauty from Mexico and Central America is well used by resident hummingbirds throughout its range and likely visited by southwestern species passing through on their way to or from wintering grounds as well. Blue-throated and Magnificent Hummingbirds are both known to favor the rich rosy-pink tubular flowers, and they and other hummingbirds probably contribute significantly to pollination.

With an enormous native range, najicoli can be found as far northward as the Mexican border states of Sonora and Chihuahua, southward from there through the middle elevations of the Sierra Madre Occidental and Sierra Madre del Sur the entire length of Mexico, and continuing southward through Central America all the way to Panama. Found over a wide range of elevations, it is probably most commonly encountered between 3,000 and 6,000 feet but has been observed both higher and lower. Its many diverse habitats include pine-oak forests, open oak woodland, disturbed tropical deciduous forest, steep volcanic slopes, rocky canyons, road cuts, limestone outcrops, and grassy springs.

Typically solitary, its slender, erect, pinkish-tinged stems arise from a stout woody root and bear thick, prominently veined, lime green leaves that are lance-shaped, have toothed margins, and are pointed at the tips. The entire plant is covered with minute, sticky hairs, as the botanical name suggests. The pale pink to deep rose-colored flowers emerge from the upper leaf axils and are held horizontally, requiring hovering in order to access the nectar within. Interesting seed capsules, with a netlike covering concealing the numerous oblong seeds, develop as the blooms fade.

Despite its wide distribution in the wild and its showy blooms, najicoli presently does not seem to be known in cultivation and little to no information on its culture is available. A close cousin of this plant, *Lamourouxia longiflora,* occurs over a much smaller range (mainly Chihuahua and Durango), has deep red flowers that are likely to be primarily hummingbird-pollinated, and truly deserves a spot in this book were it not for the regrettable fact that even less is currently known about it than najicoli.

Lobelia cardinalis

Cardinal Flower, Scarlet Lobelia

Family:	Campanulaceae	**Water use:**	High
Type:	Perennial	**Cold hardiness:**	Roots to -34°F
Size:	2–4' high x 1–2' wide	**USDA zone:**	5–9
Bloom:	June–October, with water		

Author citation: Linneaus

This classic hummingbird flower is a staple of the Ruby-throated Hummingbird in the eastern United States, and in the scattered niches in which it occurs in the Southwest it is also well used by hummingbirds for both nectar and the insects attracted. Lucifer, Broad-tailed, Rufous, Black-chinned, White-eared, Costa's, and Anna's Hummingbirds have been known to visit the gorgeous crimson tubular blossoms and serve as important pollinators. Swallowtail and sulfur butterflies take nectar as well. Interestingly, biologists have found that some populations of this plant produce no nectar at all, their irresistible blooms apparently still successfully luring in enough hummingbirds for pollination to take place.

Cardinal flower has an extremely spotty distribution, with populations occurring in southeastern California, Nevada, southern Utah, Arizona, New Mexico, Texas, and southeastern Colorado, continuing eastward to the Atlantic Ocean and southward into northern and eastern Mexico. In the Southwest this beauty is confined exclusively to wet mountain habitats such as moist meadows, streambanks, canyon creek beds, springs, and seeps, at elevations of 3,000 to 7,500 feet. Its stout, erect, unbranched stems grow from a usually evergreen basal rosette anchored by a fleshy taproot. The glossy dark-green leaves are lance-shaped with toothed margins, those at the base up to six inches long and those alternating along the stem smaller. The exquisite flowers occur in a spike-like cluster at the top of the stem. Each is two-lipped, the lower with three spreading ovate lobes, and has a very slender corolla that is one-and-a-half inches long. With regular water, the blooms often continue through autumn, then producing round seedpods.

The need for nearly constant water cannot be overemphasized with this wetland indicator. In our region it prefers a moist, humous soil and part or dappled shade, and in cold winter areas appreciates an organic mulch. For a pond margin, woodland garden, or shady oasis planting, cardinal flower adds a breathtaking brush of red that is as red as red gets. Propagate by cold-stratified seed, cuttings, layering, or division of basal offshoots, and plant in groups for the most impact.

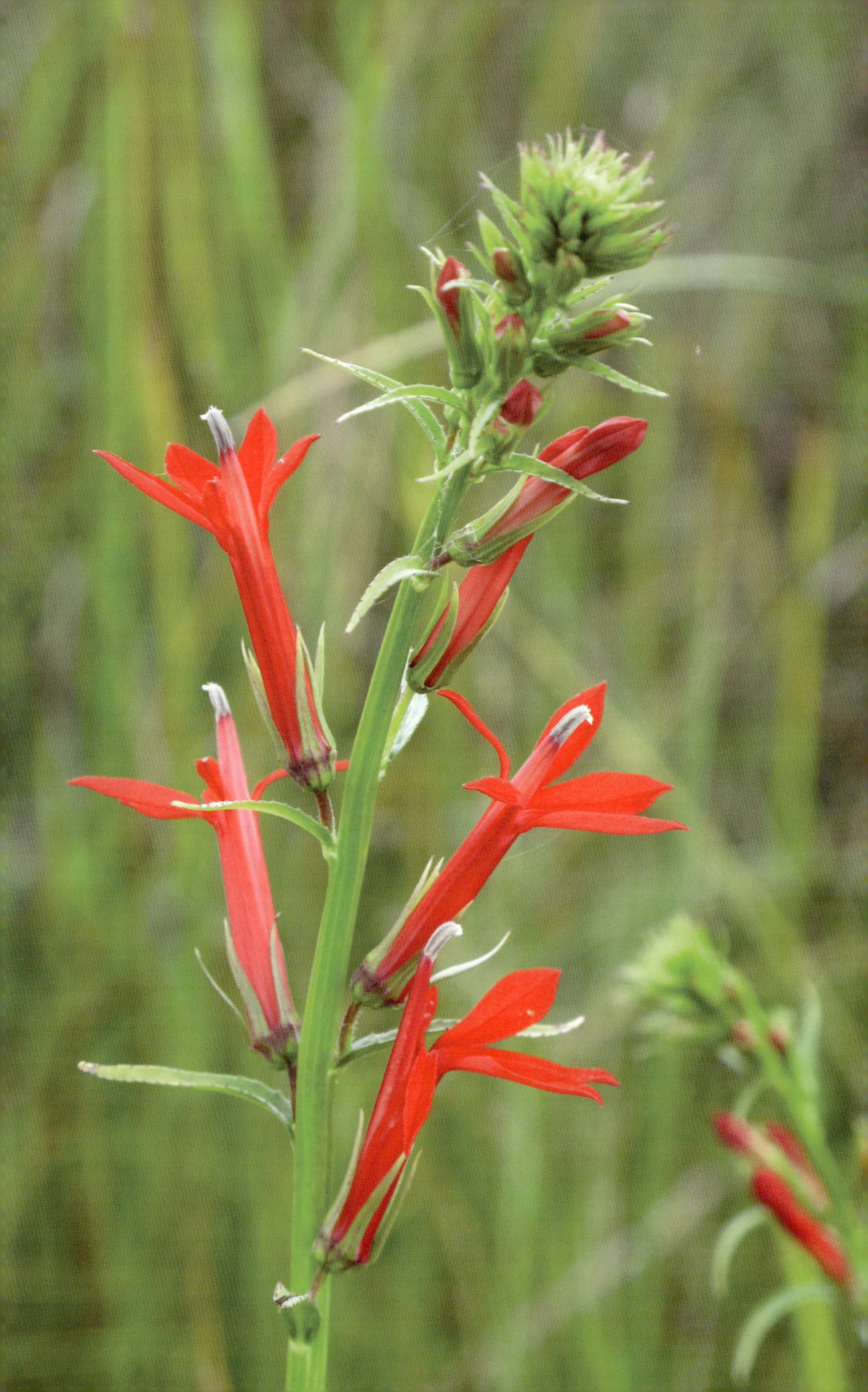

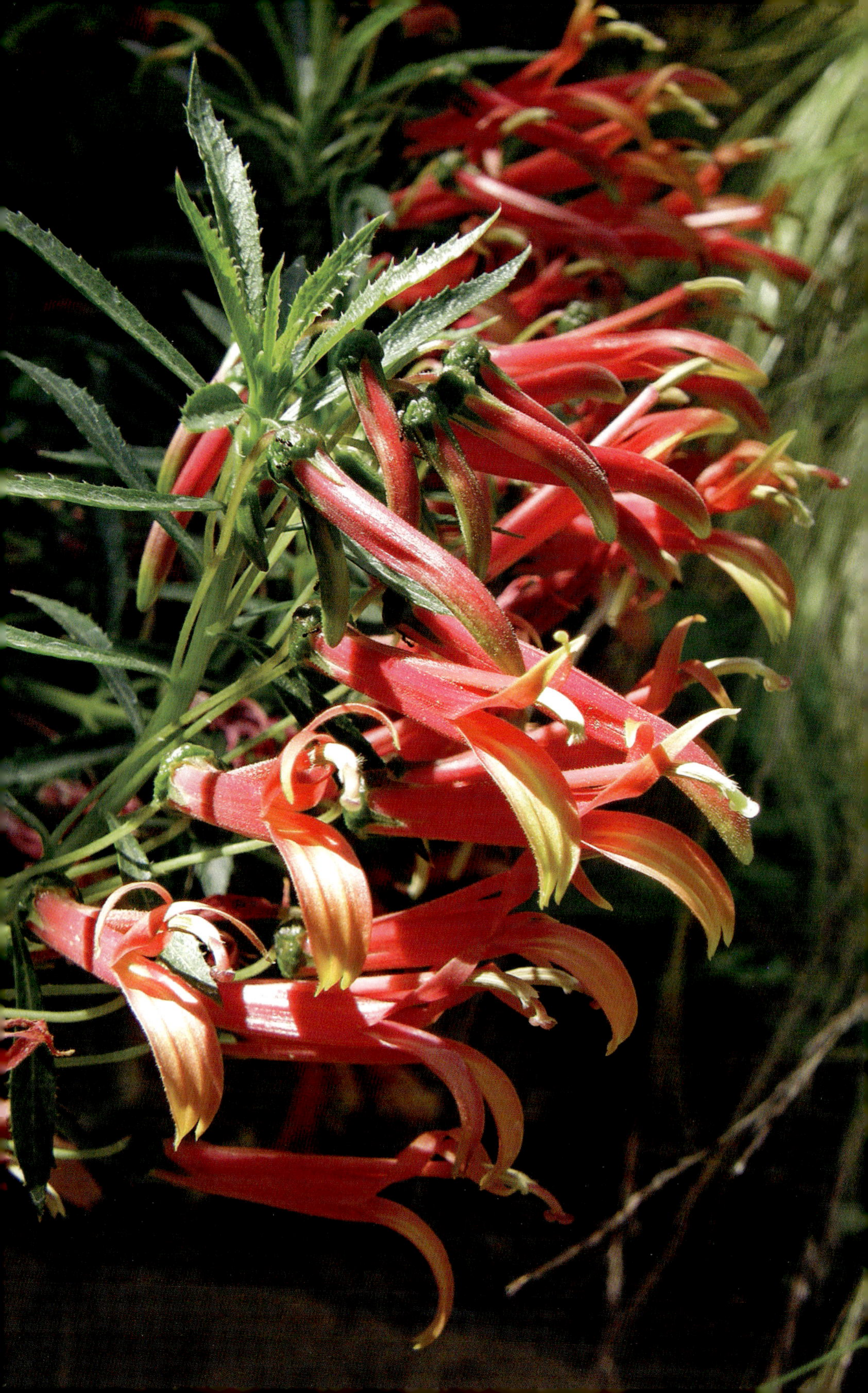

Lobelia laxiflora

Sierra Madre Lobelia, Loose-flowered Lobelia, Aretitos

Family:	Campanulaceae	**Water use:**	Moderate
Type:	Perennial	**Cold hardiness:**	Top to 25°F, roots to -10°F
Size:	2–3' high x 3–6' wide	**USDA zone:**	8–10
Bloom:	April–June, to September if deadheaded		

Author citation: Kunth

SIERRA MADRE LOBELIA IS A TERRIFIC PLANT FOR THE SPRING AND SUMMER hummingbird garden, in its native habitats beckoning Magnificent, Blue-throated, Broad-billed, Broad-tailed, Rufous, Black-chinned, and Lucifer Hummingbirds with its flashy, fire-engine-red tubular blooms. Xantus's Hummingbirds in Baja California also take nectar from the flowers, and Anna's and Allen's Hummingbirds are known to visit garden plantings. Hummingbirds appear to be the plant's chief pollinators.

Occurring in the United States only in southern Arizona in Santa Cruz County and ranging southward through the Sierra Madre Occidental to Colima and Oaxaca in central Mexico, this attractive perennial can be found in dry washes and canyon bottoms, on rocky slopes, and in pine-oak forests at elevations of 3,500 to 8,000 feet. Its erect, fleshy, often purplish stems originate from creeping underground roots, and if left to its own devices the plant will sprawl considerably, occasionally even becoming invasive in some situations. The shiny bright green, narrow, lance-shaped leaves are evergreen in mild climates. The one-and-a-half-inch flowers, which range from red-orange to bright red with yellow-tipped lobes and yellow throats, are festooned with fuzzy white anthers and occur in loose clusters.

In the landscape, bright or partial shade is preferred—even deep shade at the lower elevations—along with moderately rich, well-drained soil. A thick layer of organic mulch will help to keep the roots cool and moist in summer and warm and cozy in winter. Sierra Madre lobelia is fairly drought tolerant and puts up with considerable neglect but looks best if deep watered two or three times a month during the hot summer months. The bloom season can easily be extended into early fall by deadheading spent flowers; any necessary pruning of stems should be performed in late autumn. This is a delightful easy-care plant for a simulated dry wash or desert garden oasis, especially for low-desert areas. It also works well in a small swale that it can spread to fill, under the filtered shade of a palo verde or other small tree. Propagation is fairly easy by seed, stem cuttings, or division of rootstocks after flowering ceases.

Loeselia mexicana

Espinosilla, Hierba de la Virgen, Mexican False Calico

Family:	Polemoniaceae	**Water use:**	Moderate
Type:	Evergreen subshrub	**Cold hardiness:**	To 25°F
Size:	3–5' high x 2–4' wide	**USDA zone:**	9–11
Bloom:	August–December or longer		

Author citation: (Lamarck) Brand
Synonyms: *Loeselia coccinea* (Cav.) G. Don; *Hoitzia coccinea* Cavanilles

THIS BEGUILING BEAUTY FROM MEXICO, with its lovely scarlet blooms tailor-made for hummingbirds, enjoys an enormous natural range and provides valuable nectar over an unusually long season, making it doubly significant to a variety of hummingbird species. In central Mexico espinosilla commonly flowers later and longer than do northern populations, often continuing through the entire winter. Lucifer, Rufous, and White-eared Hummingbirds have been observed at the flowers but doubtless additional southwestern species partake of the nectar too. Hummingbirds are the primary pollinators.

Ranging throughout the Sierra Madre Occidental and Sierra Madre del Sur, espinosilla occurs from Sonora, Chihuahua, and Durango southward as far as Chiapas, most often at the middle elevations between 4,000 and 8,000 feet. Favored habitats include oak and pine-oak woodlands, juniper stands, mixed pine-hardwood semitropical forests, rocky canyons, cliff ledges, volcanic hills, old fields, and desert scrublands.

Its erect, branching, hairy stems arise from a woody base and bear narrow lance-shaped sage-green leaves with pointed tips and coarsely toothed margins. Emerging from the leaf axils near stem tips and held horizontally, the inch-long tubular blossoms, scarlet red with fine white markings in the throat, have five flaring lobes and are surrounded by dense clusters of spiny green bracts. A yellow-flowering form has been described near Mexico City. Small round three-celled capsules containing two to five winged seeds each follow the flowers. Espinosilla is reported to have a wide variety of medicinal properties, including hair loss prevention, and can be used as a soap substitute as well, by crushing the plant in water until suds form.

North of its native haunts, this beauty is suited only for locations that enjoy mild winters with little to no frost, but where appropriate it would make a colorful backdrop to a fall hummingbird garden. Full sun to part shade, good drainage, and regular water until established and as needed afterward are suggested. Plants can reportedly be propagated either by seed or by stem cuttings taken in late spring.

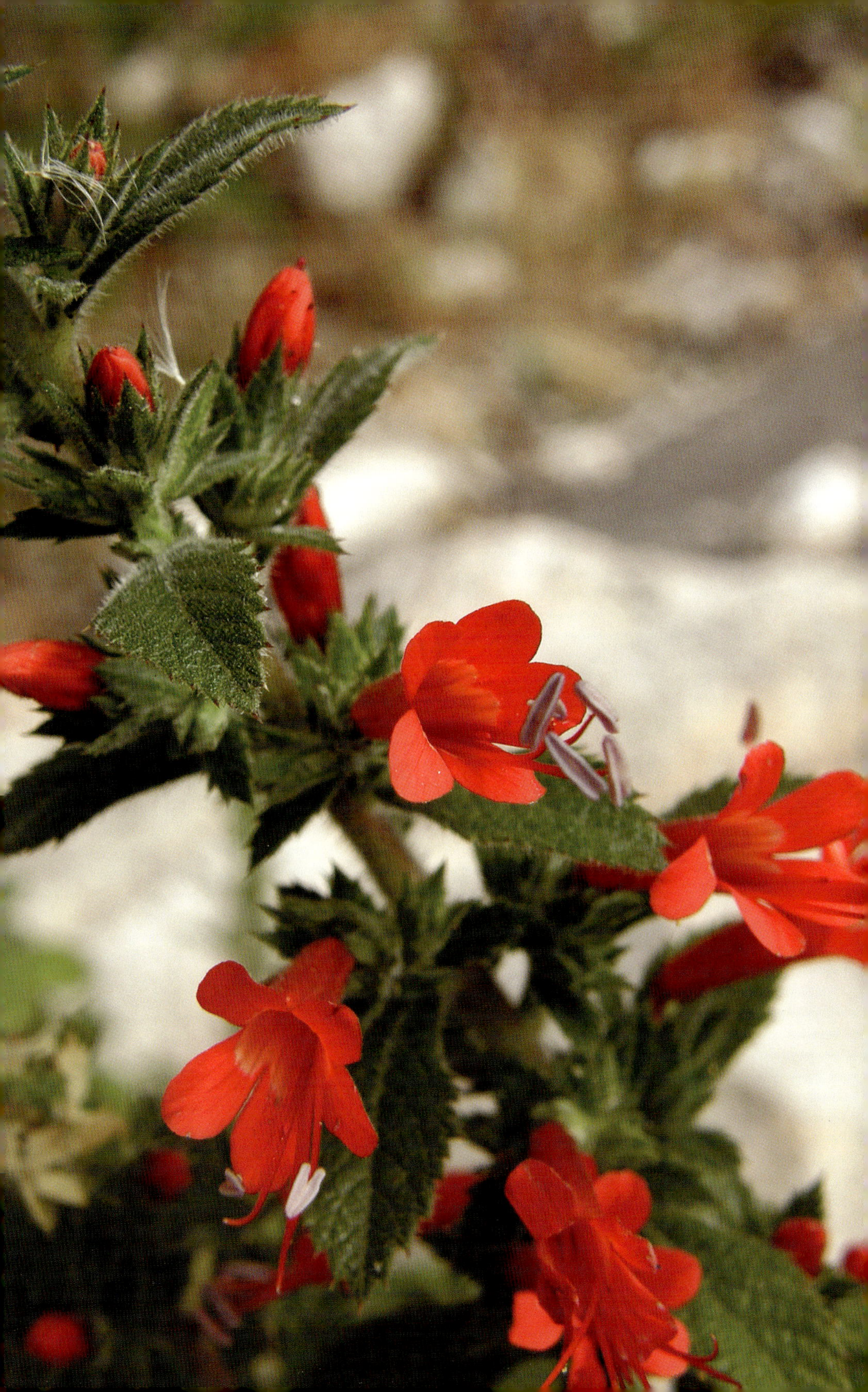

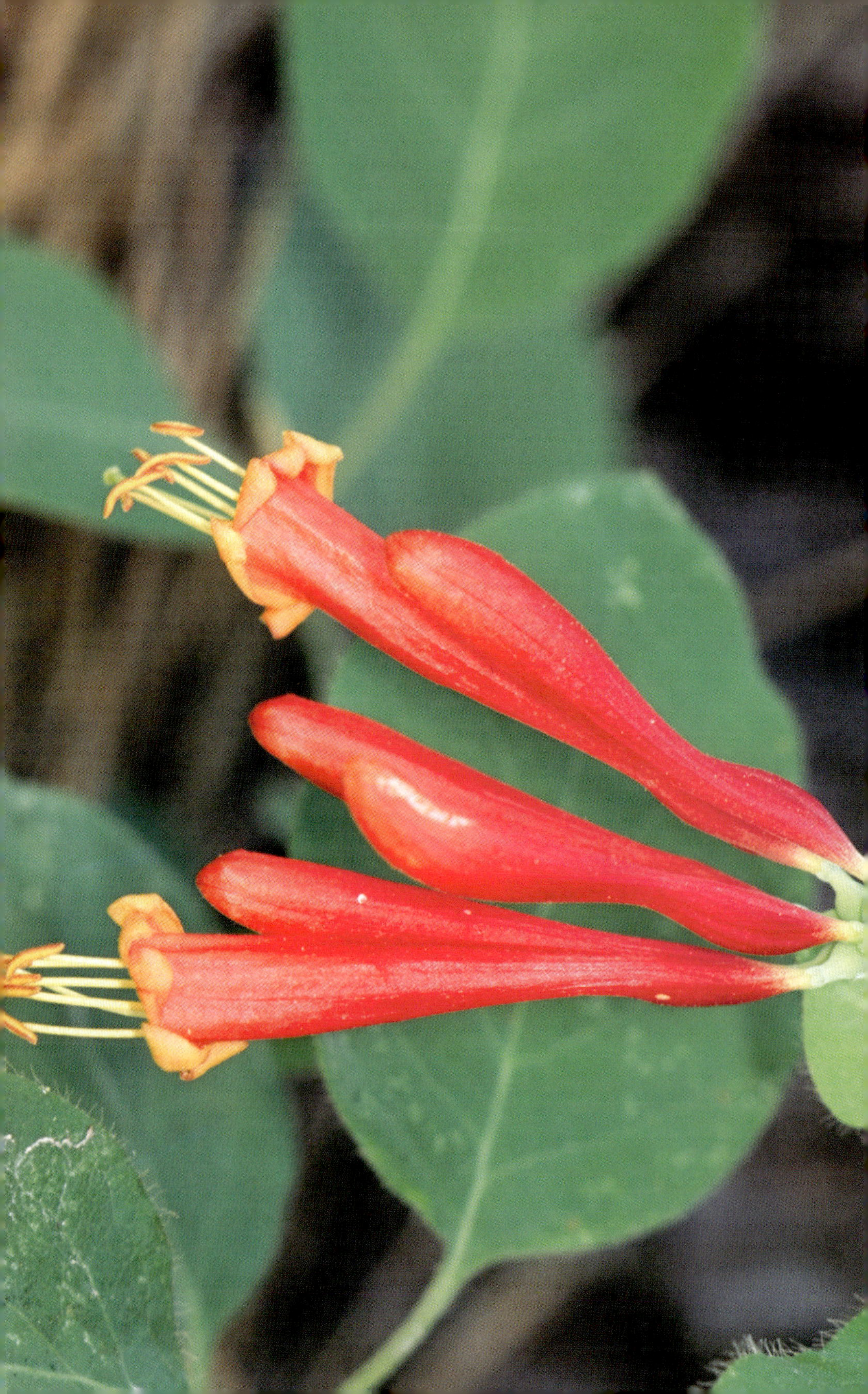

Lonicera arizonica

Arizona Honeysuckle, Madreselva

Family:	Caprifoliaceae	**Water use:**	Moderate
Type:	Deciduous vine or shrub	**Cold hardiness:**	Roots to -10°F
Size:	2–10' high	**USDA zone:**	6–9
Bloom:	May–July, sporadically through summer		

Author citation: Rehder

THIS CLAMBERING VINE IS QUITE SIMILAR TO BOTH ITS EASTERN COUSIN, coral honeysuckle (*L. sempervirens*), and a cousin from the Pacific Northwest, orange honeysuckle (*L. ciliosa*). Its showy tubular blossoms, coral red with orange throats, are avidly visited by Broad-tailed Hummingbirds and occasionally Broad-billed, Black-chinned, and Costa's Hummingbirds as well. No doubt other species use it too, for hummingbirds play the lead role in the plant's pollination. Orioles are also known to avail themselves of the sucrose-rich nectar. The round, bright red berries that ripen in autumn are relished by many small mammals and a variety of birds, including Hermit Thrushes, American Robins, Western and Mountain Bluebirds, Mountain Chickadees, and Spotted Towhees.

Arizona Honeysuckle is largely an Arizona native, occurring in most of the state save the westernmost counties, but it also ranges into western and south-central New Mexico, the Guadalupe Mountains that spill into western Texas, and Chihuahua in northern Mexico. It is typically found growing along streams or in open coniferous forests in the mountains, at elevations of 6,000 to 9,000 feet. This rather stiff, woody vine, sometimes shrubby but more often twining over shrubs and up the trunks of trees, has grayish young stems and stringy brown bark when mature. Like those of most honeysuckles, the leaves occur in opposite pairs along the stems. They are bright green, smooth, and ovate, with a fringe of tiny hairs on the margins. The eye-catching flowers are borne in whorled clusters at stem tips.

Arizona honeysuckle seems to be somewhat tricky to grow and difficult to find in the nursery trade. It needs a well-drained soil and will grow in either full sun to part shade, but it tends to languish in hot locations regardless. A deep soaking once or twice a month during the summer is recommended for best appearance and continual flowering. Propagate by seed that has been stratified for one to two months or by softwood or semi-hardwood cuttings. This handsome vine would seem to be ideal for growing on walls, arbors, and fences, or trailing over shrubs in a naturalistic wildlife garden. Hopefully in the future this native beauty will be more widely available.

Lonicera involucrata

Twinberry Honeysuckle, Twinflower, Bearberry Honeysuckle

Family:	Caprifoliaceae	**Water use:**	Moderate–high
Type:	Deciduous shrub	**Cold hardiness:**	Roots to -30°F
Size:	3–8' high x 3–5' wide	**USDA zone:**	4–9
Bloom:	March–May in south, June–July in north		

Author citation: (Richardson) Banks ex Sprengel

THIS IS ANOTHER NATIVE HONEYSUCKLE THAT IS AN EXCELLENT SOURCE of high-sucrose nectar in the springtime. Its fuzzy yellow funnel-shaped flowers, often tinged with red and framed by green to reddish-purple bracts, are known to be visited by Blue-throated, Magnificent, Broad-tailed, Rufous, and Anna's Hummingbirds. A California cousin, Ledebour's honeysuckle (var. *ledebourii*), is a variety of this species that is pollinated entirely by Allen's Hummingbirds along the Pacific Coast. Both produce purplish-black berries in late summer that are relished by numerous songbirds, including American Robins, Townsend's Solitaires, Cedar Waxwings, Wrentits, and several thrasher species. Chipmunks and bears also consume the fruits.

Twinberry honeysuckle ranges from northern and eastern Arizona into central and northern New Mexico as far eastward as the Sangre de Cristo Mountains, north through parts of Colorado, Utah, Nevada, and central and northern California, and northward into Canada. It occurs strictly in moist montane habitats, including open pine and mixed coniferous forests, canyon bottoms, wet meadows, and streamsides at elevations of 6,000 to 10,000 feet.

Growing either singly or in thickets, its upright shrubby form is often vine-like and the exfoliating bark on older stems is distinctive. The large, bright green leaves have hairy margins and occur in opposite pairs along the stem. Flowers, and later the berries as well, occur in pairs on long stems in the leaf axils and are encircled (or involucred) by large leaf-like bracts that turn deep red and showcase the maturing fruits.

This upland dweller prefers a moist, well-drained soil and protection from hot mid-afternoon sun. A deep soaking twice a month in the summer and once a month the rest of the year should keep it looking its best. Twinberry honeysuckle is definitely not appropriate for hot, low-desert locations, but given the right niche is perfect for informal hedges, mixed shrub borders, and wildlife habitat gardens. If you prefer it to grow as a vine, give young plants a support to climb. Propagate by young stem or hardwood cuttings, root division, or cold-stratified seed. Note that the berries of this honeysuckle may be mildly toxic to humans.

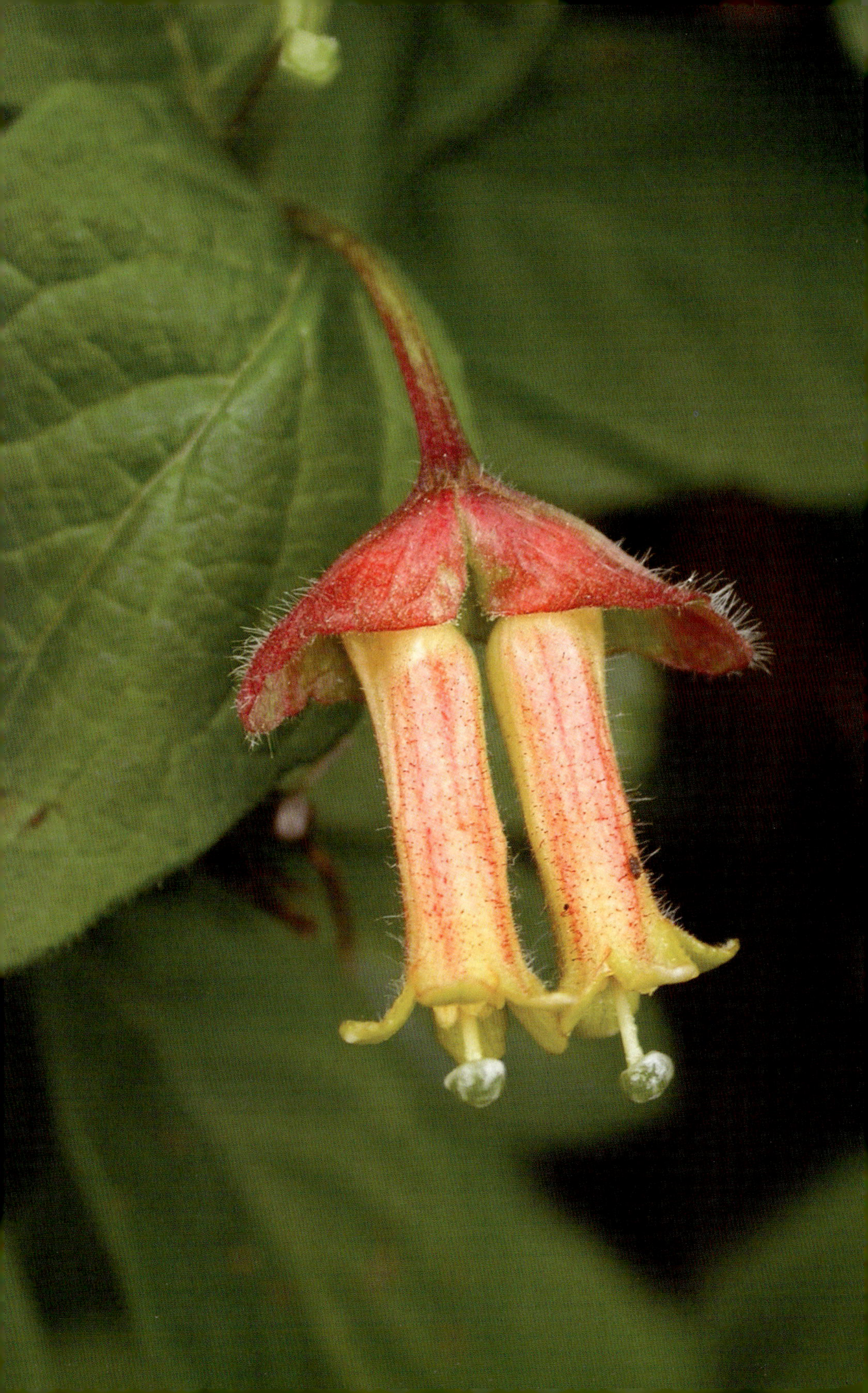

Family:	Solanaceae	**Water use:**	Low–moderate
Type:	Deciduous shrub	**Cold hardiness:**	To -10°F (*pallidum*),
Size:	6' high x 6' wide		10°F (others)
Bloom:	January–April (*exsertum, parishii*), February–May (others)	**USDA zone:**	6–10 (*pallidum*), 7–10 (others)

Author citation: Lycium andersonii A. Gray
　　　　　　　　Lycium exsertum A. Gray
　　　　　　　　Lycium pallidum Miers
　　　　　　　　Lycium parishii A. Gray

Lycium species
Wolfberry, Thornbush, Waterjacket, Cacaculo, Frutilla

It may come as a surprise that wolfberries, which are bee-pollinated members of the nightshade family, are used by hummingbirds, but nearly all of them provide nectar at times when other flowering plants are scarce. Parish's thornbush (*Lycium parishii*) is of tremendous importance to wintering Costa's Hummingbirds, for its tiny lavender flowers begin appearing quite early, usually by January, and are a primary midwinter nectar source in some parts of the bird's range. Arizona thornbush (*L. exsertum*) and Anderson's thornbush (*L. andersonii*) are also particularly important to Costa's Hummingbirds, who seek out their creamy white to pale purplish flowers in late winter, and they are visited by Broad-billed and returning Black-chinned Hummingbirds as well. The greenish-white, lavender-tinged blossoms of pale wolfberry (*L. pallidum*) often draw Black-chinned or Costa's Hummingbirds in early spring. All these thorny shrubs provide choice fruits along with useful cover and nest sites for a variety of birds.

Both Anderson's thornbush and Parish's thornbush are denizens of the Sonoran and Mojave/Colorado deserts, occurring in southern California, southern Nevada, Arizona, and Sonora in Mexico; Anderson's thornbush also occurs northward into Utah on the Colorado Plateau and southward in Mexico to Sinaloa. Arizona thornbush has a much more limited range in western and southern Arizona and southward in Mexico from Baja California and Sonora south to northern Sinaloa. With the largest distribution, pale wolfberry occurs from southeastern California through most of Arizona, southern Nevada, Utah, and Colorado, much of New Mexico, and western Texas, and southward into Mexico to Zacatecas. Their preferred habitats are all quite similar, and include desert washes, rocky slopes, and dry plains of the lower elevations, often in the company of ironwoods, palo verdes, or mesquites.

In the landscape, these dense, fast-growing shrubs favor a sunny exposure, sandy or gravelly soils, adequate drainage, and a hands-off approach to pruning, which butchers their carefree form. Once established, they require no supplemental water, but a deep soaking during extended dry periods will prevent leaf drop. Plants can be easily propagated by fresh seed, by gently dividing suckers in early spring, or by rooting semi-hardwood cuttings taken in late summer in moist sand or vermiculite. All wolfberries are terrific for security barriers, erosion control on slopes, and desert habitat gardens.

Mandevilla foliosa

Hierba del Piojo, Chupil, Hierba de la Cucaracha

Family:	Apocynaceae	**Water use:**	Moderate
Type:	Subshrub	**Cold hardiness:**	To -20°F
Size:	3–6' high x 3–6' wide	**USDA zone:**	9–11
Bloom:	June–August or longer		

Author citation: (Müller Argoviensis) Hemsley
Synonym: *Mandevilla foliosa* Hemsl.

FIELD RESEARCHERS FROM THE ARIZONA-SONORA DESERT MUSEUM report that this handsome Mexican plant is the most common flowering shrub that attracts hummingbirds in the Sierra Madrean barrancas of Sonora and western Chihuahua. Though not dependent upon hummingbirds for pollination (bees are likely the primary pollinators), its wide distribution makes it a highly dependable summer nectar source. The pretty yellow pinwheel blooms are especially important to migrating Rufous Hummingbirds in late summer and are known to be visited by Broad-billed, Black-chinned, Berylline, Violet-crowned, and White-eared Hummingbirds as well.

Occurring in Sonora and Chihuahua and southward through the Sierra Madre Occidental and Sierra Madre del Sur to Durango, Sinaloa, Jalisco, Michoacán, and Guerrero, hierba del piojo is chiefly a lower to middle elevation plant, found as low as 500 feet at Batopilas to as high as 6,500 feet in Zacatecas. Its varied habitats include oak and pine-oak woodlands, piñon-juniper woodlands, rock outcrops, canyon slopes, foothill grasslands, and tropical deciduous forest.

Rounded and bushy in form, its upright, branching stems bear densely clustered whorls of bright-green, oval-shaped leaves that are two to six inches long, prominently veined, and pointed at the tips. The sweetly scented, cheery flowers, each with five twisted tubular petals about a half-inch long and ruffled at the edges, form in clusters in the leaf axils. When mature the seeds are reddish brown and sport a tuft of creamy white hairs. Hierba del piojo (translated as "herb of the louse") is reportedly harvested and used to make an insecticide to kill lice and cockroaches.

Although not presently known in the nursery trade, this appealing shrub merits consideration for the landscape, especially in upland locations where winters are mild and mainly frost-free. If seeds can be obtained, the best results will likely be had planting on a partly shaded site with good drainage and providing regular water until established and as needed thereafter. The sunny yellow flowers would make a lovely foil for the many reds so prevalent in the typical hummingbird garden, and are certain to be welcomed by summering and migrating hummingbirds.

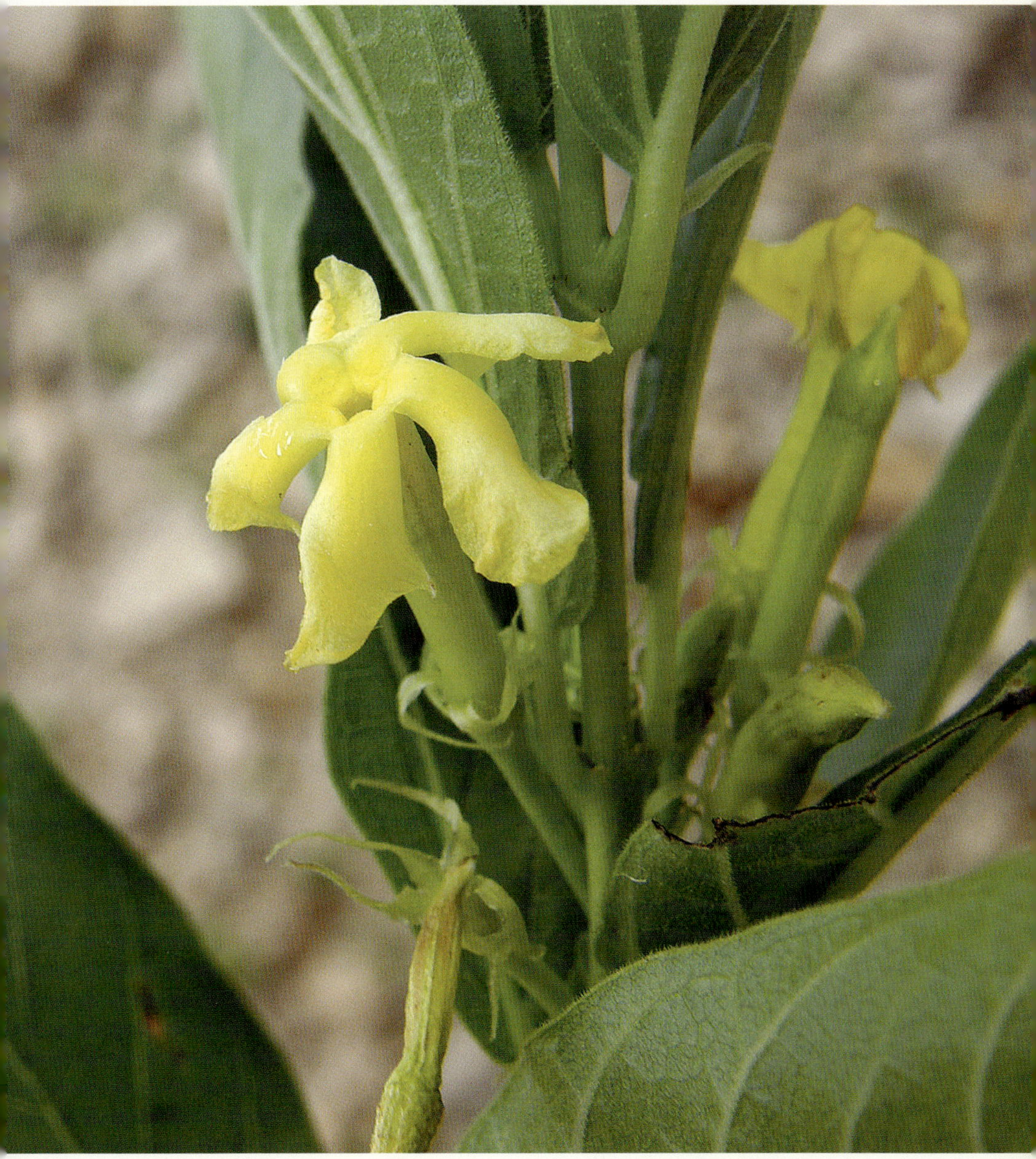

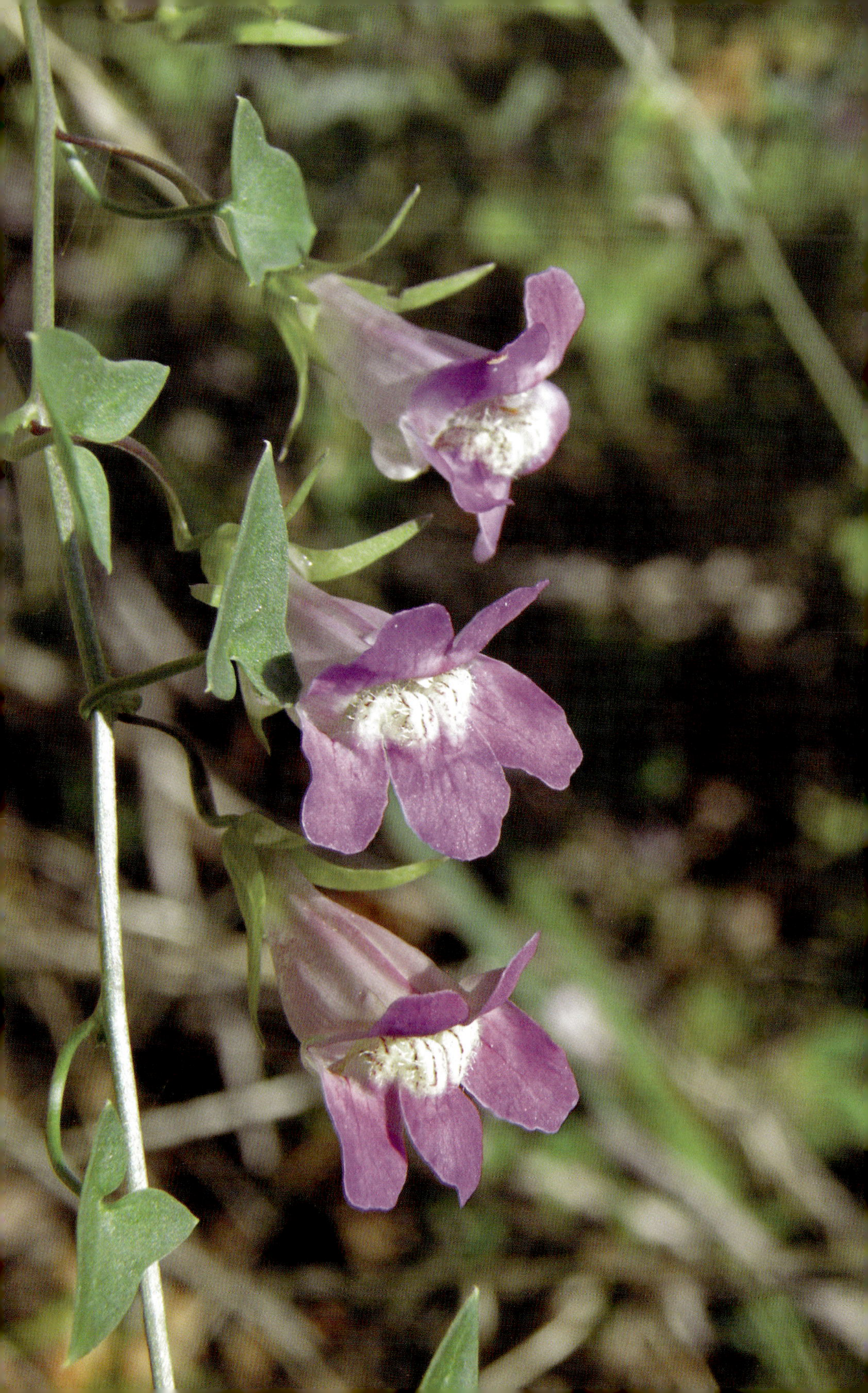

Maurandella antirrhiniflora
Snapdragon Vine, Twining Snapdragon, Roving Sailor

Family:	Plantaginaceae (Scrophulariaceae)	**Bloom:**	May–September, with rainfall or irrigation
Type:	Perennial vine	**Water use:**	Moderate
Size:	8–10' high with support, 3' high without	**Cold hardiness:**	Top to 20°F, roots to 10°F
		USDA zone:	8–10

Author citation: (Humb. & Bonpl. ex Willd.) Rothmaler
Synonym: *Maurandya antirrhiniflora* Humboldt & Bonpland ex Willdenow

Even if it didn't appeal to hummingbirds, this delightful vine merits a spot along some fence or wall in the garden for its unique snapdragon-like flowers that appear all summer long. The purplish-blue or wine-red blossoms—the former typical in Texas, the latter more common in Arizona—have creamy yellow tufts in their throats and are often visited by Black-chinned, Broad-tailed, Magnificent, and Lucifer Hummingbirds, along with their more important pollinators, the bees. The plant is both a nectar source and larval host for the buckeye butterfly.

Snapdragon vine can be found twining along most any watercourse or wooded canyon in the Southwest, its range extending from southeastern California through southern Nevada and southwestern Utah, south through Arizona, New Mexico, and southwestern Texas, and southward to central Mexico. Occurring over a broad elevation range, from 800 to 7,000 feet, it occurs on dunes and bluffs, on limestone foothills, among piñon-juniper stands, and at coniferous forest edges. Look for it to be hugging whatever vegetation is nearby, its slender wiry stems tangling with anything they contact and forming dense mats of foliage.

The deep green leaves, on twisting and curling petioles, are about an inch long and narrowly arrow-shaped. In late spring, plants begin presenting their elegant one-inch flowers, which are borne over a long period. Each is two-lipped, both lips lobed and bent outward, with a cream-colored patch of hair at the base of the lower lip. In winter the entire top freezes back, but even in cold climates plants usually self-sow readily.

This is an easy-to-grow vine that will in one season climb and bloom on whatever support it is given, whether trellis, fence, or shrub. Sandy or gravelly limestone soils are preferred, but plants are fairly tolerant as long as drainage is good, even doing well in salty soils. They will grow in full sun to part or dappled shade, but do like their roots cool. For continual bloom they should be watered two or three times a month during the summer. Propagation is easy by seed and requires no pre-treatment. This delicate beauty should be placed near a walkway or entryway for up-close enjoyment. It can be tucked into a rock crevice or allowed to spill its charms over a hanging basket.

Mimulus cardinalis

Scarlet Monkeyflower, Cardinal Monkeyflower

Family:	Phrymaceae (Scrophulariaceae)	**Bloom:**	April–October, especially June–August
Type:	Perennial	**Water use:**	Moderate–high
Size:	2' high x 3' wide	**Cold hardiness:**	Roots to -28°F
		USDA zone:	5–10

Author citation: Douglas ex Bentham
Synonym: *Diplacus cardinalis* (Douglas ex Benth.) Groenland

This long-blooming plant is a beacon for both breeding and migrating hummingbirds. Its lavish scarlet blossoms are avidly visited by Anna's, Allen's, and Blue-throated Hummingbirds, and to a lesser extent Costa's and Rufous Hummingbirds. Where cultivated in gardens, the flowers are likely to be popular with other species as well, but hummingbirds are the chief pollinators. Carpenter bees are known to slit the blooms at the base to access the high-sucrose nectar. The foliage hosts the larvae of buckeye and checkerspot butterflies.

Scarlet monkeyflower is native to coastal and interior mountains and forest openings across a broad geographic area, from California and southwestern Oregon eastward through parts of Nevada and southwestern Utah, with scattered populations southward through Arizona and southwestern New Mexico into northwestern Mexico. Occurring at elevations of 1,800 to over 8,000 feet, it is usually a denizen of damp shady places, including spring margins, seeps, caves, hanging gardens, and streambanks, where its floppy stems of bright green, sticky, coarsely toothed leaves are distinctive and pop out of the shadows. Flowering peaks in the summer, but blossoms occur intermittently from spring through fall, and in late summer it may be one of the only hummingbird plants in bloom. The one-inch tubular flowers have two lips, the upper pointing straight up and the lower swept backward and thus discouraging insects from attempting to steal the nectar.

Preferring sandy or loamy soil with a neutral pH, this handsome perennial is usually happiest in bright or filtered shade—even deep shade in very hot locations. It performs best when its roots are constantly moist, and it is not at all drought tolerant. The lengthy bloom time can be prolonged even further by cutting back spent flower stalks. Scarlet monkeyflower tends to be a short-lived plant, particularly when coaxed to maximize its bloom, but well worth planting in a desert garden oasis. It combines nicely with golden columbine (*Aquilegia chrysantha*) in shady plantings around water features. Plants reseed freely, with the two-sided seedpods appearing about three weeks after flowering ceases. Propagate by seed, cuttings rooted in moist sand, or root division.

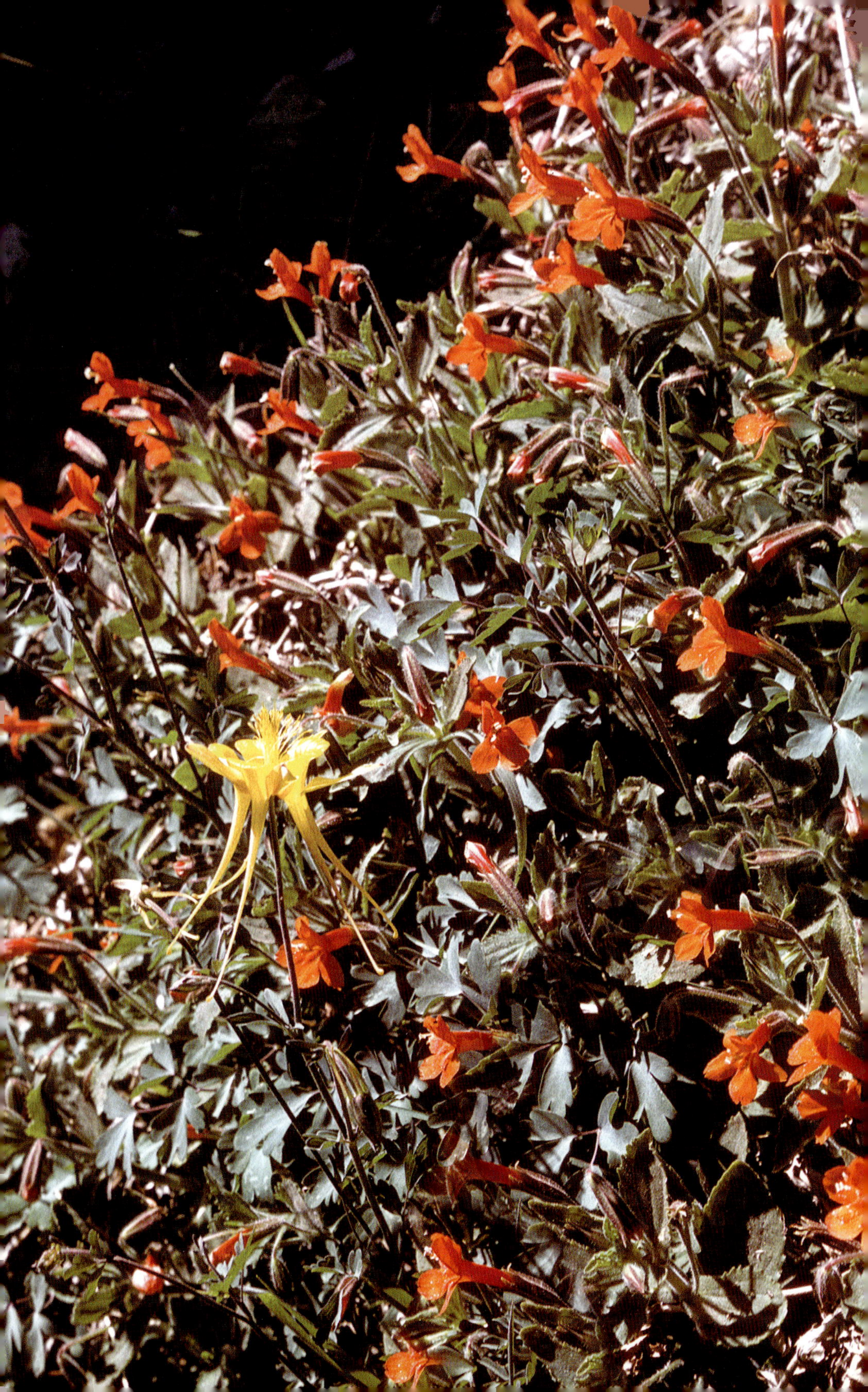

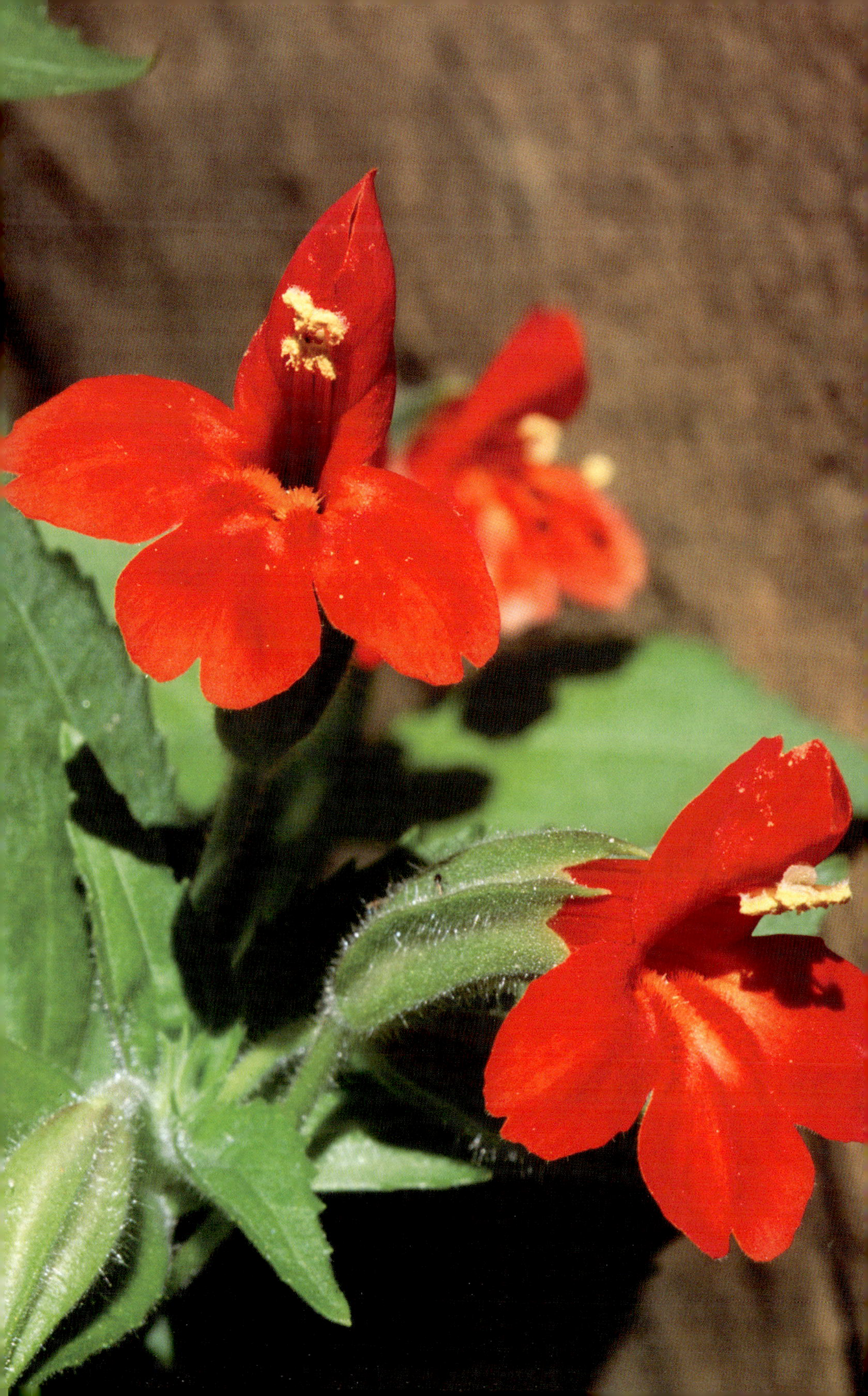

Mimulus eastwoodiae

Eastwood's Monkeyflower

Family:	Phrymaceae (Scrophulariaceae)	**Bloom:**	June–September
		Water use:	Moderate
Type:	Perennial	**Cold hardiness:**	Roots to -20°F
Size:	1–1.5' high x 2' wide	**USDA zone:**	5–8

Author citation: Rydberg

THE RICH RED-ORANGE FLOWERS OF THIS STRIKING MONKEYFLOWER crank out nectar all summer long and are pollinated at least in part by hummingbirds. Broad-tailed Hummingbirds likely are the most attendant species, but other species such as Rufous and Calliope Hummingbirds on their southward migration in late summer no doubt take advantage of the blossoms as well.

Eastwood's monkeyflower is quite rare in portions of its limited range, occurring in high desert habitats of the Colorado Plateau in the Four Corners region of northern Arizona, northwestern New Mexico, southeastern Utah, and southwestern Colorado; small populations exist in southern Arizona as well. Occasionally encountered by hikers at Grand Canyon, Arches, and Canyonlands national parks, its favored haunts include shady rock crevices in canyon walls, or hanging gardens as they are sometimes picturesquely described, springs, streamsides, and sandstone cave seeps at elevations of 3,000 to over 6,000 feet.

Spreading by rhizomes and frequently forming large mats, the stems bear bright green, opposite, unstalked leaves, those at the base scallop-edged and those on upper stems oblong or elliptical, deeply veined, and coarsely toothed. The tubular flowers, with upper lips that project straight outward, flaring one-inch corollas, and protruding butter-yellow or white stamens, are nestled in a five-pointed calyx that after drying and turning brown may persist through the winter. Two-chambered seed capsules form after flowering ceases.

This beauty is a shade and moisture lover and not at all suitable for the intense heat of most desert landscapes, even with regular water. It is said to prefer a gravelly, humous soil and often occurs on sandstone cliffs. A deep soaking twice a month during the growing season is recommended, particularly during periods of drought. If seeds or potted plants can be located from a specialty grower in the region this pretty perennial might do beautifully in a cool upland garden, gracing a water feature or tucked into a shady nook between large boulders. It is certain to be noticed and used by any hummingbirds summering in the vicinity. Reportedly plants can be propagated by seed, stem cuttings taken in late summer, or root division.

Mirabilis coccinea

Red Four-o'clock, Red Umbrellawort, Scarlet Four-o'clock

Family:	Nyctaginaceae	**Water use:**	Low–moderate
Type:	Perennial	**Cold hardiness:**	Roots to 5–10°F
Size:	1–3' high x 1' wide	**USDA zone:**	7–10
Bloom:	May–September		

Author citation: (Torrey) Bentham & Hooker f.
Synonyms: *Oxybaphus coccineus* Torrey; *Allionia coccinea* (Torr.) Standley

The rather spindly form of this plant certainly will not make or break a landscape, but its carmine to purplish-red flowers appear over a lengthy bloom season and offer nectar to both breeding and migrating hummingbirds, who return the favor by playing at least a supporting role in pollination. Sphinx moths are likely the chief pollinators.

Red four-o'clock ranges over the southern portion of our region, from the Mojave Desert of southeast California, where it is rare and occurs only in far eastern San Bernardino County, east through the southern tip of Nevada, central and southern Arizona, and southwestern New Mexico, and southward into Sonora in northwestern Mexico. It can be found on dry rocky hillsides or brushy slopes, in piñon-juniper or ponderosa pine woodlands, and along seasonal washes or sycamore-lined streams, typically at middle elevations of 3,500 to 6,500 feet but occasionally as high as 8,900 feet.

Unlike many of its cousins that tend to be spreading and bushy, this four-o'clock is upright and lanky, with narrow leaves to three inches long in widely spaced opposite pairs along the stems. When the plant blooms, it makes up for its gangly form. The appealing half- to three-quarter-inch blossoms, occurring in small clusters, are funnel-shaped with extremely long stamens and a gradually narrowing tube like that of a classic salvia. Unfortunately, the blooms are rather short-lived and curl up shortly after they unfurl. Papery fruits develop from the calyces after flowering, containing quarter-inch seeds shaped like tiny clubs and with five rounded ribs around the sides.

Red four-o'clock should do well in any sandy or rocky fast-draining soil, in the wild growing in full sun to light shade exposures. While plants are not readily available in the nursery trade, check with local native plant growers for seeds or potted starts. Given a wild corner of the yard, this long-bloomer would be an attractive and worthwhile addition to the summer hummingbird garden. Propagate by scarified seed either sown in fall or cold stratified for at least a month and sown in spring.

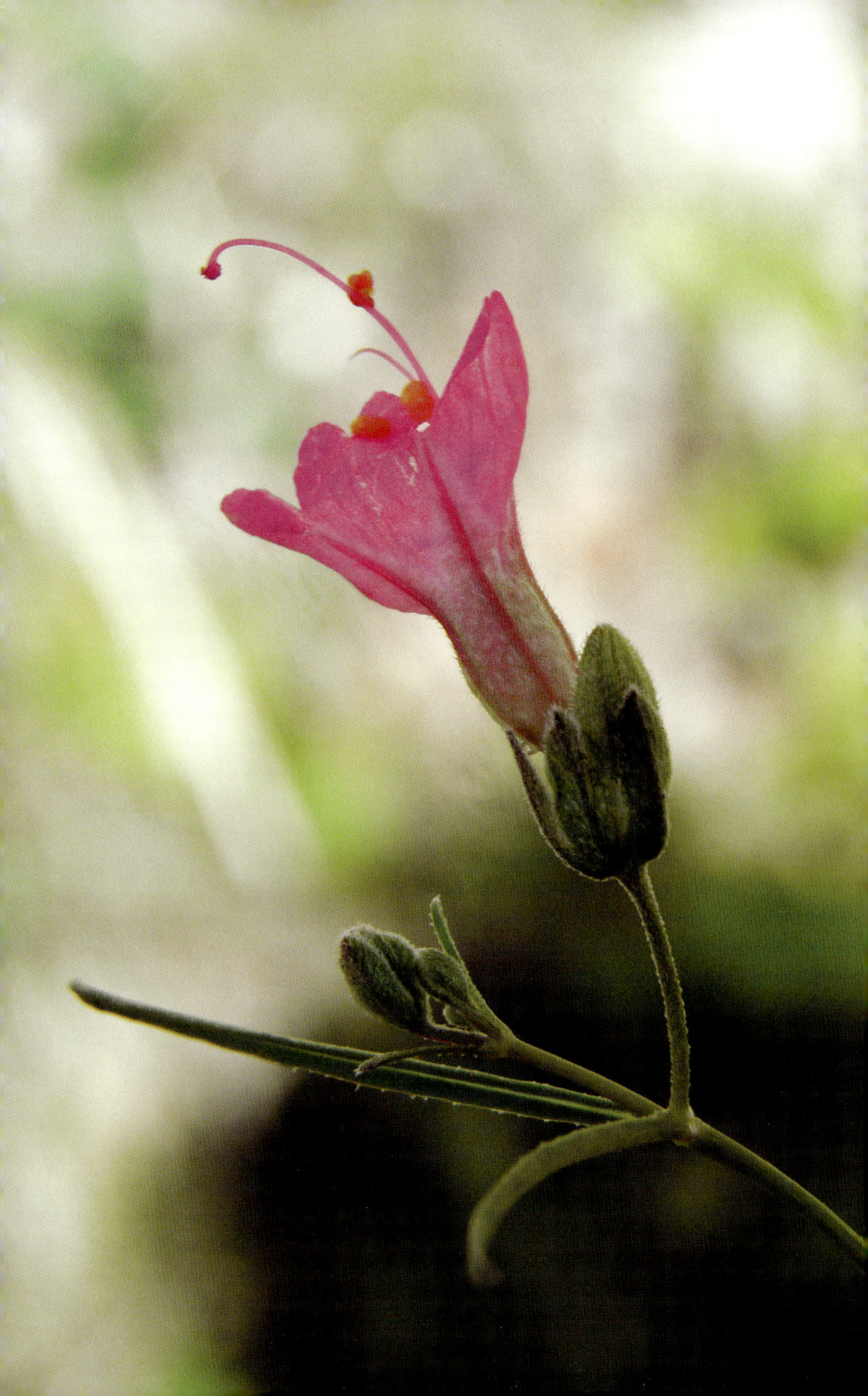

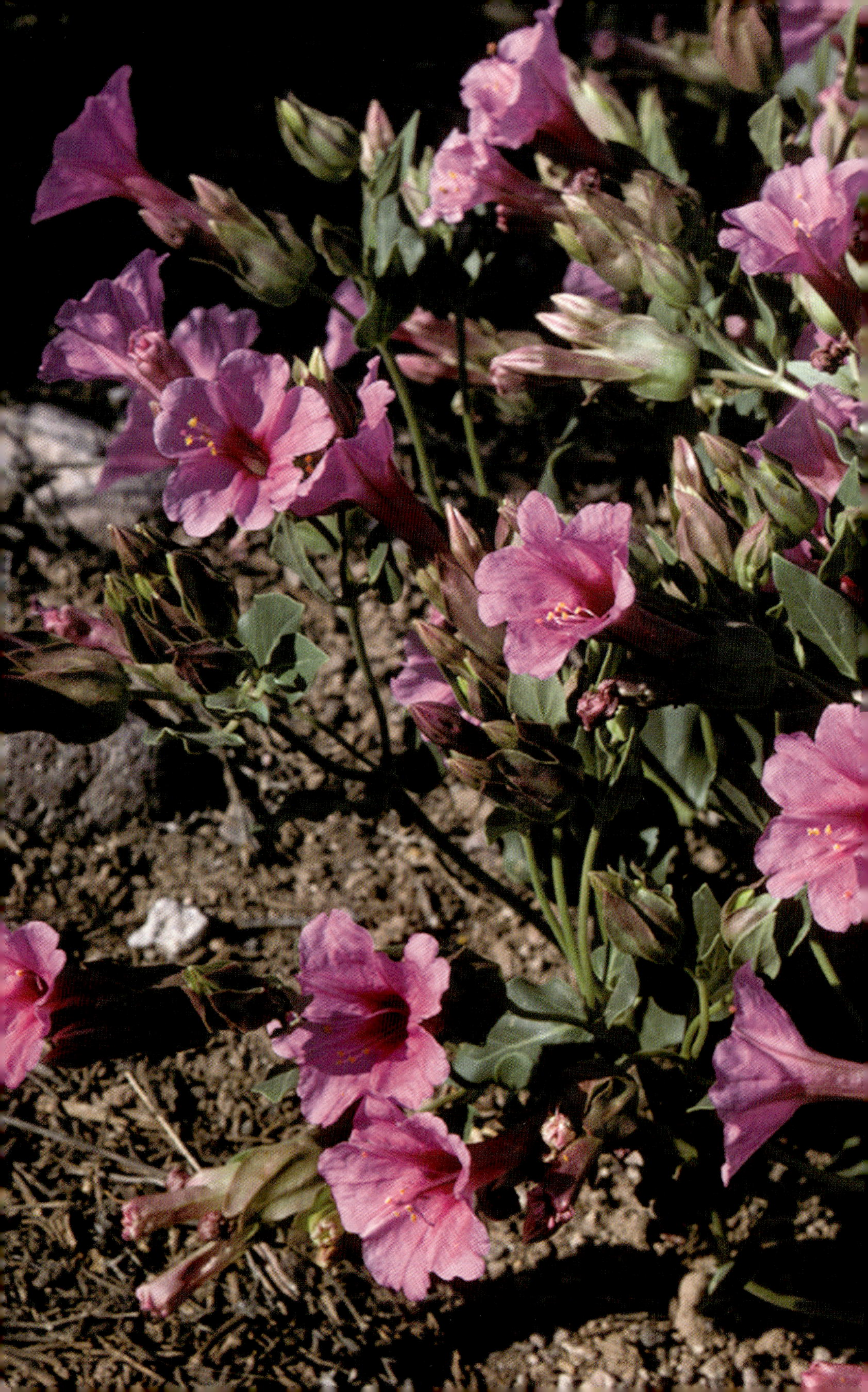

Mirabilis multiflora

Desert Four-o'clock, Colorado Four-o'clock, Maravilla

Family:	Nyctaginaceae	**Water use:**	Low–moderate
Type:	Perennial	**Cold hardiness:**	Roots to -20°F
Size:	1–3' high x 3–5' wide	**USDA zone:**	5–10
Bloom:	May–September		

Author citation: (Torrey) A. Gray
Synonym: *Oxybaphus multiflorus* Torrey

THIS SPECTACULAR BEAUTY graces all of our southwestern deserts, boasting lavish magenta to purple funnel-shaped flowers that crank out nectar over an incredibly long bloom season. While pollinated mostly by sphinx moths, the blossoms are also quite attractive to hummingbirds. Broad-tailed and Rufous Hummingbirds are among the many patrons of the nectar, which is reportedly much more copious than that of cultivated four-o'clocks.

Desert four-o'clock enjoys a broad geographical range that extends from southern California east through southern Nevada, southern and eastern Utah, and western and southern Colorado south through Arizona, New Mexico, and western Texas, and southward into northern Mexico. Its typical haunts include sandy or rocky plains, mesas, piñon-juniper grasslands, and ponderosa pine forests at elevations ranging from 2,500 to over 8,000 feet.

Plants have large, up to four-inch-diameter tuberous roots that extend several feet below the surface and store most of the moisture needed for growth and flowering. In the spring, strong magenta-colored stems emerge and rapidly develop into a shrubby, mounding or trailing form that in the fall will again disappear completely. The large, fleshy, opposite leaves are dark gray-green and ovate to heart-shaped with a pointed tip. The colorful one- to two-inch flowers, presented in clusters in the leaf axils, flare broadly at the mouth and are slightly fragrant. They open in the late afternoon and close early the next morning except in cloudy or cool weather.

This sturdy perennial is long-lived, drought tolerant, and stands up to heat well. It prefers a sunny exposure—except in the hottest deserts—and seems to favor sandy soil among rocks but is fairly adaptable as long as drainage is excellent. Desert four-o'clock works beautifully as a ground cover under the filtered shade of a palo verde or desert-willow or draped over a retaining wall, and it will be a welcome addition to any hummingbird garden. Plants typically self-sow readily. Propagate by seeds that have been scarified and stratified for one month and plant in late spring or fall. Alternatively, root pieces can be divided and transplanted in autumn.

Monardella macrantha

Scarlet Monardella, Red Mountainbalm, Hummingbird Mint

Family:	Lamiaceae	**Water use:**	Low–moderate
Type:	Perennial	**Cold hardiness:**	To -20°F
Size:	To 1' high x 1–2' wide	**USDA zone:**	9–10
Bloom:	May–August		

Author citation: A. Gray

THE SHOWY, FIRE-ENGINE-RED TUBULAR FLOWERS of this perennial are quite popular with hummingbirds and depend at least partially upon them for pollination. Presumably Anna's Hummingbirds count among its regular nectar customers, and many butterflies visit the flowers as well. The long bloom season makes this a wonderful addition to the summer hummingbird garden, particularly in upland environments.

This cousin of the bee balms is native to the Coast, Transverse, and Peninsular ranges of central and southern California, from the Santa Lucia Range near Monterey southward into Mexico in northern Baja California. Most commonly encountered in San Diego County, it is typically found on dry slopes or rocky outcrops in montane chaparral or burned areas and openings in ponderosa pine forests, at elevations of 2,500 to over 6,000 feet.

Growing from a woody rootstock, it is low and sprawling in form, the stems that hold the two-inch flower clusters turning upward at the ends. Established plants often form expansive mats. The small oval evergreen leaves are glossy dark green and aromatic and occur in opposite pairs along the stems. The inflorescence resembles those of bee balms, with several long tubular blossoms that are two-lipped and held upright in whorls. The scarlet flowers are sometimes accented with pointed, yellow-tipped lobes and have toothed purple bracts.

Plants prefer a coarse, even gravelly, well-drained soil that is low in organic matter, and while they frequently occur on sunny sites in the wild they seem to prefer partly shady exposures under cultivation. Scarlet monardella can be finicky in desert landscapes but seems to do much better in coastal gardens. While quite drought-tolerant, established plants will benefit from an occasional deep soaking during dry periods in the summer. In suitable conditions, this long-blooming perennial works nicely as a ground cover, an accent in rock gardens, or a container plant. To elevate the flowers and make them more safely accessible to hummingbirds, plant in a raised bed or large pot or allow it to spill over a hanging basket. Propagate by untreated seed sown in spring, by stem cuttings, or by root division.

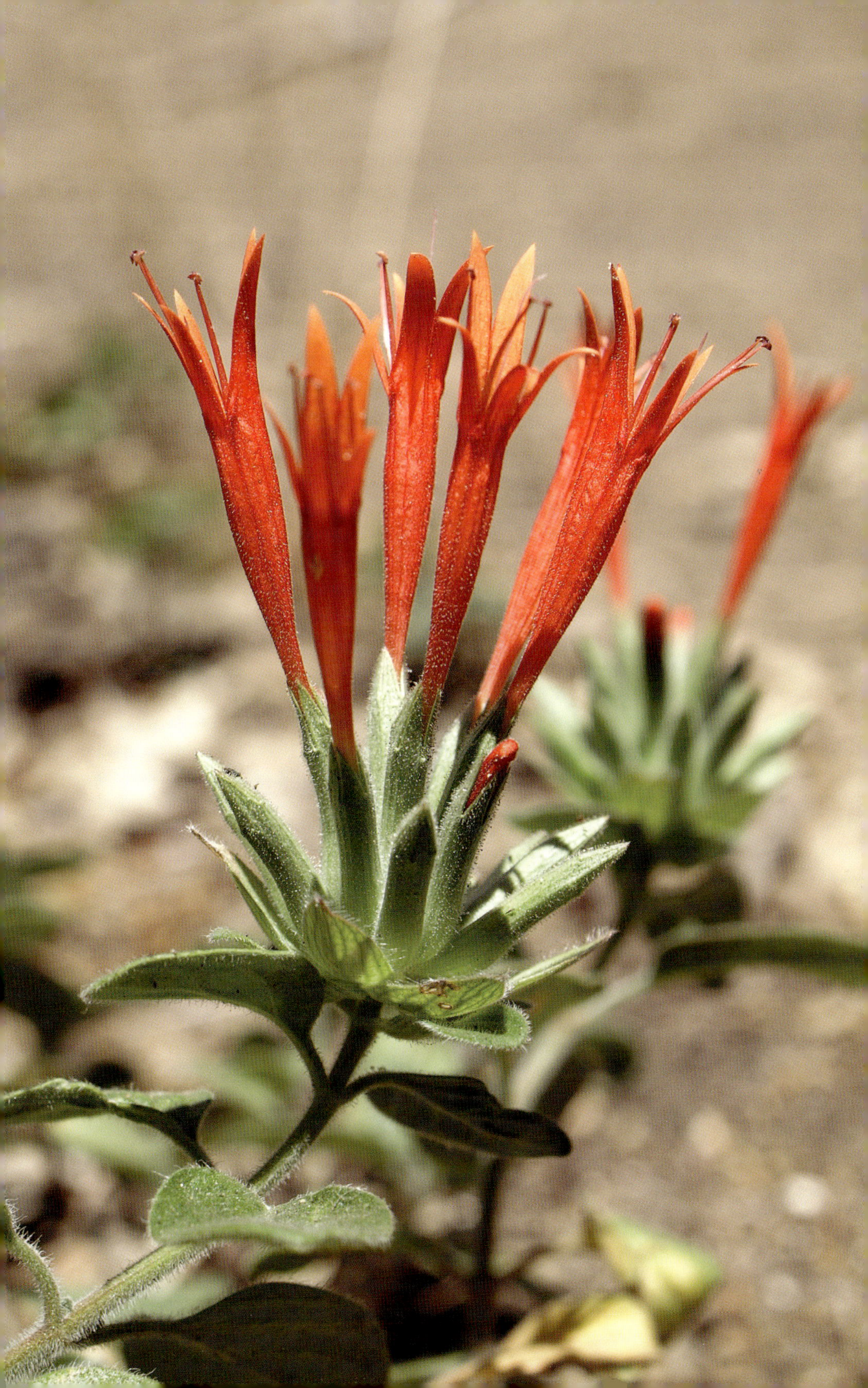

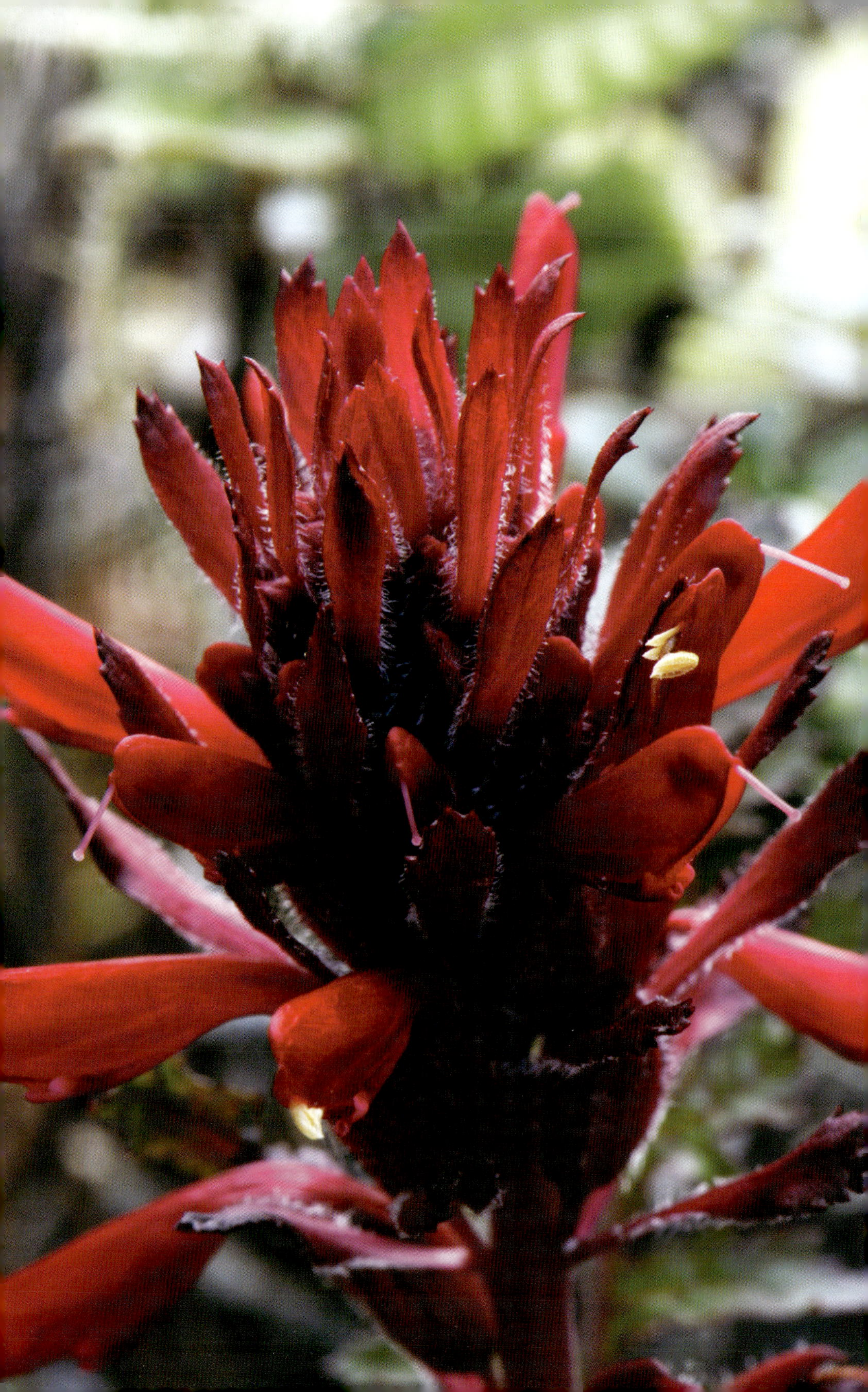

Pedicularis densiflora
Indian Warrior, Red Lousewort

Family:	Orobanchaceae (Scrophulariaceae)	**Bloom:**	January–June
		Water use:	Low–moderate
Type:	Perennial	**Cold hardiness:**	To -10°F
Size:	1–2' high x 1–2' wide	**USDA zone:**	8–10
Author citation:	Bentham ex Hooker		

THE DEEP WINE-RED COWLED FLOWERS of this pretty perennial provide valuable nectar to Anna's, Allen's, and Black-chinned Hummingbirds over an incredibly long bloom season, often when little else is blooming. While most species in its genus are bee-pollinated, this interesting plant is primarily dependent upon hummingbirds for pollination. It is also a larval host for checkerspot butterflies.

Indian warrior can be found in a variety of habitats below 6,000 feet in elevation, from southwestern Oregon and southward through California, occurring in the Cascade Range, in the Sierra Nevada foothills, in the Coast, Transverse, and Peninsular ranges, and along the central and southern coastline. It is said to be semi-parasitic on the roots of other plants—particularly heaths such as manzanita—and is most commonly found on dry slopes and foothills in chaparral, oak-pine, and ponderosa pine communities, often growing in the shade of shrubs or at woodland edges; it also seems to repopulate burned areas quickly.

The erect stems rise from a basal rosette of foliage and are brownish and covered with hairs. The large, pinnately divided leaves are quite fern-like, with 13 to 41 linear to ovate leaflets that when new are red as a protection against strong ultraviolet rays. Gradually the foliage turns to bright green, contrasting with the predominant grays of coastal scrub or the browns of fallen pine needles. The flat tubular flowers, each with a stout hooded upper lip and three small spreading lower lobes halfway down the corolla, occur in clusters at stem tips.

Indian warrior needs a well-drained soil and shaded exposure to thrive, and once established seems quite drought tolerant. This attractive perennial is reputed to be quite difficult to cultivate and as such is not readily available in the nursery trade, but if an appropriate niche can be created, it would make a lovely addition to a shady wildflower bed or border. In natural areas it is unquestionably a plant to be cherished. One can try to propagate this wildflower by planting seed on site or in pots along with manzanita, or inquire about it at native plant sales.

Penstemon alamosensis

Alamo Penstemon, Alamo Beardtongue

Family:	Plantaginaceae (Scrophulariaceae)	**Bloom:**	May–June
Type:	Perennial	**Water use:**	Low–moderate
Size:	1' high x 1' wide, with flower stalk to 3' high	**Cold hardiness:**	Roots to -15°F
		USDA zone:	6–9
Author citation:	Pennell & G. T. Nisbet		

First in the alphabet among the many penstemons that have evolved to cater especially to hummingbirds is this striking plant, with its bright orange-red funnel-shaped blooms. Offering sucrose-rich nectar during a critical period of the nesting season, it likely depends significantly on hummingbirds for pollination.

In the wild, Alamo penstemon is quite rare, occurring only in the Sacramento and San Andres mountains of south-central New Mexico and on one site in western Texas. Its common name refers to the location in the Sacramento Mountains where it was first described, Alamo Canyon. A denizen of limestone slopes, boulder crevices, arroyos, and dry streambeds in the middle elevations between 4,300 and 6,000 feet, this handsome perennial has an evergreen rosette of large, smooth, leathery leaves that are blue-gray in color and broadly lance-shaped. In spring the plant sends up one or more thick, bluish-gray, sparsely leafed flower stalks. Each bears one or two widely spaced clusters of pendant blooms that are one inch long and covered with tiny hairs.

In the garden, plants prefer a lean, rocky or gravelly soil that is slightly alkaline and well drained. They stand up to heat well and after establishment require supplemental water only during extended drought, although while in flower will perform best with a deep soaking once or twice a month. In coldest winter areas, the basal rosette may need to be protected with pine boughs or other such covering. Given the rarity of this plant, one might not expect it to be commercially available, but it was widely grown for a time and is still offered for sale on occasion. Tucked among boulders in a dry wash, it would make a splendid addition to a middle-elevation hummingbird garden and is certain to draw any Broad-tailed Hummingbirds in the vicinity within view. When seed capsules dry and turn brown, the seeds within are ripe and can be harvested and planted elsewhere if desired. If planting in fall, no treatment is necessary. Because of the combined past impacts of overgrazing and over-collecting, Alamo penstemon is listed as a Rare/Sensitive Plant Species in New Mexico, and collection from the wild is illegal.

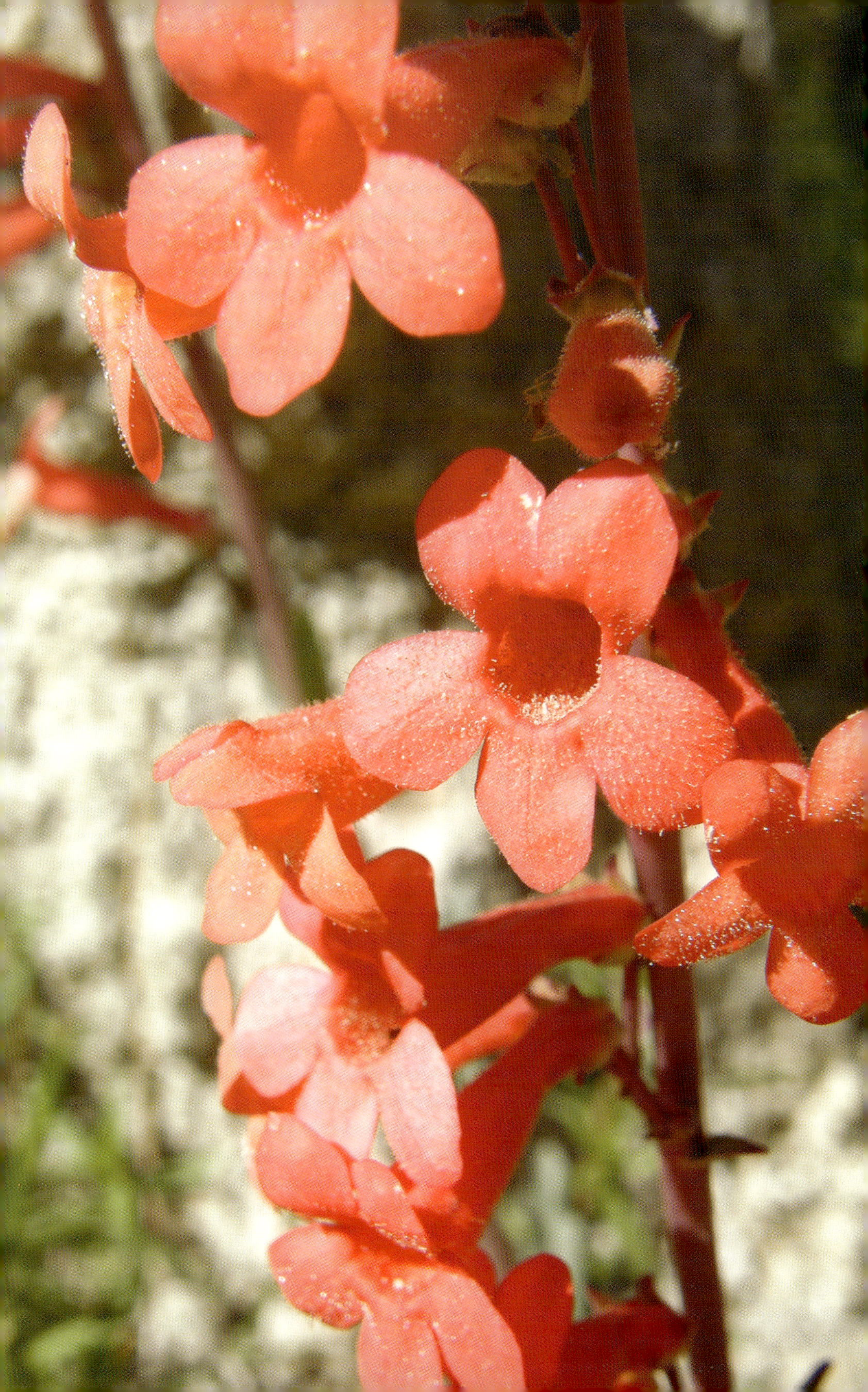

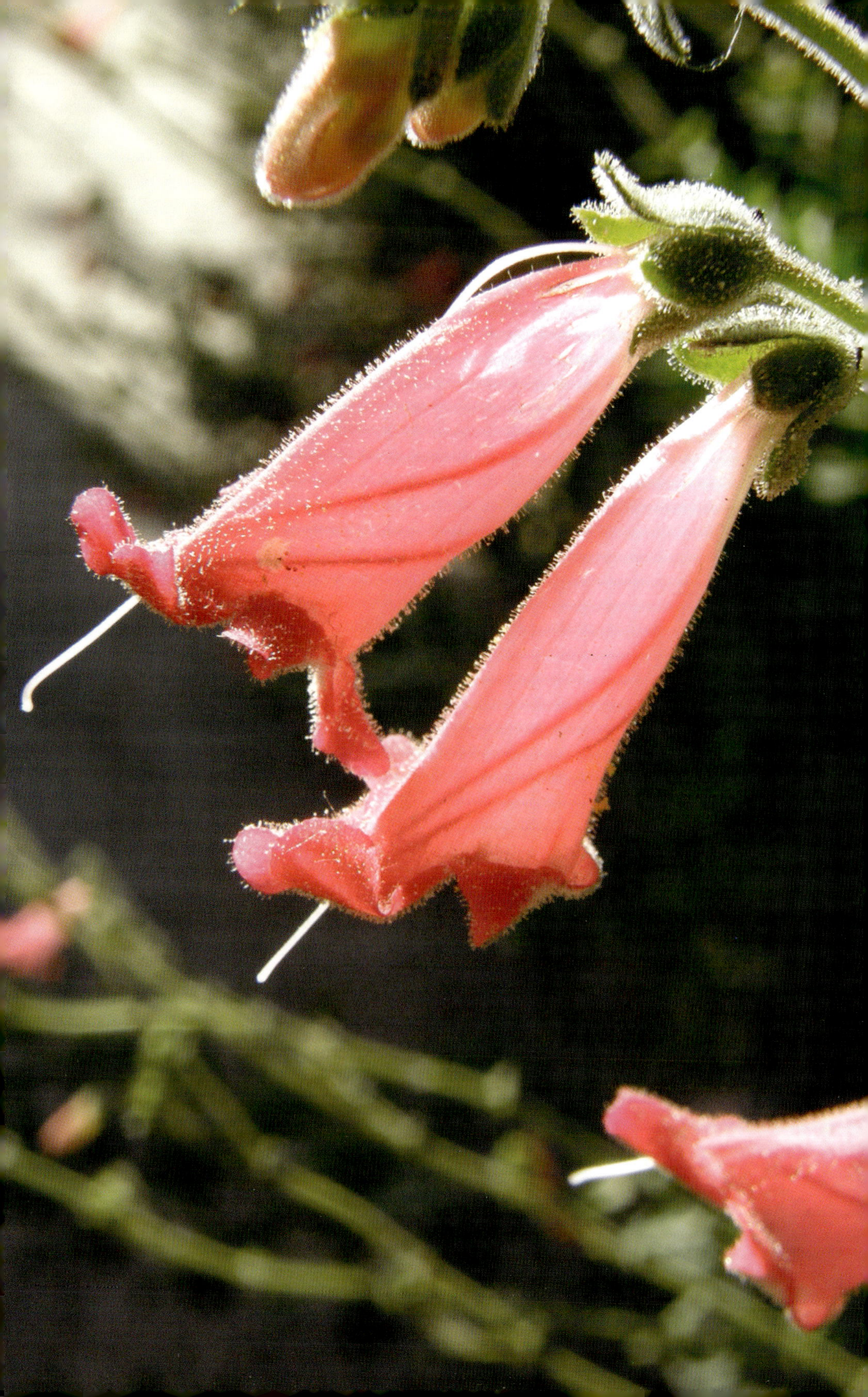

Penstemon baccharifolius

Baccharisleaf Penstemon, Rock Penstemon

Family:	Plantaginaceae (Scrophulariaceae)	**Bloom:**	June–September or longer
Type:	Perennial subshrub	**Water use:**	Low–moderate
Size:	1.5' high x 2' wide, with flower stalk to 2' high	**Cold hardiness:**	Top to 15°F, roots to 0°F
		USDA zone:	7–10

Author citation: Hooker

THIS TEXAS BELLE IS AN ADAPTABLE AND ATTRACTIVE SUMMER-BLOOMING penstemon, its nodding cherry-red flowers offering nectar over a long period of time. Black-chinned Hummingbirds are avid visitors to the blooms and along with bees shoulder most of the pollination duties.

In the United States baccharisleaf penstemon occurs only in Texas, but in Mexico it can be found from Coahuila to San Luis Potosi. In Texas its usual domicile is on limestone bluffs and outcrops of the Edwards Plateau in the south-central part of the state or the Chihuahuan Desert of the Big Bend region to the west, at elevations ranging from 1,100 to 7,000 feet.

Its shrubby, much-branched form is distinctive and unlike that of most penstemons. Its multiple downy stems originate from a woody base and can be upright or spreading, with thick, fleshy, one-inch leaves that are an attractive rich green year-round in mild winters and may or may not have toothed margins. The one-inch sticky, tubular flowers have flaring lobes and are occasionally rimmed in white. Held on short stalks above the foliage, they appear nonstop throughout the summer and with supplemental water often well into fall.

This drought-tolerant charmer prefers fast-draining, alkaline soil and a mostly sunny exposure, with afternoon shade and a protective cover of rocks or mulch around the crown advisable in low desert gardens. After establishment, plants usually need only a deep soaking once a month, twice a month during summer droughts. In cold climates, cut back any frost damage in late winter. Long-lived and adaptable, baccharisleaf penstemon is well suited for rock gardens, perennial borders, and planting en masse as a ground cover. It complements cacti and other succulents nicely and works equally well in more traditional garden plantings. It may also be grown in containers, which will elevate the flowers to a height more appealing to hummingbirds, but will then need more frequent watering. Propagate by fresh seed sown directly on site in the fall or by stem cuttings. Protect young seedlings from deer, sheep, and other browsers.

Penstemon barbatus

Beardlip Penstemon, Beardtongue, Scarlet Bugler, Jarritos

Family:	Plantaginaceae (Scrophulariaceae)	**Bloom:**	May/June–September/October, varies with altitude
Type:	Perennial		
Size:	1' high x 1' wide, with flower stalk to 5' high	**Water use:**	Low–moderate
		Cold hardiness:	Roots to -30°F
		USDA zone:	4–9
Author citation:	(Cavanilles) Roth		

The fire-engine-red tubular blooms of this classic hummingbird flower are wildly popular with and extremely important to a host of hummingbirds, including Black-chinned, Broad-tailed, Magnificent, Blue-throated, Broad-billed, Calliope, and Rufous Hummingbirds. In some areas its most important pollinator is the Black-chinned Hummingbird.

Beardlip penstemon is native to high desert and montane habitats from southern Utah and southwestern Colorado south through western Texas, most of New Mexico, northern and eastern Arizona, and well southward into Mexico, from 4,000 to 10,000 feet in elevation. Typically seen along roadsides, in coniferous forest openings, or on rocky aspen-conifer slopes, it is usually the most common hummingbird flower at upper elevations within its range.

The plant has an open, somewhat sprawling form, and before the flower stalk shoots up bides its time as a clump of glossy gray-green narrow foliage that may be lance-shaped, spatulate, or oval. The one-inch flowers have a reflexed lower lip that deters bees and depending upon the variety may be covered with tiny white or yellowish hairs, giving rise to the common name of "beardlip."

This iconic penstemon prefers coarse well-drained soil but will tolerate heavier soils if sloped for drainage. Plants do well in sun or part shade, but in hot low-desert areas will appreciate afternoon shade and supplemental water two or three times a month during periods of summer drought. Peak flowering is in May and June, but if deadheaded right away it will bloom again in late summer. Cut back flower stems to the basal rosette in late fall to encourage new shoots and more blooms the following year.

Beardlip penstemon is marvelous for rock gardens, in shrub borders, in a woodland understory, or massed in beds, and it is one of the best penstemons for cold winter and/or humid summer climates. Plants are short-lived, usually about five years, but fortunately they reseed readily if at least one stalk is allowed to set seed. When the seeds ripen, looking like flattened poppy seeds within the dry capsule, cut the stalk back and shake it over the ground where plants are desired. If planting in spring, cold stratifying improves germination rates.

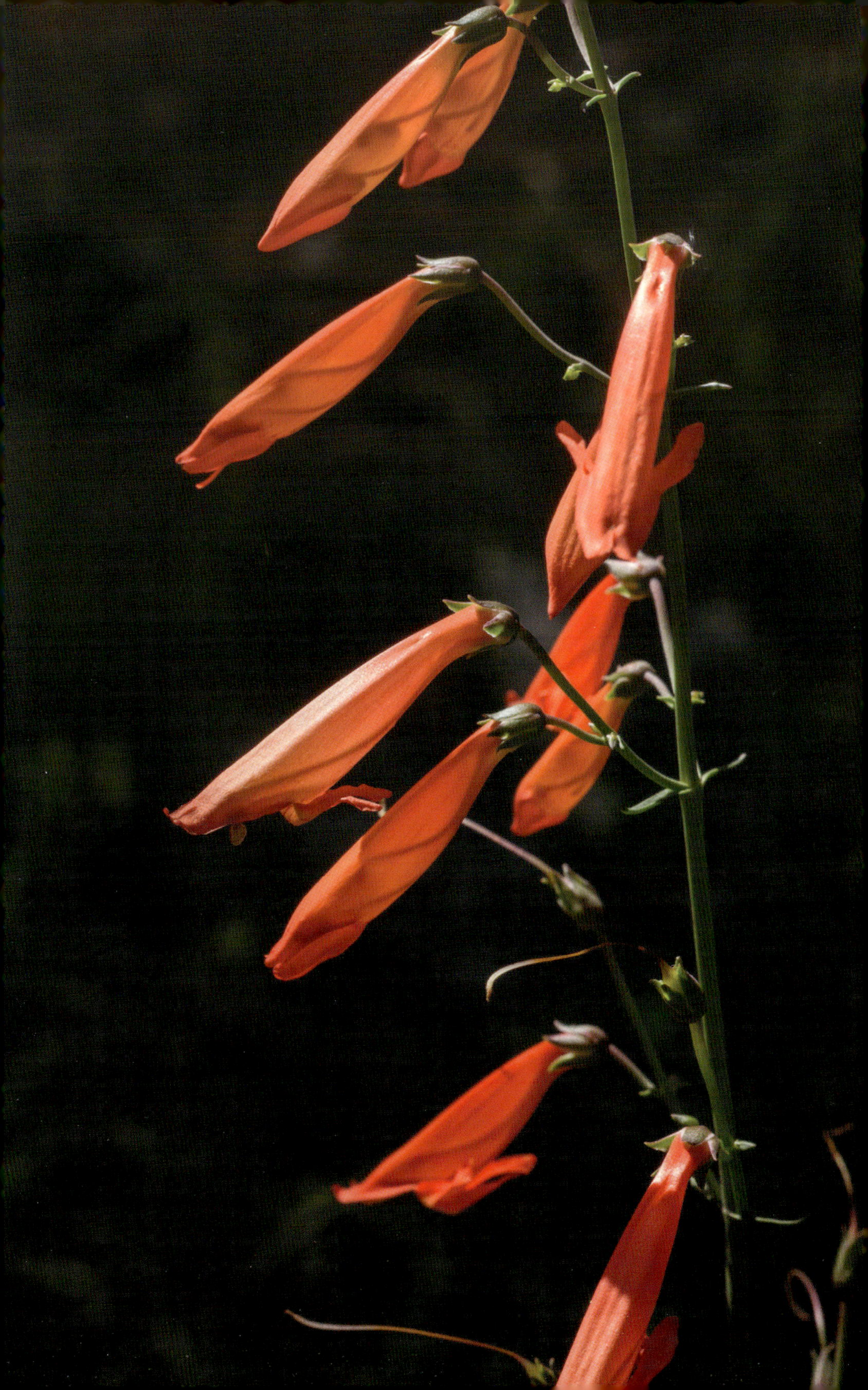

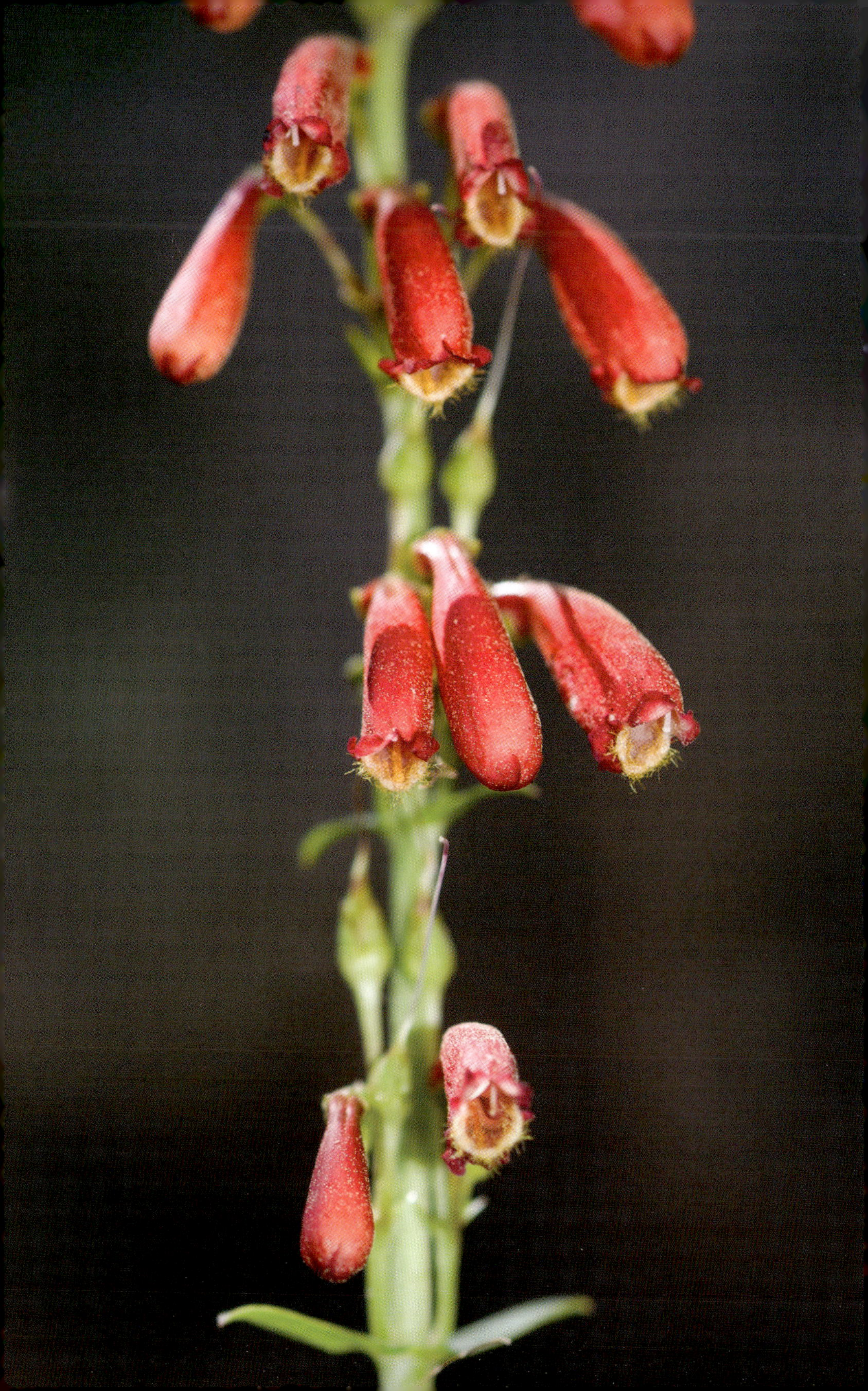

Penstemon cardinalis
Cardinal Penstemon, White Mountain Beardtongue

Family:	Plantaginaceae (Scrophulariaceae)	**Bloom:**	May–July in south, July–October in north
Type:	Perennial	**Water use:**	Low–moderate
Size:	1' high x 1' wide, with flower stalk to 3' high	**Cold hardiness:**	Roots to -10°F
		USDA zone:	5–9

Author citation: Wooton & Standley

This is another mountain penstemon whose deep red tubular blooms positively scream out to hummingbirds. Broad-tailed Hummingbirds in particular tap into this nectar source throughout the breeding season and no doubt contribute significantly to pollination.

Cardinal penstemon resides within a quite limited geographical area, occurring only in the Guadalupe Mountains of southern New Mexico and western Texas (subspecies *regalis*) and in three additional south-central New Mexico mountain ranges (subspecies *cardinalis*). Typically dwelling in the company of ponderosa pines or Douglas-firs, it forms large clumps of basal rosettes on steep limestone slopes or in rocky canyon bottoms, at elevations that range from 4,500 to over 9,000 feet.

The large, heart-shaped leaves of the rosette and those paired along the upright flower stems are bluish-green and waxy. The one-inch blossoms are borne in loose one-sided spikes atop the stalk and are puffy with a slight constriction behind the opening—aptly likened to a partly closed drawstring by author Jean Heflin—with a tuft of flaxen hair at the mouth.

Cardinal penstemon establishes quickly in any fast-draining, sandy or loamy soil in full sun to part or filtered shade, especially when given a cozy cranny next to a rock wall or tucked between boulders for warmth and the extra bits of moisture from condensation and runoff. In such niches it is fairly drought tolerant and reportedly hardy north even to the Denver area. In late summer after flowering, plants go into dormancy and need much less water than during growth and flowering; in fall they resume growing and may need a bit more water. Like most penstemons it is most effective in mass plantings, where it can colonize a corner or swale. Its early summer bloom period makes it a valuable addition to most any hummingbird garden, whether cool oasis in the low desert or sunny slope in the mountains, and it will roll out the welcome mat for any and all hummingbirds that may be nesting in the vicinity. Collect seeds when the pods turn brown in early fall, and scatter where new plants are desired.

Penstemon centranthifolius
Scarlet Bugler

Family:	Plantaginaceae (Scrophulariaceae)	**Bloom:**	April–June
		Water use:	Low–moderate
Type:	Perennial	**Cold hardiness:**	To -10°F
Size:	2' high x 2' wide, with flower stalks to 4' high	**USDA zone:**	8–10

Author citation: (Bentham) Benth.

WHEN THIS PENSTEMON OF THE FOOTHILLS FLOWERS IN LATE spring, it is the most prevalent and sometimes the only hummingbird flower in bloom, and thus is a critically important source of nectar for nesting Costa's and to a lesser extent Anna's and Black-chinned Hummingbirds. According to biologists, each bloom produces a veritable wellspring of 5.37 milligrams of sugar per day—nearly twice that of many hummingbird flowers. In turn, the brilliant scarlet-red blossoms are pollinated primarily by hummingbirds.

Scarlet bugler is native to an extremely narrow zone that stretches from northern California southward to northern Baja California in Mexico and encompasses the Sierra Nevada foothills, margins of the Central Valley, the Coast, Transverse, and Peninsular ranges, and the southwestern edge of the Mojave Desert. Found at elevations ranging from sea level to 6,000 feet, it occurs on both eastern and western slopes of the mountains, where it is common on dry brushy hillsides along with oaks, piñons, or digger pines, as well as in desert canyons. Its several stout, upright, sparsely leafed stems are bluish-green and clasped by opposite, waxy, blue-green leaves that vary from oval to lanceolate and are evergreen. In spring the plant sends up long spikes of narrow one- to one-and-a-half-inch tubular flowers that have short, barely spreading lobes and are held horizontally on the stem, necessitating that any prospective partaker of the nectar within be able to hover while feeding.

Scarlet bugler prefers a coarse, gravelly, fast-draining soil and will grow in full sun to part shade, although in hottest climates it should have afternoon shade. While fairly drought tolerant, it will benefit from a deep soaking twice a month during extended dry periods, but be careful not to overwater during its summer dormancy. After the seed ripens, cut stalks back and collect seed or shake above ground where plants are desired. Plants usually self-sow readily, but like other penstemons nearly always germinate during the colder months. This extremely showy penstemon is appropriate for both coastal and desert gardens, and is an absolute must in areas of southern California where Costa's Hummingbirds are known to breed.

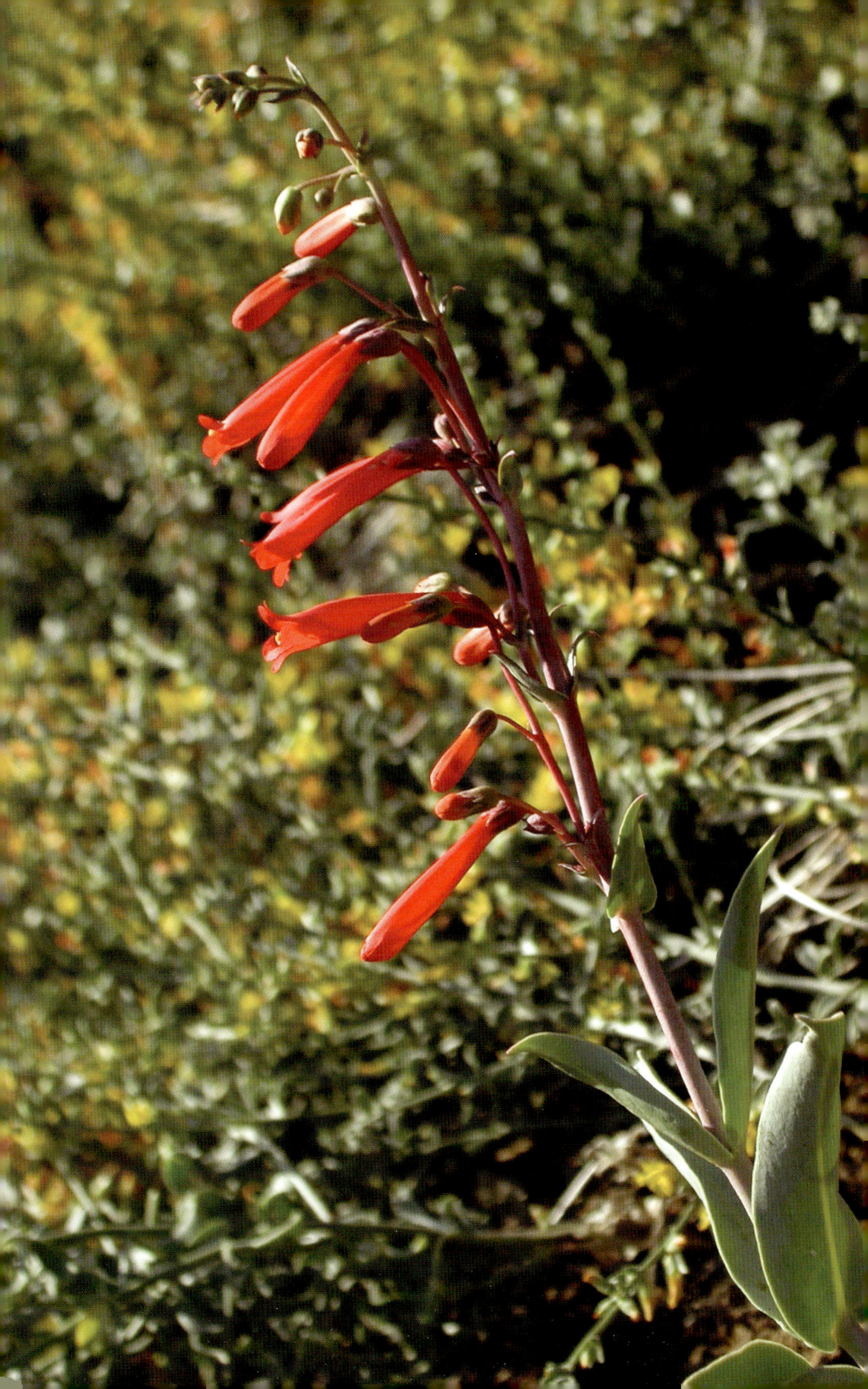

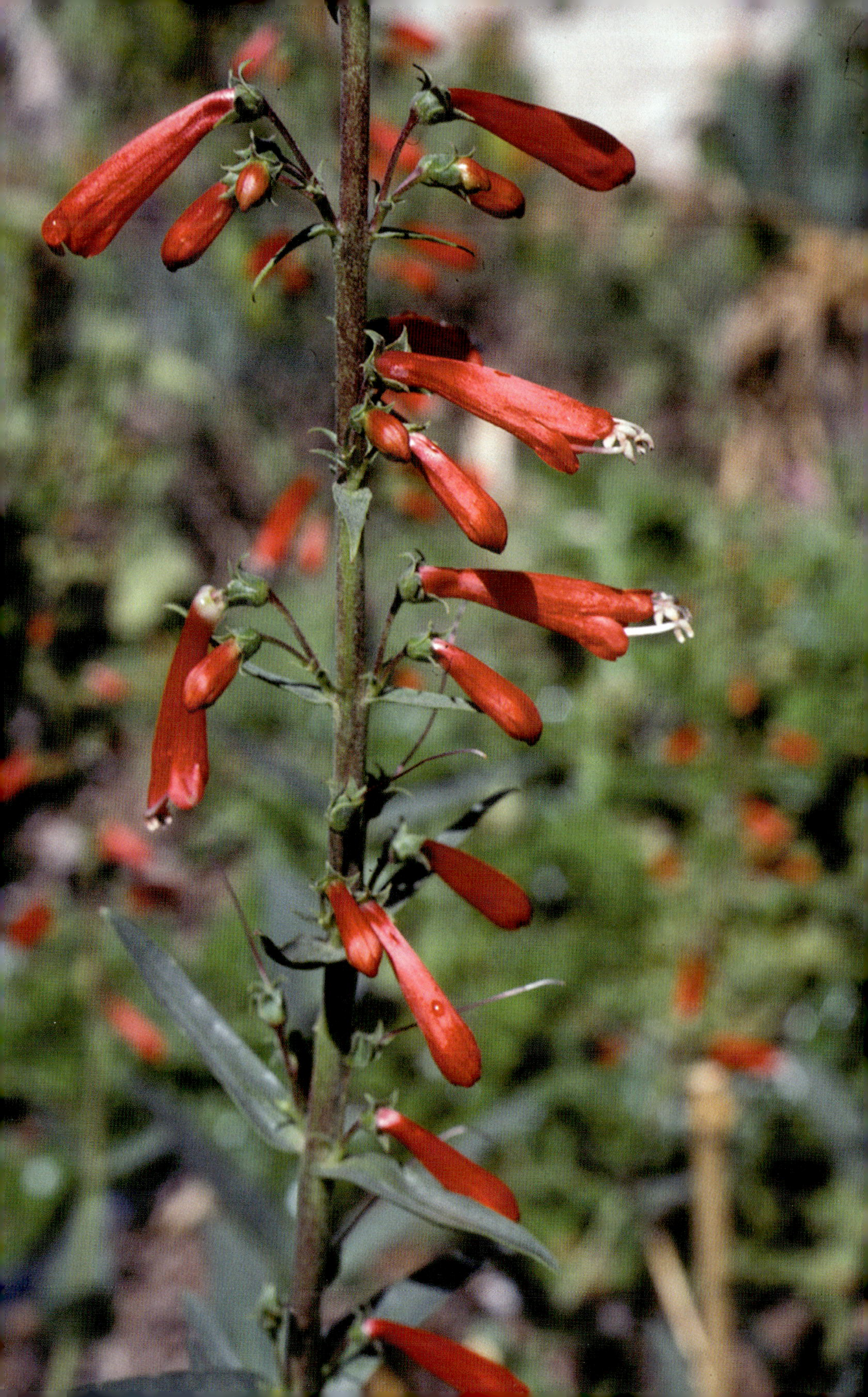

Penstemon eatonii

Firecracker Penstemon, Eaton's Firecracker

Family:	Plantaginaceae (Scrophulariaceae)	**Bloom:**	April–June
Type:	Perennial	**Water use:**	Low–moderate
Size:	1–2' high x 2' wide, with flower stalks to 3' high	**Cold hardiness:**	Top to 15–18°F, roots to -18°F
		USDA zone:	6–9

Author citation: A. Gray

WHEN IN BLOOM, FIRECRACKER PENSTEMON more than lives up to its name. Its showy spikes of fiery red tubular flowers are pollinated by, and an important nectar source for, migrating and nesting Broad-tailed and Black-chinned Hummingbirds. Anna's, Costa's, and Rufous Hummingbirds also take nectar from the flowers, and some butterflies use it as a larval plant.

This desert mountain penstemon ranges from southeastern California, southern Nevada, much of Utah, and southwestern Colorado southward through northwestern New Mexico and northern, central, and parts of southeastern Arizona, at elevations of 2,000 to over 9,000 feet. It is found in a wide variety of habitats, including rocky slopes, mesas, sandy washes, sage scrublands, piñon-juniper woodlands, and ponderosa pine forests.

For much of the year the plant is a tidy evergreen basal rosette, and then in spring it sends up one to several two-foot flower stalks with large, deep-green, leathery leaves that are shaped like elongated triangles. Stems may be erect or may loop around picturesquely. The distinctive narrow tubular flowers, appearing in clusters along one side of the stalk, often dangle from the stem and have lobes that do not spread as those of many penstemons do.

Soil must have excellent drainage and should be on the lean side with respect to organic content, but otherwise this penstemon is not persnickety. It is quite heat tolerant and normally prefers full sun, but in extremely hot summer regions it may appreciate some filtered or afternoon shade. Mulching lightly in the summer will help keep roots cool. A deep soaking once or twice a month during summer will keep foliage looking more attractive, but otherwise firecracker penstemon is quite drought tolerant. This is a great accent plant for rock gardens or courtyards and is particularly striking when massed in borders, in beds, or along walkways, where it can form self-perpetuating colonies. When the seed capsule dries and turns brown, cut the stalk back and shake it over the ground where you would like to start plants. Sowing in late fall or cold stratifying the seeds for one to two months before planting in spring may improve germination rates.

Penstemon fasciculatus
Fascicled Penstemon

Family:	Plantaginaceae (Scrophulariaceae)	**Bloom:**	July–September or longer
Type:	Subshrub	**Water use:**	Low–moderate
Size:	2' high x 2' wide	**Cold hardiness:**	Roots to at least 20°F
Author citation:	A. Gray	**USDA zone:**	9–10

First of the several Mexican penstemons covered by this book is this little charmer from the Sierra Madre Occidental, its crimson blooms offering nectar to both resident and southbound southwestern hummingbird species in late summer. Although observations in the literature are scarce, the flowers are doubtless well visited by hummingbirds because the plant relies primarily on them for pollination.

Known only from Sonora and Chihuahua, fascicled penstemon is perhaps most common in the Rio Mayo region along the border between the two states and in the Copper Canyon complex between Creel and Guachochi. Usually encountered at the middle elevations of 5,000 to 7,000 feet, its shrubby clump of leafy stems is commonly found in open pine-oak woodlands, on rocky slopes or outcroppings, on bluff tops, and on cliff ledges.

The green to reddish-brown stems arise from a woody base and rootstock and bear linear needlelike leaves very similar to those of pineleaf penstemon (*Penstemon pinifolius*) but differing in that they are arranged in dense bunches, or fascicles, which encircle the stem; a few scattered single leaves may also appear along the upper stems. Usually a bright lime-green to grayish-green in color, the one- to two-inch-long leaves typically have a slightly hairy surface. The one-and-a-quarter-inch-long tubular flowers, with short petal lobes that flare slightly at the opening, are borne singly or in pairs near stem tips and held horizontally above the foliage. Small rounded but sharply pointed capsules each containing numerous tiny seeds develop after flowering ceases.

Fascicled penstemon would seem to be an ideal candidate for an upland rock garden where winters are fairly mild. Although typically found on volcanic ash flows in its native haunts, it appears to be somewhat flexible in its requirements. Full sun to light shade, a thin soil with decent drainage, and moderate water should yield the best results. If seed can be obtained, one might try direct sowing on the site in late summer or fall and allowing the winter chill to stratify the seeds naturally.

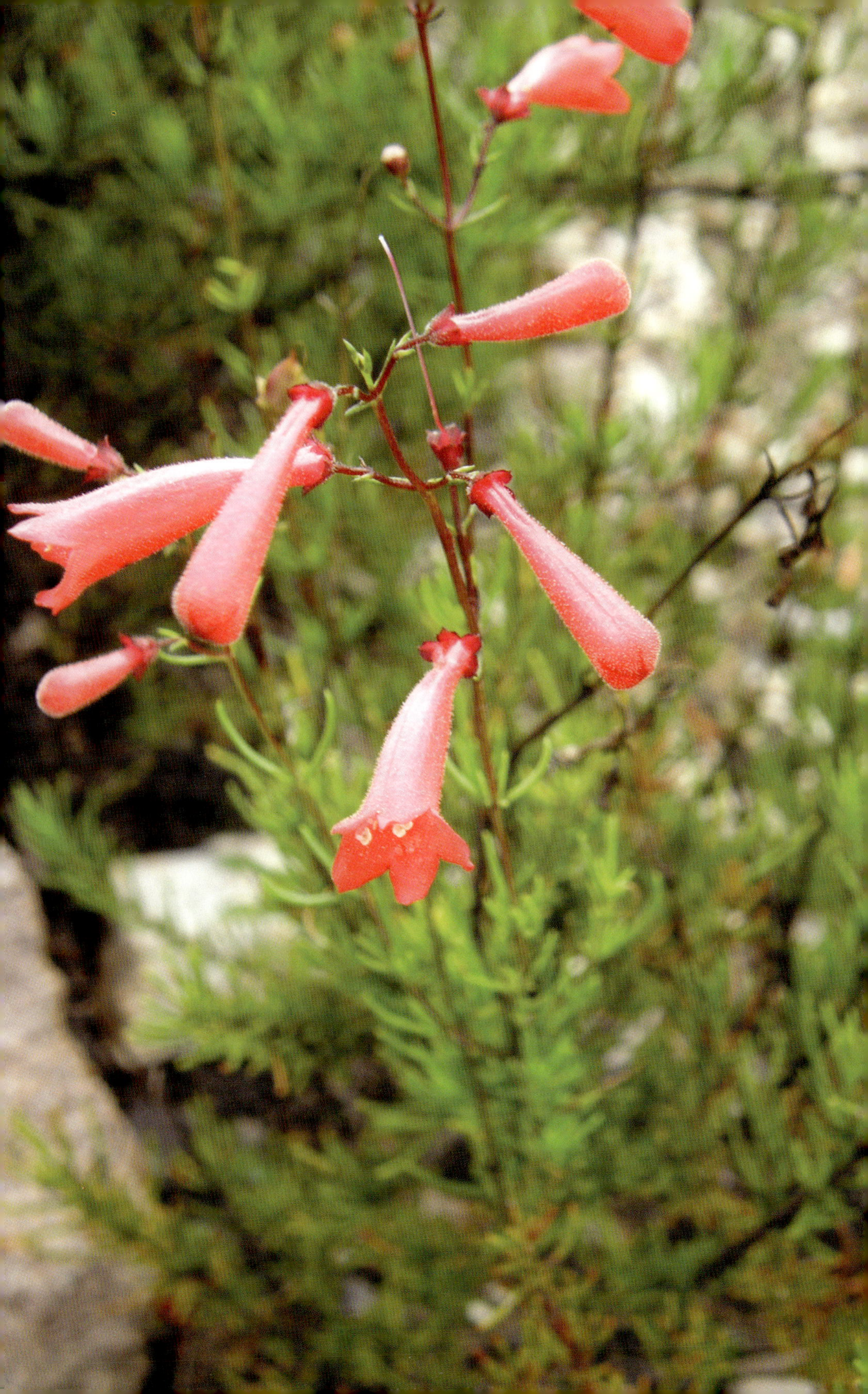

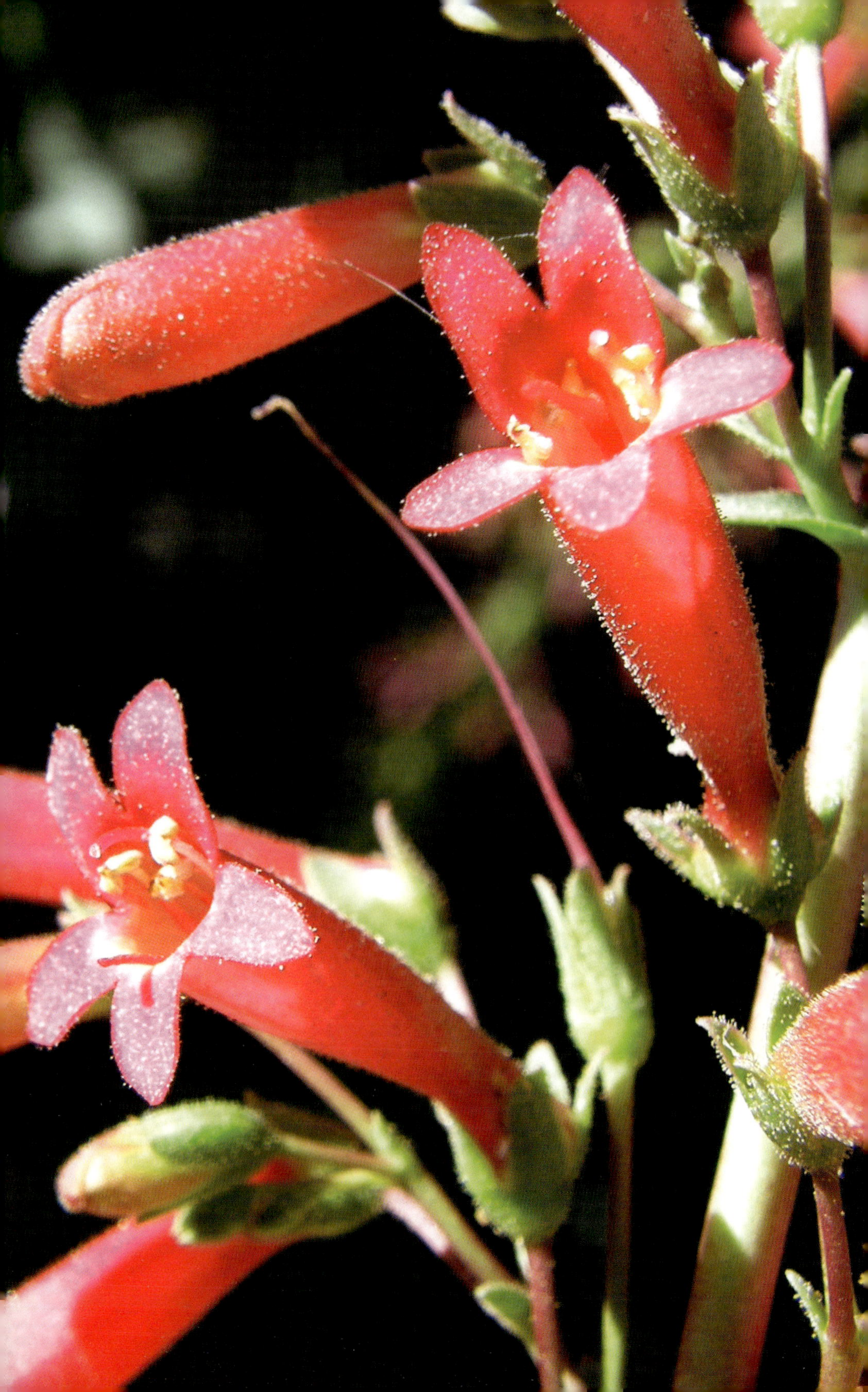

Penstemon havardii

Havard's Penstemon, Big Bend Beardtongue

Family:	Plantaginaceae (Scrophulariaceae)	**Bloom:**	April–June, sporadic summer, often again October
Type:	Perennial		
Size:	1–2' high x 1–2' wide, with flowers stalks to 5' high	**Water use:**	Low–moderate
		Cold hardiness:	To 0°F
		USDA zone:	7–10

Author citation: A. Gray

THIS LONG-BLOOMING BEAUTY is the preeminent hummingbird-adapted penstemon of the Big Bend region of Texas. Its scarlet tubular flowers supply extremely important nectar to breeding Lucifer Hummingbirds, who actively defend stands of flowering plants in April and May. Black-chinned and Broad-tailed Hummingbirds likewise visit the blossoms, which depend chiefly on hummingbirds for pollination.

Havard's penstemon occurs on desert grasslands, in arroyos, and on limestone slopes of the Chihuahuan Desert, from the Trans-Pecos region of west Texas and southward into Mexico from Chihuahua to Coahuila. In Chihuahua it has been encountered in the Sierra San Ignacio and Sierra La Esperanza just across the border from Fort Hancock, Texas. In the Big Bend area it is most common along the road from Study Butte to Government Springs and at Green Gulch.

Most of the year the plant bides its time as a basal rosette of large, thick, fleshy, pale blue-green leaves that are narrowly wedge-shaped. In springtime it sends up multiple unbranched four-foot flower stalks that are clasped by pairs of small oval leaves and topped with clusters of blooms. The showy one- to two-inch flowers have spreading lobes and glandular hairs, and will bloom spring to fall with irrigation. Wynn Anderson tells of a plant at the Chihuahuan Desert Gardens whose seeds he harvested from the bases of the stalks in midsummer when blossoms still adorned the tips.

Havard's penstemon prefers a gravelly or sandy soil but will tolerate loam or clay as long as it is fairly well drained. It will grow in full sun to part shade and is very heat and drought tolerant, requiring supplemental water only while getting established and during extended dry periods during the bloom season. Leave spent flower stalks to encourage continuous bloom. Seeds can be harvested as with other penstemons and scattered wherever plants are desired; they typically germinate in late fall and the young seedlings are fairly easy to transplant. This is an outstanding penstemon for the spring hummingbird garden, particularly in western Texas, and works well in rock gardens, perennial borders, and massed in beds.

Penstemon kunthii

Kunth's Penstemon, Painted Red Penstemon

Family:	Plantaginaceae (Scrophulariaceae)	**Bloom:**	June–October
Type:	Perennial	**Water use:**	Low–moderate
Size:	2–4' high x 2' wide	**Cold hardiness:**	To 20°F or below
		USDA zone:	9–10

Author citation: G. Don

This voluptuous Mexican penstemon occurs over a huge geographic range, offering prime nectar to various southwestern hummingbird species migrating southward along the Sierra Madre in late summer as well as to year-round residents near the southern end of the plant's range. Kunth's penstemon is said to be particularly important to Magnificent Hummingbirds in Oaxaca and is also well used by resident Blue-throated Hummingbirds, who have been observed defending large stands. Not surprisingly, hummingbirds are the plant's primary pollinators.

A denizen of the higher mountains, this beauty begins occurring in southern Sonora, western Chihuahua, and Durango, with disjunct populations in parts of Coahuila, Nuevo Leon, and Tamaulipas, and ranges southward along the Madrean highlands all the way to Chiapas in far southern Mexico. Mixed pine or pine-oak forests and open meadows bordering or within them are typical habitats, most often at elevations ranging from 6,000 to 10,000 feet.

Erect, freely branching, and open in form, its sometimes reddish, willowy stems are softly pubescent and leafy, with two narrow, finely toothed, lance-shaped leaves up to several inches long at each node. The foliage is evergreen in its native range. The lovely flowers, presented in a loose spike above the foliage, are one-and-a-half inches long, slightly inflated, and minutely fuzzy. They range from deep red to rosy purple to magenta in color, with fine white guidelines down the throat. Sharply pointed, tulip-shaped seedpods containing numerous tiny seeds develop shortly after the bloom ceases and tend to self-sow readily where conditions are favorable.

Kunth's penstemon is by no means common in the nursery trade but seems to be growing in popularity among gardeners, so perhaps its large range of occurrence will expand even more. Those purveying seeds recommend giving it full sun, sandy or gravelly soil, and average water, and some maintain that it is significantly more cold hardy than indicated here. Its showy blooms and value to hummingbirds certainly make it worth trying, especially for higher elevation gardens where winters are mild.

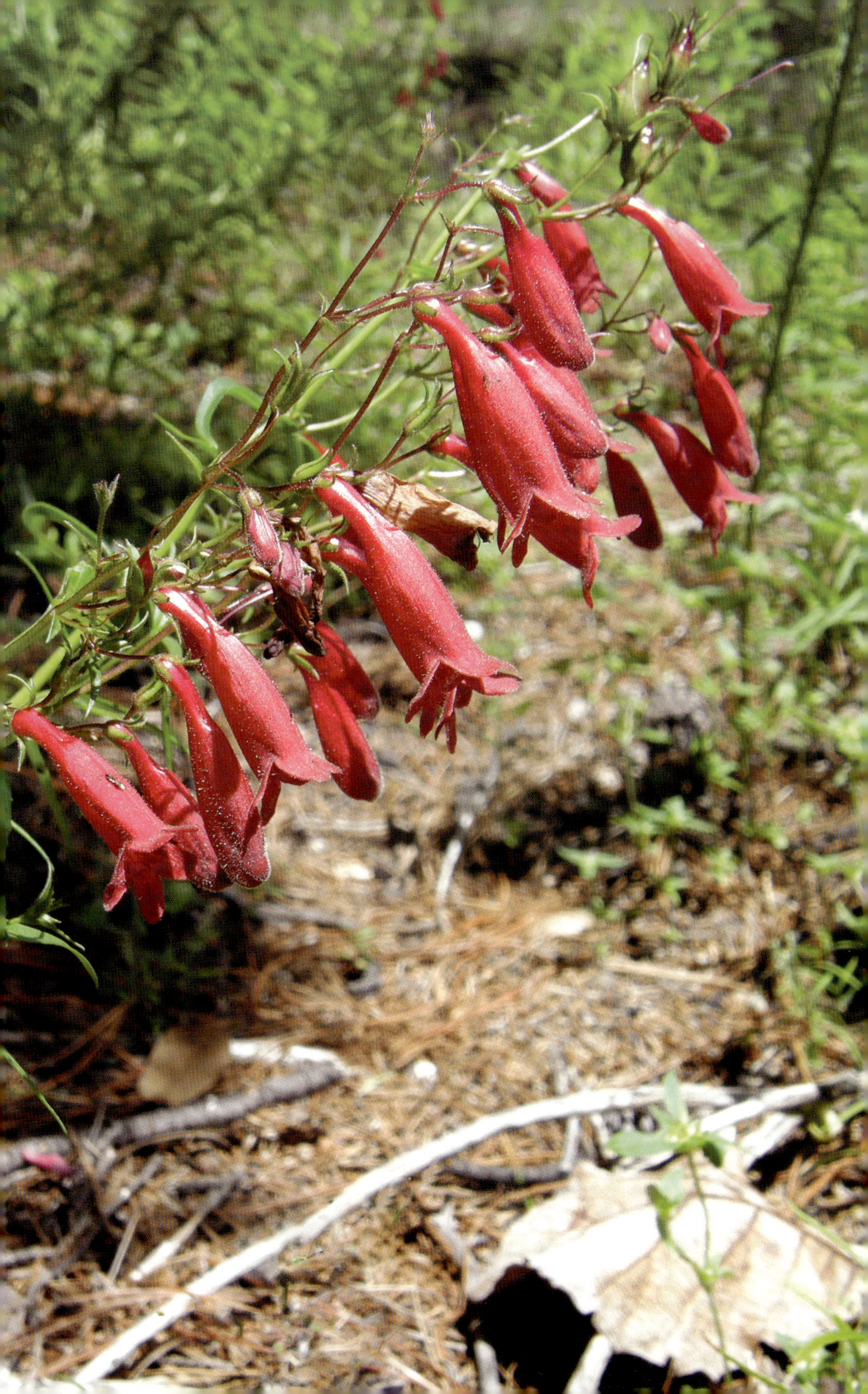

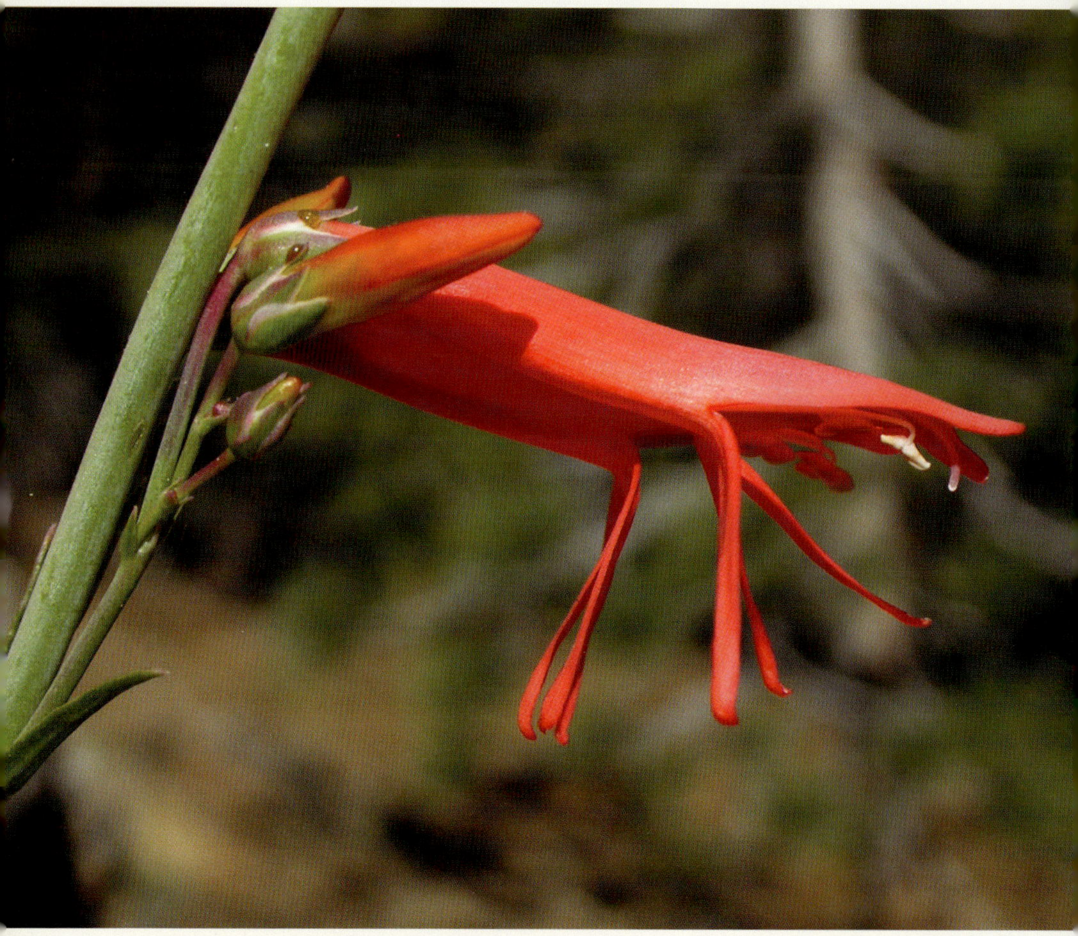

Penstemon labrosus

San Gabriel Beardtongue, Mountain Bugler

Family:	Plantaginaceae	**Bloom:**	July–September
	(Scrophulariaceae)	**Water use:**	Moderate
Type:	Perennial	**Cold hardiness:**	To 0°F
Size:	1–3' high x 1' wide	**USDA zone:**	6–10

Author citation: (A. Gray) Hooker f.
Synonym: Penstemon labrosus (A. Gray) Masters ex Hooker f.

THIS MAINLY CALIFORNIA PENSTEMON UNFURLS ITS SATURATED ORANGE-red blooms from mid to late summer, beckoning nearby resident hummingbirds that move up to higher elevations after breeding as well as those from further north that are slowly making their way southward to wintering areas. Rufous Hummingbirds have been observed at the flowers and no doubt other species make use of them as well, for hummingbirds are presumed to be the plant's chief pollinators.

Quite limited in its distribution, San Gabriel beardtongue is confined to the mountain ranges of southern California and northern Baja California in Mexico, with observations distributed across the Transverse (including the namesake San Gabriel Mountains) and Peninsular ranges. Varied associated habitat types include mixed coniferous forests (often including red fir, ponderosa pine, Jeffrey pine, and/or lodgepole pine), pine-mixed hardwood forests, and piñon-juniper woodlands, where it graces dry slopes and benches at elevations ranging from 3,000 to 10,000 feet.

Its footprint is quite small, with its clump of basal foliage often lying nearly flat among the pine needles or gravelly scree where it grows. The linear leaves usually roll inward and are largest at the base of the plant and decrease in size up the stems. Often plants have only one or two erect flower stalks, bearing the beguiling blooms near their tips. The narrow tubular flowers are nearly two inches in length, the upper lobes forming a lavish hood and the three long narrow lower lobes strongly reflexed downward. After flowering, plants go to seed quickly and the plant may die back to the ground and disappear entirely until the next spring.

Native plant and seed purveyors that grow this penstemon recommend a partly shaded exposure, good drainage, moderate water, and some freezing temperatures in the winter for optimal results, and they further note that it absolutely cannot tolerate intense reflected heat, particularly in hot climates. Plants may be easily propagated by seed or with luck by stem cuttings. Since they reportedly spread by creeping rootstocks, it is also quite possible that they could be gently divided while dormant.

Penstemon miniatus

Sierra Madrean Penstemon

Family:	Plantaginaceae (Scrophulariaceae)	**Bloom:**	July–September
		Water use:	Moderate
Type:	Perennial	**Cold hardiness:**	To 20°F
Size:	2–4' high x 1' wide	**USDA zone:**	9–10

Author citation: Lindley

Precious little information exists in the literature about this widespread Mexican species, which offers nectar to resident and southbound migrant hummingbirds alike from midsummer to early fall. Its colorful blooms of deep scarlet red depend largely upon hummingbirds for pollination and are likely to be used by the larger butterflies as well.

Of the few observation records of Sierra Madrean penstemon with details, nearly all come from western Chihuahua, but scattered sightings also exist from western Durango east to San Luis Potosi and southward along the Sierra Madre Occidental and Sierra Madre del Sur all the way to Oaxaca. In Chihuahua, plants are perhaps most common between Nuevo Casas Grandes and Madera, with additional sightings reported south of Madera, close to the Sonora border near the Cascada de Basaseáchic, and in the vicinity of Creel, near the eastern portion of the Barranca del Cobre (Copper Canyon). Favored sites include open pine woodlands, pine-oak forests, and rocky canyons, typically at elevations ranging from 6,000 to 8,000 feet.

Solitary plants are rather spindly in stature, with just a few slender stems, sparse stem leaves, and a small clump of low-lying basal foliage, but where stands of numerous plants occur, they appear as robust, multi-stemmed, willowy clumps. The lance-shaped to elliptic green leaves are about three inches long at the base of the stem and become progressively smaller toward the tip. The elegant flowers are held above the foliage, and feature a one-and-a-half-inch-long corolla that is slightly puffy and gradually widens toward the mouth. As is true with many other penstemons, rounded seedpods with sharply pointed tips form after the bloom ceases. In habit and foliage this penstemon closely resembles beardlip penstemon (*P. barbatus*), but its flowers do not have the two elongated lower lobes that reflex strongly backward, which are characteristic of that species.

This penstemon is not currently known in the nursery trade but if seeds can be obtained it would likely be fairly easy to grow, especially in an upland hummingbird garden where winters are mild. Full sun to part shade, good drainage, and regular water until established and as needed afterward are likely to yield the best results. Propagation by seed in fall or winter is apt to be most successful.

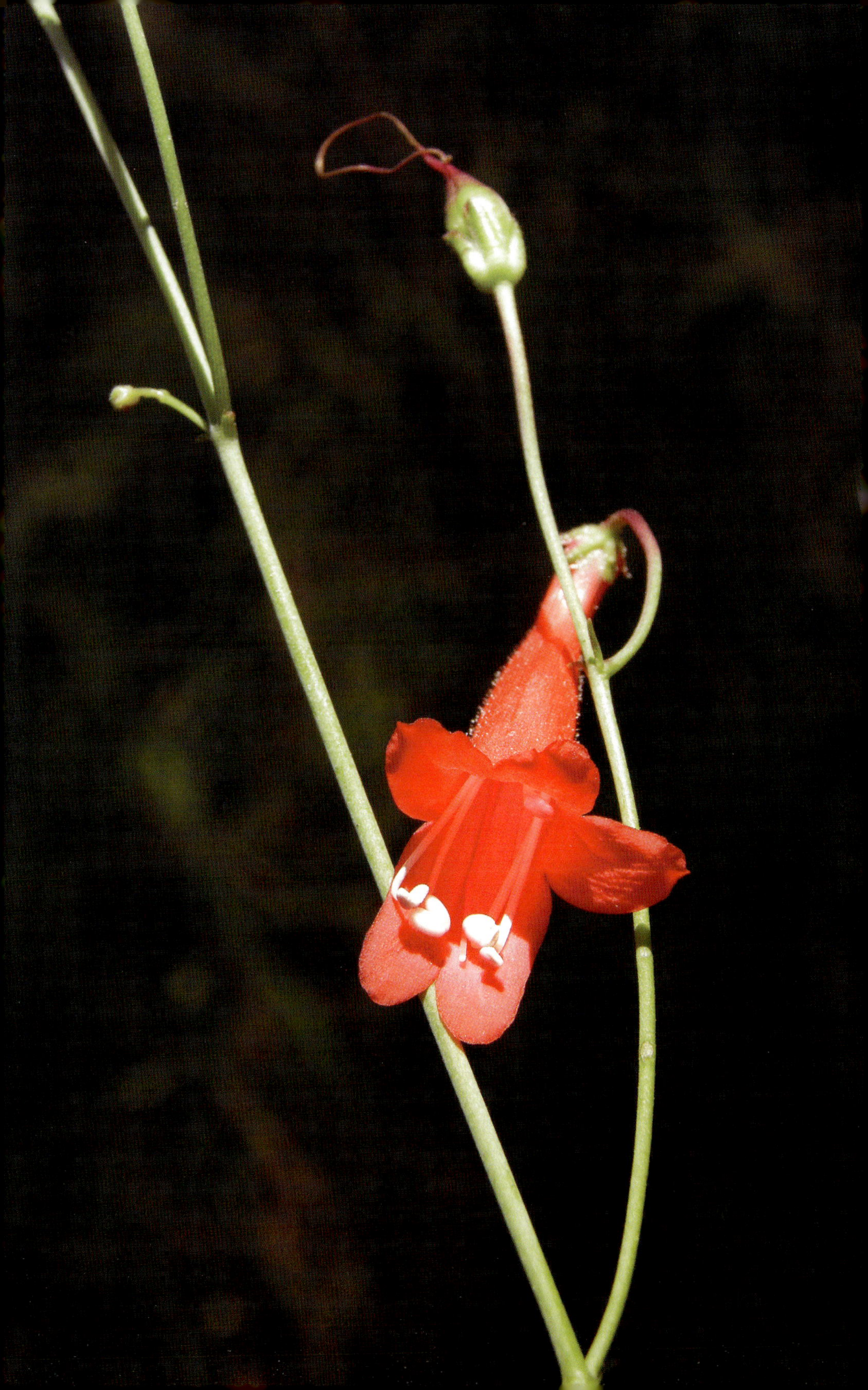

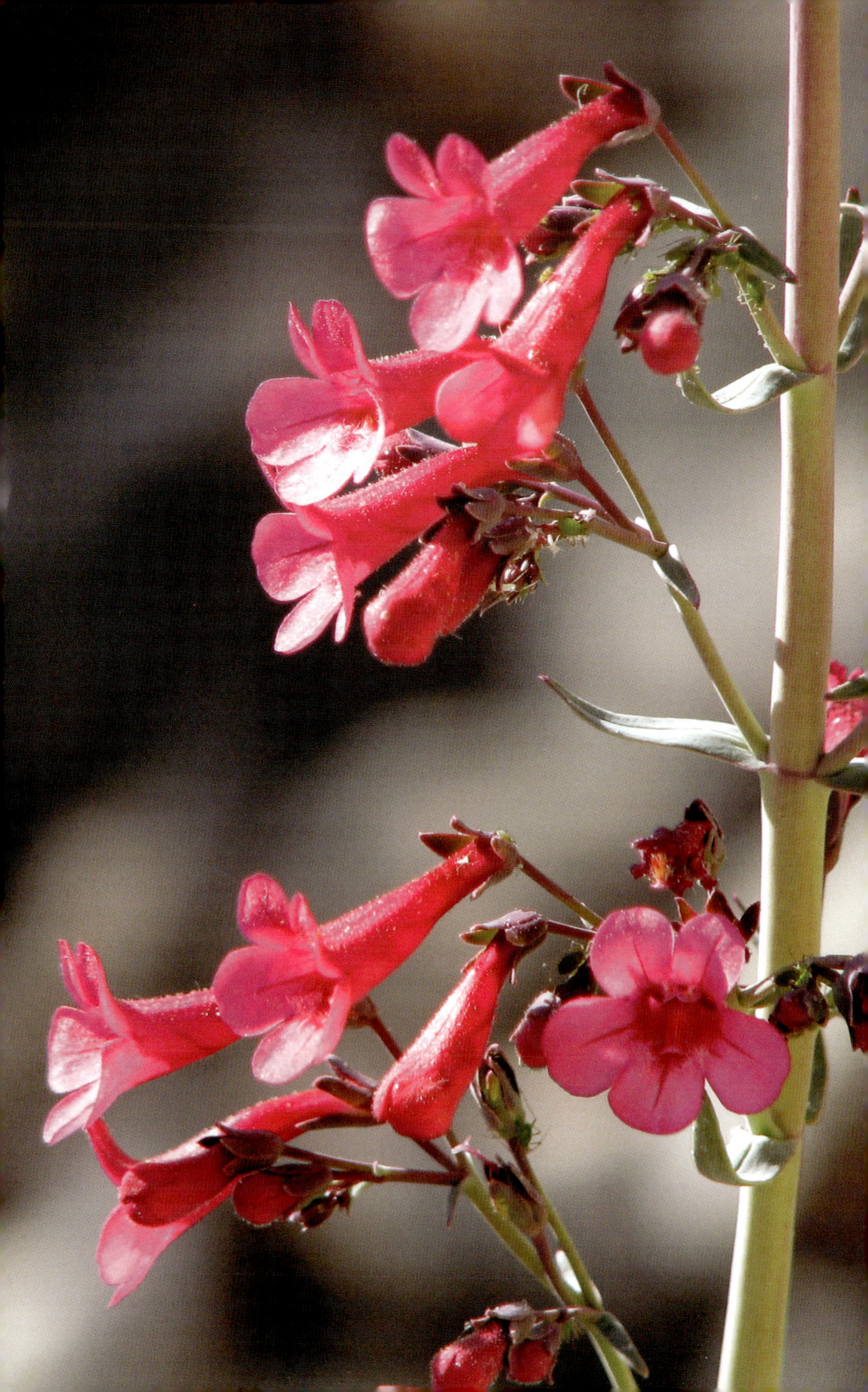

Penstemon parryi

Parry's Penstemon, Varita de San José, Pichelitos

Family:	Plantaginaceae (Scrophulariaceae)	**Bloom:**	March–April
		Water use:	Low–moderate
Type:	Perennial	**Cold hardiness:**	Top growth to 15°F
Size:	1' high x 1–2' wide, with flower stalks to 3' high	**USDA zone:**	8–10

Author citation: (A. Gray) A. Gray

The enchanting funnel-shaped flowers of deep rosy pink are reason enough to plant Parry's penstemon, but they are also a valuable source of nectar for nesting Costa's Hummingbirds, Arizona populations of Anna's Hummingbird, and northbound Broad-tailed Hummingbirds at a time when few other flowers are in bloom. Black-chinned, Lucifer, Broad-billed, Magnificent, and Rufous Hummingbirds are known to visit the blossoms as well. Hummingbirds appear to be the chief pollinators, with bees earning an honorable mention. Parry's penstemon is also a larval host plant for butterflies.

This Sonoran Desert native has a relatively small geographic range, from central and southern Arizona southward into Sonora, Mexico, but particularly in Arizona it is fairly common. It can be found in desert washes, on rocky north slopes, in mountain canyons, and in grasslands, at elevations of 1,500 to 5,000 feet.

In late winter the evergreen basal rosette of fleshy, pale sage green foliage sends up several erect three-foot stalks that are punctuated with narrow clasping leaves and clusters of flower buds that are among the first of the spring penstemons to bloom.

A coarse, well-drained soil that is low in organic content is preferred. Plants thrive in full sun in most areas but also do not mind a bit of afternoon shade, particularly in extremely hot locations. Too much shade, on the other hand, tends to result in leggy growth and sparse bloom. When the seed capsule dries and turns tan-colored, cut the stalk back, shake it over the ground where you would like to establish plants, and scratch in the tiny black seeds. Sally Wasowski recommends lightly covering seeds of this and other penstemons with a mulch of decomposed granite to hide them from birds and insects—a great idea! Deer and rabbits browse on the foliage, so protect plants where necessary. When starting a new garden plant at least three of a species for good cross-pollination. Parry's penstemon works beautifully in rock gardens, borders, and massed plantings, and is especially suitable for difficult low-desert landscapes in the filtered shade of palo verdes or mesquites.

Penstemon pinifolius

Pineleaf Penstemon, Pine-needle Penstemon

Family:	Plantaginaceae (Scrophulariaceae)	**Bloom:**	Late May–July, sporadic through August
Type:	Perennial	**Water use:**	Low–moderate
Size:	1–1.5' high x 2' wide	**Cold hardiness:**	Roots to -20°F
		USDA zone:	5–9

Author citation: Greene

THIS IS A TERRIFIC EARLY SUMMER–BLOOMING PENSTEMON for an upland hummingbird garden, its profusion of tiny orange-red flowers offering valuable nectar when often few other nectar flowers are yet in full bloom. Broad-tailed and White-eared Hummingbirds especially favor the blossoms, and Black-chinned, Rufous, and Calliope Hummingbirds are avid customers as well. Hummingbirds are likely the primary pollinators.

Pineleaf penstemon has a fairly small native range, occurring only in southeast Arizona, where it is mostly limited to the Chiricahua Mountains, southwest and south-central New Mexico, where it is more widely distributed, and Sonora and Chihuahua in northern Mexico. It is confined to montane habitats, typically steep rocky slopes or outcroppings, gravelly arroyos, and openings in ponderosa pine forests, at elevations of 5,500 to 10,000 feet.

Its slender green stems grow from a woody base, forming a dense, spreading, shrubby clump quite unlike most penstemons. The distinctive needle-like bright green leaves often nearly cover the stems. In winter the foliage on some forms turns red. The one-inch flowers are borne on one side of the stem and have extremely narrow corollas, with the two upper lobes projecting outward and the lower three reflexed slightly backward. The throat is yellow-orange and coated with sticky yellow hairs that trap tiny insects, offering a nutritional bonus for hummingbirds.

This copiously flowering penstemon needs a sunny exposure and a well-drained, gravelly soil for best performance. In the lower elevations it will benefit from some filtered afternoon shade and a deep soaking two or three times per month during the summer growing season; even then it may be tricky at best. Pineleaf penstemon makes a nice plant for the front of a border planting, as an accent in rock gardens, or massed for a ground cover. It also can be grown in containers, which will elevate the flowers and make them more accessible to hummingbirds, but they must then be watered regularly. Propagate by seed sown on site in spring after cold stratifying for two months. Stems that grow prostrate along the ground may take root and these can be divided fairly easily. Soft stem cuttings are also said to root readily, atypical of the majority of penstemons.

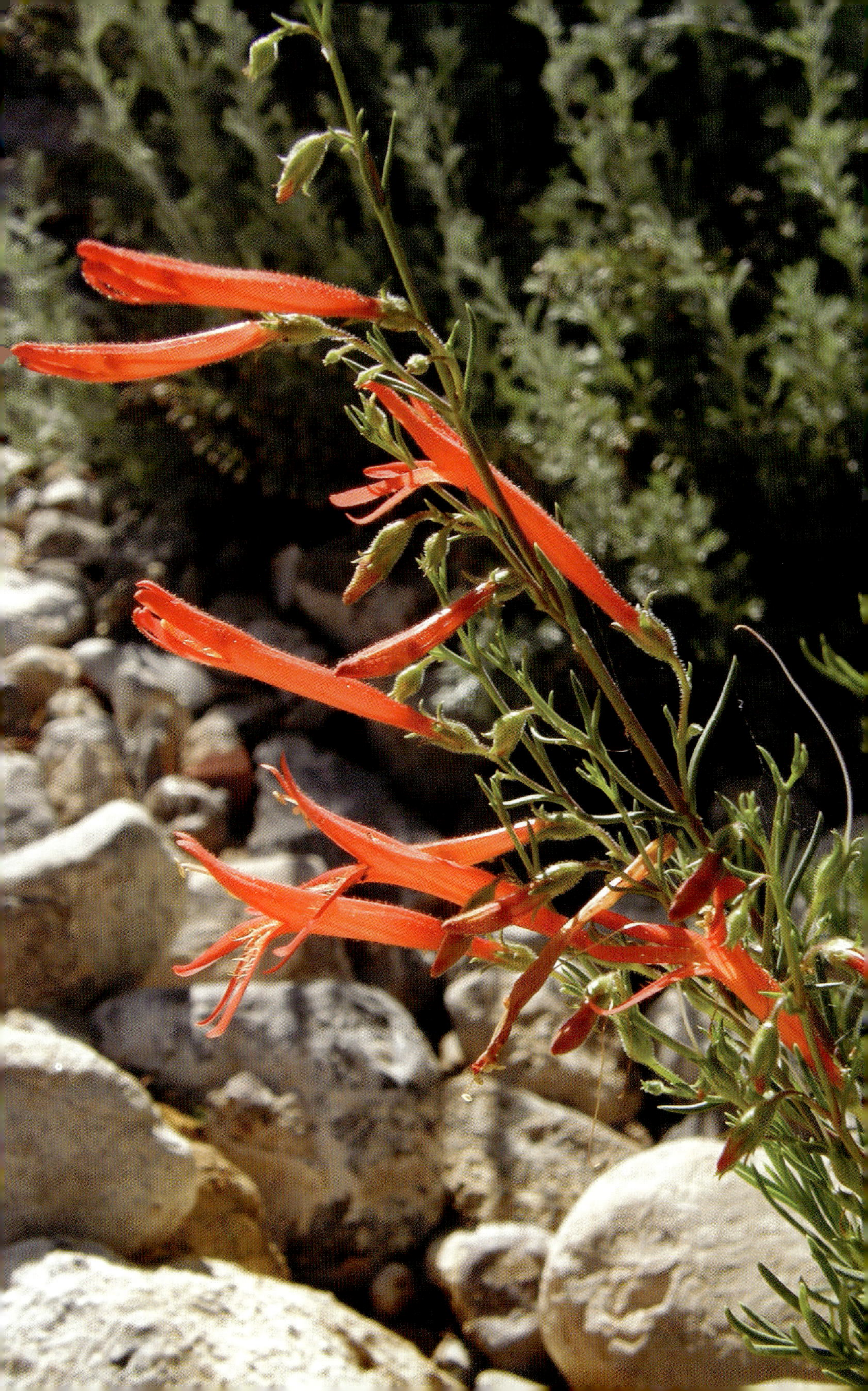

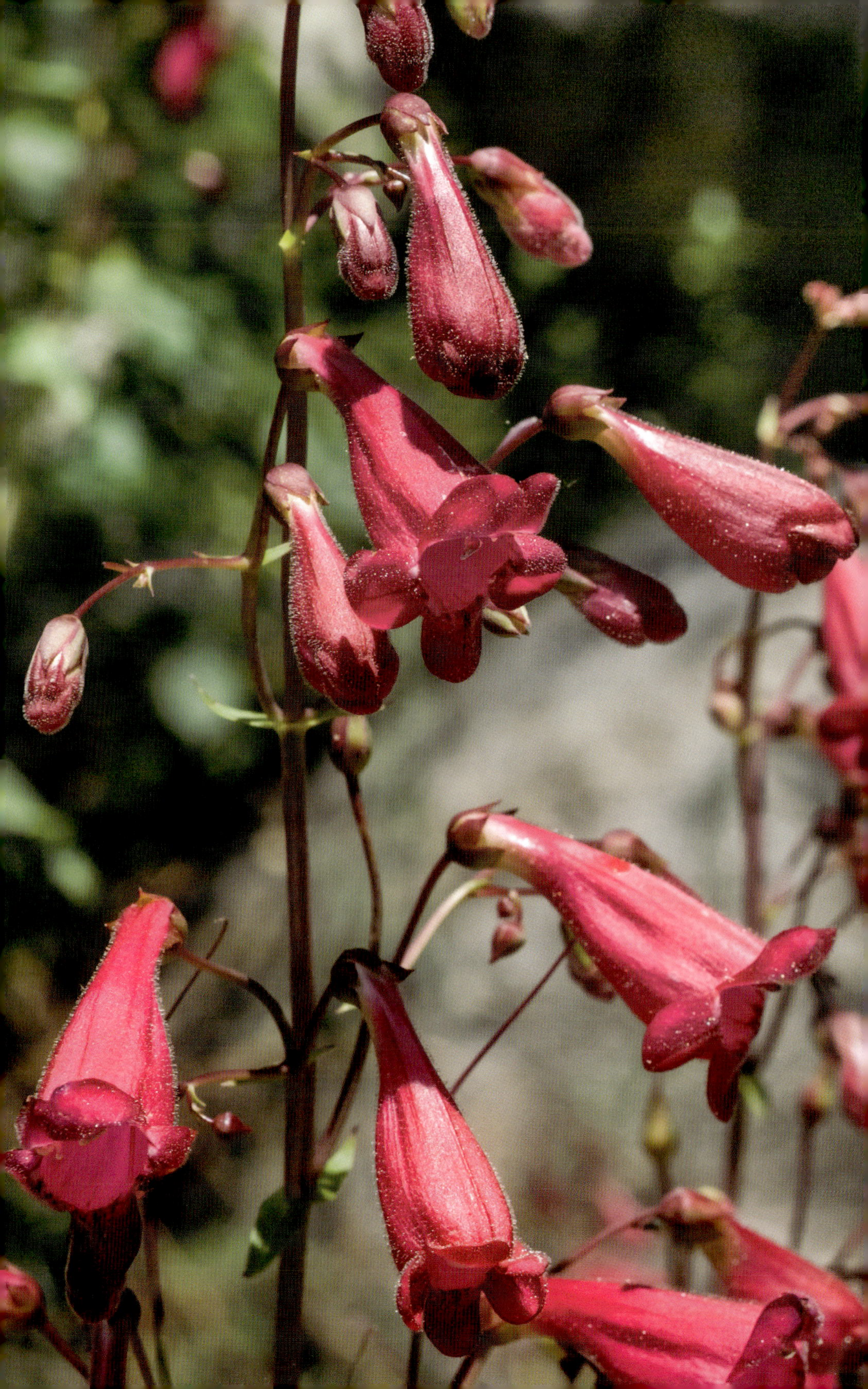

Penstemon pseudospectabilis

Desert Beardtongue, Canyon Penstemon, Mojave Beardtongue

Family:	Plantaginaceae (Scrophulariaceae)	**Bloom:**	March–June
Type:	Perennial	**Water use:**	Low–moderate
Size:	1' high x 2' wide, with flower stalks to 5' high	**Cold hardiness:**	Top to 10°F, roots to -20°F
		USDA zone:	5–8
Author citation:	M. E. Jones		

Desert beardtongue is a captivating perennial with deep rose to salmon-pink flowers that provide valuable spring nectar for nesting Broad-billed and Costa's Hummingbirds. Black-chinned, Anna's, Broad-tailed, Magnificent, and migrating Rufous Hummingbirds are also known to visit the flowers. Cranking out nectar that is both ample (nearly four milligrams of sugar per flower per day) and sweet (averaging about 27 percent sugar), the plants are pollinated by both bees and hummingbirds. In Guadalupe Canyon on the southern Arizona–New Mexico border, desert beardtongue supplies the bulk of nectar during the month of May for the various hummingbirds breeding there.

This delightful penstemon has a fairly broad range, extending from southeastern California through most of Arizona and southern Utah into southwestern New Mexico and just the northern fringe of Mexico in northwestern Sonora. Typically, it occurs in desert washes, on dry rocky slopes and canyon walls, and in piñon-juniper and ponderosa pine forests at elevations of 350 to 7,000 feet.

Its shrubby evergreen rosette is grayish green, as are the large triangular ragged-toothed leaves that clasp the tall but often sprawling flower stalks that emerge in early spring. Cold weather may give the foliage a reddish-purple tinge. The tubular flowers differ from those of many other penstemons used by hummingbirds because one side of the corolla billows out, reportedly to give bee pollinators easier access to the nectar. The blossoms appear in whorls along the flower stalk and bloom from early to late spring.

As with many others in its family, desert beardtongue needs a gravelly, well-drained soil, filtered or afternoon shade in all but the coolest locations, and a deep soaking once a month during the summer to prevent dormancy. In extremely windy areas, protect it from drying winter winds by planting it on the lee side of walls, shrub borders, or boulders. Allow some stalks to go to seed as plants tend to be short-lived. Typically, seeds will germinate during the cooler months; if sowing stored seeds, plant in fall or cold stratify for one to two months before planting. This showy hummingbird magnet is marvelous for rock gardens, seasonal washes, mixed borders, raised beds, and mass plantings.

Penstemon ramosus
Branching Penstemon, Lanceleaf Beardtongue

Family:	Plantaginaceae (Scrophulariaceae)	**Bloom:**	May–July (*ramosus*), July–September (*lanceolatus*)
Type:	Perennial	**Water use:**	Low–moderate
Size:	1–2' high x 1.5' wide, flower stalks to 2.5' high	**Cold hardiness:**	To at least 10°F
		USDA zone:	7–9

Author citation: Crosswhite
Synonym: *P. lanceolatus* auct. non Bentham

THIS DESERT MOUNTAIN BEAUTY MAY NOT BE WELL KNOWN OR WIDESPREAD, but where it does occur it is certain to be much used by hummingbirds. Its long narrow tubular flowers of deep scarlet red offer nectar during the breeding season of Black-chinned, Broad-billed, and Violet-crowned Hummingbirds, all species that share the same habitat. Undoubtedly, hummingbirds are the principal pollinators.

Branching penstemon hails from southeastern Arizona, where it is extremely rare, southwestern New Mexico, where it is slightly more common, and the Big Bend region of Texas, beyond which its status is rather murky as its very close cousin, *Penstemon lanceolatus*, begins to appear and occurs southward through northern Mexico in Chihuahua, Coahuila, Nuevo Leon, and Durango. Its favored haunts are rocky slopes, desert grasslands, arroyos, and canyon bottoms at elevations ranging from 4,000 to 7,000 feet. Populations are scattered in distribution but perhaps most common along the Gila River drainage.

The densely hairy stalks originate from a woody crown, with branching stems that distinguish it from *Penstemon lanceolatus*. The two- to four-inch gray-green leaves are somewhat downy and narrowly lance-shaped, the edges typically turning backward. The one- to one-and-a-half-inch-long pendulous flowers also wear a layer of sticky hairs, and are borne singly or in pairs on branchlets from stem nodes. When fertile, the anthers are twisted.

Occurring on rocky or gravelly sites in the wild, often with northern or northeastern exposures, this attractive penstemon needs a fast-draining soil and full sun to part shade in the garden. At low elevations some protection from mid-afternoon sun would be wise. Allow at least one flower stalk to set seed and when capsules turn brown and woody, collect the seeds and scatter them on the desired site. As with other penstemons, seeds tend to germinate during the cooler months and may benefit from prior stratification. Branching penstemon would make a valuable addition to a middle-elevation hummingbird garden, filling an important nectar slot for breeding birds, and would work beautifully in a natural or simulated rocky wash. Look for it at specialty suppliers or native plant sales in its home region.

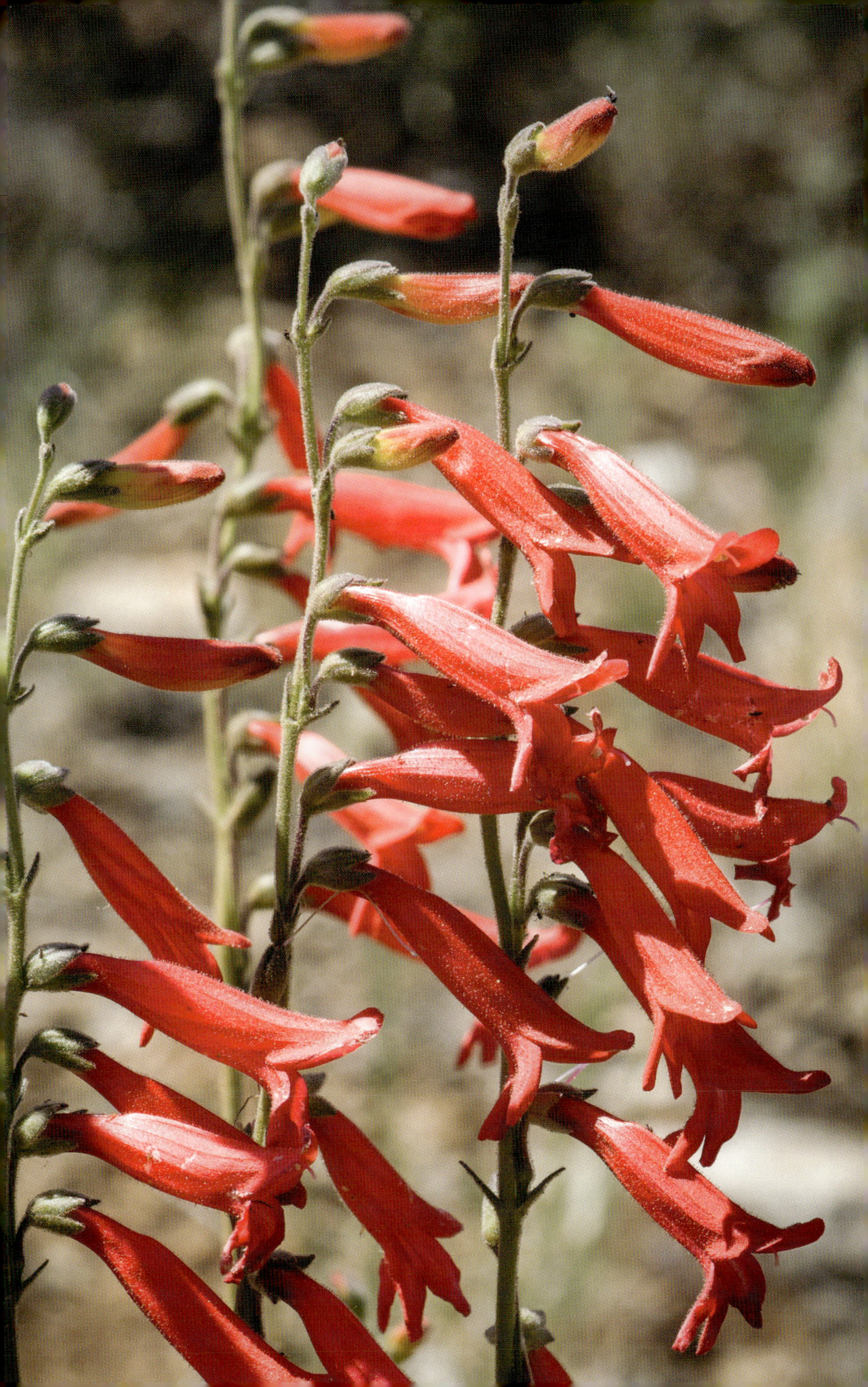

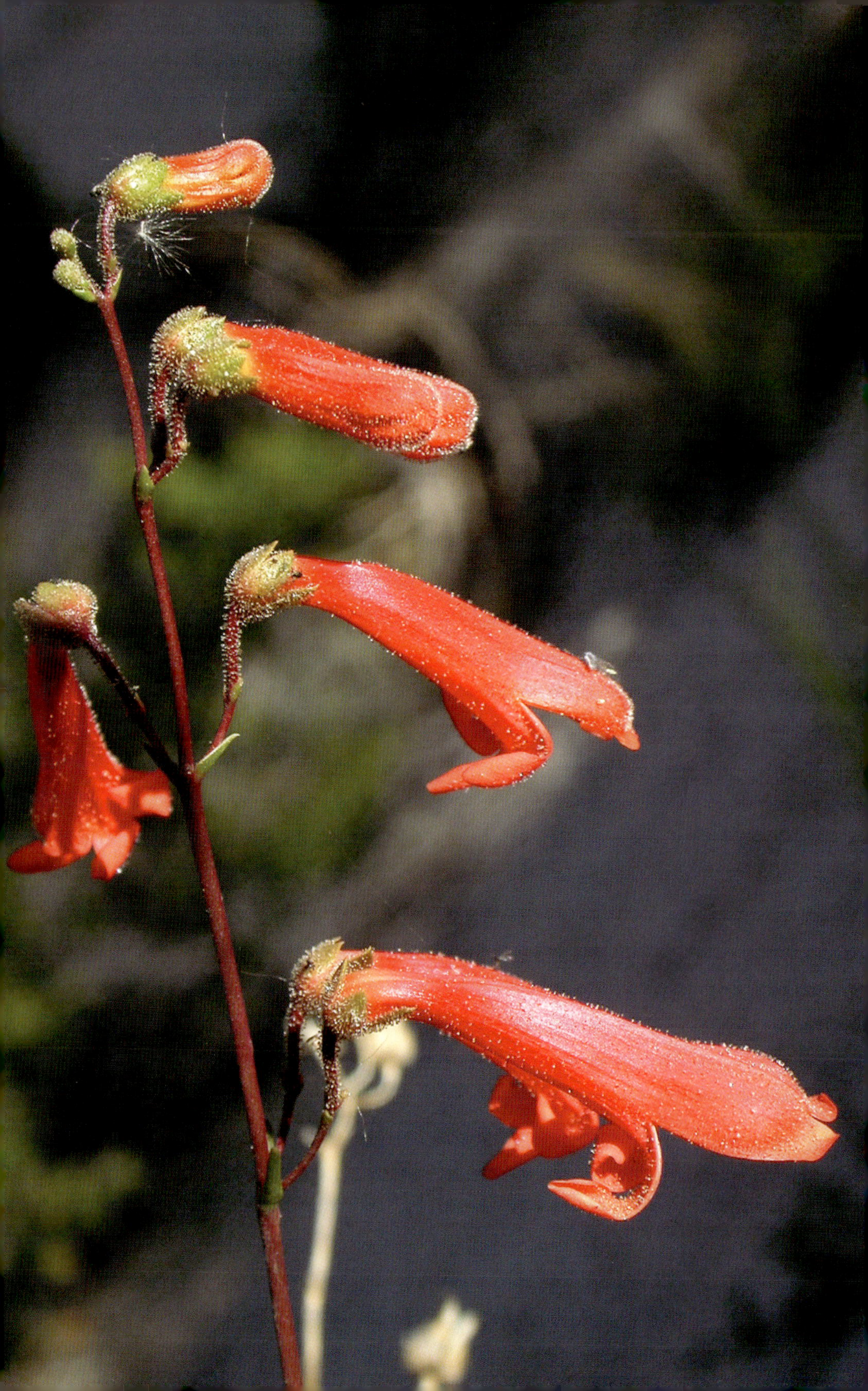

Penstemon rostriflorus
Beaked Beardtongue, Bridges' Penstemon

Family:	Plantaginaceae (Scrophulariaceae)	**Bloom:**	May–September
		Water use:	Moderate
Type:	Perennial	**Cold hardiness:**	To -20°F
Size:	1' high x 1' wide, with flower stalks to 3' high	**USDA zone:**	5–10
Author citation:	Kellogg		
Synonym:	*P. bridgesii* A. Gray		

This striking penstemon's long bloom season enables it to snag both breeding and migrant hummingbirds throughout its range. The scarlet to deep red tubular flowers offer abundant nectar to Calliope, Rufous, Allen's, Costa's, Anna's, and probably Broad-tailed Hummingbirds, who in return perform pollination services. Many insects are also attracted to the blossoms.

Beaked beardtongue enjoys a broad geographical distribution, from California, where it occurs from the Sierra Nevadas south through the Lower Coast, Transverse, and Peninsular ranges, eastward through southern Nevada, southern Utah, and southwestern Colorado, and southward through northern Arizona and western New Mexico. The habitats in which it is found are quite diverse and include sage scrub, Joshua tree scrub, piñon-juniper woodlands, and lodgepole or ponderosa pine forests. Most often it occurs on dry slopes at elevations between 4,500 and 10,000 feet, where it tends to form large, sprawling clumps and may become quite shrubby.

The sometimes erect, sometimes droopy flower stems are woody at the base and bear numerous one- to three-inch linear leaves that are a rich green in color. Both the stems and the undersides of the leaves are often purplish early in the season. The one-inch flowers, which like the stems are covered in sticky glandular hairs that trap insects, are borne along a one-foot spike and are held horizontally. Each blossom has a reflexed lower lip that deters bees and an upper lip that forms a hood or beak over the horseshoe-shaped anthers and gives the plant its common name. The tan seedpods may persist for a year or more.

Plants need a sunny exposure, excellent drainage, and an occasional deep soaking during the summer to thrive, flourishing in lean dry soils as well as those enriched with organic matter. To propagate, simply collect the seed when it ripens and scatter where new plants are desired. Cold stratification, unless planting in late fall, will often improve germination rates. Beaked beardtongue reportedly performs best in areas with cool summer temperatures, so it would make an excellent choice for an upland hummingbird garden or rockery, especially in the northern portion of our range.

Penstemon subulatus

Little Beardtongue, Hackberry Beardtongue

Family:	Plantaginaceae (Scrophulariaceae)	**Bloom:**	March–May
Type:	Perennial	**Water use:**	Low–moderate
Size:	<1' high x 1' wide, with flower stalk 2–3' high	**Cold hardiness:**	To -10°F
		USDA zone:	8–9

Author citation: M. E. Jones

THIS PENSTEMON MAY BE RATHER DIMINUTIVE, but nesting Costa's Hummingbirds zero in on its fiery orange-red nectar-bearing flowers as soon as they begin to unfurl in early spring. Hummingbirds most likely perform the lion's share of pollination duties.

Little beardtongue is endemic to Arizona, making its home in Sonoran Desert scrublands in and among a number of mountain ranges that traverse the midsection of the state at elevations ranging from 1,500 to 5,500 feet. The Pinaleño, Santa Rita, Tucson, Santa Catalina, Picacho, Tortilla, Hieroglyphic, Eagletail, Bradshaw, Vulture, and Harcuvar mountains are some of the locations where it occurs, typically forming small colonies on dry rocky slopes, mesas, and outcrops, in canyons, or along seasonal washes. Plants with which it is commonly found include foothills palo verde, ironwood, brittlebush, creosote bush, and presumably spiny hackberry (*Celtis pallida*).

The evergreen foliage is gray-green, ovate in shape in the basal rosette and more linear (*subulatus* means awl-shaped, as penstemon grower and author Robert Nold points out) along the erect, pink-tinged flower stems. The tubular flowers are held horizontally and are among the narrowest in the family (only those of pineleaf penstemon, *P. pinifolius,* are narrower).

This, like most penstemons, insists on a fast-draining, sandy or gravelly soil that is low in organic matter. It is extremely drought tolerant and handles full or reflected sun well, but also does beautifully in part or filtered shade. Clipping spent spikes may encourage a second bloom, but allow some to go to seed to guarantee some new plants. A search may be required to locate a source for plants or seeds, but if one can be found, little beardtongue would make a perfect ground cover for a desert hummingbird garden, especially apropos in the vicinity of any natural areas where Costa's Hummingbirds are known to breed. It would also work well in a raised bed, where the height of the flowers would be elevated and more accommodating to the hummingbirds. Propagate by fresh seed sown in fall. If planting in spring, cold stratifying the seeds for one to two months may improve germination rates.

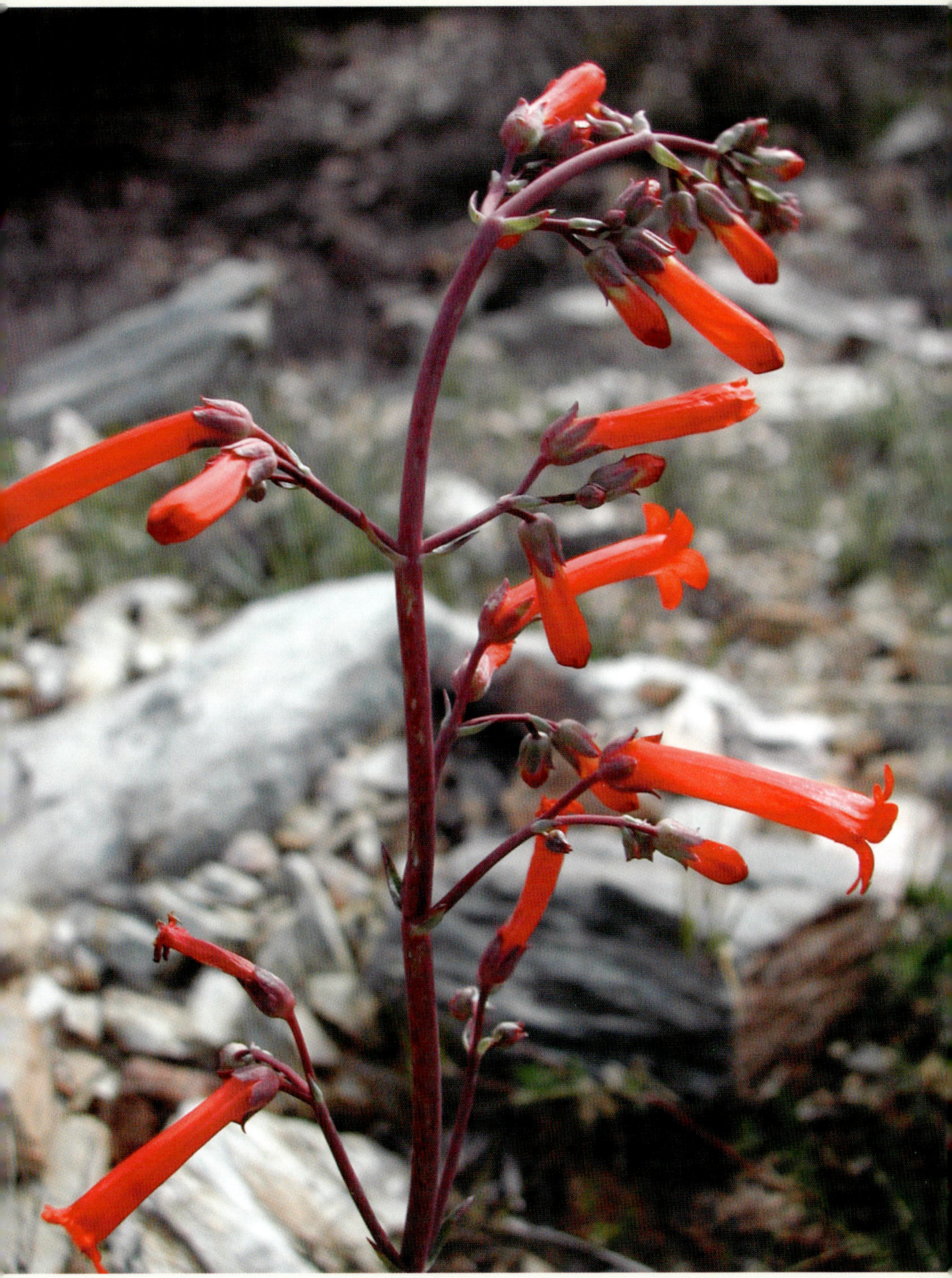

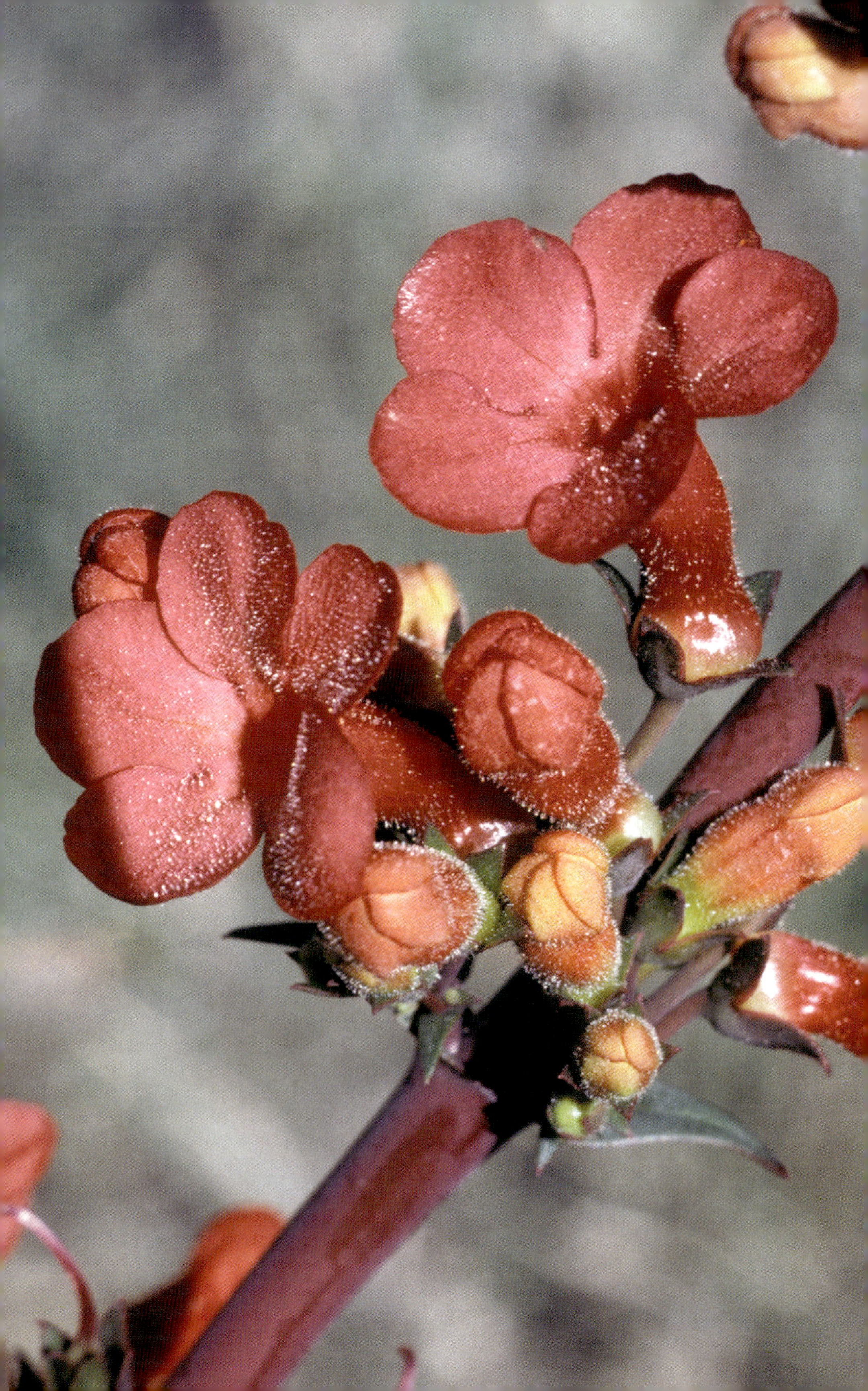

Penstemon superbus

Superb Penstemon, Coral Penstemon

Family:	Plantaginaceae (Scrophulariaceae)	**Bloom:**	March–May
Type:	Perennial	**Water use:**	Low–moderate
Size:	1' high x 1–2' wide, with flower stalks 3–6' high	**Cold hardiness:**	To 5–10°F
		USDA zone:	7–10

Author citation: A. Nelson

THIS PENSTEMON TRULY *IS* SUPERB! It is a vigorous grower and if allowed to colonize a bed or corner of the garden, will delight humans and hummingbirds alike for many years. Its vivid coral-red tubular flowers are packed with high-sucrose nectar and are avidly visited by Broad-billed, Black-chinned, Lucifer, Violet-crowned, and Costa's Hummingbirds. Note that House Finches occasionally may eat the buds just as they start to open, and Lesser Goldfinches are fond of the seeds.

Superb penstemon is a transitional plant of the Chihuahuan and Sonoran deserts, ranging from central and southeastern Arizona through southwestern New Mexico and southward into Mexico in northeastern Sonora and northwestern Chihuahua, at elevations of 3,200 to 5,800 feet. In its favored grassland habitats, it often forms large colonies, but it may also be found in rocky canyons, on piñon-juniper slopes, among ponderosa pines, in seasonal washes, and along roadsides.

The evergreen basal rosette is bluish-green, as are the fleshy, ovate leaves that clasp or may even surround the upright, three- to four-foot flower stalk. Both stems and leaves sometimes have a purplish tinge.

Plants prefer a sandy or gravelly well-drained soil and are fairly drought tolerant, in most situations needing only a deep soaking once or twice a month during the summer if not on drip irrigation. They abhor overhead watering, including roof runoff. In most instances they do well in full sun to part shade but prefer filtered shade in very hot low-desert regions, where the shade of mesquites or acacias provides an ideal niche. Superb penstemon is terrific for rock gardens, borders, and mass plantings. In late summer, when the seed capsule dries and turns tan-colored, cut the stalk back, shake it over the ground where plants are desired, and scratch in the tiny black seeds. A swale that can harbor a self-perpetuating colony of plants is ideal. Young basal rosettes are fairly easy to transplant in winter as well. Note that superb penstemon is quite similar to and blooms at the same time as Parry's penstemon (*P. parryi*), and the two will hybridize where they occur together.

Penstemon utahensis

Utah Firecracker, Utah Penstemon

Family:	Plantaginaceae (Scrophulariaceae)	**Bloom:**	April–June
Type:	Perennial	**Water use:**	Low–moderate
Size:	1' high x 1–2' wide, with flower stalks to 3' high	**Cold hardiness:**	To -10°F
		USDA zone:	6–8

Author citation: Eastwood

THE VOLLEY OF BLOOMS THAT THIS EYE-POPPING PENSTEMON SENDS UP in early spring are undoubtedly cause for celebration among the ranks of northbound hummingbirds returning to their breeding territories in the intermountain West. The narrow, slightly flaring tubular blossoms range from hot pinkish red to bright red-orange, and offer valuable nectar when few other plants are blooming. Pollination appears to be a joint venture of both hummingbirds and bees, some botanists speculating that the species is still in the process of evolving toward hummingbird pollination.

Utah firecracker is an uncommon resident of desert mountains from eastern California (where rare) through southern Nevada, northern Arizona, the southern and eastern portions of its namesake state of Utah, and southwestern Colorado, at elevations of 3,500 to 6,500 feet and occasionally much higher. Sometimes forming large colonies, its diverse natural haunts include rocky mesas, brushy slopes, sage scrub flats, canyons, and piñon-juniper woodlands.

The evergreen basal rosette consists of thick, waxy, blue-green leaves that are narrowly triangular in shape and roll inward. In late winter the two- to three-foot glaucous flower stalk appears, sparsely dressed with pairs of lance-shaped leaves. The one-inch trumpet-shaped flowers, held horizontally and with lobes that spread at right angles to the corolla tube, unfurl a short time afterward.

This penstemon is reportedly difficult to find in the nursery trade, challenging to cultivate, and frustratingly short-lived, even for a penstemon. The best odds will come from planting in a lean, coarse soil with excellent drainage, minimal water, a sunny exposure, and some winter chill. It is not a good choice for the intense heat of the low deserts. If it can be located at a native plant sale or specialty seed supplier, Utah firecracker would make a fine addition to a wildflower garden or higher-elevation desert planting. Regardless, it is a beauty to be enjoyed and appreciated in its natural habitats. Propagate by fresh seeds sown in place in early fall and seedlings will usually begin to emerge by early winter. Stratifying the seeds for one to two months may improve the germination rate.

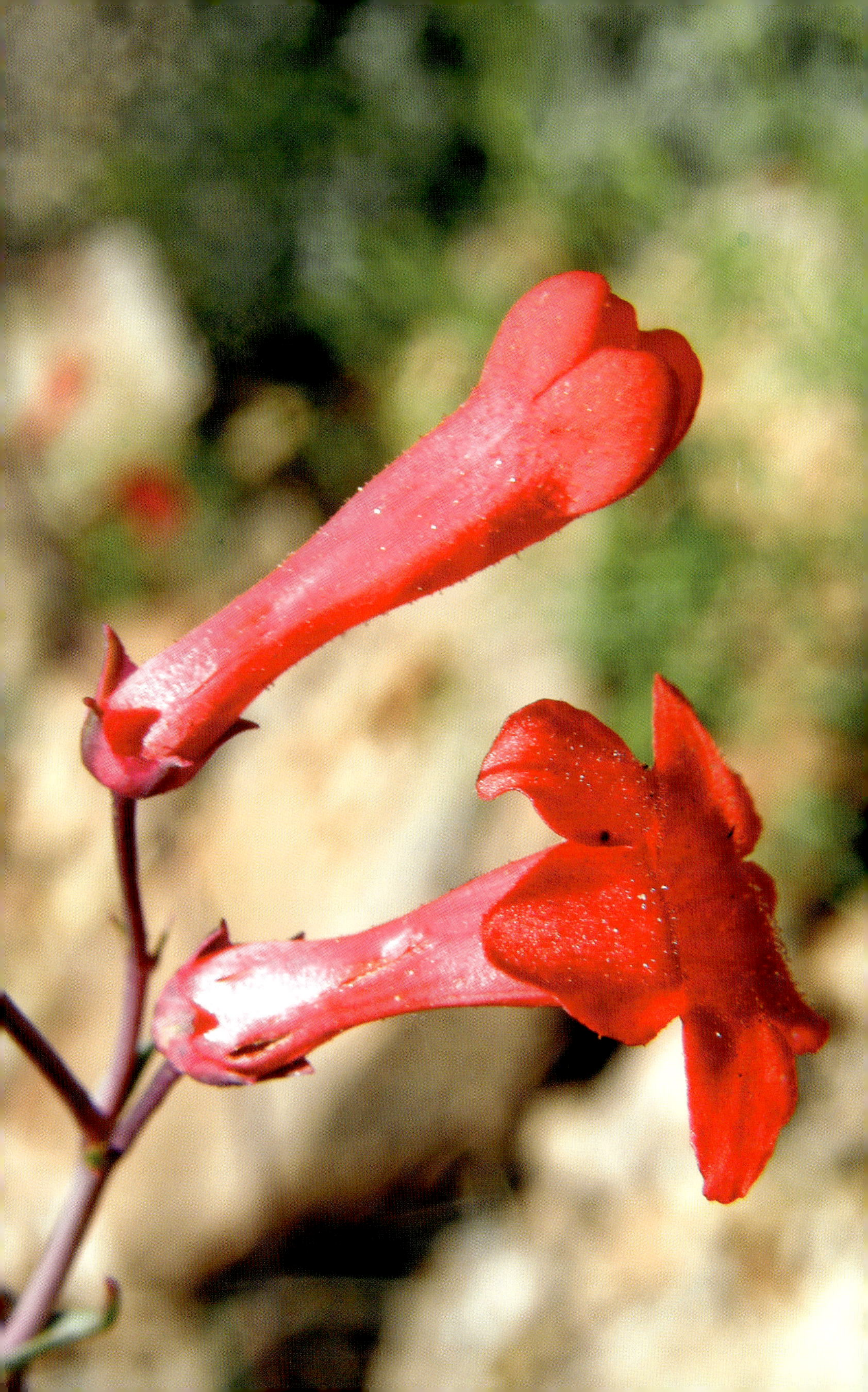

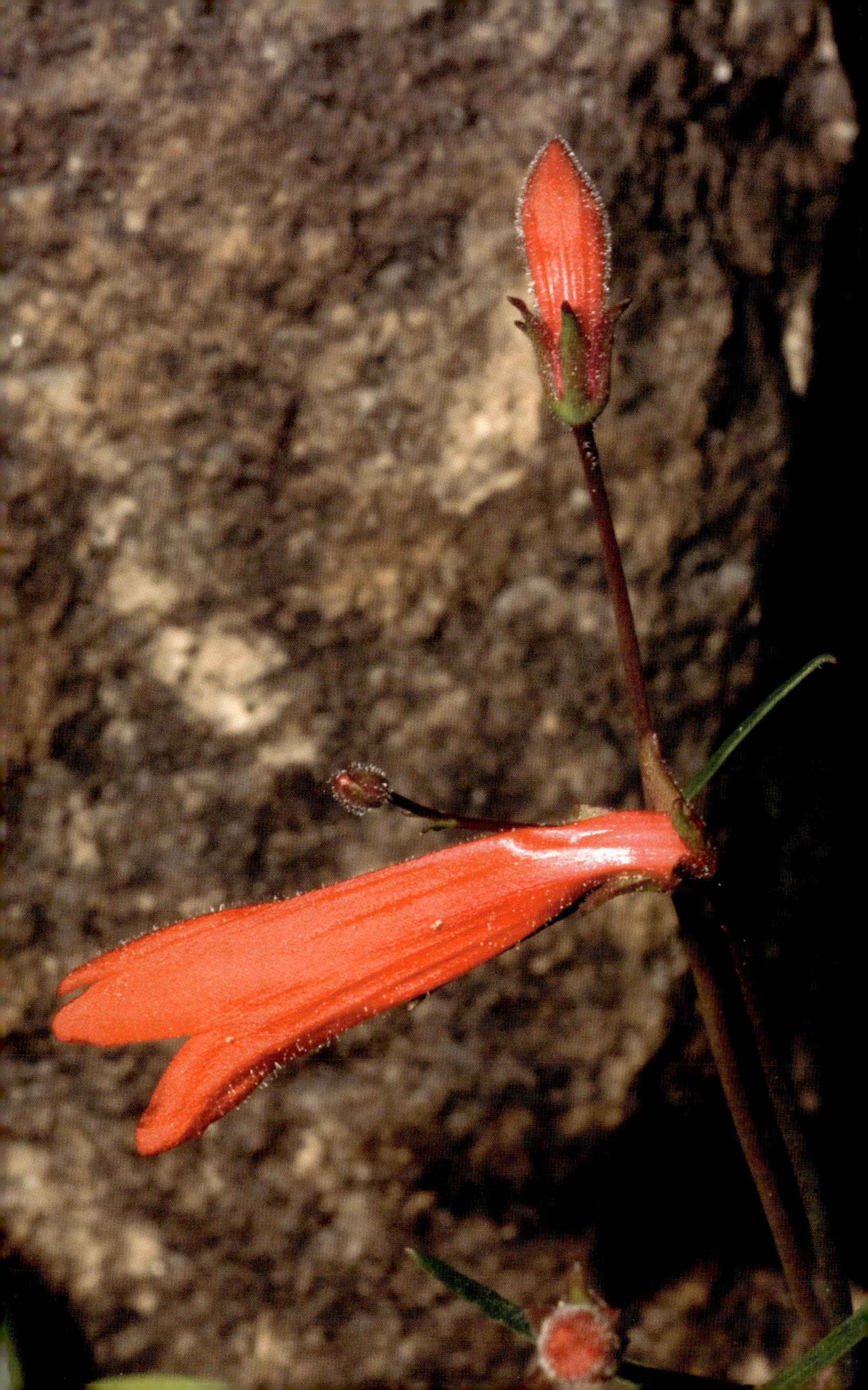

Penstemon wislizenii

Madrean Beardtongue, Wislizenius' Penstemon

Family:	Plantaginaceae (Scrophulariaceae)	**Bloom:**	May–September
		Water use:	Low–moderate
Type:	Perennial	**Cold hardiness:**	To 20°F
Size:	2–3' high x 1' wide	**USDA zone:**	9–10
Author citation:	(A. Gray) Straw		

THIS MEXICAN BEAUTY IS ANOTHER PENSTEMON SPECIES about which relatively little information exists in the literature. Researchers from the Arizona-Sonora Desert Museum believe that although the plant is primarily dependent upon hummingbirds for pollination, it is probably not common enough to be of great importance to hummingbirds. Regardless, its late spring and summer scarlet tubular flowers are well used where they do occur. Migrating Rufous Hummingbirds in particular have been observed nectaring at the flowers as they move southward toward their wintering grounds in late summer.

Rare and limited solely to northern Mexico in its distribution, Madrean beardtongue inhabits mountainous areas of eastern Sonora, western Chihuahua, and principally Durango in the Sierra Madre Occidental. Nearly always found in dry pine-oak forests and grassy openings, it typically occurs at elevations of about 5,000 to 7,500 feet. Solitary plants may appear somewhat spindly, with one to three fuzzy, mostly leafless, upright flower stems and a small clump of dark green, spatula-shaped leaves at the base, whereas stands of blooming plants are much more attractive. Flowers are presented near stem tips, each with a long narrow tubular corolla that is slightly puffy and flares at the mouth and a shortened lower petal lobe that flares or reflexes backward to allow a hovering hummingbird access. The blossoms open from bottom to top, and when the stalk is spent the rounded seedpods begin to form.

If little is known about this plant's natural habits, then next to nothing is currently known about cultivating it, which is unfortunate because it is likely a fairly easy plant to grow. If seeds can be obtained from a specialty supplier or nursery, best results will probably come from planting on a middle elevation site with mild winters, full sun to part shade, good drainage, and regular watering until established and as needed afterwards. Mulching lightly with pine needles will not only help to keep plants cool in summer and warm during winter but also may add some nutrients to the soil that will make the young plants feel at home. Propagation by seed is simplest.

Penstemon wrightii

Wright's Beardtongue, Wright's Penstemon, Texas Rose

Family:	Plantaginaceae (Scrophulariaceae)	**Bloom:**	March–May
Type:	Perennial	**Water use:**	Low–moderate
Size:	1' high x 1–2' wide, with flower stalks to 3' high	**Cold hardiness:**	To 5–10°F
		USDA zone:	8–10
Author citation:	Hooker		

Rounding out the long honor roll of penstemons that are particularly attractive to hummingbirds is this Chihuahuan Desert beauty, whose intense deep coral blossoms beckon breeding Black-chinned Hummingbirds and others from spring into early summer. Presumably, hummingbirds are its primary pollinators.

Wright's beardtongue is endemic to Trans-Pecos Texas, occurring only in four counties in the Big Bend region of the state (namely Brewster, Presidio, Jeff Davis, and Reeves). Even on its home turf it does not seem to be very well known or described, but it seems to favor rocky streambeds and washes in foothills and canyons of desert mountains, to about 5,500 feet in elevation.

In flower structure and color it is quite similar to an Arizona cousin, superb penstemon (*P. superbus*), but it is more compact in habit. It has an evergreen basal rosette of large, fleshy, light green, egg-shaped leaves, from which the two- to three-foot flower stalks shoot up in springtime, bearing clusters of one-inch, richly colored tubular flowers.

Wright's beardtongue, while strongly associated with limestone soils in the wild, does well in any well-drained coarse soil in full sun or partial shade. It is extremely drought tolerant, although a deep soaking once a month during flowering or prolonged drought will keep plants performing their best. Cutting back the spent stalks will often prolong the bloom, but keep in mind that in order for plants to self-sow, at least one stalk must be allowed to go to seed. After the seedpods dry and turn brown, collect the seeds in late summer or early fall and scratch them in wherever you would like to establish a new bed. Seedlings typically begin appearing by late fall, and these very young plants usually can be transplanted fairly easily. If storing seeds, cold stratification for one to two months before planting will yield the best results. Give this showy penstemon a corner to colonize, and it will make a sensational addition to a rock garden, simulated dry wash, or Chihuahuan Desert hummingbird habitat planting.

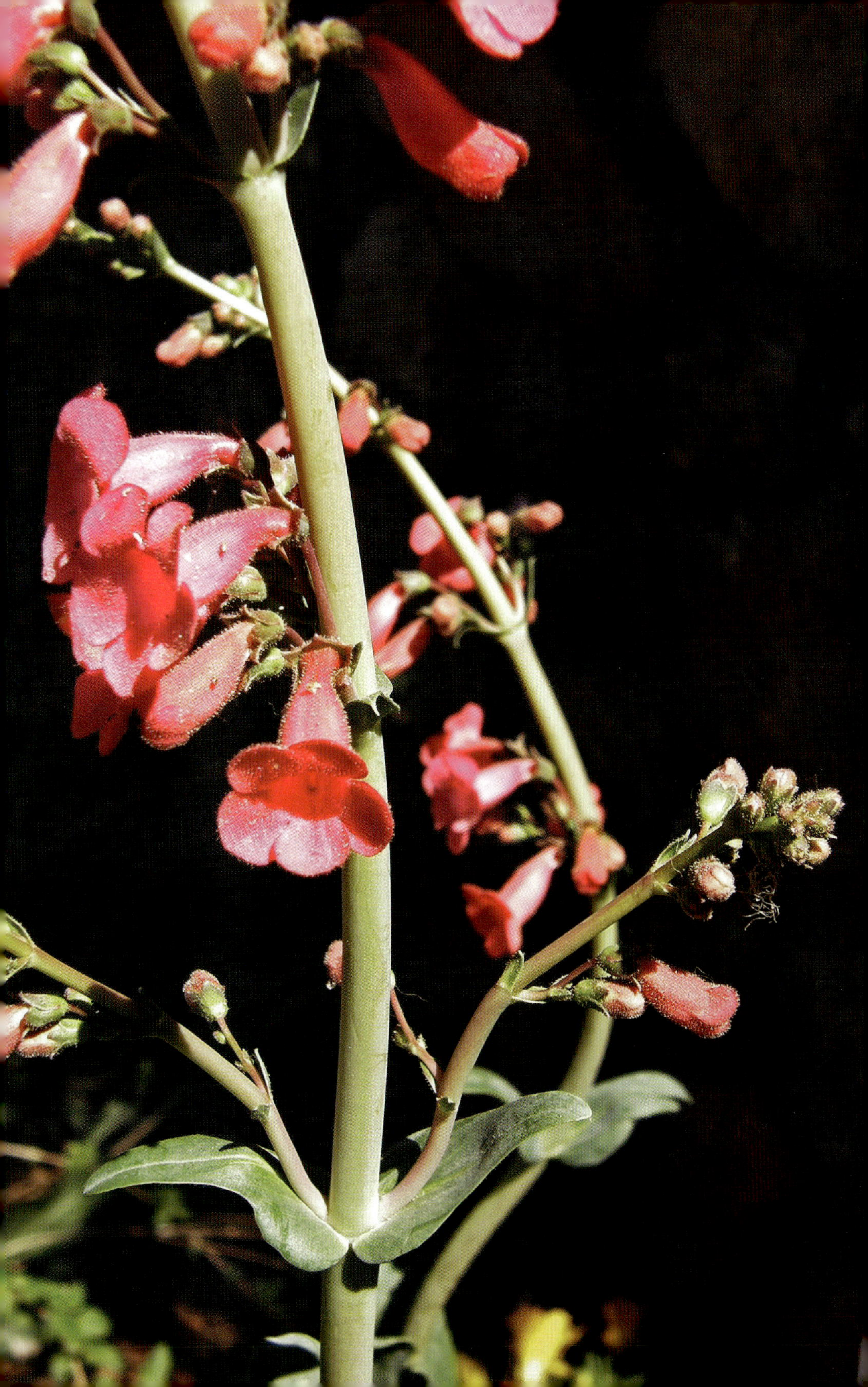

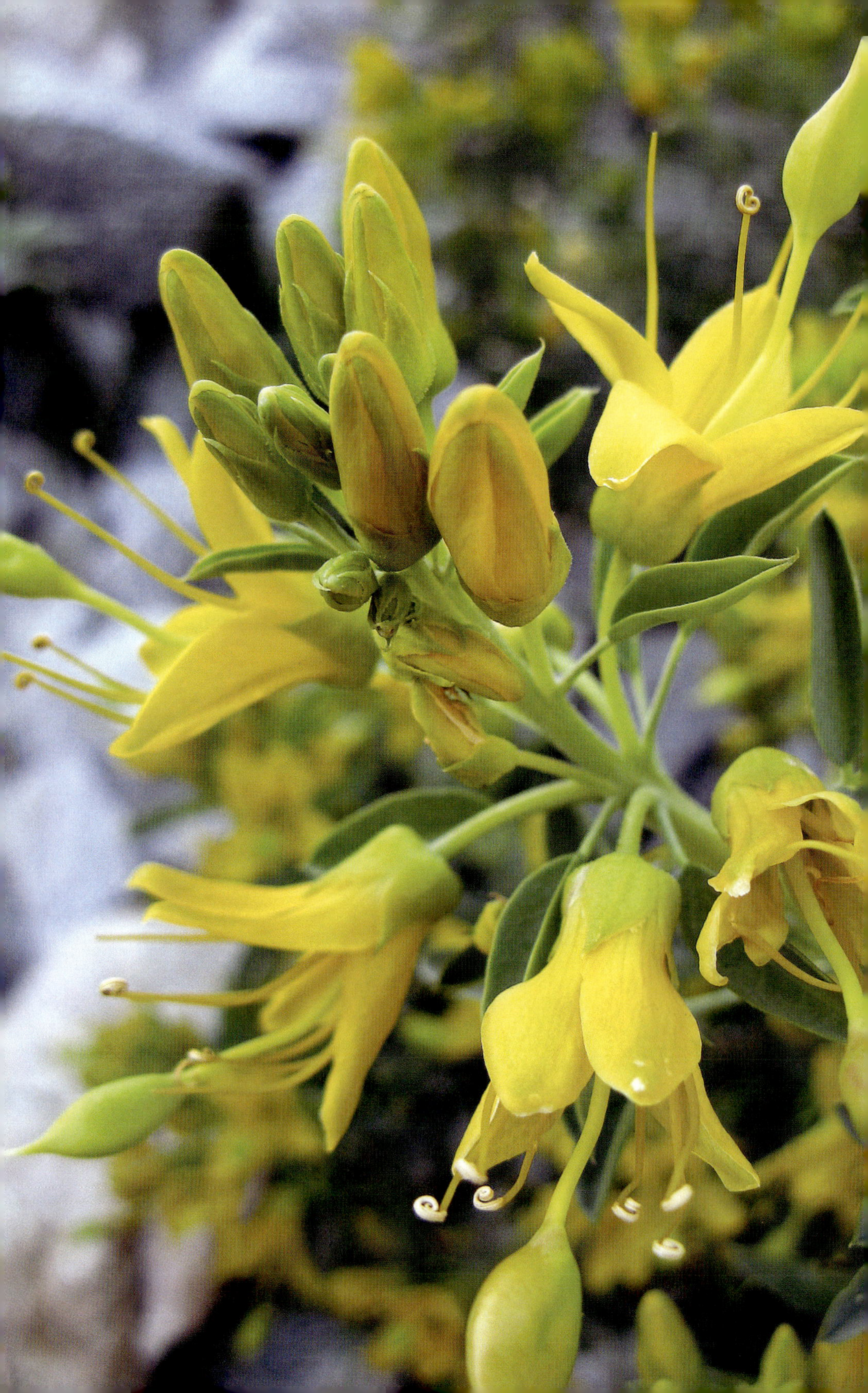

Peritoma arborea

Bladderpod Spiderflower, Burro Fat

Family:	Cleomaceae (Capparaceae)	**Water use:**	Low–moderate
Type:	Evergreen shrub	**Cold hardiness:**	To 15°F
Size:	3–5' high x 4-6' wide	**USDA zone:**	8–10
Bloom:	January–May, sporadic nearly all year		

Author citation: (Nuttall) H. H. Iltis
Synonyms: *Cleome isomeris* Greene; *Isomeris arborea* Nuttall

THE SUNNY YELLOW SNAPDRAGON-LIKE FLOWERS OF THIS SHRUB are an important source of nectar for California hummingbirds in the late winter and early spring, when other natural nectar sources are often scarce. Nesting Costa's and Anna's Hummingbirds, as well as northbound Allen's Hummingbirds returning to their breeding grounds, make good use of the blooms. Pollination is primarily performed by carpenter bees, but the hummingbirds undoubtedly play at least a minor role as well.

Bladderpod spiderflower resides in sandy washes of the Colorado and Mojave deserts of southern California, southwestern Arizona, and in Mexico in northern Baja California, as well as on coastal bluffs and dry slopes of interior valleys north to Monterey, at elevations that range from sea level to 4,000 feet. It also occurs on the Channel Islands.

It is densely branched, usually rounded in form, and fast growing, with dense light green aromatic foliage that is divided into three narrow oblong leaflets from one to two inches in length. Clusters of small, oddly scented four-petaled flowers begin to appear at stem tips in midwinter and usually peak in early spring but may occur almost any time of year. The puffy oval seed capsules that follow look like inflated bladders and give the plant its common name.

Plants prefer a well-drained, alkaline soil and full sun but can tolerate partial shade. A deep soaking once or twice a month in the summer will prolong the bloom during its natural dormant period when water requirements are very low. Bladderpod stands up to wind well and is reputed to be deer proof. It makes a nice addition to mixed shrub borders, informal hedges, slopes for erosion control, and naturalistic desert gardens. Plant this attractive evergreen with chuparosa (*Justicia californica*) for a colorful hummingbird duo, particularly in natural areas where Costa's Hummingbirds are known to occur. Any necessary pruning should be performed in late winter. Propagate either by seed or root cuttings. The distinctive seed capsules are dry and tan-colored when mature and contain both light and dark seeds, the latter of which are said to germinate more readily.

Peritoma serrulata
Rocky Mountain Bee Plant

Family:	Cleomaceae (Capparaceae)	**Water use:**	Moderate
Type:	Annual or biennial	**Cold hardiness:**	To -30°F
Size:	2–4' high x 1–2' wide	**USDA zone:**	4–9
Bloom:	June–September		

Author citation: (Pursh) de Candolle
Synonym: *Cleome serrulata* Pursh

In July and August when hummingbird migration is at its peak, seas of these rosy-pink to pinkish-purple blossoms cover hillsides and plains, offering nectar and the many insects they attract for the taking. As the name implies, the plants are pollinated by bees, but they are also an important source of energy for migrating Rufous, Calliope, and to a lesser extent Black-chinned and White-eared Hummingbirds. Caterpillars of the checkered white butterfly feed upon the foliage of this showy annual, and Mourning Doves are reportedly fond of the seeds.

Rocky Mountain bee plant has an enormous geographical range that extends from Canada nearly to Mexico, occurring in at least parts of all the western states. It is most at home on sandy riparian flats, overgrazed range lands, and disturbed soil along roadsides and trails, at elevations ranging from 4,000 to 8,000 feet and most commonly below 6,000 feet.

Its erect slender pink stems, usually branching toward the top, have medium-green or blue-green lance-shaped leaves with toothed margins, the upper ones single and the lower trilobed. The foliage gives off a skunk-like odor when brushed against. The winsome half-inch flowers occur in showy clusters at the top of the stem and are four-petaled with long, threadlike stamens tipped with green anthers. Even before flowering ceases, curved seedpods dangle from the stems on arched stalks.

Plants need a well-drained, sandy soil and full sun to thrive. They are reportedly not salt tolerant but handle heat very well, though during extended dry periods will benefit from an occasional deep soaking. Rocky Mountain bee plant makes a lovely addition to a wildflower garden or a meadow of native grasses, and can also be grown in containers. Seeds germinate in fall or early spring and the plants flower within the year. In autumn after flowering ceases and the seeds ripen to brown, cut off or pull up the stalks, shake the seeds out where you want to establish plants, and tamp them in lightly. If planting in spring, soaking the seeds in hot water for several hours before sowing may improve germination rates.

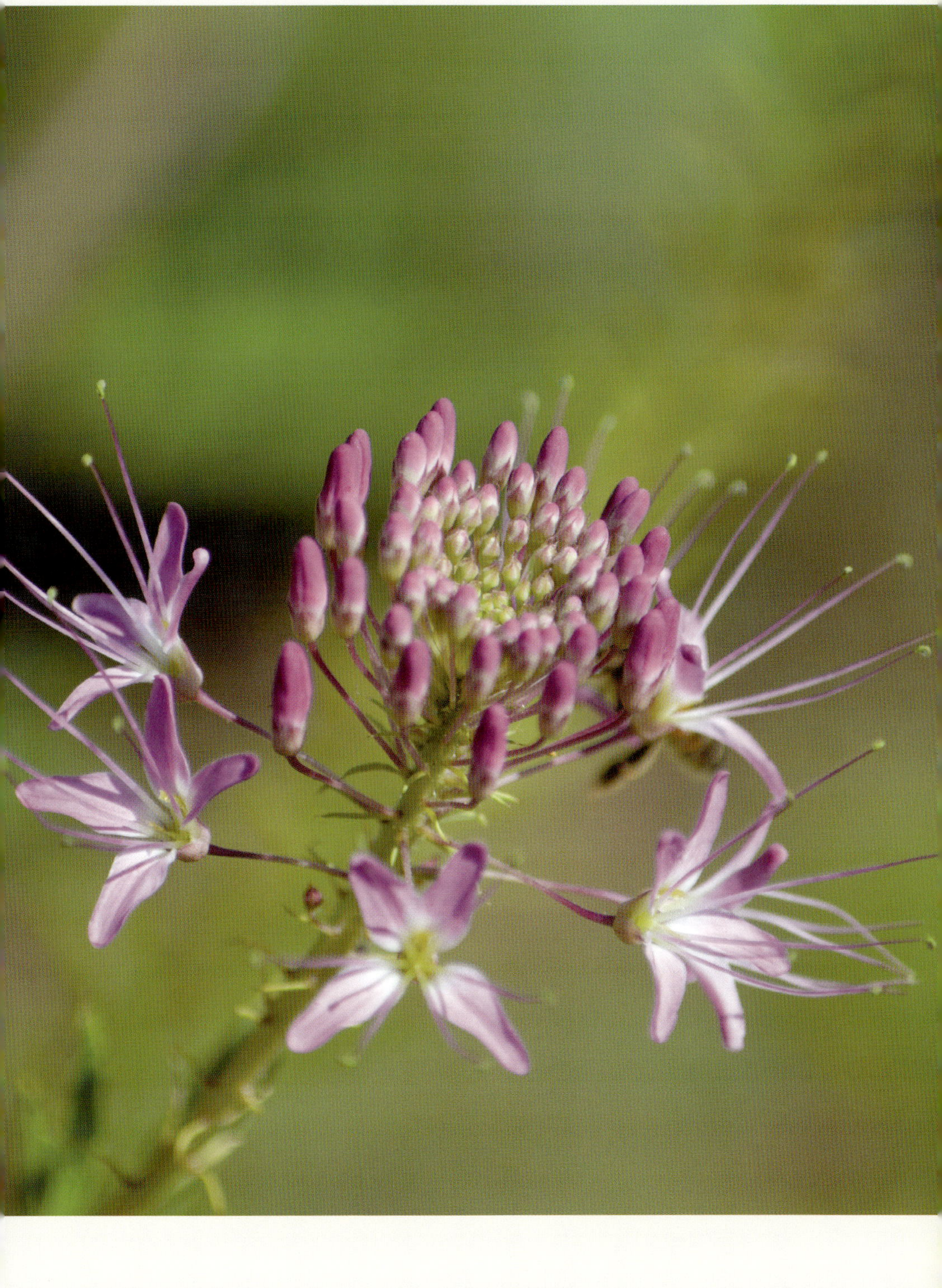

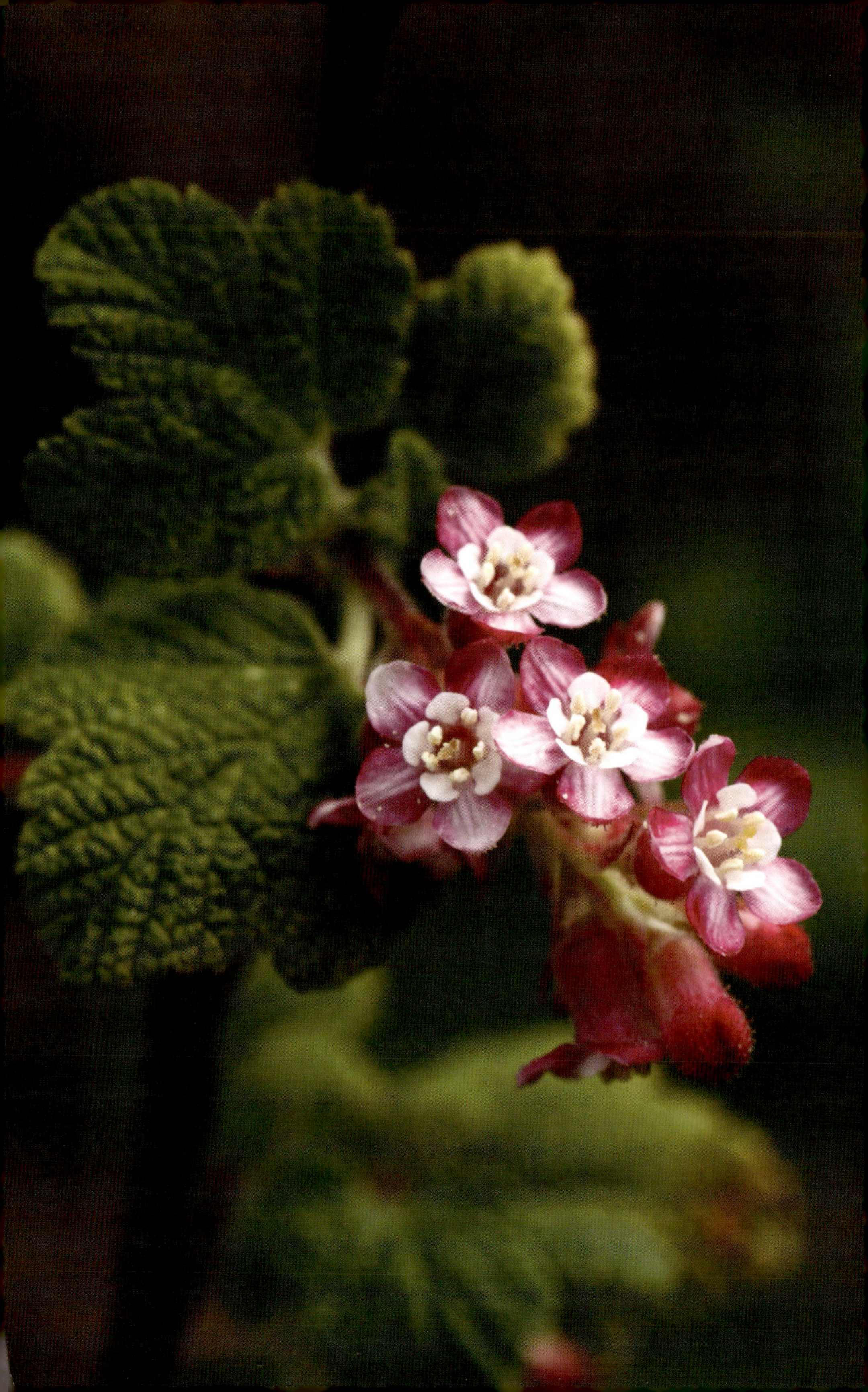

Ribes malvaceum
Chaparral Currant

Family:	Grossulariaceae	**Water use:**	Low–moderate
Type:	Deciduous shrub	**Cold hardiness:**	To -15°F
Size:	5' high x 5' wide	**USDA zone:**	8–10
Bloom:	November–May, especially January–March		

Author citation: Smith

T*HE LOVELY PALE PINK FLOWERS* of this shrub provide vitally important nectar to wintering Anna's and to a lesser extent Allen's Hummingbirds, both of which probably figure significantly in pollination. Butterflies are occasional nectar patrons as well. A variety of birds take the choice reddish-purple berries as soon as they appear, and the leafy branches provide valuable cover.

Chaparral currant makes its home in central and southern California and the Mexican state of Baja California, occurring in all of the Coast Ranges from Tehama County southward as well as in the Transverse and Peninsular ranges, the Sierra Nevada foothills, the San Francisco Bay Area, and the Channel Islands. It inhabits chaparral slopes, sandy coastal bluffs, dry creek beds, shaded ravines, oak woodlands, and pine-studded foothills below 4,500 feet in elevation.

Upright and bushy in form, its spineless, erect stems bear two-inch, mildly scented green leaves that are fuzzy with double-toothed lobes. The plant bursts into bloom with the winter rains, usually by January in the lower elevations and continuing into May at higher locations. Flowering is profuse, with hundreds of blooms on a mature plant. The blossoms occur in drooping clusters of ten to twenty-five flowers and have a pleasant fragrance. Each has sepals of pink to purple and petals of white to pale pink that encircle the throat.

This fast-growing charmer requires a well-drained soil and is quite drought tolerant, although it normally copes with the dry summertime by going dormant so will need periodic watering if you wish it to retain its foliage throughout the year. A sunny exposure is best for coastal or cool upland gardens, while afternoon shade is better for hot inland locations. Propagate by semi-hardwood cuttings or root division. Although this particular currant is not specifically mentioned in the literature as a host to pine blister rust, it should probably not be planted near pine woodlands or plantations. This is a terrific shrub for naturalizing on brushy slopes or massing under live oaks, and it is particularly appropriate for southern California hummingbird gardens.

Ribes pinetorum

Orange Gooseberry

Family:	Grossulariaceae	**Water use:**	Moderate
Type:	Deciduous shrub	**Cold hardiness:**	Root hardy to -20°F
Size:	4–6' high x 4–6' wide	**USDA zone:**	5–9
Bloom:	April–September		

Author citation: Greene

This attractive gooseberry, while not likely to be offered for sale at the local garden center, nonetheless merits mention because it likely depends almost entirely upon hummingbirds for pollination. In turn its orange tubular flowers provide plentiful high-sucrose nectar throughout the breeding season of several hummingbird species, the most widespread being the Broad-tailed Hummingbird. The berries, which turn from red to purple when ripe, are thickly covered with stout yellow thorns, and, although not considered tasty by human standards, are taken by many birds and mammals in summer and fall.

Orange gooseberry has a fairly small range that is confined to Arizona and New Mexico but within these two states can be rather common in suitable habitat. Strictly a high elevation plant, occurring between 6,000 and 11,500 feet, it is a denizen of open coniferous forests and mountain parks, below about 9,000 feet tending to frequent north-facing slopes or canyon bottoms.

Unlike those of the currants, the branches of gooseberries are armed, this particular one with one to three needlelike spines at each node. The bright green alternate leaves are heart-shaped at the base and have five irregularly toothed lobes. The handsome flowers, with hairy calyces and five recurving petals, are solitary or presented in loose clusters.

On its home turf in the mountains, orange gooseberry thrives in sun or shade and once established seems to be fairly drought tolerant. At lower elevations it is likely to languish without supplemental water and some protection from the mid-afternoon sun, and even then it may sulk. One might try to propagate this gooseberry by scarified seed or semi-hardwood cuttings. As this plant is an alternate host to a devastating bark disease known as white pine blister rust, it should not be grown in the vicinity of mixed pine forests or plantings of five-needled pine species. If a source for seeds or potted plants can be located and an appropriate niche exists, however, this ornamental shrub would be an excellent addition to an upland wildlife habitat garden and is certain to draw in summering Broad-tailed Hummingbirds. It can be enjoyed in the wild regardless.

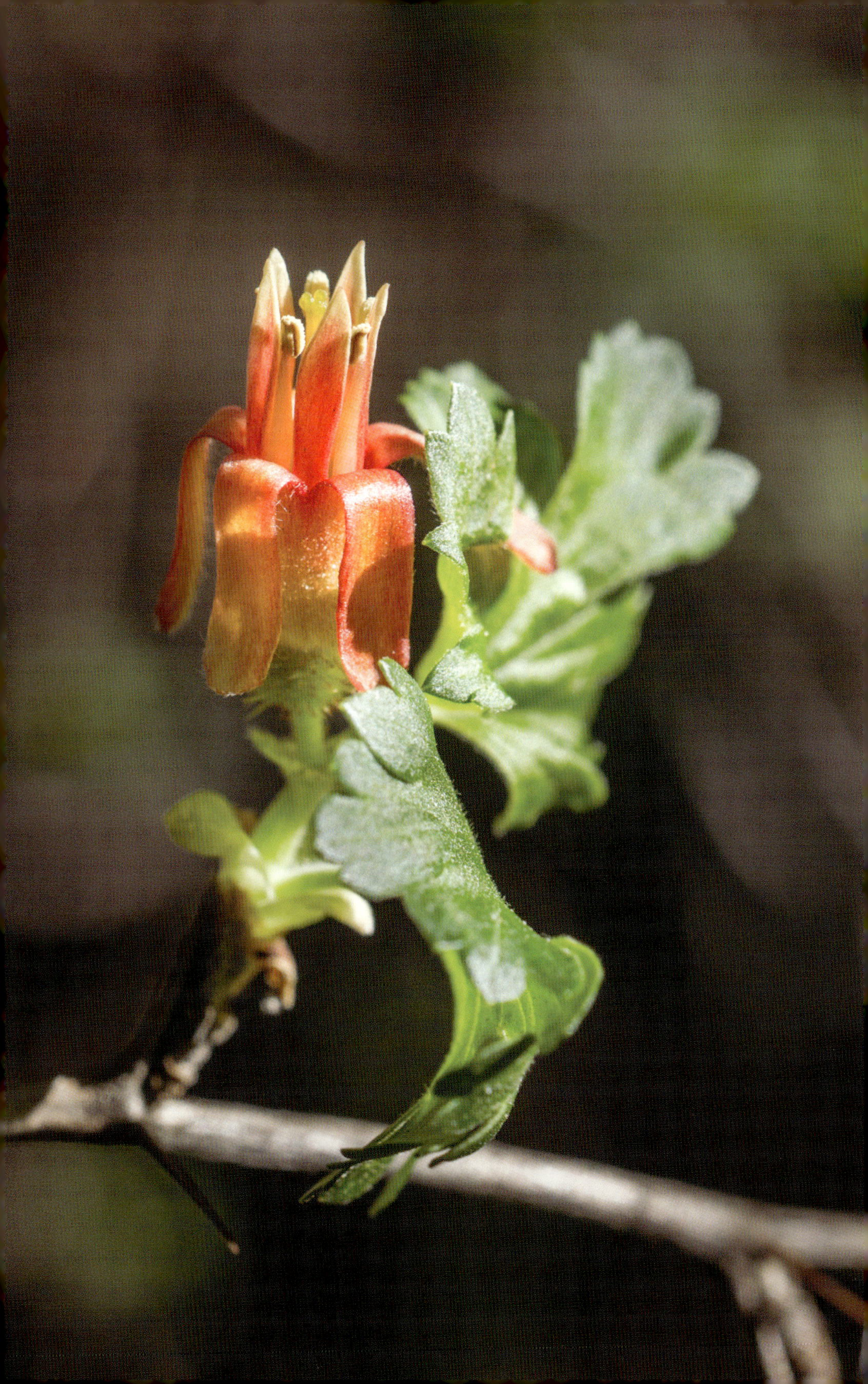

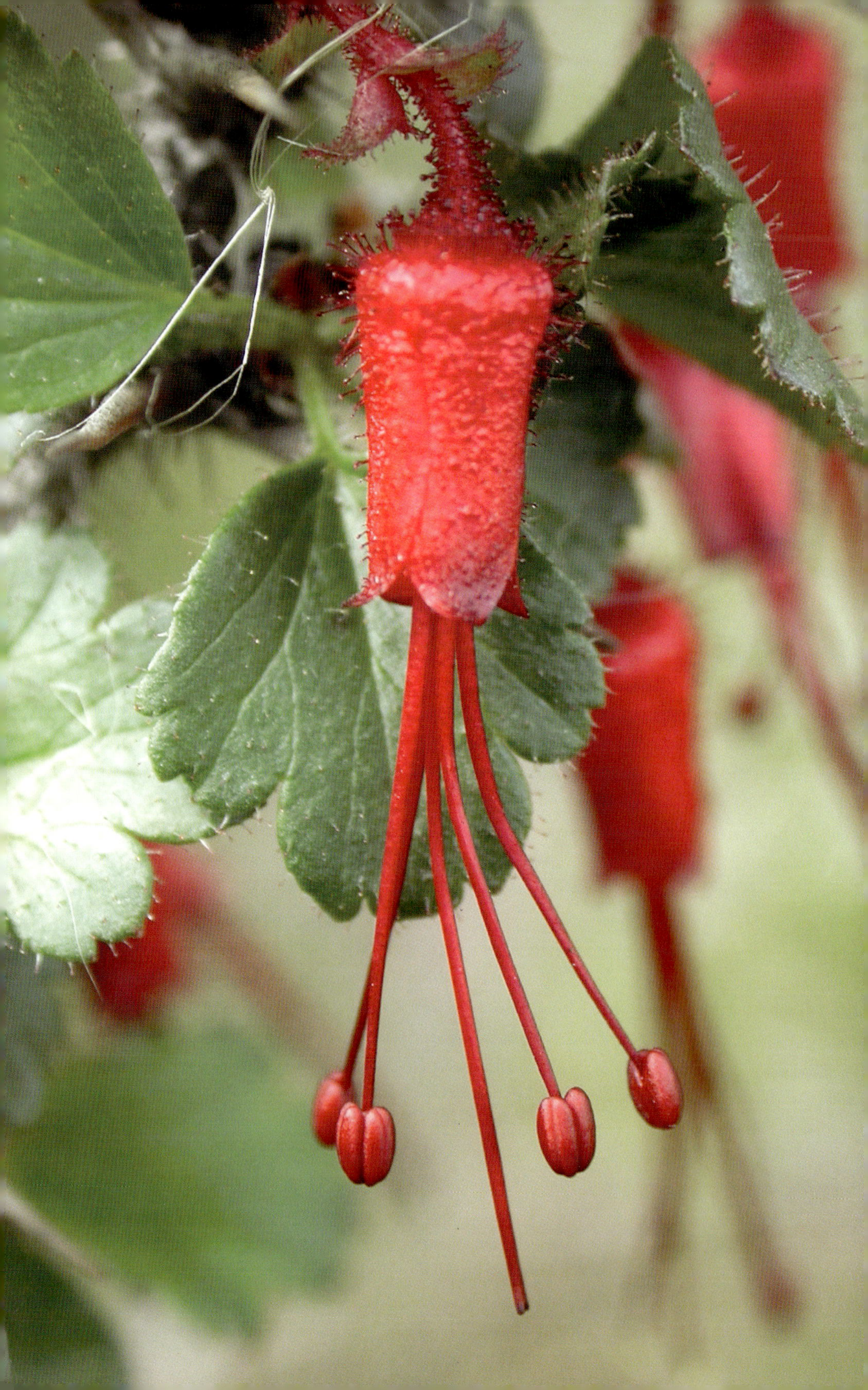

Ribes speciosum

Fuchsia-Flowering Gooseberry

Family:	Grossulariaceae	**Bloom:**	December–May, especially January–March
Type:	Deciduous to semi-evergreen shrub	**Water use:**	Low–moderate
Size:	4–6' high x 6' wide	**Cold hardiness:**	Roots to -10°F
		USDA zone:	7–9

Author citation: Pursh
Synonym: *Grossularia speciosa* (Pursh) Coville & Britton

THE LATE WINTER CHERRY-RED FLOWERS OF THIS SHRUB are often lifesavers for wintering hummingbirds, offering critical nectar when little else is in bloom in return for pollination services. Each blossom is said to produce over twenty-five microliters of nectar per day—a comparatively ample amount. Anna's Hummingbirds in particular rely heavily on this abundant nectar source, and their early breeding season is said to have coevolved with the plant's unusual flowering period. Costa's and Allen's Hummingbirds are also avid visitors to the blooms. The bristly red berries that appear in late spring and summer are prized by many songbirds, and the spiny branches provide excellent cover.

This winter-flowering member of the currant family is native to the coastal sage and chaparral communities of central and southern California, from the San Francisco Bay Area southward, and Baja California in Mexico. Most common between Los Angeles and San Diego, it is typically found below 1,600 feet in elevation, on north slopes, in shady canyons, on coastal bluffs with sage scrub, or in the understory of live oaks and toyon (*Heteromeles arbutifolia*).

Its arching, red, bristly branches bear sharp thorns and are clad in glossy dark-green, maple-like foliage. The drooping tubular flowers have long protruding stamens and resemble fuchsias.

Plants are not fussy about soil as long as it is well-drained, and do best if given a fairly shady exposure, particularly in the hot mid-afternoon. While quite drought tolerant, plants will drop leaves in extended dry periods, which can be avoided with a deep soaking once or twice a month during the summer. Propagate by fresh seed sown in a cold frame in fall or by semi-hardwood cuttings. Because this gooseberry may be a host for white pine blister rust, it is best to avoid planting it near pine woodlands or plantations. Fuchsia-flowering gooseberry is extremely frost tender, but where winters are mild works well in a shady mixed border, as a barrier planting, or on banks for erosion control, and is an absolute must for southern California hummingbird gardens. Be sure to locate its thorny stems away from walkways.

Russelia sonorensis

Sonoran Firecracker Plant

Family:	Plantaginaceae (Scrophulariaceae)	**Bloom:**	March–May and September–December
Type:	Subshrub	**Water use:**	Low–moderate
Size:	3' high x 3' wide, occasionally larger	**Cold hardiness:**	To about 20°F
		USDA zone:	9–10
Author citation:	M. Carlson		

With its bright red tubular flowers tailor-made for hummingbirds, this Mexican shrub serves up nectar over a remarkably long period of time, with blooms occurring anytime from fall into winter and again in spring. Somewhat surprisingly, no observations of any southwestern hummingbirds nectaring at the plant are recorded in the literature, for it is likely that multiple species encounter the blooms in spring as they are heading north from central Mexico and again in fall as they return to wintering grounds. Certainly, hummingbirds of some ilk are the primary pollinators.

Sonoran firecracker plant is mostly confined to its namesake state of Sonora, with a few records from Chihuahua and another couple from Sinaloa and Nayarit. In Sonora it is most common in the southern portion, especially in the Rio Mayo region, where it occurs in a wide variety of habitats. Riparian forests, rocky stream canyons, cliff faces, stony arroyo bottoms, seeps, foothill thornscrub, palm ravines, and tropical deciduous forests are common haunts, at elevations ranging from about 700 to over 4,000 feet.

Its upright shrubby form and slender, rather gangly stems are inconspicuous until it begins flowering in spring, when the lower stems are usually still leafless and the small, heavily veined teardrop-shaped leaves are just starting to emerge on the branch tips. The flowers occur in clusters of three to five blossoms, with very narrow half-inch-long corollas and short flaring petal lobes, and may range in color from coral red to scarlet to cherry red. Small seed capsules about an eighth-of-an-inch long develop after flowering and bear tiny oval seeds.

This long-blooming plant is not presently known in cultivation but it could be a valuable addition to a naturalistic hummingbird garden where winters are relatively mild. As it is similar to others in its genus that are commercially available, it is likely to do well in containers. Full sun to part shade and regular water until established are suggested. Other *Russelias* are sometimes propagated by partly burying stems so that roots will form at the nodes; this procedure might work well with this species also.

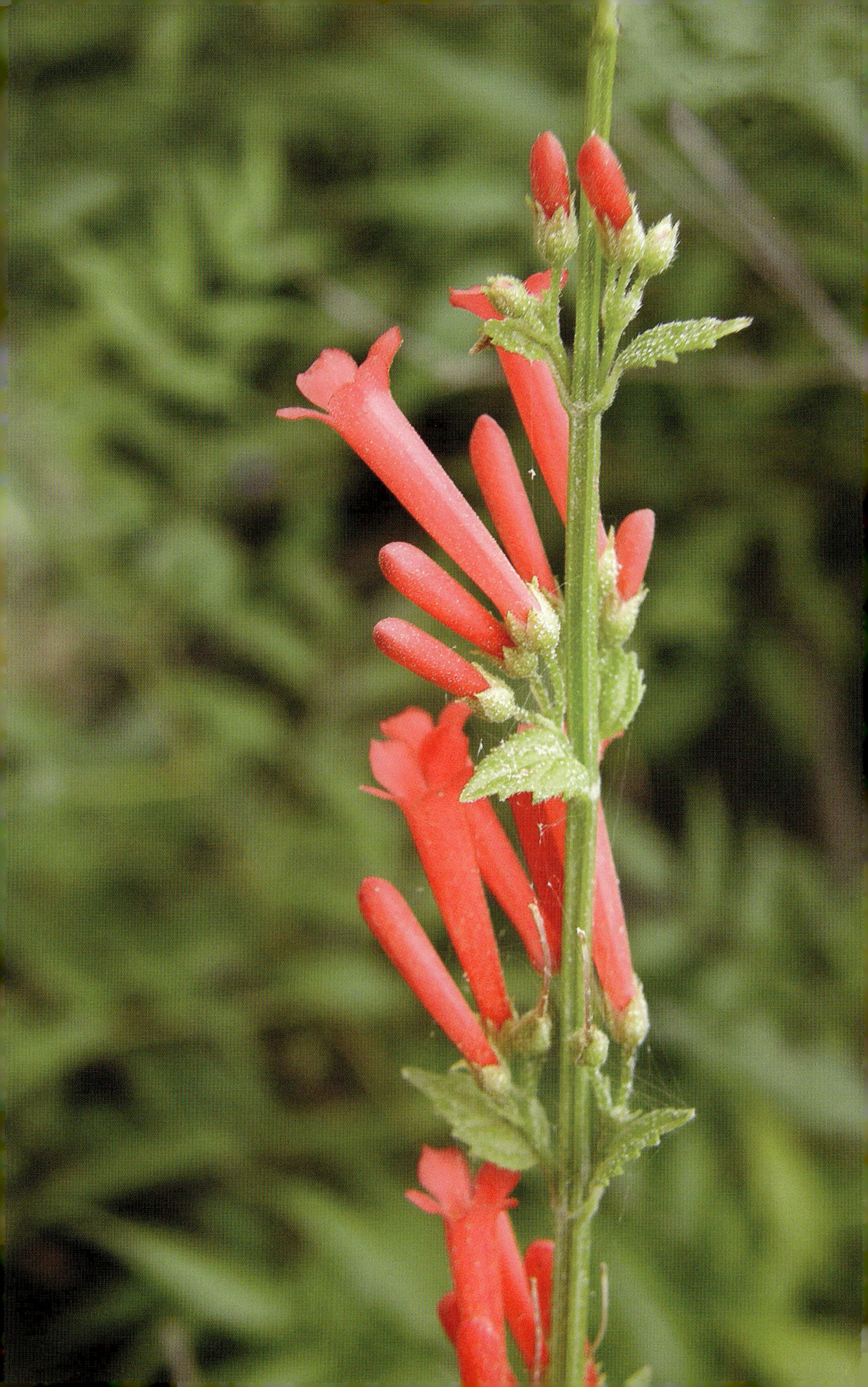

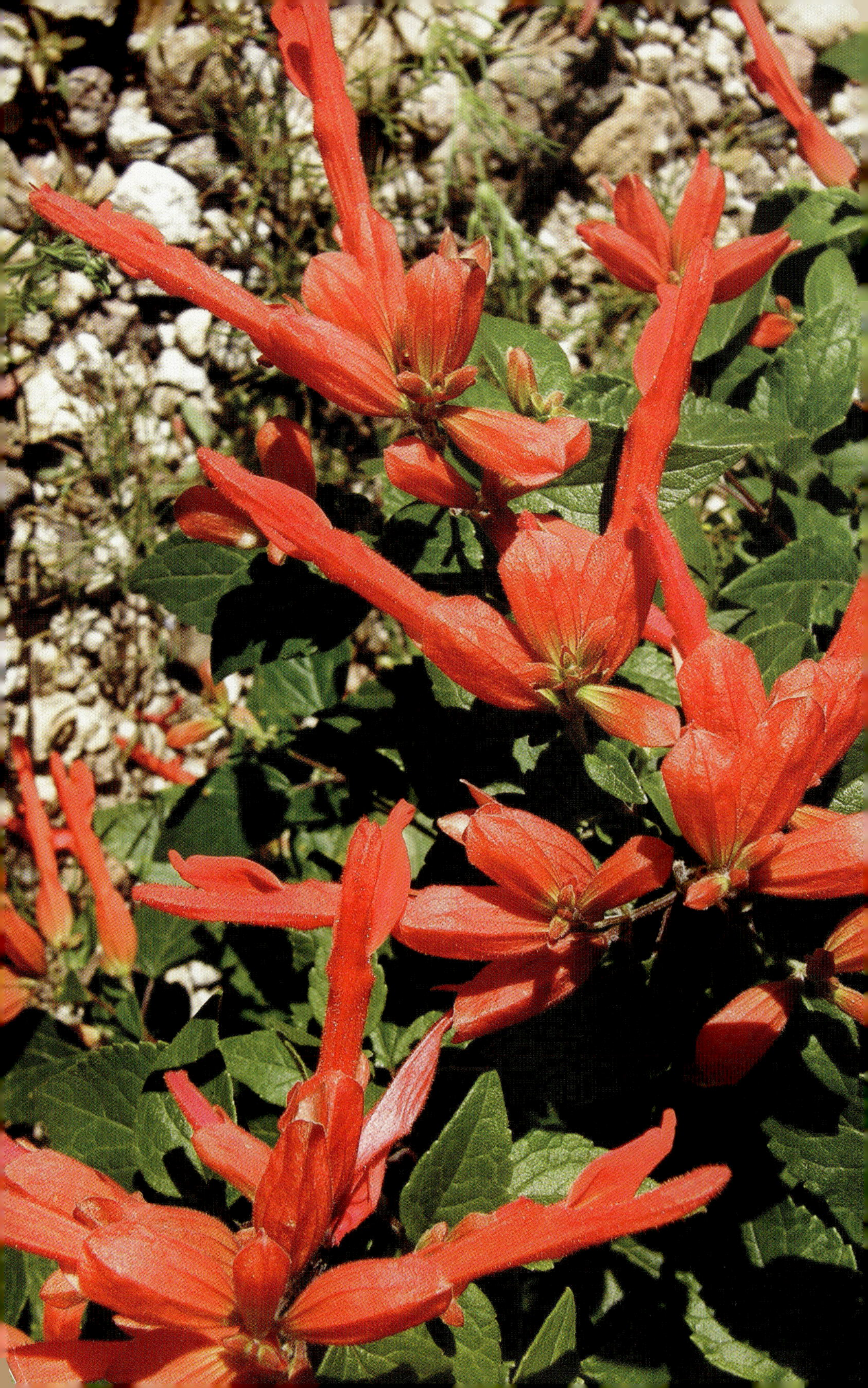

Salvia betulifolia

Maycoba Sage, Birchleaf Sage

Family:	Lamiaceae	**Water use:**	Moderate
Type:	Subshrub	**Cold hardiness:**	To at least 20°F
Size:	3–5' high x 3–4' wide	**USDA zone:**	9–10
Bloom:	August–October		

Author citation: Epling

Though its natural range is limited and its flowering season fairly short, this bright red Mexican bloomer is sensational when it is in bloom, providing valuable nectar to resident and migrating hummingbirds alike. Berylline, Violet-crowned, Black-chinned, Broad-billed, and White-eared Hummingbirds have all been observed at the flowers, and are likely the chief pollinators.

A true treasure of the Sierra Madre, this lovely salvia is found only in the heart of the Sierra Madre Occidental in southeastern Sonora, western Chihuahua, and western Durango, typically at elevations of 4,000 to 8,000 feet. Particularly common around the town of Maycoba and the nearby headwaters of the Rio Mayo, it is also often encountered in the Copper Canyon area and drainages to the south. Some of its preferred habitats include rocky stream canyons, oak, pine-oak, and juniper-oak woodlands, lava rocks and outcrops, moist rock seeps, grassy river terraces, and cliff faces. Upright and shrubby, its square, often purplish stems bear bright green, prominently veined, toothed leaves shaped like those of a birch tree. They occur in pairs at each stem node and become smaller toward the tip. Ranging in color from scarlet red to deep salmon-pink, the beguiling flowers feature long narrow tubular corollas and strongly reflexed lower petal lobes that provide easy access to hummingbirds. As is true of many salvias, several tiny seeds form within the calyces of the spent flowers.

Maycoba sage is unfortunately not presently known in cultivation but it would appear to be an ideal candidate for a late summer hummingbird garden, especially in upland locations where winters are mild. Sun to part shade, the latter necessary in hot locations, and regular water until established and as needed afterward, will likely make plants happiest. As they occur in varying soils in their native haunts—including volcanic tuff, roadside gravels, and silty river sand—they are probably fairly tolerant of different soil types, but providing good drainage to new plants is probably wise. Plants can be propagated either by seed, if a source can be found, or by stem cuttings.

Salvia elegans

Pineapple Sage, Salvia Roja, Mirto

Family:	Lamiaceae	**Bloom:**	September to frost, through spring in mild winter areas
Type:	Perennial		
Size:	3–4' high x 3–4' wide, larger in frost-free areas	**Water use:**	Moderate–high
		Cold hardiness:	To 25°F, roots to -15°F
		USDA zone:	8b–10 or as annual
Author citation:	Vahl		
Synonym:	*S. rutilans* Carrière		

W**IDELY PLANTED IN THE SOUTHEASTERN** U**NITED** S**TATES**, this veritable hummingbird magnet actually has closer ties to southwestern hummingbirds, occurring along the migratory route or within the wintering range of many species. Black-chinned, Rufous, Blue-throated, Magnificent, Violet-crowned, Berylline, White-eared, and Broad-billed Hummingbirds are strongly attracted to the bright red tubular blooms that appear from fall through spring in Mexico, and Anna's and Allen's Hummingbirds happily patronize garden plantings. Butterflies may also visit the flowers.

Pineapple sage has a fairly large native range, extending from southern Sonora and Chihuahua in Mexico south through the Sierra Madre Occidental and Sierra Madre del Sur to Guatemala. Typically occurring at oak or pine forest edges and along drainages at elevations ranging from 3,200 to over 9,000 feet, this brittle-stemmed perennial is usually shrubby in form, with thick bright green leaves that are heart-shaped to oval with pointed tips and densely covered with hairs. The foliage has a delightful scent that is reminiscent of ripe pineapple and is often used in salads and beverages. In autumn the plant sends up six- to ten-inch stems that bear narrow one-and-a-half-inch-long flowers in loose whorls of up to a dozen, and will continue to crank out blossoms until frost or through spring in frost-free areas.

This salvia needs a fast-draining, humus-enriched soil and regular watering throughout the growth period. It will grow in full sun, but in very hot locations will do better with some afternoon shade, particularly in midsummer. Protection from frost is mandatory, but if no suitable planting spot exists, it can either be grown in a large pot that can be brought indoors for the winter or planted as an annual for the fall color extravaganza. In mild winter climates, pineapple sage works beautifully as a ground cover under the filtered shade of a tree or as an accent for a courtyard, patio, or oasis planting. Propagate by fresh seed, softwood cuttings, or division of rootstocks. Many different cultivars of this plant are available, with different growth habits and a veritable rainbow of color choices.

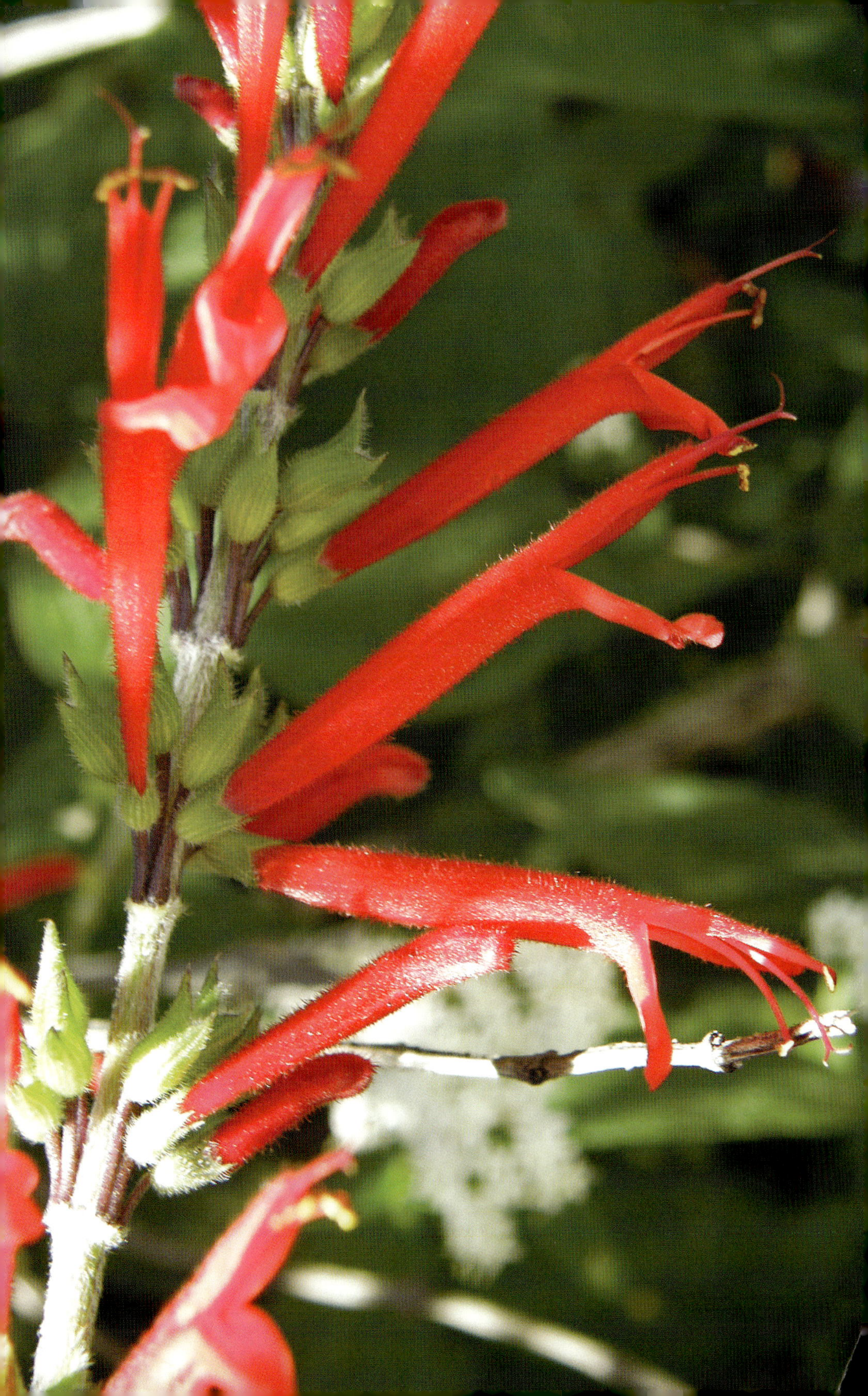

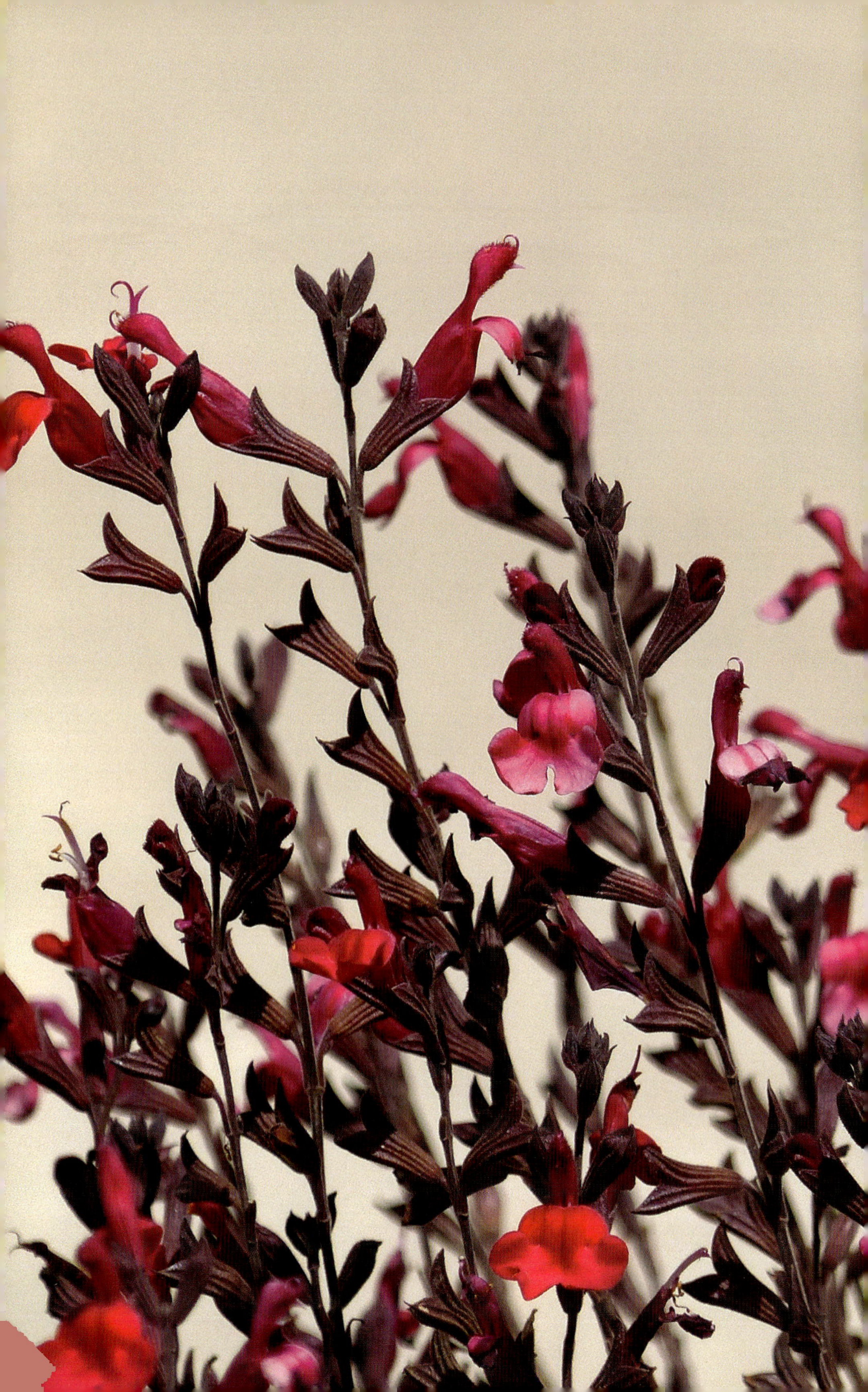

Salvia greggii

Autumn Sage, Cherry Sage, Gregg Salvia

Family:	Lamiaceae	**Water use:**	Moderate
Type:	Semi-evergreen subshrub	**Cold hardiness:**	Top to 15°F, roots to 0°F
Size:	2' high x 2–3' wide	**USDA zone:**	7–10
Bloom:	August–November, again March–May, sporadic summer		

Author citation: A. Gray

THIS IS A TOUGH AND WELL-BEHAVED LITTLE SHRUB, whose charming hot pink to cherry-red flowers blanket the plant in autumn and again in spring. Black-chinned Hummingbirds are perhaps its most regular visitors, with Rufous and Broad-tailed Hummingbirds joining in during migration, and Costa's, Anna's, and Calliope Hummingbirds visit garden plantings. Other customers include orioles, butterflies, and carpenter bees, the latter slashing the base of the corolla to access the high-sucrose nectar.

Autumn sage has a limited range in the United States, occurring only in central, southwestern, and western Texas, but it enjoys a broader distribution in Mexico, from southeastern Chihuahua, Coahuila, and Nuevo Leon south to San Luis Potosi. Favored niches include sandy washes, rocky hillsides, and canyons from 2,200 to 9,000 feet in elevation.

The square stems branch from a woody base into a naturally rounded form. The small, oval, glossy dark-green leaves grow in dense clusters at the nodes and have a pungent fragrance when crushed. The one-inch tubular flowers appear in loose spikes and are quite showy, flowering in successive waves from spring to fall.

This is a very forgiving plant with ample irrigation, requiring only fast-draining soil and an eastern exposure or filtered afternoon shade. A deep soaking twice a month during the summer will keep it looking its best, but avoid over-watering. Clip spent flower spikes to prolong the bloom, and prune some of the old woody stems each year in late winter to keep plants dense and compact. In cooler areas, plant on the south or southeast side of a wall for winter warmth.

Autumn sage works beautifully in courtyards, patios, and perennial beds, or massed as a low hedge or ground cover, and it also makes a delightful container plant. Happily, it self-sows freely and volunteer seedlings are easy to transplant. As with most members of the mint family, propagation is also easy by rooting softwood or semi-hardwood cuttings. Note that this salvia readily hybridizes, and many salvias available in the nursery trade are hybrids of this species and baby sage (*Salvia microphylla*), a very similar shrub from eastern and central Mexico.

Salvia henryi

Crimson Sage, Henry's Sage

Family:	Lamiaceae	**Water use:**	Low–moderate
Type:	Perennial	**Cold hardiness:**	To -0°F
Size:	2' high x 2' wide	**USDA zone:**	7–9
Bloom:	April–June, to September in higher elevations		

Author citation: A. Gray
Synonym: *S. davidsonii* Greenman

The slender, vivid red tubular flowers of this perennial sage offer nectar not only to nesting hummingbirds, such as Broad-tailed and Black-chinned Hummingbirds, but also to Rufous and Calliope Hummingbirds hopscotching southward through desert mountains in late summer. Hummingbirds are presumed to be the most important pollinators. A variety of birds feasts on the small seeds in the fall.

Crimson sage is the most widely distributed red salvia of the Southwest, ranging across much of Arizona in a broad diagonal swath from the Grand Canyon to the southeast corner of the state, and eastward through central and southern New Mexico and far western Texas. Typically found at middle elevations between 4,000 and 7,500 feet and sometimes lower, it occurs on rocky desert slopes and in canyons, often in the company of piñon pines, junipers, oaks, and mountain mahogany.

Its slender square stems, sometimes woody at the base, are covered with gray down and bedecked with opposite, grayish green, pinnately divided leaves that usually have three or five leaflets. The terminal leaflet is the largest and is coarsely toothed. The one-and-a-half-inch flowers occur in pairs or small clusters in axils along the upper stem and under cultivation may vary in color from deep pink to rich crimson. The upper lip of each projects straight out, while the three-lobed lower lip curves downward to discourage bees from landing, thus preserving nectar for its hovering pollinators.

Crimson sage needs a lean, fast-draining soil and can be grown in full sun to part shade, although in hot low-elevation locations it may prefer dappled to full shade during the mid-afternoon. Although remarkably drought tolerant, it will perform best with a deep soaking once a month during the growing season, particularly during extended dry spells. Pinching back spent flowers will maximize the bloom period. This beguiling, long-blooming perennial with its fern-like foliage is occasionally available at native plant sales or through specialty nurseries and makes a lovely accent for the spring hummingbird garden. It performs beautifully in containers. Propagation is easy by seed direct sown in fall or started in a cold frame in winter. Rooting stem cuttings taken in early spring or late summer is trickier but possible. Plants tend to be fairly short-lived, so propagating new individuals will help ensure a continuous population.

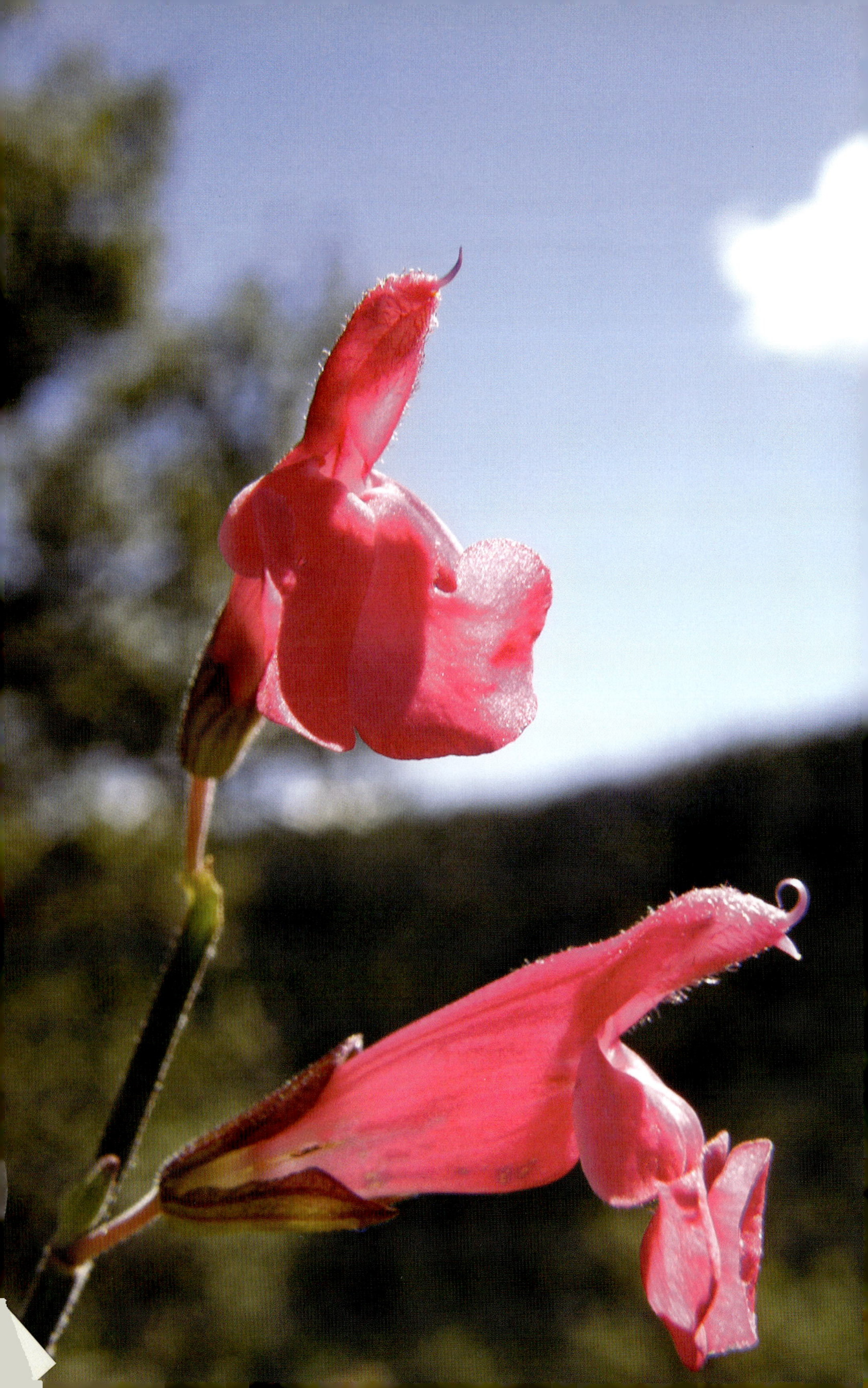

Salvia lemmonii

Lemmon's Sage, Salvia del Monte

Family:	Lamiaceae	**Water use:**	Moderate
Type:	Semi-evergreen subshrub	**Cold hardiness:**	Top to 10°F, roots to -10°F
Size:	3–4' high x 3–5' wide	**USDA zone:**	6–9
Bloom:	July–October		

Author citation: A. Gray
Synonyms: *Salvia microphylla* var. *wislizenii* A. Gray; *S. microphylla* Kunth

This pretty salvia of the Arizona sky islands stages an extended open house for hummingbirds with its long bloom season. Its luscious fuchsia-colored blooms are held in high favor by Broad-tailed, Rufous, Black-chinned, Broad-billed, Berylline, Blue-throated, and Magnificent Hummingbirds. Not surprisingly, the primary pollinators are hummingbirds. Early in the season carpenter bees provisioning their nest chambers sometimes plunder the sucrose-packed nectar by slashing the base of the corolla.

Lemmon's sage has a fairly small natural range, occurring in canyons, on rocky slopes, and in oak and pine forest openings of desert mountains and the sky islands, at elevations of 5,000 to 8,000 feet and occasionally higher, in southeastern Arizona, extreme southwestern New Mexico, and in the Sierra Madre Occidental of Sonora and Chihuahua in Mexico.

Sometimes shrubby in form, sometimes sprawling and irregular, the numerous woody-based branches bear small bright-green oval leaves with toothed margins. The foliage, which has a minty fragrance when bruised, occurs in tight clusters, unlike that of its close cousin, baby sage (*S. microphylla*), with which it has been often confused—even by botanists. The tubular blossoms have a hooded upper lip and a three-lobed lower lip. As a hummingbird hovers in front of the corolla, the upper part of its bill contacts the stigma and two anthers sheltered under the upper lip of the flower, and it carries this yellow dusting along to the next flower it visits.

This sage is a tough performer, needing only a fast-draining soil, protection from hot mid-afternoon sun, and a deep soaking twice a month during extended summer dry periods. Propagate by seed sown in fall or late winter or by rooting stem cuttings taken in spring or late summer in moist vermiculite. This is one of the most cold tolerant salvias but unfortunately is not widely available in the nursery trade. If a source can be found for seeds or potted plants, Lemmon's sage makes a fine plant for low hedges, mixed borders, and courtyards. It also performs well in containers but will need to be watered more often.

Salvia penstemonoides
Big Red Sage, Penstemon Sage

Family:	Lamiaceae	**Bloom:**	June–September
Type:	Perennial	**Water use:**	Moderate
Size:	3' high x 2–3' wide, with 1' flower stalks	**Cold hardiness:**	To at least 10°F
		USDA zone:	7b–10

Author citation: Kunth & Bouché
Synonyms: *Salvia pentstemonoides* Kunth & Bouché; *S. pentstemonoides* K. Koch & Bouché

FEATURING EXQUISITE BLOSSOMS OF BRIGHT MAGENTA clasped by burgundy calyces, this rare beauty cannot help but attract hummingbirds. Black-chinned and Rufous Hummingbirds are probably the most common visitors and primary pollinators. The foliage is a highly favored browse for deer, which along with habitat loss is a contributing factor to the plant's endangered status.

Known from only a handful of locations in south-central Texas on the Edwards Plateau, big red sage occurs below 2,000 feet in elevation in seasonally wet silt or clay along streams and on limestone slopes and outcrops where seeps provide moisture. The first plants to be discovered were along a creek near San Antonio, and the species was brought into cultivation by the Lady Bird Johnson Wildflower Center.

The species name *penstemonoides* refers to its penstemon-like form, with a basal rosette of evergreen foliage from which the numerous flower stalks emerge. The leaves are lance-shaped and lime green in color, often with tinges of purple. The flower stems also have leaves and rise to a foot or more above the foliage, bearing open whorls of narrow tubular flowers an inch in length. Flowering may begin as early as May or as late as August depending upon location.

Plants can be grown in full sun to part shade but reportedly do best with morning sun and dappled afternoon shade. While native to a variety of soil types including silt, clay, limestone, and caliche, in the garden they seem to prefer average, sandy or loamy, slightly alkaline, well-drained soil to which some organic material has been added. They are somewhat drought tolerant but for optimum bloom should receive a deep soaking once a week during the active growth season. Propagation is easy by seed, and established plants self-seed readily. Cuttings are said to be a bit more challenging. Though quite rare in the wild, both seeds and plants are increasingly available from native plant growers. Big red sage makes a big red splash of color in a perennial border, oasis garden, or patio container, and will roll out the welcome mat for the parade of migrating hummingbirds in late summer.

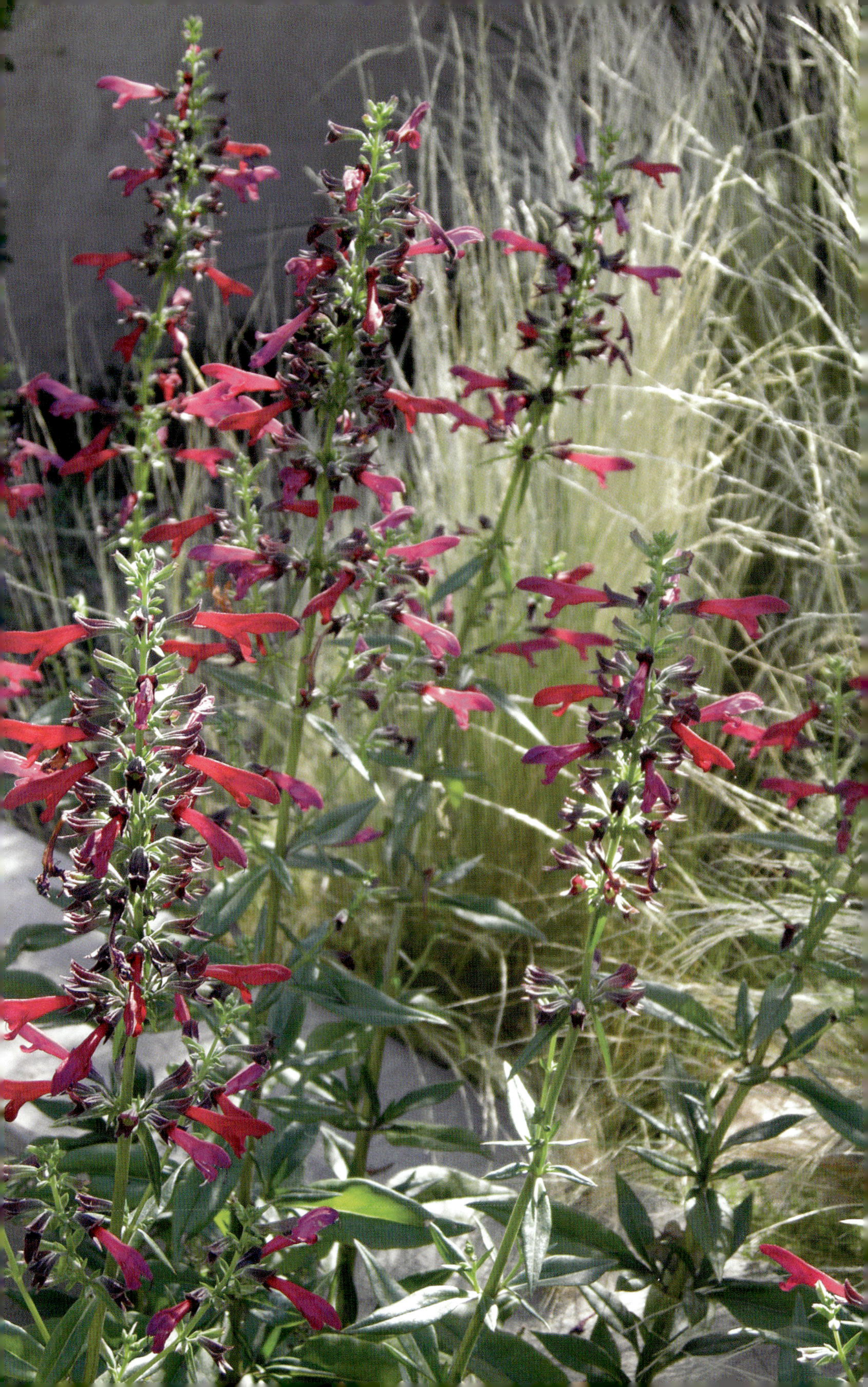

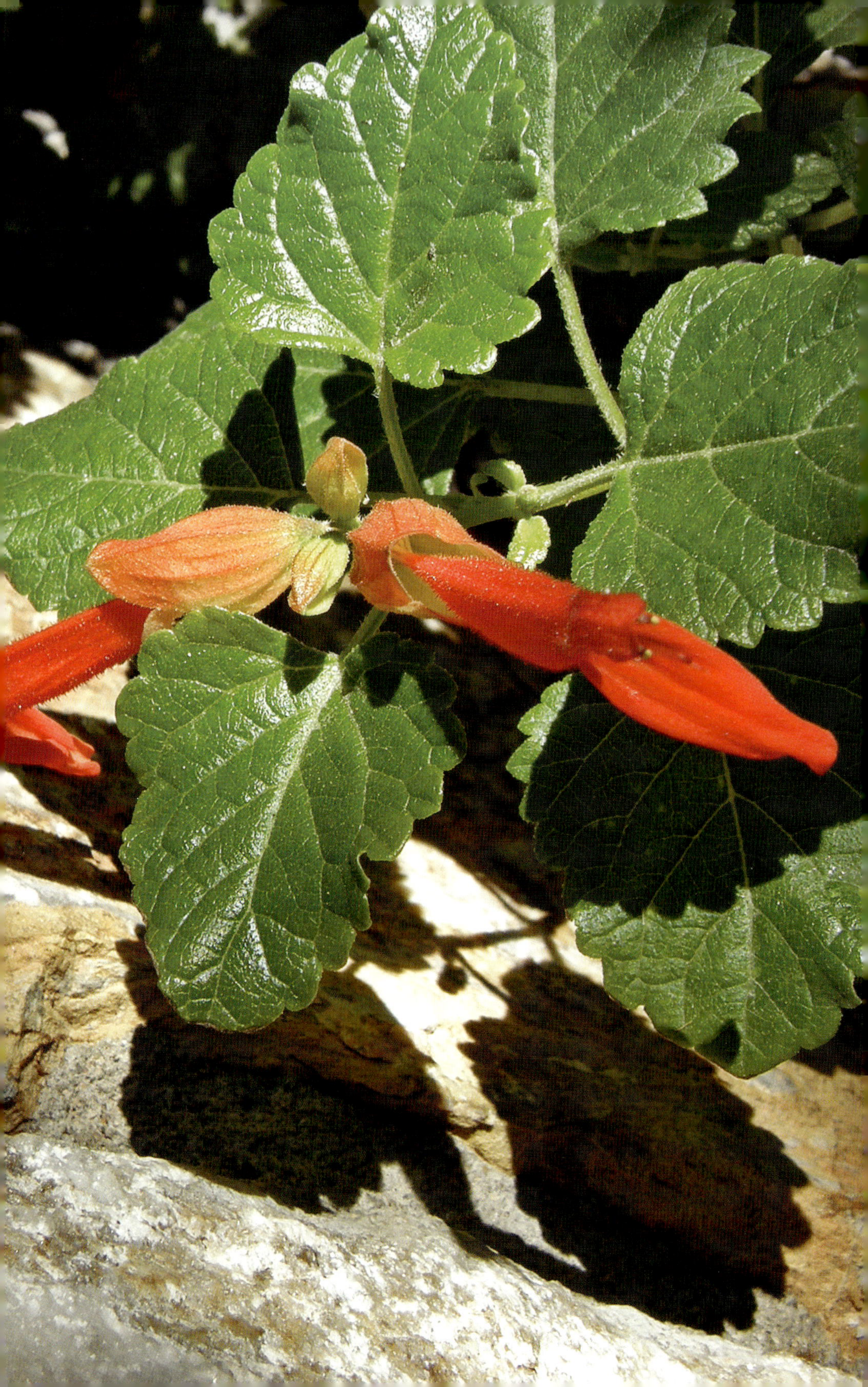

Salvia regla

Mountain Sage, Royal Sage, Cardinal Sage, Salvia de Montaña

Family:	Lamiaceae	**Water use:**	Low–moderate
Type:	Deciduous shrub	**Cold hardiness:**	Top to -20°F, root hardy to 5°F
Size:	3–6' high x 3–5' wide		
Bloom:	June–September, through winter in mild areas	**USDA zone:**	7b–10

Author citation: Cavanilles

This salvia, dubbed "the queen of the Chisos Mountains" by naturalist Barton Warnock, is simply stunning when in flower. The long scarlet blossoms with their flaring, orange-red calyces are avidly sought out by no fewer than eight hummingbird species: Blue-throated, Broad-tailed, Rufous, Lucifer, Magnificent, Broad-billed, Black-chinned, and Calliope Hummingbirds. The nectar is reported to be abundant and quite sweet, averaging 32 percent sugar. Hummingbirds are undoubtedly the plant's primary pollinators, although butterflies also visit the flowers.

Mountain sage makes itself at home on cool slopes and cliff ledges and in wooded canyons, typically at elevations between 4,000 and 9,000 feet. In the United States it occurs only in the Chisos Mountains in the Big Bend region of Texas, but it ranges from there well south into Mexico through the Sierra Madre Oriental from Coahuila to at least Hidalgo and at scattered locales in the Sierra Madre Occidental.

Its multiple stems are woody, dense, and arching in form. The glossy light green leaves are deeply veined and have scalloped edges. They are triangular in shape and deciduous, dropping at temperatures below 28°F but quickly growing back in spring. The one-and-a-half-inch tubular flowers, with widely gaping lower lips, appear in short clusters at stem tips and last for several days.

The plant is said to like slightly alkaline well-drained soil, and prefers an eastern exposure or dappled shade. Mountain sage absolutely will not stand the intense heat of low deserts, and also withers when exposed to drying winds. A deep soaking twice a month during the summer and minimal watering during winter dormancy are recommended. Older stems may occasionally need to be pruned back, which should be done only during the growing season. Given the right growing conditions, this shrub makes an outstanding specimen for courtyards, patios, poolsides, and oasis plantings and can be easily grown in a large container as well. Plants usually set seed readily, and they can also be propagated by softwood or semi-hardwood tip cuttings. 'Mount Emory' is a selection that has larger flowers and leaves and is reportedly root hardy to 0°F.

Salvia roemeriana

Cedar Sage, Roemer's Sage, Salvia Peluda

Family:	Lamiaceae	**Water use:**	Moderate
Type:	Perennial	**Cold hardiness:**	To 0°F
Size:	1–2' high x 1' wide	**USDA zone:**	7–10
Bloom:	March–July, into fall with water		

Author citation: Scheele

This is the kind of plant that can melt the heart of even the most field-worn of botanizers, with its nodding crimson flowers that ooze with both nectar for hummingbirds and charm for their human admirers. Black-chinned and Broad-tailed Hummingbirds are avid nectar customers and probably chiefly responsible for pollination, although butterflies may visit the blooms as well. The dark brown nut-like seeds are popular with quail and goldfinches, and the foliage is (unfortunately) well liked by deer.

Although its stronghold is the Edwards Plateau of south-central Texas, cedar sage ranges westward to the Chisos Mountains of the Big Bend region and southward into northeastern Mexico from southeastern Chihuahua to Nuevo Leon. Found at elevations ranging from about 600 feet in Texas to over 8,000 feet in Mexico, it forms small colonies on limestone outcrops and in canyons. In Texas it seems to favor dense thickets of Ashe juniper (*Juniperus ashei*) known as cedar brakes or shady spots beneath oaks such as Texas red oak (*Quercus buckleyi*) or Lacey oak (*Q. laceyi*).

In form cedar sage somewhat resembles a penstemon, with a tidy basal rosette of leaves and flowering stems that emerge from the crown. The few-branched stems are often purplish, and may be erect or sprawling. The attractive bright green foliage is heart-shaped to rounded with scalloped edges and has a velvety texture. The sigh-inducing flowers dangle in loose whorls about the stems.

This beguiling perennial will grow in sand, clay, or loam but seems to do best in a light, well-drained soil enriched with plenty of organic material. A location in dappled shade is ideal but plants will also thrive with morning sun and afternoon shade. A deep soaking once a week during the growing season will encourage continued flowering, but in full sun or in a container more water will be required. Plants are short-lived but self-sow readily, particularly where ample moisture exists, and volunteer seedlings can be transplanted elsewhere. Propagation is also fairly easy by direct-sown seed or by stem cuttings if lengths with multiple nodes are available. Cedar sage makes a lovely ground cover under the high shade of trees and is delightful lining a pathway or spilling out of a rock crevice.

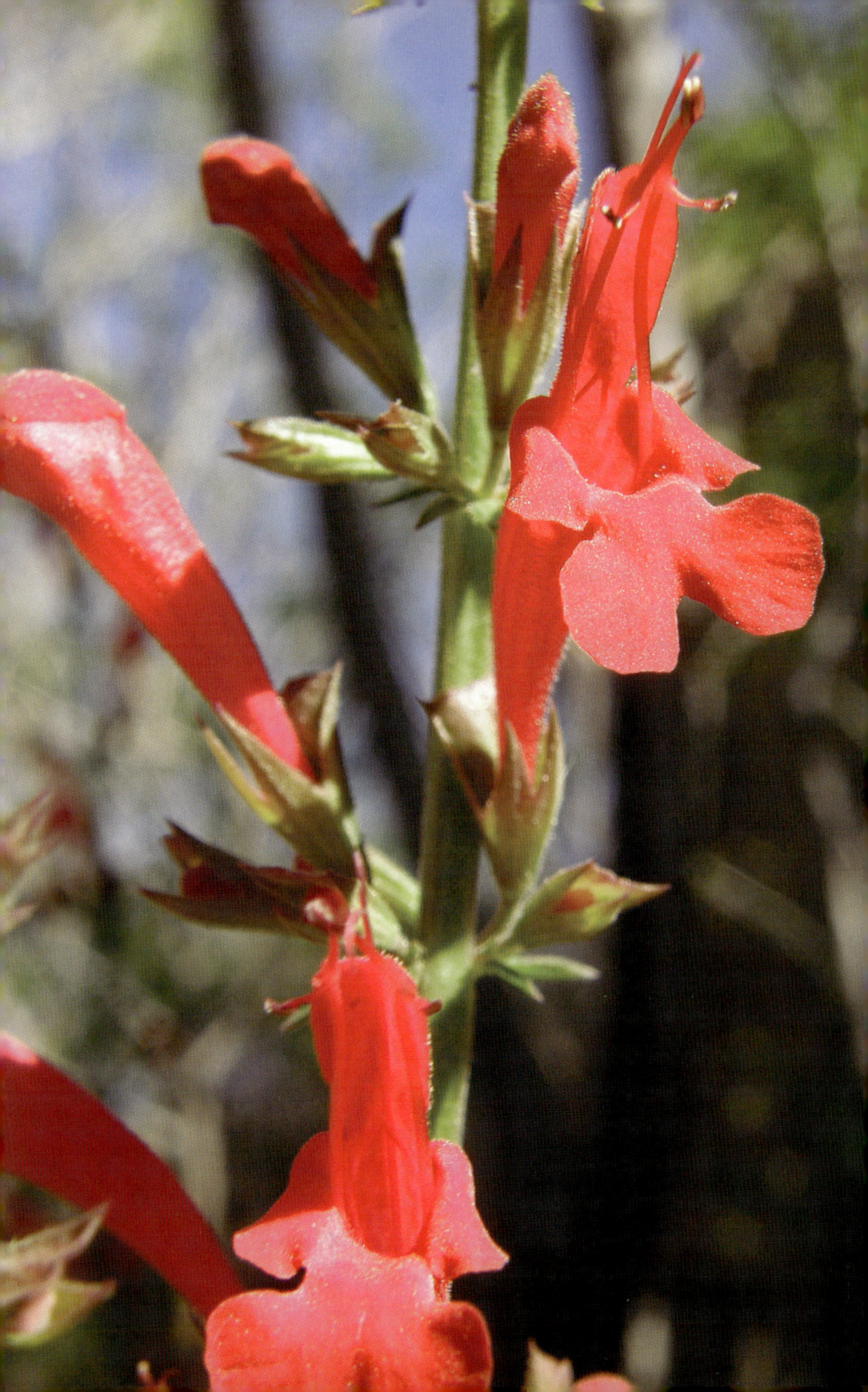

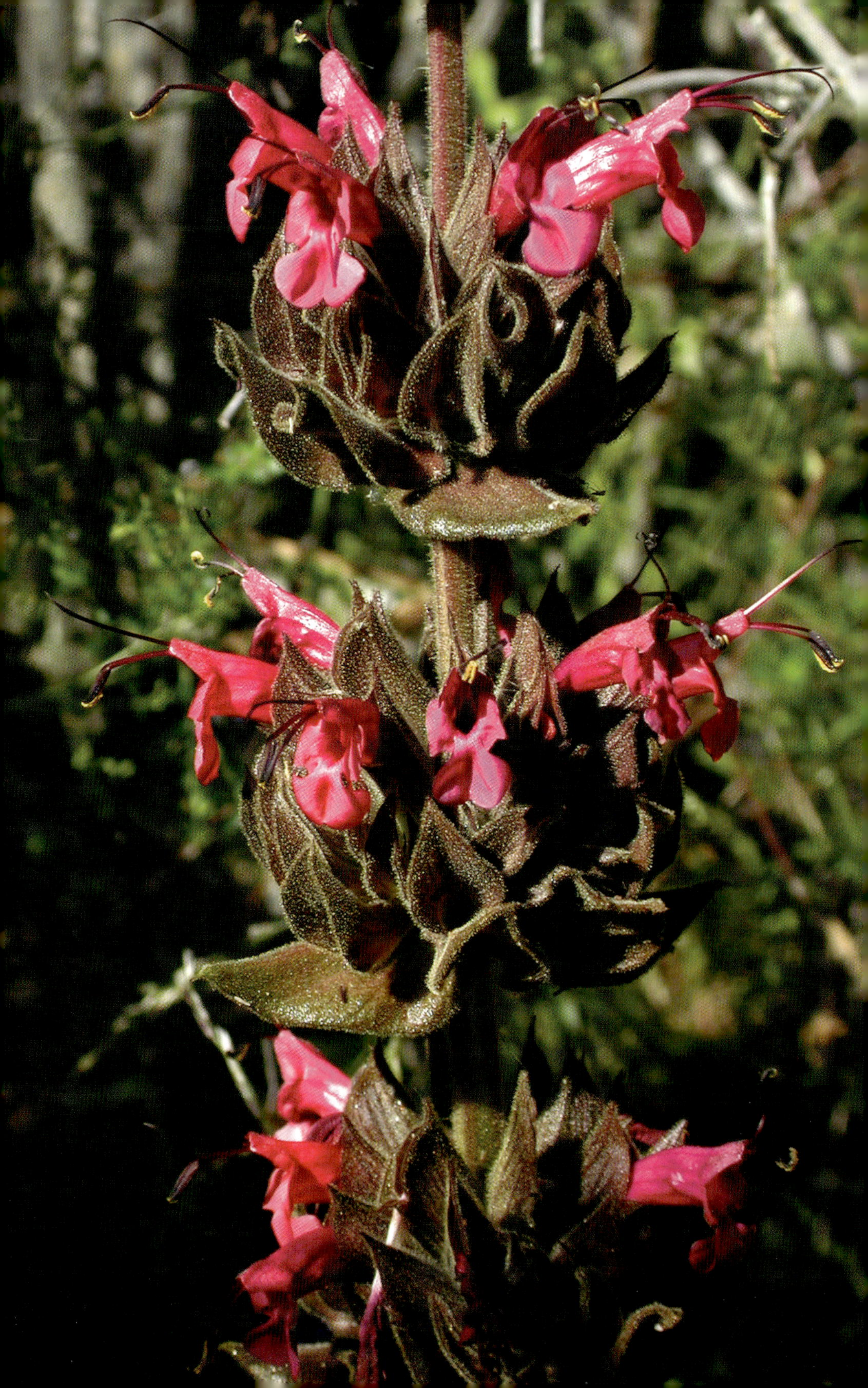

Salvia spathacea

Hummingbird Sage, Pitcher Sage, Crimson Sage

Family:	Lamiaceae	**Water use:**	Moderate
Type:	Perennial	**Cold hardiness:**	Top to 20°F, roots to below 10°F
Size:	2–3' high x 3–4' wide, with 1–3' flower stalks	**USDA zone:**	8–10
Bloom:	March–May, usually repeats in fall		
Author citation:	Greene		

This showy beauty of the West Coast is also suited to interior gardens. As billed by its common name, it is a veritable beacon to hummingbirds and relies upon them for pollination. In turn its deep rosy-red flowers, with their maroon bracts and calyces, supply extremely important sucrose-rich nectar for Anna's, Allen's, and Black-chinned Hummingbirds during the nesting season. Various butterflies and bees also visit the blossoms. Finches and quail are among the birds that relish the seeds, which are said to be particularly rich in protein.

Hummingbird sage is a California endemic, native to the coast sage and chaparral communities of the central and southern coast, from the San Francisco Bay Area southward to San Diego County and usually below 2,500 feet in elevation. It is typically found on grassy hillsides, both open and shady, often in the understory of native oaks or on north slopes next to seeps.

Spreading by rhizomes to form shrubby clumps, the upright stems are clad in very large, triangular, scallop-edged leaves that are dark green and wrinkled above and pale green and downy below. Unless drought-stressed, the foliage is evergreen, and when brushed emits a fruity fragrance. The flowers too are relatively large, up to two inches long, with tubular corollas that terminate in a pitcher-like spout. They occur in dense whorls spaced two inches apart along flower stems that rise two to three feet above the foliage.

Hummingbird sage is not particular about soil as long as it is well drained, and it seems to do best in part or filtered shade. While moderately drought tolerant, it will look nicer with a deep soaking once or twice a month during extended dry periods. This distinctive plant lends a vivid splash of spring color to borders or beds under the high shade of trees, and it is especially appropriate for California hummingbird gardens. Propagate by seed, cuttings, or careful division of the rootstocks of established plants. 'Kawatre' is a variety with larger leaves and more deeply colored flowers that is reportedly hardier than the species, to about 10°F.

Salvia townsendii
Townsend's Sage

Family:	Lamiaceae	**Water use:**	Moderate
Type:	Subshrub	**Cold hardiness:**	To 20°F
Size:	3' high x 3–5' wide	**USDA zone:**	9–10
Bloom:	August–October		

Author citation: Fernald

THIS GORGEOUS PLANT FROM THE SIERRA MADRE OCCIDENTAL may not be very common or well known, but its velvety, deeply hued, reddish pink flowers provide late summer nectar to both resident hummingbirds and migrants moving southward toward their wintering grounds in central Mexico. Rufous Hummingbirds are the only species specifically mentioned in the literature but others partake of the nectar as well and are at least partially responsible for pollination.

Charles Townsend first collected this pretty sage in Chihuahua, near a mine in the pine-oak forest of the Sierra Madres at 7,500 feet high, and scattered populations are still found in the west-central part of the state, but it also occurs in eastern Sonora and has been found in Sinaloa and Nayarit as well. Preferred habitat niches include sparse oak woodlands, open pine-oak forests, rocky slopes, barren volcanic hilltops, gravelly roadsides, and canyon bottoms, usually from 4,000 to 8,000 feet in elevation, although some Nayarit populations occur at lower elevations.

In open oak grasslands, it comes into its own as a commanding presence, with its erect, spreading, branching stems generously cloaked in smooth dark-green leaves that are narrowly oval in shape with pointed tips. Flowers occur in dense clusters near branch tips and have inch-long corollas, drooping lower lips that afford hummingbird access, and styles and stamens that extend beyond the corolla and brush the crowns of the birds as they feed on nectar.

Its handsome habit and spectacular floral display have led multiple field botanists that have encountered Townsend's sage in its natural haunts to exclaim that it ought to be brought under cultivation. If seeds can be obtained, it is likely to prefer full sun to part shade, gravelly soil with good drainage, and regular water until established, and it would be particularly suited to middle elevation gardens where winters are fairly mild. One would expect that plants should be easy to propagate by either seed or stem cuttings taken in spring. As plants are reported to be somewhat rhizomatous, they likely can be propagated by root division as well.

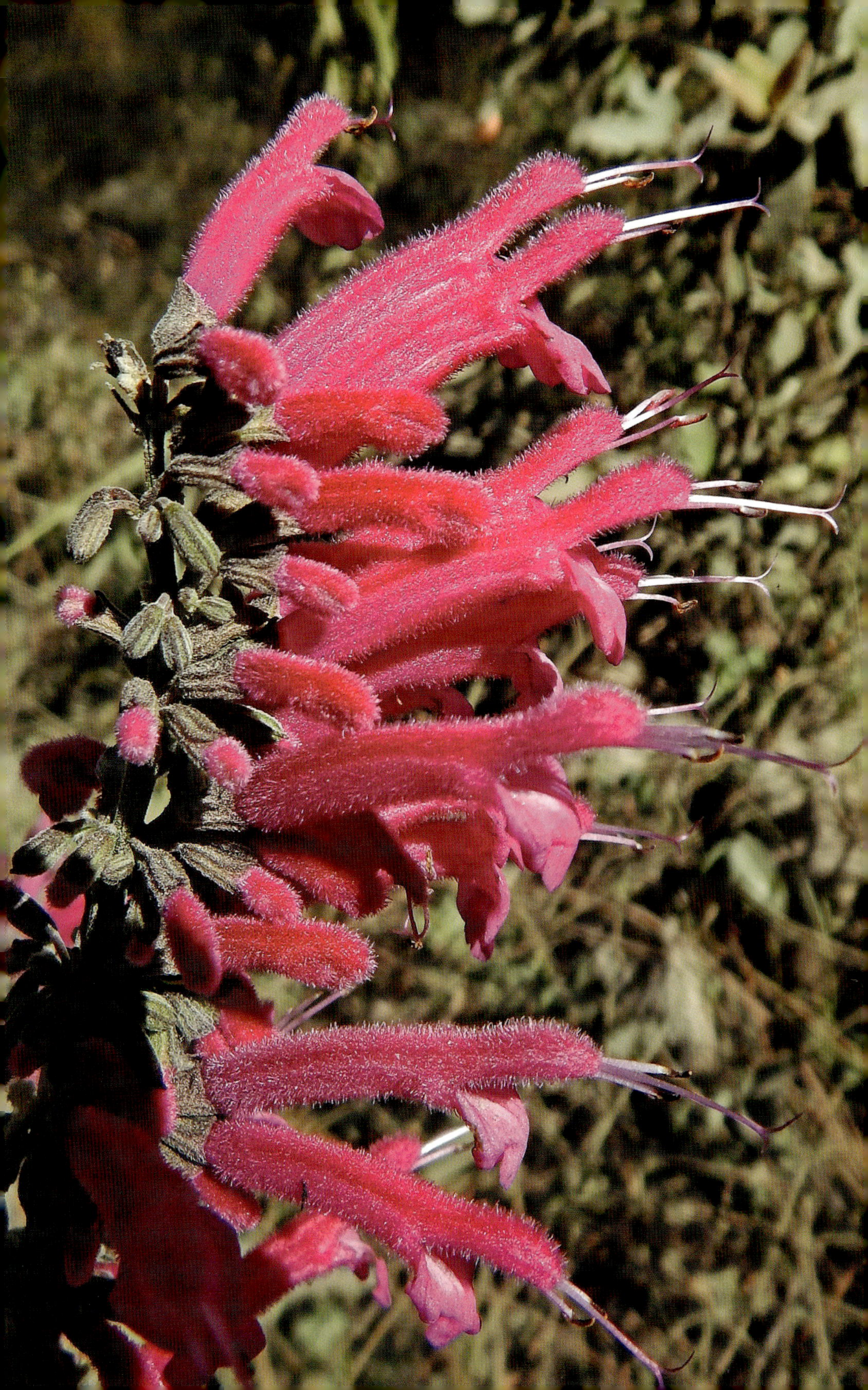

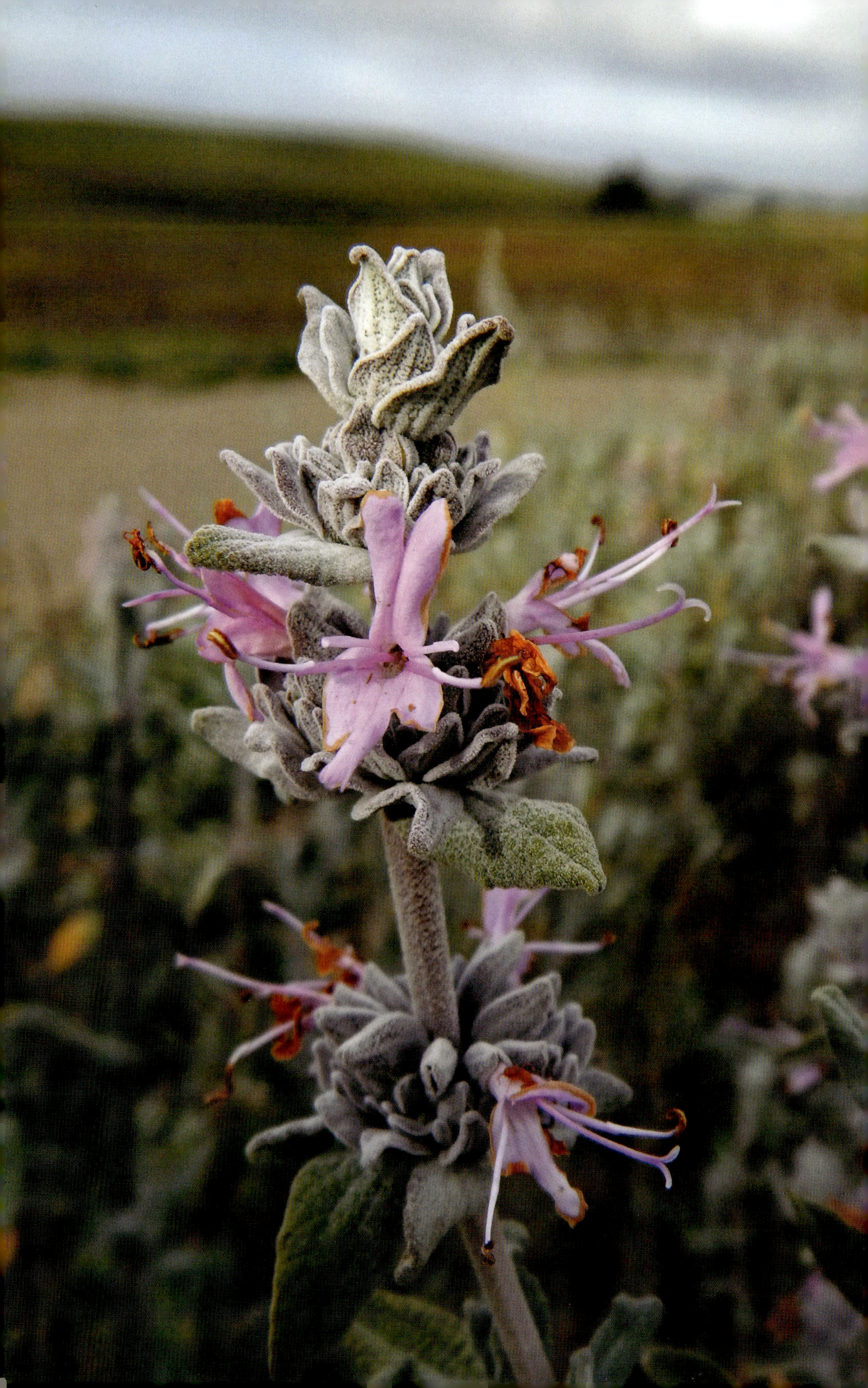

Salvia species
Sage

Family:	Lamiaceae	**Water use:**	Low–moderate
Type:	Evergreen shrub	**Cold hardiness:**	To 15°F or below
Size:	3–5' high x 3–5' wide	**USDA zone:**	8b–10
Bloom:	March–June (*mellifera*), April–June (others)		

Author citation: *Salvia apiana* Jepson
Salvia clevelandii (A. Gray) Greene
Salvia leucophylla Greene
Salvia mellifera Greene

UNLIKE THEIR RED-FLOWERING COUSINS THESE CALIFORNIA SALVIAS ARE primarily pollinated by bees, but their spring blooms are extremely important to both Anna's and Costa's Hummingbirds, especially in early spring when other nectar producers may be few and far between. Black-chinned Hummingbirds, along with various butterflies, also visit the blossoms, which are white or pale lavender in white sage (*Salvia apiana*) and black sage (*S. mellifera*), pinkish purple in purple sage (*S. leucophylla*), and vivid blue-violet in chaparral sage (*S. clevelandii*). Quail, goldfinches, and sparrows polish off the shiny brown seeds soon after they appear.

All of these sages belong to the coast sage and chaparral communities of southern California and northern Baja California in Mexico, with black sage ranging as far north as the San Francisco Bay area and chaparral sage mostly limited to San Diego County. Black sage also occurs on some of the Channel Islands. Typically, these shrubs inhabit dry coastal bluffs, gravelly slopes in foothills of the coastal ranges, and occasionally oak savanna, usually at elevations below 4,000 feet but sometimes higher.

All are upright to spreading in form, with herbaceous stems arising from a woody base, and have wrinkled, aromatic foliage that is silvery gray in color, with the exception of black sage with its olive green leaves. Flower clusters are spaced at intervals on stalks above the foliage.

These sages especially thrive in areas of summer drought, requiring only a sunny exposure, a loose, fast-draining soil low in organic matter, and perhaps a monthly watering during extended dry periods. They benefit from winter moisture but are prone to rot with too much water during their summer dormant period, and they reportedly cope better with summer monsoons when planted in the ground rather than in a container. All of these shrubs are excellent for stabilizing dry banks or a chaparral restoration planting. Plants may be propagated by stem cuttings taken in early spring before new growth appears or by spring-sown seed that has been cold-stratified for one month.

Scrophularia macrantha

Mimbres Figwort, New Mexico Figwort, Redbirds in a Tree

Family:	Scrophulariaceae	**Water use:**	Moderate
Type:	Perennial	**Cold hardiness:**	Roots to -20°F
Size:	3–4' high x 1.5' wide	**USDA zone:**	5–10
Bloom:	July–October		

Author citation: Greene ex Stiefelhagen
Synonyms: *Scrophularia neomexicana* R. J. Shaw; *S. coccinea* A. Gray

WHEN BROAD-TAILED HUMMINGBIRDS STREAM SOUTHWARD from the Southern Rockies in late summer en route to the Sierra Madre Occidental and their Mexican wintering grounds, they're apt to make a rest stop wherever this intriguing plant is in bloom. Black-chinned and Rufous Hummingbirds are avid visitors as well. The bright rosy-red, white-lipped flowers offer both nectar and abundant small insects for quick energy, and unlike most others in the genus are pollinated to a significant extent by hummingbirds. Mining, overgrazing, and road construction are among the threats to this appealing plant's future in the wild.

Mimbres figwort is endemic to just a few scattered mountain ranges in Catron, Grant, Sierra, Luna, and Doña Ana counties in southwestern New Mexico, occurring in the piñon-juniper belt and in lower montane coniferous forests at elevations ranging from 6,500 to 8,200 feet. Quite rare, it is typically found growing on steep talus slopes, on north-facing igneous cliffs, and less frequently in moist canyon bottoms.

Its reddish stems are rather coarse and floppy, and sport dark green, opposite or whorled, narrowly triangular leaves that are coarsely toothed and deeply veined. The small puffy two-lipped tubular flowers occur in loose clusters on showy foot-long spikes above the foliage. Two-chambered, oblong seed capsules containing numerous tiny seeds develop after flowering and mature by late fall.

Plants require a fast-draining soil and full sun to light shade for best growth but in low deserts will bake without afternoon shade, and they absolutely will not tolerate reflected heat. A deep soaking once or twice a month during hot dry periods is recommended. Quite rare in the wild but occasionally available from nurseries, this charming perennial benefits from being planted with taller plants to help support its lanky stems. It works nicely in mixed borders or beds, naturalistic plantings, and niche gardens and can also be grown in containers if given more regular watering. Propagate by seed or stem cuttings. Mountain figwort *(S. montana)* is a close cousin that ranges from north-central to southwestern New Mexico and is also much visited by Broad-tailed and Rufous Hummingbirds.

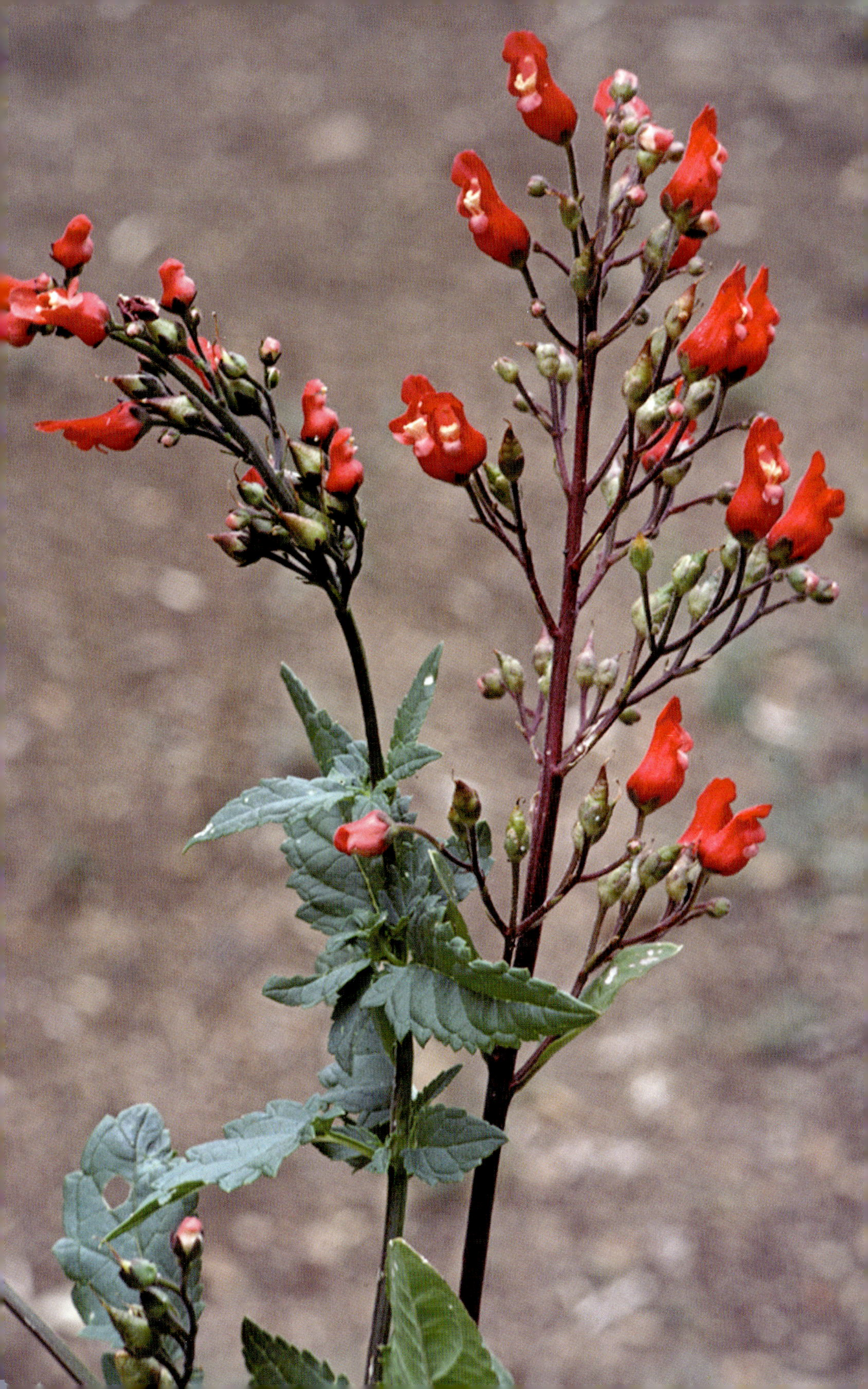

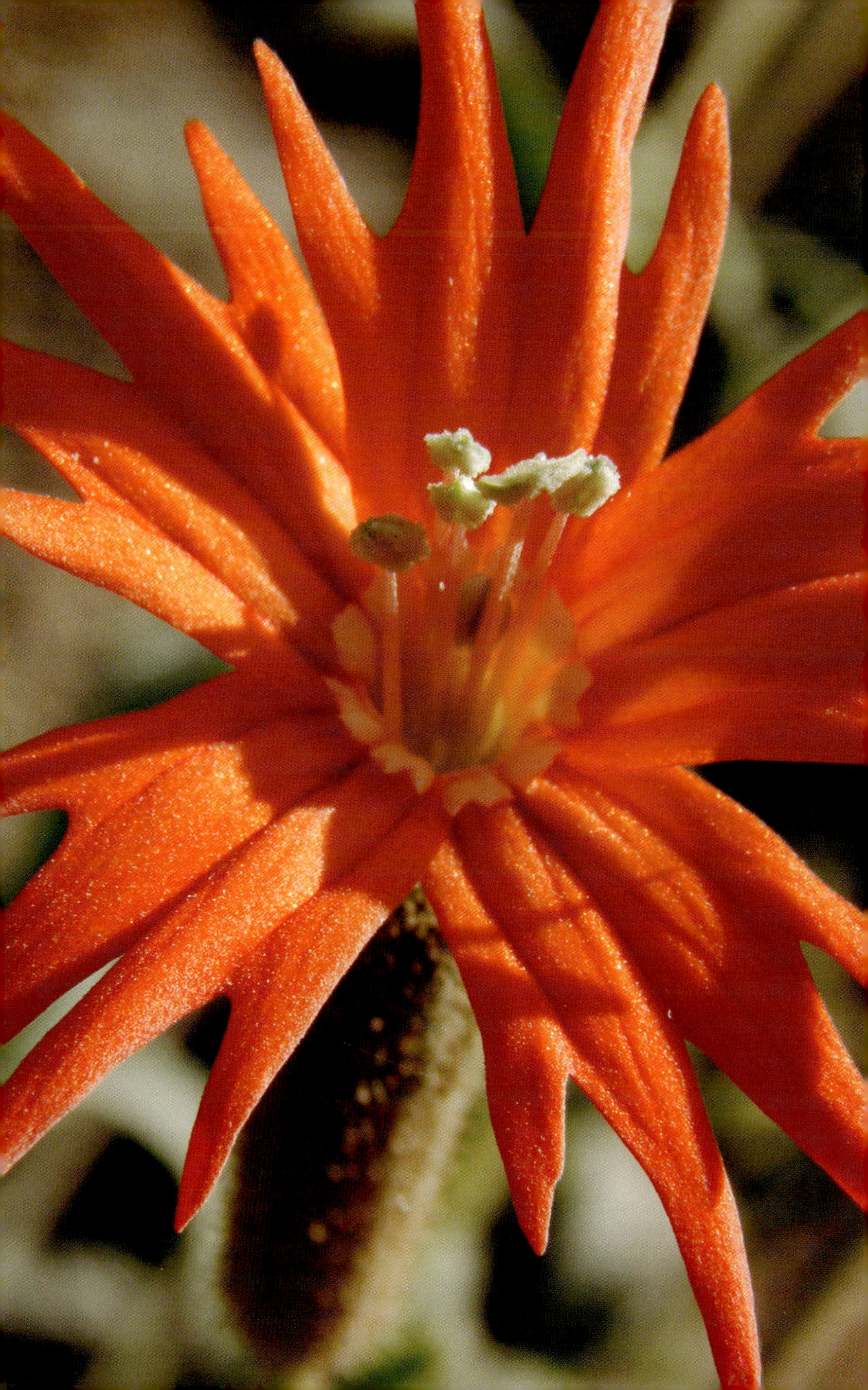

Silene laciniata

Mexican Catchfly, Mexican Campion, Cardinal Catchfly

Family:	Caryophyllaceae		April–July on Pacific Coast
Type:	Perennial	**Water use:**	Moderate
Size:	1–2' high x 1–2' wide	**Cold hardiness:**	To -10°F
Bloom:	May–October in Southwest,	**USDA zone:**	6–9

Author citation: Cavanilles
Synonym: *Melandrium laciniatum* (Cavanilles) Rohrbach

For a tiny perennial this fringed beauty commands a lot of notice from hummingbirds when in bloom. The unusual scarlet flowers are an important source of nectar for Anna's, Allen's, Broad-tailed, and Magnificent Hummingbirds and are popular with Black-chinned, Rufous, and Calliope Hummingbirds as well. In their studies of hummingbird-pollinated plants, Karen and Verne Grant noted that hummingbirds seemed to remain a long time at the blossoms, suggesting that the nectar is either copious or particularly sweet, or both. The sticky hairs below the petals trap numerous insects seeking to rob the nectar—a protein bonus that may also contribute toward the plant's tremendous appeal to hummingbirds.

Mexican catchfly ranges from California eastward through Arizona and New Mexico to western Texas, and southward into Mexico to at least Durango. It occurs on brushy slopes and canyonsides of interior mountains and coast ranges at elevations ranging from below 1,000 to nearly 10,000 feet, often in the company of pines, oaks, or madrones.

Not commonly encountered but fairly easy to recognize, the pubescent stems are typically lanky, often sprawling against other plants. The bright green linear leaves have toothed margins and are densely coated with sticky hairs. The small orange-red flowers are tubular with five petals, each with four pointed, flaring lobes, and have a faint white ring at the throat.

Plants can be somewhat finicky in cultivation, preferring moist, well-drained, gravelly soil. In the north they can take full sun, but afternoon shade is preferred in the south and at lower elevations. Given the perfect niche, they are relatively carefree but will languish in humid regions or areas with high rainfall. A deep soaking twice a month during the summer will prolong the bloom and keep plants looking their best. Cut stems back after flowering to encourage density. Where snails are a problem, try planting in a hanging basket, which will also make the flowers more accessible to hummingbirds. Plants can be propagated from seed sown on site in fall or by root division. Mexican catchfly makes a delightful addition to rock gardens, oasis plantings, and perennial borders and is particularly suited to upland locales.

Stachys coccinea

Scarlet Betony, Texas Betony, Scarlet Hedgenettle

Family:	Lamiaceae	**Water use:**	High
Type:	Perennial	**Cold hardiness:**	Top to 10°F, roots to below 0°F
Size:	1–2' high x 2–3' wide		
Bloom:	April–October, but sporadic midsummer	**USDA zone:**	7–10

Author citation: Ortega

THIS CHARMER IS A TERRIFIC LITTLE PLANT FOR A HUMMINGBIRD OASIS. No fewer than twelve hummingbird species are known to visit its scarlet red blossoms, including Blue-throated, Magnificent, Violet-crowned, Berylline, White-eared, Broad-tailed, Rufous, Calliope, Broad-billed, Black-chinned, Costa's, and Anna's Hummingbirds. The plant depends to a large extent on hummingbirds for pollination, but butterflies take nectar from the flowers as well.

Scarlet betony hails from central and southeastern Arizona and southwestern New Mexico, ranging well southward into Mexico as far as Oaxaca. It is a denizen of wet niches—riparian springs, rock crevices on steep slopes, canyon bottoms, arroyos, and seeps—at elevations ranging from 1,500 to 8,000 feet.

In warm climates the plant is evergreen, the square stems rising from a basal rosette into an irregularly rounded form. The triangular sage-green leaves are wrinkled with toothed margins and have a unique odor that some people adore and some find distasteful. The small tubular flowers appear in whorls on short spikes above the foliage, the bloom peaking in spring and fall in desert regions but providing little splashes of color most any time of year.

Plants thrive in moist, nitrogen-rich soil but are quite tolerant as long as drainage is good. They will grow in full sun to heavy shade but do best in partial or filtered shade, especially in low desert regions. During periods of drought, plants respond by dying back and then re-growing when moisture is adequate. To keep plants looking their best, give them a weekly soaking during the hot summer months, or locate near a hose bib or other perpetually wet spot. Remove spent flower spikes to encourage more blooms. When old clumps die out in the center, the outer sections can be divided and replanted. Propagation is easiest by cuttings taken in spring or late summer and kept under mist until rooted. Germination by seed yields stronger plants but is a bit more challenging; for best results sow on site or in a cold frame in fall. Scarlet betony is perfect for gracing a water feature, in rock gardens nestled next to boulders, in beds, or in containers. Golden columbine (*Aquilegia chrysantha*) is an ideal companion plant; the two complement each other nicely in planters.

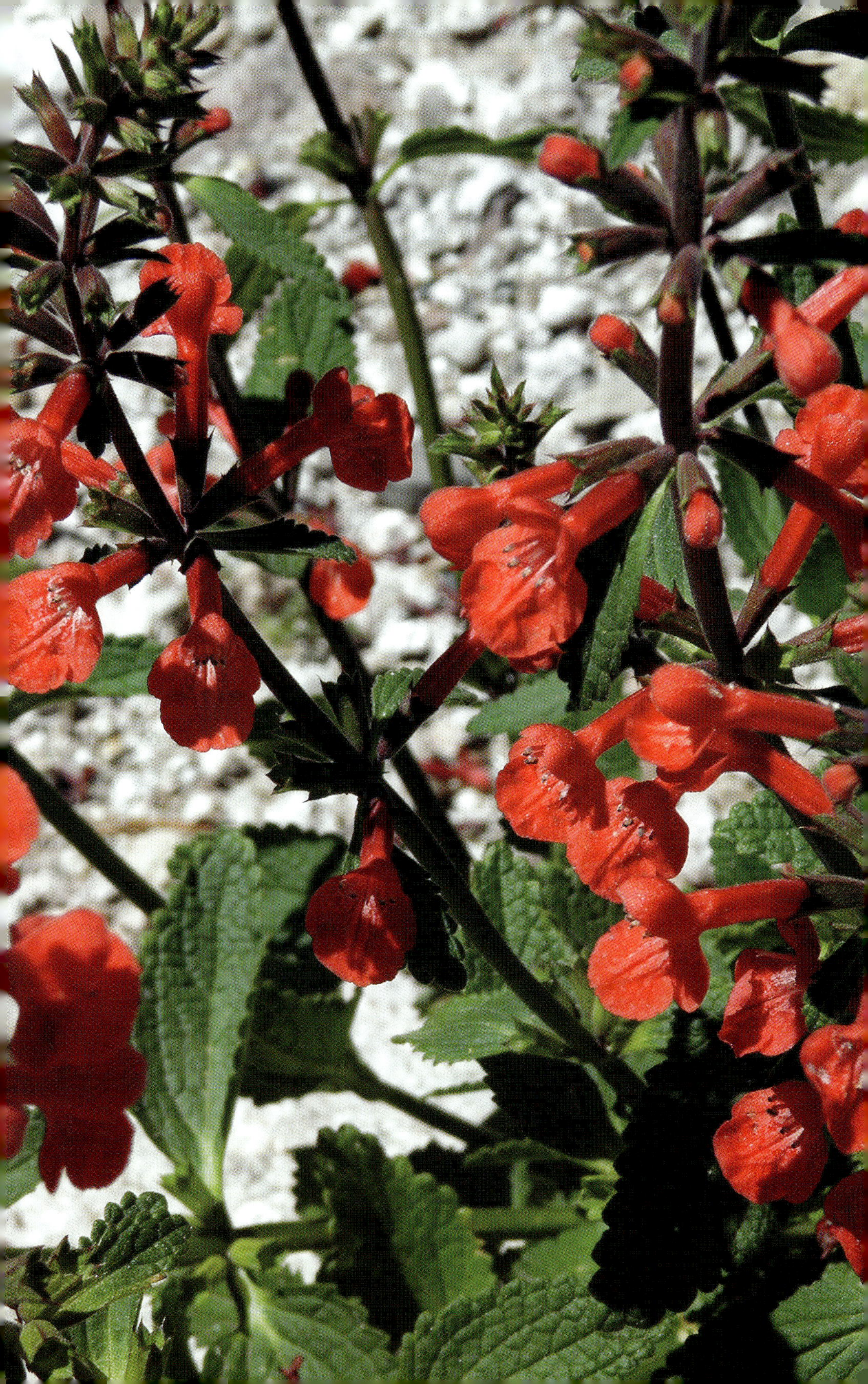

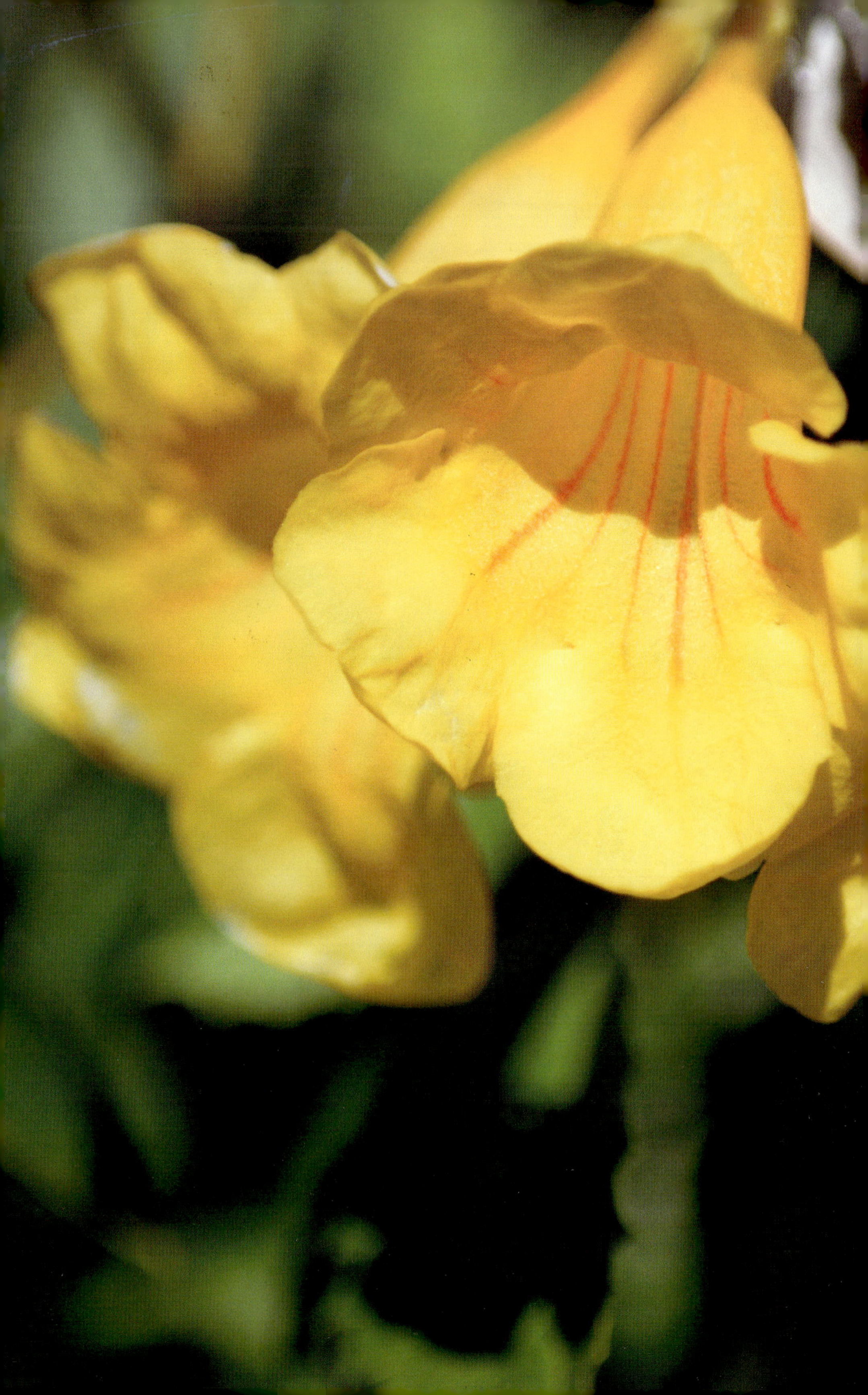

Tecoma stans

Yellow Bells, Esperanza, Tronadora, Palo del Arco, Caballito

Family:	Bignoniaceae	**Water use:**	Low–moderate
Type:	Deciduous or evergreen shrub	**Cold hardiness:**	Top to low 20s°F, roots to 5°F
Size:	3–6' high x 5' wide (to 15' high in frost-free areas)	**USDA zone:**	8–10
Bloom:	April–June, sporadic summer, August–October		

Author citation: (L.) Jussieu ex Kunth
Synonyms: *Tecoma stans* var. *angustatum* Rehder; *Bignonia stans* Linneaus

THIS PRETTY SHRUB IS IRRESISTIBLE WHEN IN BLOOM, with its clusters of large, bright yellow, trumpet-shaped flowers. Lucifer, Black-chinned, and Broad-billed Hummingbirds are known to take nectar from the blossoms, but some gardeners report little apparent interest from visiting hummingbirds. Bumblebees are the primary pollinators, and the plant is both a nectar source and larval host for the dogface butterfly.

The narrow-leafed form of yellow bells (variety *angustatum*) ranges from southeastern Arizona eastward through southern New Mexico and western Texas, and southward into Mexico, occurring on limestone and igneous soils on rocky slopes, among boulders in arroyos and dry washes, and on gravelly plains, from 2,000 to 5,500 feet in elevation.

Even when not in bloom, its upright form, dressed in lush dark green pinnately divided foliage, stands out from the typical grays and sage greens of neighboring vegetation. Plants bloom on new growth in late spring, continue through summer with sufficient moisture, and bloom again in fall. Long brown pods form after flowering, containing flat seeds with white papery wings.

Yellow bells will grow in sand, loam, gravel, and even caliche, demanding only excellent drainage. It can be grown in full sun or part shade, and benefits from a deep soaking once or twice during the hot summer months. After late summer it should not be watered, so as to harden it off for winter. A hard freeze will damage the leaves and it will die back to the ground in the low 20s, but it usually recovers quickly in the springtime. Damaged stems can be cut back in late winter. This tough, fast-growing plant makes a luxuriant accent for courtyards, water features, and rock gardens. It works beautifully as a backdrop to perennial beds and also can be grown in a large container. Propagate by fresh seed or softwood cuttings taken in late spring or fall. Occasionally, cutter bees can badly mutilate the foliage. Wide-leafed forms of yellow bells, native to southern Texas and southward through Central America, seem be less attractive to hummingbirds, are hardy to only 28°F, and the lusher foliage requires more water.

Trichostema lanatum

Woolly Blue Curls, Romero

Family:	Lamiaceae	**Water use:**	Low–moderate
Type:	Evergreen shrub	**Cold hardiness:**	Top to 15°F, roots to 0°F
Size:	2–5' high x 4–5' wide		
Bloom:	April–June, also summer–fall if spent flowers removed	**USDA zone:**	8–10

Author citation: Bentham

THIS PLANT'S COMMON NAME SUITS IT PERFECTLY. Its showy clusters of cobalt blue flowers, with their coats of blue, pink, or whitish wool and their long, curling, exserted stamens, provide valuable nectar to both Anna's and Costa's Hummingbirds and are especially important during the nesting season when other nectar sources can be scarce. Each blossom reportedly produces from about six to twenty-five microliters of sucrose-rich nectar per day, the upper end of that range considered a relatively high amount. Butterflies also visit the flowers, but hummingbirds are the most important pollinators.

Woolly blue curls occurs only in central and southern California from near Monterey southward and in Mexico in northern Baja California. Typically it is found on dry sunny slopes of the Coast and Transverse ranges and in the coastal sage scrub and chaparral communities, at elevations below 3,800 feet.

Its many branches are woolly, as are the undersides of the narrow, curling, glossy dark green leaves. When bruised, the leaves have a minty fragrance that may discourage browsing except in times of extreme drought. The mint-like flower clusters appear on one-foot spikes that rise above the foliage. As a hummingbird feeds from the short, narrow corolla tube, its crown is dusted with pollen by the long stamens, to be transferred to the next flower visited.

This distinctive shrub is fairly short-lived, usually lasting only about five years, and can sometimes be rather fussy but is well worth the effort. It will grow in full sun to part shade and does not require any irrigation, but it demands perfect drainage and detests heavy wet soils, particularly during summer. Its usual form is neat and airy, but if it gets too lanky, cut it back hard to promote denser growth. To maximize bloom time, pinch back spent flowers and cut back spent stalks. Propagate by seed sown in fall or by stem cuttings. Woolly blue curls can be used singly as an interesting accent or massed in groups, working well at the perimeter of native live oaks, in mixed shrub borders, and in herb gardens.

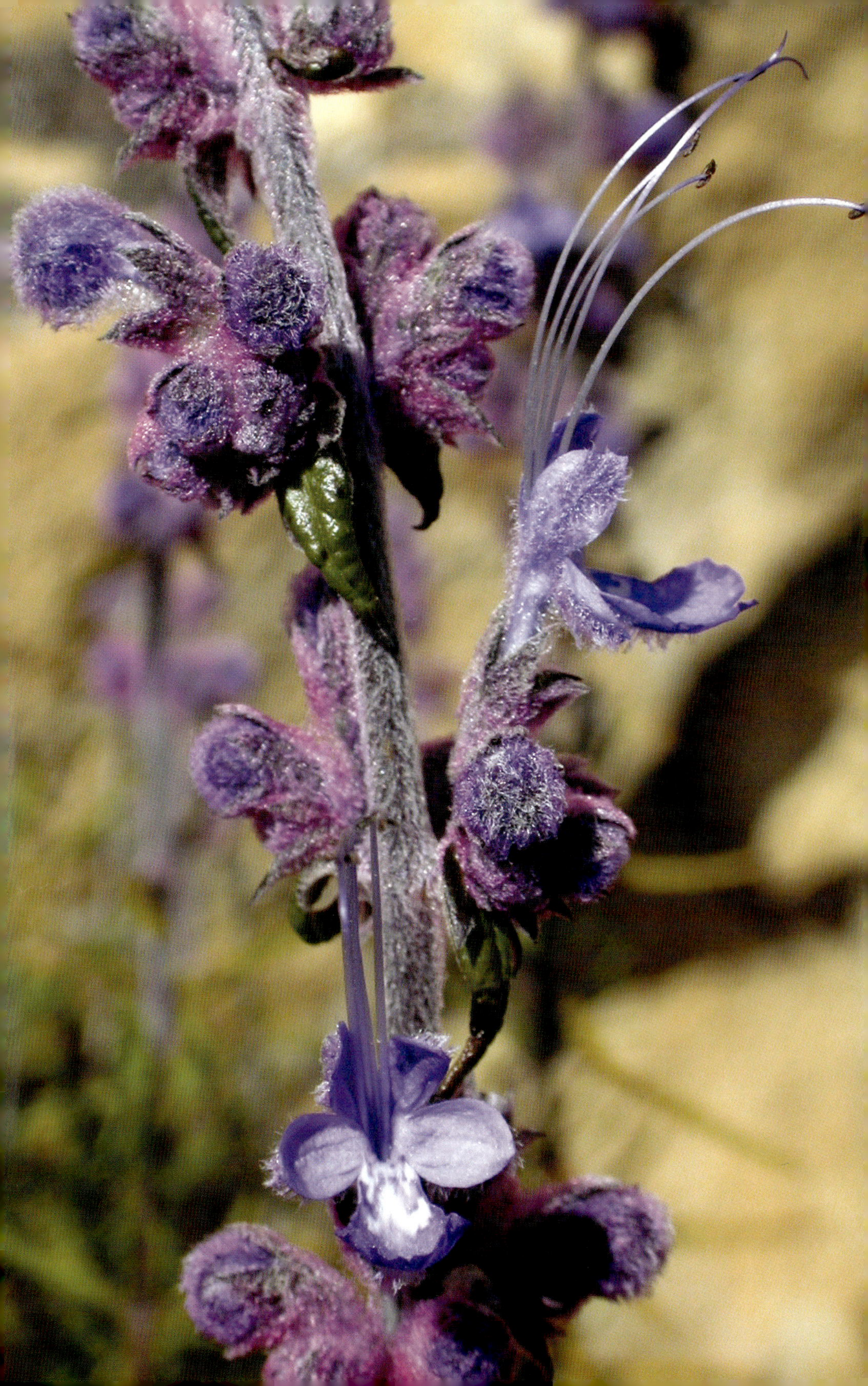

Acknowledgments

Of the many blessings of living in the Southwest, its people—whether recent transplants or those whose taproots span multiple generations—are right there at the top. Throughout the lengthy process from research to publication, nearly everywhere I turned for help, someone would not only answer my questions but offer a great deal more, thus I have many people to thank for this project coming to fruition. I have been little more than a compiler in this entire effort, gathering and processing data generated by the hard work of a multitude of others, including field biologists, ornithologists, hummingbird banders, botanists, horticulturalists, landscape designers, and the authors among them who have made a lot of this information available. Without the benefit of their combined wealth of knowledge, this book would be impossible—it is truly theirs in many respects.

"Well, hurry up and write something for me to rip apart," invited Wynn Anderson with a twinkle in his eye when I first told him of my idea for this book. With these words, Wynn, founder and past curator of the Chihuahuan Desert Gardens at the University of Texas–El Paso and dear friend (still, inexplicably, even after this project), bestowed upon me the fundamental confidence to proceed. He has since read and critiqued nearly every word I've written, in some cases multiple times, and yet somehow unfailingly manages to convey nothing short of unbridled enthusiasm. His wisdom has saved me from untold embarrassments and his unwavering encouragement has been invaluable. His many fine photographs that grace the book really make it more his production than mine, and I'm profoundly humbled to have my name on it.

Another esteemed gentleman whose input, support, and friendship have been pivotal is Dale Zimmerman, noted ornithologist, systematic botanist, author, illustrator, and photographer. He generously shared his wealth of knowledge born of uncountable hours in the field observing hummingbirds and the flowering plants they use, and he provided a fair number of exquisite images of each for the book as well. His discerning eye and wise counsel on many matters have nudged me to raise the bar on this project, and the end product is that much stronger as a result.

I am also indebted to Mary Irish, prolific author on southwestern gardening, whom I solicited for advice on the various agave species and who graciously volunteered to look over all of the plant profiles; her cheerfully offered contributions have been a tremendous blessing. Jon Stewart of the Albuquerque BioPark was kind enough to review a number of California plant profiles and provide key propagation advice. Barry Zimmer and Joan Day-Martin both read and contributed valuable feedback on the hummingbird profiles and primer and Susan Wethington of the Hummingbird Monitoring Network generously reviewed and critiqued the entire manuscript. Leslie Scott and Jackye Meinecke both gave helpful feedback on some of my early work, and Al Schneider provided valuable assistance with taxonomic proofreading down the home stretch.

This being a research-driven project I must give due recognition to my most important sources, without which there would be no book at all. My principal references on hummingbird biology were the various species abstracts in *The Birds of North America* (a project of the American Ornithologists' Union, the Academy of Natural Sciences, and the Cornell Laboratory of Ornithology), Sheri Williamson's *A Field Guide to Hummingbirds of North America*, Paul Johnsgard's *The Hummingbirds of North America*, and Karen Grant & Verne Grant's *Hummingbirds and Their Flowers*. Botanical references were much more numerous, but I would still be wandering in taxonomic purgatory were it not for the Flora of North America, John Kartesz and the Biota of North America Program (BONAP), the Southwest Environmental Information Network (SEINet), *The Plant List*, Encyclopedia of Life, and the USDA PLANTS database. (Doubtless I'll still manage to offend some taxonomists and for that I hereby apologize.) Thanks also to both New Mexico State University and the University of Texas–El Paso for granting access to their periodicals.

For miscellaneous key information, crucial assistance, and/or sage advice I thank Lois Balin, Troy Corman, Jeanne Fredericks, Jeff Grass, David Griffin, the HUMNET-L message board, Dan Johnson, Manuel Jurado, Kathy Kiseda, Sarada Krishnan, Carl Lundblad, Lisa Mandelkern, Molly McCormick, Tim McKimmie, Gary Nabhan, Jim Paton, Jane Poss, Ron Pulliam,

Janet Rademacher, Joan Silagy, Ken Stinnett, Mel Stone, Tom Van Devender, Sally Wasowski, John White, Sandy Williams, Sarah and Ron Wood, and Eleanor Wootten. Thanks also go to all my friends and family who didn't roll their eyes whenever I droned on about the book and especially my head cheerleader and mom, Pat Scott.

For making this book so visually spectacular, I extend my heartfelt appreciation to artful designer Preston Thomas and all of the talented photographers who contributed images. I am deeply grateful to Rio Nuevo Publishers for taking on this project and I particularly want to thank Aaron Downey for his respectful patience with my publishing naïveté and his unflappably positive attitude.

My most profound gratitude goes to my husband and primary sounding board Jimmy Zabriskie, who taught me much of what I know about plants of the Southwest. He quietly took on virtually all of my usual household and nursery chores as I readied the manuscript for publication and from the beginning has been both my inspiration and patient champion, putting tacos on the table and a smile in my heart for the duration of this seemingly interminable endeavor.

APPENDIX

Fifteen Ways to Help Hummingbirds and Their Flowers

1. Acquire and set aside tracts of land that contain vital habitat for hummingbirds, particularly major riparian corridors, desert oases, and watered canyons, and/or lend whatever support you can to organizations with the wherewithal to do so, such as The Nature Conservancy.

2. Support organizations conducting ongoing research about hummingbirds, such as the Arizona-Sonora Desert Museum, the Hummingbird Monitoring Network, and the Southeast Arizona Bird Observatory.

3. Support local and regional seed banks, herbaria, and botanical gardens, and/or help with planting and maintaining a pollinator garden.

4. Volunteer your time helping a Master Hummingbird Bander in your area, and lend financial support to such efforts if you are able.

5. On property that you own, protect streamside vegetation from livestock and restrict access points to water to limit erosion. Prohibit the use of all-terrain vehicles (ATVs) in sensitive arroyos and canyon bottoms.

6. Preserve existing native trees and shrubs as much as is feasible, and when adding new plantings consider native plants whenever possible.

7. Plant a succession of flowering plants native to your region that will offer nectar throughout the season when hummingbirds are expected in your area. Group at least two of a species together to optimize pollination.

8. Keep your cat indoors or confined to an enclosure, and do not permit free-roaming cats on your property. Support humane enclosure programs such as Trap-Evaluate-Neuter-Vaccinate-Adopt-Contain (TEN-VAC) for feral cats in your community.

9. Avoid or limit the use of pesticides—particularly insecticides—in the home landscape.

10. Practice water conservation whenever possible. Lawns and swimming pools are both huge and unnecessary consumers of water, which if left in the water table could otherwise nourish a great many flowering plants.

11. Avoid planting exotic plants that are known to be invasive, and limit others that seem potentially so by planting in containers, deadheading flowers so they don't go to seed, or periodic root pruning.

12. If you maintain a feeding station, make sure that feeders are kept clean and solution is fresh.

13. Take a birding trip to interior Mexico, where most of our hummingbirds spend the winter and where our tourist dollars are greatly appreciated. Landowners there need to know that viable alternatives to deforestation and overgrazing exist.

14. Speak up and make your opinion heard when particularly productive natural areas in your community face development pressures.

15. Share your enthusiasm and knowledge with everyone you possibly can, especially children.

GLOSSARY

acequia: An irrigation canal.
alkaline: Pertaining to soil with a pH greater than 7.0.
alluvial fan: A fan-shaped deposit of soil left by the flow of a watercourse at the base of a mountain.
alpine: Above timberline.
alternate: Arranged singly, as in leaves or branches.
annual: A plant that lives out its entire life within one year.
anther: The part of the stamen that bears pollen.
arroyo: A drainage or gully carved by water, usually dry.
axil: The upper angle between the stem and a leaf.
bajada: The broad lower slopes of a mountain.
banner: Uppermost petal of a flower.
barranca: A steep, narrow, winding river gorge or canyon.
basal rosette: Radiating cluster of leaves at the base of a plant.
berm: An artificial ridge or raised bank.
biennial: A plant that takes two years to grow to maturity, flowering and setting seed in its second year.
bilobed: Divided into two lobes or parts, as in a leaf or flower petal.
bipinnate: Twice pinnate, with the divisions also pinnately divided.
biternate: Twice divided into three parts.
bosque: A woodland.
bract: A reduced leaf that is part of an inflorescence.
browse: To feed on leaves, twigs, or other vegetation; the plants on which grazing animals feed.
calcareous: Containing calcium carbonate.
caliche: Limestone that has leached out and been redeposited in a hard, sometimes impermeable, layer.
calyx: The outermost part of a flower; collectively, the sepals; plural is calyces or calyxes.
compound leaf: A leaf that is composed of multiple leaflets.
cordillera: Group of parallel mountain ranges.
corolla: The inner part of a flower; collectively, the petals.
cultivar: A naturally occurring plant selected for cultivation because of certain characteristics.
deadhead: To remove a flower or cluster of flowers that has completed blooming before it goes to seed.
deciduous: Pertaining to leaves that drop all at once, usually in fall, and are replaced each year.

endemic: Native to and restricted to a particular geographic area.
escarpment: Long steep slope.
exotic: Originating in another country.
exserted: Extending past the length of the flower corolla.
filament: Threadlike part of the stamen.
fledgling: A young bird that has recently left its nest.
genus: A group of organisms having common characteristics distinct from other such groupings.
glandular: Covered with tiny dark or clear glands.
glaucous: Covered with a whitish powdery or waxy film.
gorget: The iridescent throat feathers of a hummingbird.
herbaceous: Having soft or fleshy stems.
humus: Organic matter in soil.
hybrid: The offspring of two or more plants of different species.
igneous: Created by intense heat.
indigenous: Originating in a particular place.
inflorescence: The arrangement of flowers on a stalk.
insectivorous: Pertaining to an animal that feeds on insects and other invertebrates.
involucre: Group of bracts that encircles a flower or fruit.
lanceolate: Lance-shaped, or narrowly elongated with the widest point at the base.
lichen: Crust-like growth composed of algae and fungi that forms on rocks.
limestone: Sedimentary rock consisting mainly of calcium carbonate.
loam: Soil that contains equal parts of sand, silt, and clay.
mesa: Flat-topped hill with steep sides.
mesic: Associated with or favoring environments with a moderate amount of moisture.
microliter: One-millionth of a liter.
monsoon: The rainy season, as it is usually used in the Southwest.
montane: Pertaining to mountains.
native: Originating in a particular region.
naturalized: Not native but reproducing without human encouragement.
nectary: The organ of a flower that secretes nectar.
nectivorous: Pertaining to an animal that feeds on flower nectar.
nestling: A young bird that has hatched but is still developing in its nest.
node: Position on stem from which branches or leaves emerge.
obovate: Shaped like an egg, with the narrowest part at the base.
offset: Plant originating from and connected to another plant.
outcrop: Rock formation.
ovate: Shaped like an egg, with the narrowest part at the tip.
palmate: Radiating from a common point.
panicle: A branched inflorescence.
perennial: A plant that lives more than two years.
perlite: A lightweight material derived from volcanic glass and often used in soil mixes to improve drainage.
petal: A unit of the corolla.
petiole: The stalk that connects a leaf to the stem.

pinnate: Arranged on both sides of the leaf axis.
pip: Split open, as a seed capsule when it is ripe.
pistil: Female reproductive part of a plant.
pubescent: Covered with short soft hairs.
raceme: An unbranched inflorescence of flowers on stalks.
rhizome: An underground stem that travels horizontally.
rhyolite: Pale, fine-grained volcanic rock composed of granite (common in the Sierra Madre Occidental).
riparian: Pertaining to the banks of a river or other watercourse.
rosette: A radiating arrangement of spreading leaves.
scarified: Scratched, as may be done to penetrate the hard coating of some seeds.
scree: A mass of small loose stones that covers a mountain slope.
sepal: A unit of the calyx.
silt: Sediment deposited by running water and having particles between sand and clay in size.
sky island: A mountain range of considerable elevation surrounded on all sides by desert.
species: A group of living organisms consisting of similar individuals capable of interbreeding. (See also *spp.*)
spicate: Pertaining to an inflorescence that is unbranched.
spp.: An abbreviation for multiple species.
spur: Projection of a flower that is hollow and usually contains nectar.
ssp: An abbreviation for subspecies.
stamen: Male reproductive part of a plant.
staminode: Sterile stamen.
stigma: The part of the pistil that receives pollen.
stolon: A runner that extends horizontally atop the ground.
stratified: Placed in moist sand, peat, or perlite, as seeds prior to germination.
style: Stalk that connects the ovary of a plant to the stigma.
subalpine: Just below timberline.
subshrub: A plant that is woody at the base with herbaceous upper parts.
succulent: A plant that has the capacity to store water.
swale: A low spot or depression.
talus: Sloping accumulation of large pieces of rock.
taproot: Main root that grows straight down.
taxonomy: The branch of science concerned with the classification of organisms.
ternate: Divided into three parts.
trilobed: Having three lobes or parts, as in a leaf or flower petal.
tripinnate: Pinnately divided three times.
tuff: Light porous rock formed by the consolidation of volcanic ash.
umbel: Cluster of flowers originating from a central point.
var.: An abbreviation for variety.
vermiculite: A mica-based mineral used in soil mixes for its water-retentive properties.
whorl: A circular arrangement of leaves or flowers around the stem of a plant.
xeric: Associated with or preferring arid environments.
xeriscape: A landscape that has relatively low water requirements.

RESOURCES

ABQ BioPark Botanic Garden, 2601 Central Ave. NW, Albuquerque, NM 87104. (505) 764-6200. www.cabq.gov/culturalservices/biopark/garden.

American Bird Conservancy, 4249 Loudoun Ave., The Plains, VA 20198-2237. (540) 253-5780 or (888) 247-3624. www.abcbirds.org.

American Penstemon Society. http://apsdev.org.

The Arboretum at Flagstaff, 4001 S. Woody Mountain Rd., Flagstaff, AZ 86001. (928) 774-1442. www.thearb.org.

Arizona Native Plant Society, P. O. Box 41206, Sun Station, Tucson, AZ 85717. http://aznps.com.

Arizona-Sonora Desert Museum. 2021 N. Kinney Rd., Tucson, AZ 85743-8918. (520) 883-2702. www.desertmuseum.org.

Borderlands Habitat Restoration Initiative, P. O. Box 1191, Patagonia, AZ 85624. http://borderlandsrestoration.org.

The Botanical Gardens at the Springs Preserve, 333 S. Valley View Blvd., Las Vegas, NV 89153. (702) 822-7700. www.springspreserve.org/gardens/gardens.html.

Boyce Thompson Arboretum State Park, 37615 U.S. 60, Superior, AZ 85273. (520) 689-2723. http://arboretum.ag.arizona.edu/, azstateparks.com/Parks/BOTH.

California Native Plant Society, 2707 K Street, Suite 1, Sacramento, CA 95816. (916) 447-2677. http://cnps.org.

Chihuahuan Desert Gardens of the Centennial Museum, The University of Texas at El Paso, El Paso, TX. (915) 747-5565. www.museum.utep.edu.

Chihuahuan Desert Nature Center, 43869 State Highway 118, Fort Davis, TX 79734. (432) 364-2499. http://cdri.org.

Denver Botanic Gardens, 1005 York St., Denver, CO 80206. (720) 865-3501. www.botanicgardens.org.

Desert Botanical Garden, 1201 N. Galvin Parkway, Phoenix, AZ 85008. (480) 941-1225. www.dbg.org.

The Hummingbird Monitoring Network, P. O. Box 115, Patagonia, AZ 85624. www.hummonnet.org.

Hummingbirds.net. www.hummingbirds.net.

The Hummingbird Society, 6560 State Route 179, Suite 124, Sedona, AZ 86351. (800) 529-3699. www.hummingbirdsociety.org.

The Huntington Botanical Gardens, 1151 Oxford Rd, San Marino, CA 91108. (626) 405-2100. www.huntington.org.

Lady Bird Johnson Wildflower Center, 4801 La Crosse Ave., Austin, TX 78739. (512) 232-0100. www.wildflower.org.

The Living Desert, 47900 Portola Avenue, Palm Desert, CA 92260. (760) 346-5694. www.livingdesert.org.

National Audubon Society, 225 Varick St., New York, NY 10014. (212) 979-3000. www.audubon.org.

Native Plant Society of New Mexico, P. O. Box 35388, Albuquerque, NM 87176-5388. (505) 424-3019. www.npsnm.org.

Native Plant Society of Texas, 320 W. San Antonio St., Fredericksburg, TX 78624. (830) 997-9272. http://npsot.org/wp.

Native Seeds/SEARCH Administration & Seed Bank, 3584 E. River Road, Tucson, AZ 85718. (520) 622-0829. www.nativeseeds.org.

Nativescapes Garden, San Diego Zoo Safari Park, 15500 San Pasqual Valley Rd., Escondido, CA 92027-7017. (760) 747-8702. www.sdzsafaripark.org/parkwildlife/nativescapes_garden.html.

Nevada Native Plant Society, P. O. Box 8965, Reno, NV 89507-8965. https://nvnps.org.

Rancho Santa Ana Botanic Garden, 1500 North College Ave., Claremont, CA 91711. (909) 625-8767. www.rsabg.org.

Red Butte Garden, 300 Wakara Way, Salt Lake City, UT 84108. (801) 585-0556. www.redbuttegarden.org.

San Antonio Botanical Garden, 555 Funston Place, San Antonio, TX 78209. (210) 207-3250. www.sabot.org.

San Diego Botanic Garden, 230 Quail Gardens Drive, Encinitas, CA 92024. (760) 436-3036. www.sdbgarden.org.

Santa Barbara Botanic Garden, 1212 Mission Canyon Rd., Santa Barbara, CA 93105. (805) 682-4726. www.sbbg.org.

Santa Fe Botanical Garden, 715 Camino Lejo, Santa Fe, NM 87505. (505) 471-9103. www.santafebotanicalgarden.org.

Sky Island Alliance, 300 E. University Blvd., Tucson, AZ 85705. (520) 624-7080. www.skyislandalliance.org.

Southeastern Arizona Bird Observatory, 2899 Hidden Meadow Ln., Bisbee, AZ 85603. (520) 432-1388. www.sabo.org.

Theodore Payne Foundation, 10459 Tuxford St., Sun Valley, CA 91352. (818) 768-1802. www.theodorepayne.org.

Tohono Chul Park, 7366 N. Paseo Del Norte, Tucson, AZ 85704. (520) 742-6455. www.tohonochulpark.org/gardens.

Tree of Life Nursery. 33201 Ortega Highway, San Juan Capistrano, CA 92675. (949) 728-0685. www.californianativeplants.com.

Tucson Botanical Gardens, 2150 N. Alvernon Way, Tucson, AZ 85712. (520) 326-9686. http://www.tucsonbotanical.org.

University of Nevada–Las Vegas Arboretum, 4505 S. Maryland Parkway, Las Vegas, NV 89154-1064. (702) 895-3392. http://facilities.unlv.edu/landscape/arboretum.html.

Utah Native Plant Society, P. O. Box 520041, Salt Lake City, UT 84152-0041. www.unps.org.

Western Colorado Botanical Gardens, 641 Struthers Ave., Grand Junction, CO 81501. (970) 245-3288. www.wcbotanic.org.

BIBLIOGRAPHY

HUMMINGBIRD REFERENCES

Arizona-Sonora Desert Museum. 2014. Migratory pollinators program. Tucson, AZ: Arizona-Sonora Desert Museum. www.desertmuseum.org/pollination/hummingbirds.php.

Baltosser, W. H. 1989. "Nectar availability and habitat selection by hummingbirds in Guadalupe Canyon." *Wilson Bulletin* 101: 559–578.

Baltosser, W. H., and S. M. Russell. 2000. "Black-chinned Hummingbird (*Archilochus alexandri*)." No. 495 in *The Birds of North America,* edited by A. Poole and F. Gill. Philadelphia: The Birds of North America, Inc.

Baltosser, W. H., and P. E. Scott. 1996. "Costa's Hummingbird (*Calypte costae*)." No. 251 in *The Birds of North America,* edited by A. Poole and F. Gill. Philadelphia: The Birds of North America, Inc.

Bent, A. C. 1940. *Life Histories of North American Cuckoos, Goatsuckers, Hummingbirds, and Their Allies.* Washington, DC: U. S. Government Printing Office [Smithsonian Institution, U. S. National Museum Bulletin 176].

Calder, W. A. 1999. "Hummingbirds in Rocky Mountain meadows." In *Gatherings of Angels: Migrating Birds and Their Ecology,* edited by K. P. Able. Ithaca, NY: Comstock Books (Cornell University Press).

———. 2004. "Rufous and Broad-tailed Hummingbirds." In *Conserving Migratory Pollinators and Nectar Corridors in Western North America,* edited by G. P. Nabhan. Tucson, AZ: The University of Arizona Press and The Arizona-Sonora Desert Museum.

Calder, W. A., and L. L. Calder. 1994. "Calliope Hummingbird (*Stellula calliope*)." No. 135 in *The Birds of North America,* edited by A. Poole and F. Gill. Philadelphia: The Birds of North America, Inc.

Camfield, A. F., W. A. Calder, and L. L. Calder. 2013. "Broad-tailed Hummingbird (*Selasphorus platycercus*)." *The Birds of North America Online,* edited by A. Poole. Ithaca, NY: Cornell Lab of Ornithology. http://bna.birds.cornell.edu/bna/species/016.

Clark, C. J., and D. E. Mitchell. 2013. "Allen's Hummingbird (*Selasphorus sasin*)." *The Birds of North America Online,* edited by A. Poole. Ithaca, NY: Cornell Lab of Ornithology. http://bna.birds.cornell.edu/bna/species/501.

Clark, C. J., and S. M. Russell. 2012. "Anna's Hummingbird (*Calypte anna*)." *The Birds of North America Online,* edited by A. Poole. Ithaca, NY: Cornell Lab of Ornithology. http://bna.birds.cornell.edu/bna/species/226.

Grant, K. A., and V. Grant. 1968. *Hummingbirds and Their Flowers.* New York: Columbia University Press.

Healy, S., and W. A. Calder. 2006. "Rufous Hummingbird (*Selasphorus rufus*)." *The Birds of North America Online,* edited by A. Poole. Ithaca, NY: Cornell Lab of Ornithology. http://bna.birds.cornell.edu/bna/species/053.

Howell, S. N. G. 2003. *Hummingbirds of North America: The Photographic Guide.* Princeton, NJ: Princeton University Press.

Johnsgard, P. A. 1997. *The Hummingbirds of North America,* 2nd edition. Washington, DC: Smithsonian Institution Press.

Kuban, J. F., J. Lawley, and R. L. Neill. 1980. "Feeding ecology of hummingbirds in the highlands of the Chisos Mountains, Texas." *Condor* 82: 180–185.

Martinez del Rio, C. M. 1990. "Sugar preferences in hummingbirds: the influence of subtle chemical differences on food choice." *Condor* 92: 1022–1030.

Nabhan, G. P. 2004. "Stresses on Pollinators during Migration." In *Conserving Migratory Pollinators and Nectar Corridors in Western North America,* edited by G. P. Nabhan. Tucson, AZ: The University of Arizona Press and The Arizona-Sonora Desert Museum.

Powers, D. R. 2013. "Magnificent Hummingbird (*Eugenes fulgens*)." *The Birds of North America Online,* edited by A. Poole. Ithaca, NY: Cornell Lab of Ornithology. http://bna.birds.cornell.edu/bna/species/221.

Powers, D. R., and S. M. Wethington. 1999. "Broad-billed Hummingbird (*Cyanthus latirostris*)." No. 430 in *The Birds of North America,* edited by A. Poole and F. Gill. Philadelphia: The Birds of North America.

Schondube, J. E., S. Contreras-Martinez, I. Ruan-Tejeda, W. A. Calder, and E. Santana C. 2004. "Migratory Patterns of the Rufous Hummingbird in Western Mexico." In *Conserving Migratory Pollinators and Nectar Corridors in Western North America,* edited by G. P. Nabhan. Tucson, AZ: The University of Arizona Press and The Arizona-Sonora Desert Museum.

Scott, P. E. 1994. "Lucifer Hummingbird (*Calothorax lucifer*)." No. 134 in *The Birds of North America,* edited by A. Poole and F. Gill. Philadelphia: The Birds of North America.

Stiles, F. G. 1976. "Taste preferences, color preferences, and flower choice in hummingbirds." *Condor* 78: 10–26.

Stromberg, M. R., and P. B. Johnsen. 1990. "Hummingbird sweetness preferences: taste or viscosity?" *Condor* 92: 606–12.

Van Devender, T. R., W. A. Calder, K. Krebbs, A. L. Reina G., S. M. Russell, and R. Russell. 2004. "Hummingbird Plants and Potential Nectar Corridors of the Rufous Hummingbird in Sonora, Mexico." In *Conserving Migratory Pollinators and Nectar Corridors in Western North America,* edited by G. P. Nabhan. Tucson, AZ: The University of Arizona Press and The Arizona-Sonora Desert Museum.

Wagner, H. O. 1946. "Food and feeding habits of Mexican hummingbirds." *Wilson Bulletin* 58: 69–93.

Waser, N. M. 1978. "Food supply and nest timing of Broad-tailed Hummingbirds in the Rocky Mountains." *Condor* 78: 133–35.

Wethington, S. M. 2002. "Violet-crowned Hummingbird (*Amazilia violiceps*)." No. 688 in *The Birds of North America,* edited by A. Poole and F. Gill. Philadelphia: The Birds of North America.

Williams III, S. O. 2002. "Status of the Violet-crowned Hummingbird in New Mexico." *NMOS Bulletin* 30(3): 91–95. Albuquerque, NM: The New Mexico Ornithological Society.

Williamson, S. L. 2000. "Blue-throated Hummingbird (*Lampornis clemenciae*)." No. 531 in *The Birds of North America,* edited by A. Poole and F. Gill. Philadelphia: The Birds of North America.

———. 2001. *A Field Guide to Hummingbirds of North America.* Boston: Houghton Mifflin Company.

PLANT REFERENCES

Ajilvsgi, G. 1984. *Wildflowers of Texas.* Fredericksburg, TX: Shearer Publishing.

Allred, K. W., and R. D. Ivey. 2012. *Flora Neomexicana III: An Illustrated Identification Manual.* Lulu.com.

American Penstemon Society website. 2006–2014. http://apsdev.org/identification.descriptions.php.

Anderson, W. 2000. A bow to the royal sage. *Southwest Trees & Turf,* April 2000.

Arizona Native Plant Society, Urban Landscape Committee. 1990. *Desert Shrubs.* Tucson, AZ: Arizona Native Plant Society.

———. 1991. *Desert Wildflowers.* Tucson, AZ. Arizona Native Plant Society.

———. 1992. *Desert Accent Plants.* Tucson, AZ. Arizona Native Plant Society.

Arnberger, L. P. 1982. *Flowers of the Southwest Mountains.* Tucson, AZ: Southwest Parks and Monuments Association.

Bailey, L. H. 1949. *Manual of Cultivated Plants.* New York: Macmillan.

Balin, L. 2000. "Native and Adapted Plant List for Butterflies in El Paso." El Paso, TX: Texas Parks and Wildlife.

Bowers, J. E. 1993. *Shrubs and Trees of the Southwest Deserts.* Tucson, AZ: Southwest Parks and Monuments Association.

Buchmann, S. L., and G. P. Nabhan. 1996. *The Forgotten Pollinators.* Washington, DC: Island Press.

Busco, J., and N. R. Morin. 2003. *Native Plants for High-Elevation Western Gardens.* Golden, CO: Fulcrum Publishing, in partnership with The Arboretum at Flagstaff.

Calflora: Information on California plants for education, research and conservation [web application]. 2014. Berkeley, California: The Calflora Database [a non-profit organization]. http://www.calflora.org/.

Carter, J. L. 1997. *Trees and Shrubs of New Mexico.* Boulder, CO: Johnson Books.

Chihuahuan Desert Plant Database. 2006. El Paso, TX: The University of Texas at El Paso. http://museum2.utep.edu/chih/gardens/list/list.htm.

Clebsch, B. 2003. *The New Book of Salvias.* Portland, OR: Timber Press.

Craighead, J. J., F. C. Craighead, Jr., and R. J. Davis. 1963. *A Field Guide to Rocky Mountain Wildflowers.* Boston: Houghton Mifflin.

Crosswhite, F. S., and C. D. Crosswhite. 1981. "Hummingbirds as pollinators of flowers in the red-yellow segment of the color spectrum, with special reference to *Penstemon* and the 'open habitat.'" *Desert Plants* 3: 156–170.

Demcheck, D. K. 2003. "Sugar content of hummingbird plants in Louisiana gardens." *LOS Newsletter,* March 2003, Louisiana Ornithological Society.

Desert Botanical Garden. 1988. *Desert Wildflowers,* edited by G. P. Nabhan and J. Cole. Phoenix, AZ: Arizona Highways Books.

Dodge, N. N. 1985. *Flowers of the Southwest Deserts.* Tucson, AZ: Southwest Parks and Monuments Association.

Elisons, W. J., and C. E. Freeman. 1988. "Floral nectar sugar composition and pollinator type among New World genera in tribe Antirrhineae (*Scrophulariaceae*)." *American Journal of Botany* 75: 971–78.

Elizondo, M. G., A. G. Elizondo, and Y. H. Arneta. 1991. *Listados Floristicos de Mexico.* IX. Flora de Durango. Mexico, DF: Instituto de Biologia, UNAM.

Elmore, F. H. 1976. *Shrubs and Trees of the Southwest Uplands.* Tucson, AZ: Southwest Parks and Monuments Association.

Encyclopedia of Life website. 2014. http://www.eol.org.

Fagan, D. 1998. *Canyon Country Wildflowers.* Helena, MT: Falcon Publishing.

Flora of North America Editorial Committee, eds. 1993+. Flora of North America North of Mexico. 16+ Vols. New York and Oxford. http://floranorthamerica.org/.

Freeman, C. E., W. H. Reid, J. E. Becvar, and R. Scogin. 1983. "Nectar sugar composition in some species of *Agave* (Agavaceae)." *Madroño* 30: 153–58.

———. 1984. "Similarity and apparent convergence in the nectar-sugar composition of some hummingbird-pollinated flowers." *Botanical Gazette* 145: 132–35.

Freeman, C. E., and R. D. Worthington. 1985. "Some floral nectar-sugar compositions of species from southeastern Arizona and southwestern New Mexico." *Madroño* 32: 78–86.

Gentry, H. S. 1982. *Agaves of Continental North America.* Tucson, AZ: The University of Arizona Press.

Global Biodiversity Information Network (GBIF) website. www.discoverlife.org/.

Heflin, J. 1997. *Penstemons: The Beautiful Beardtongues of New Mexico.* Albuquerque, NM: Jackrabbit Press.

Irish, M. F. 2000. *Gardening in the Desert: A Guide to Plant Selection and Care.* Tucson, AZ: The University of Arizona Press.

———. 2006. *Perennials for the Southwest: Plants That Flourish in Arid Gardens.* Portland, OR: Timber Press.

Irish, M. F., and G. Irish. 2000. *Agaves, Yuccas, and Related Plants: A Gardener's Guide.* Portland, OR: Timber Press.

Jepson Flora Project (eds.). 2013. *Jepson eFlora.* Accessed on May 18, 2014. http://ucjeps.berkeley.edu/IJM.html.

Jepson Herbarium. 2002. *The Jepson Desert Manual: Vascular Plants of Southeastern California,* edited by B. G. Baldwin, S. Boyd, B. J. Ertter, R. W. Patterson, T. J. Rosatti, and D. H. Wilden. Berkeley, CA: University of California Press.

Johnson, E. A. 1997. *Pruning, Planting & Care: Johnson's Guide to Gardening Plants for the Arid West.* Tucson, AZ: Ironwood Press.

Kartesz, J. T., The Biota of North America Program (BONAP). 2013. Taxonomic Data Center. http://www.bonap.net/tdc.

Kearney, T. H., and R. H. Peebles. 1969. *Arizona Flora,* 2nd edition (with supplement by J. T. Howell, E. McLintock, et al.). Berkeley, CA: University of California Press.

Lange, R. S., S. A. Scobell, and P. E. Scott. 2000. "Hummingbird-syndrome traits, breeding system, and pollinator effectiveness in two syntopic *Penstemon* species." *International Journal of Plant Sciences* 161: 253–63.

Lange, R. S., and P. E. Scott. 1999. "Hummingbird and bee pollination of *Penstemon pseudospectabilis.*" *Journal of the Torrey Botanical Society* 126: 99–106.

Little, E. L. 1980. *The Audubon Society Field Guide to North American Trees, Western Region.* New York: Alfred A. Knopf.

Lott, E. J. 1985. *Listados Floristicos de Mexico.* III. La Estacion de Biologia Chamela, Jalisco. Mexico, DF: Instituto de Biologia, UNAM.

Loughmiller, C., and L. Loughmiller. 1984. *Texas Wildflowers.* Austin, TX: University of Texas Press.

Martin, P. S., D. Yetman, M. Fishbein, P. Jenkins, T. R. Van Devender, and R. K. Wilson (eds.). 1998. *Gentry's Rio Mayo Plants: The Tropical Deciduous Forest & Environs of Northwest Mexico.* Tucson, AZ: University of Arizona Press.

Martin, W. C., and C. R. Hutchins. 1984. *Spring Wildflowers of New Mexico.* Albuquerque, NM: University of New Mexico Press.

———. 1986. *Summer Wildflowers of New Mexico.* Albuquerque, NM: University of New Mexico Press.

———. 1988. *Fall Wildflowers of New Mexico.* Albuquerque, NM: University of New Mexico Press.

Mason, C. T., Jr., and P. Mason. 1987. *A Handbook of Mexican Roadside Flora.* Tucson, AZ: University of Arizona Press.

Mielke, J. 1993. *Native Plants for Southwestern Landscapes.* Austin, TX: University of Texas Press.

Miller, G. O. 1991. *Landscaping with Native Plants of Texas and the Southwest.* Stillwater, MN: Voyageur Press.

Mountain States Wholesale Nursery. 2011. Plant Database. Glendale, AZ: Mountain States Wholesale Nursery. http://www.mswn.com/plants/database/.

Native Plant Society of New Mexico. 1998. *Chihuahuan Desert Gardens: A Native Plant Selection Guide,* edited by G. Magee and T. McKimmie. Santa Fe, NM: The Native Plant Society of New Mexico.

New Mexico Forestry and Resources Conservation Division, Energy, Minerals and Natural Resources Department. 1994. *Inventory of the Rare and Endangered Plants of New Mexico,* 2nd edition, edited by R. Sivinski and K. Lightfoot. Santa Fe, NM: The State of New Mexico.

New Mexico Native Plants Protection Advisory Committee. 1984. *A Handbook of Rare and Endemic Plants of New Mexico,* edited by R. Fletcher et al. Albuquerque, NM: University of New Mexico Press.

New Mexico Rare Plant Technical Council. 1999. *New Mexico Rare Plants.* Albuquerque, NM: New Mexico Rare Plants Home Page (Latest update: January 16 2014). http://nmrareplants.unm.edu/.

Niehaus, T. F., and C. L. Ripper. 1976. *A Field Guide to Pacific States Wildflowers.* Boston: Houghton Mifflin.

Niehaus, T. F., C. L. Ripper, and V. Savage. 1984. *A Field Guide to Southwestern and Texas Wildflowers.* Boston: Houghton Mifflin.

Nokes, J. 2001. *How to Grow Native Plants of Texas and the Southwest.* Austin, TX:

University of Texas Press.
Nold, R. 1999. *Penstemons.* Portland, OR: Timber Press.
Patraw, P. M. 1959. *Flowers of the Southwest Mesas.* Tucson, AZ: Southwest Parks and Monuments Association.
Phillips, J. 1995. *Plants for Natural Gardens.* Santa Fe, NM: Museum of New Mexico Press.
———. 1998. *New Mexico Gardener's Guide.* Nashville, TN: Cool Springs Press.
Plant List. 2013. Version 1.1. http://www.theplantlist.org.
Powell, A. M. 1988. *Trees and Shrubs of Trans-Pecos Texas.* Big Bend National Park, TX: Big Bend Natural History Association.
Quintanilla, J. G., V. 2001. *Listados Floristicos de Mexico.* XXIII. Flora de Coahuila. Mexico, DF: Instituto de Biologia, UNAM.
Robertson, L. 1999. *Southern Rocky Mountain Wildflowers.* Helena, MT: Falcon Publishing.
Sanders, R. W. 1987. "Taxonomy of *Agastache* section *Brittonastrum* (Lamiaceae-Nepeteae)." *Systematic Botany Monographs* 15: 1–92.
Schuler, C. 1993. *Low Water-Use Plants for California & the Southwest.* Tucson, AZ: Fisher Books.
Scobell, S. A., and P. E. Scott. 2002. "Visitors and floral traits of a hummingbird-adapted cactus (*Echinocereus coccineus*) show only minor variation along an elevational gradient." *American Midland Naturalist* 147: 1–15.
Shultz, L. M., R. D. Ramsey, W. Lindquist, and C. Garrard. 2010. Digital Atlas of the Vascular Plants of Utah [updated]. Logan, UT: Utah State University. http://earth.gis.usu.edu/plants/.
Southwest Colorado Wildflowers. 2014. Wildflowers, Ferns, & Trees of Colorado, New Mexico, Arizona, & Utah. www.swcoloradowildflowers.com/.
Southwest Environmental Information Network, SEINet. 2013–2014. Accessed April 2013–June 2014. http://swbiodiversity.org/seinet/index/php.
Starr, G. 1985. "New World salvias for cultivation in southern Arizona." *Desert Plants* 7: 167–171,184–89, 204–7.
Sunset Books. 2007. *Sunset Western Garden Book,* edited by K. Brenzel. Menlo Park, CA: Sunset Publishing.
Thomson, J. D., P. Wilson, M. Valenzuela, and M. Malzone. 2000. "Pollen presentation and pollination syndromes, with special reference to *Penstemon.*" *Plant Species Biology* 15: 11–29.
Tidestrom, I., and T. K. Kittell. 1941. *Flora of Arizona and New Mexico.* Washington, DC: The Catholic University of America Press.
Tropicos.org, Missouri Botanical Garden. 2014. "La familia Scrophulariaceae in México: diversidad y distribución." http://www.tropicos.org/Reference/1021577.
Turner, R. M., J. E. Bowers, and T. L. Burgess. 2005. *Sonoran Desert Plants: An Ecological Atlas.* Tucson, AZ: The University of Arizona Press.
USDA, National Resource Conservation Service. 2014. The PLANTS Database. Greensboro, NC: National Plant Data Team. http://plants.usda.gov/.
Warnock, B. H. 1970. *Wildflowers of the Big Bend Country, Texas.* Alpine, TX: Sul Ross State University.
Wasowski, S., and A. Wasowski. 1988. *Native Texas Plants: Landscaping Region by Region.* Houston, TX: Gulf Publishing.

———. 1995. *Native Gardens for Dry Climates.* New York: Clarkson Potter/Publishers.
West, S. 2000. *Northern Chihuahuan Desert Wildflowers.* Helena, MT: Falcon Publishing.
Wooton, E. O., and P. C. Standley. 1915. *Flora of New Mexico.* Washington, DC: U. S. Government Printing Office [Smithsonian Institution, U. S. National Museum].

BIRD GARDENING REFERENCES

Adams, G. 1994. *Birdscaping Your Garden.* Emmaus, PA: Rodale Press.
Arizona Native Plant Society Urban Landscape Committee. 1997. *Desert Bird Gardening.* Tucson, AZ: Arizona Native Plant Society and Tucson Audubon Society.
Arizona-Sonora Desert Museum. *Hummingbirds in Your Garden: How to Attract and Maintain Hummingbirds in Your Garden or Patio.* Tucson, AZ: Arizona-Sonora Desert Museum.
Dennis, J. V., and M. Tekulsky. 1991. *How to Attract Hummingbirds and Butterflies.* San Ramon, CA: Ortho Books.
Knopf, J., S. Wasowski, J. K. Boring, F. Keator, J. Scott, and E. Glasener. 1995. *Natural Gardening: A Nature Company Guide,* R. G. Turner, consulting editor. San Francisco: Time-Life Books.
Kress, S. W. 1995. *The Bird Garden.* New York: Dorling Kindersley Publishing.
Magee, G. 1997. "Attracting hummingbirds to your garden." In *Native Plant Society of New Mexico Newsletter,* May/June 1997, Vol. XXII, No. 3. Santa Fe, NM: Native Plant Society of New Mexico.
Newfield, N. L. 1990. "A strategy for hummers: convert your backyard into a hummingbird haven." *Birder's World,* June 1990.
Newfield, N. L., and B. Nielsen. 1996. *Hummingbird Gardens: Attracting Nature's Jewels to Your Backyard.* Boston: Houghton Mifflin.
Roth, S. 1997. *Natural Landscaping: Gardening with Nature to Create a Backyard Paradise.* Emmaus, PA: Rodale Press.
Williamson, S. L. 2000. *Attracting and Feeding Hummingbirds.* Neptune City, NJ: T.F.H. Publications.
Yoder, S. 1999. *Desert Hummingbird Gardens.* Paradise Valley, AZ: Real Estate Consulting and Education.

INDEX

A

Agastache barberi, 70–71
Agastache cana, 68–69
Agastache 'Desert Sunrise,' 74
Agastache mearnsii, 73
Agastache pallida, 70–71
Agastache pallidiflora, 72–73
Agastache rupestris, 74–75
Agave chrysantha, 76–77, 85
Agave delamateri, 77
Agave deserti, 78–79
Agave havardiana, 80–81
Agave lechuguilla, 82–83
Agave murpheyi, 77
Agave neomexicana, 86–87
Agave palmeri, 77, 84–85
Agave palmeri var. *chrysantha*, 76–77
Agave parryi, 77, 86–87
Agave schottii, 88–89
Agave utahensis, 90–91
Alamo beardtongue, 222–23
Alamo penstemon, 222–23
albarda, 164–65
Aliciella subnuda, 92–93
alkalinity, soil, 60
Allen's Hummingbird, 40–41
Allionia coccinea, 214–15
Amazilia beryllina, 14–15
Amazilia violiceps, 16–17
amole, 88–89
amolillo, 88–89
amul, 78–79
Anderson's thornbush, 204–5
Anisacanthus andersonii, 94–95
Anisacanthus linearis, 96–97
Anisacanthus puberulus, 97
Anisacanthus quadrifidus, 98–99

Anisacanthus thurberi, 100–101
Anna's Hummingbird, 4, 22–23
Aquilegia chrysantha, 102–3
Aquilegia desertorum, 104–5
Aquilegia elegantula, 106–7
Aquilegia formosa, 105, 108–9
Aquilegia skinneri, 110–11
Aquilegia triternata, 104–5
Arbutus arizonica, 113
Arbutus species, 112–13
Arbutus texana, 113
Arbutus xalapensis, 113
Archilochus alexandri, 18–19
Arctostaphylos glauca, 114
Arctostaphylos pungens, 114–15
Arctostaphylos species, 114–15
aretitos, 196–97
Arizona gilia, 180–81
Arizona honeysuckle, 200–201
Arizona madrone, 113
Arizona paintbrush, 124–25
Arizona skyrocket, 180–81
Arizona thistle, 144–45
Arizona thornbush, 204–5
Arizona water-willow, 186–87
artichoke agave, 86
artificial feeders, 50–51, 312
Astragalus coccineus, 116–17
Audubon, John James, 1
autumn sage, 280–81

B

baby sage, 281, 285
baccharisleaf penstemon, 224–25
Baja bush snapdragon, 166
barrel columbine, 104–5
Basilinna leucotis, 30–31

bat-faced cuphea, 148–49
bat-faced monkeyflower, 148–49
bats, pollination by, 8
beaked beardtongue, 252–53
bearberry honeysuckle, 202–3
beardlip penstemon, 11, 226–27, 242
beardtongues, 222–23, 226–29, 236–37, 240–41, 248–55, 260–63
bee plants, 266–69
bejuco blanco, 174–75
Beloperone californica, 184–85
berms, 59, 63
Berylline Hummingbird, 14–15
Big Bend agave, 80–81
Big Bend beardtongue, 236–37
big honeysuckle, 94–95
big red sage, 286–87
bigberry manzanita, 114
Bignonia stans, 304–5
Bill Williams Mountain giant hyssop, 72–73
birchleaf sage, 276–77
birdbaths, 49–50
birding trip to Mexico, 312
black sage, 297
Black-chinned Hummingbird, 18–19
bladderpod spiderflower, 264–65
blood alum root, 170–71
bloom seasons, 48
Blue-throated Hummingbird, 32–33
Bouvardia glaberrima, 118–19
Bouvardia ternifolia, 118–19
branching penstemon, 250–51
Bridges' penstemon, 252–53
Broad-billed Hummingbird, 26–27
Broad-tailed Hummingbird, 36–37
brocha India, 126–27
bubblegum mint, 68–69
buglers, 226–27, 230–31, 240–41
burro fat, 264–65
bush monkeyflower, 154–55

C

caballito, 304–5
cacaculo, 204–5
calendar for hummingbirds, 47–48
California beloperone, 184–85
California fuchsia, 158–59
Calliope Hummingbird, 34–35
Calothorax lucifer, 20–21
Calypte anna, 4, 22–23
Calypte costae, 24–25
canary columbine, 102–3
canyon penstemon, 248–49
Canyonlands gilia, 92–93
cardinal catchfly, 300–301
cardinal flower, 194–95
cardinal larkspur, 150–51
cardinal monkeyflower, 210–11
cardinal penstemon, 228–29
cardinal sage, 288–89
cardo, 146–47
carmine gilia, 92–93
carpenter bees, 48–49
Castilleja angustifolia, 120–21
Castilleja affinis, 122
Castilleja applegatei, 122–23
Castilleja austromontana, 124–25
Castilleja chromosa, 120–21
Castilleja integra, 126–27
Castilleja lanata, 128–29
Castilleja laxa, 138–39
Castilleja linariifolia, 130–31, 134
Castilleja miniata, 132–33
Castilleja patriotica, 134–35
Castilleja scabrida, 136–37
Castilleja tenuiflora, 138–39
cat predation, 52–53, 312
Cave Creek Canyon, 10
cedar sage, 290–91
Chamaenerion angustifolium, 140–41
Chamerion angustifolium, 140–41
chaparral sage, 297
cherry sage, 280–81
chilicote, 160–61
Chilopsis linearis, 49, 142–43
Chiricahua Mountain columbine, 104–5
chunari, 162–63
chupamiel, 192–93
chuparosa, 184–85
chupil, 206–7
cigarrito, 118–19

Cirsium arizonicum, 144–45
Cirsium neomexicanum, 146–47
claretcup cactus, 156–57
Clark Mountain agave, 90–91
Cleome isomeris, 264–65
Cleome serrulata, 266–67
climbing penstemon, 188–89
coast paintbrush, 122
coastal migratory corridors, 11
Colazo, Tom, 2
Colorado four-o'clock, 216–17
columbines, 8, 102–11
comet columbine, 106–7
container plants, 63
coral bells, 170–71
coral gilia, 92–93
coral penstemon, 256–57
coralina, 160–61
Costa's Hummingbird, 24–25
crimson columbine, 108–9
crimson sage, 282–83, 292–93
crimson sheeppod, 116–17
Cuphea llavea, 148–49
cuttings, taking, 61–62
Cynanthus latirostris, 26–27

D

Delphinium barbeyi, 152–53
Delphinium cardinale, 150–51
Delphinium macrophyllum, 152–53
Delphinium nelsoni, 152–53
Delphinium nuttallianum, 152–53
Delphinium scopulorum, 152–53
Delphinium sonnei, 152–53
Delphinium species, 152–53
desert agave, 78–79
desert beardtongue, 248–49
desert columbine, 104–5
desert four-o'clock, 216–17
desert paintbrush, 120–21
desert skyrocket, 178–79
desert thistle, 146–47
desert trumpet, 178–79
desert-honeysuckle, 96–101
desert-willow, 49, 142–43
devil's coachwhip, 164–65
Diplacus aurantiacus, 154–55

Diplacus cardinalis, 210–11
Diplacus longiflorus, 154–55
Diplacus puniceus, 154–55
Diplacus species, 154–55
drip irrigation, 59
drought tolerant plants, 58–59
dwarf anisacanth, 96–97

E

Eastwood's monkeyflower, 212–13
Eastwood's paintbrush, 136–37
Eaton's firecracker, 232–33
Echinocereus arizonicus, 156–57
Echinocereus coccineus, 156–57
Echinocereus polyacanthus, 156–57
Echinocereus species, 156–57
Echinocereus triglochidiatus, 156–57
Epilobium angustifolium, 140–41
Epilobium canum, 158–59
Erythrina flabelliformis, 89, 160–61
esperanza, 304–5
espinosilla, 198–99
Eucalyptus species, 2, 56
Eugenes fulgens, 28–29
Exogonium bracteatum, 174–75

F

fascicled penstemon, 234–35
feeders, 50–51, 312
female hummingbird behaviors, 4
fertilizer, 60
firecracker bush, 118–19
firecracker penstemon, 232–33
fireweed, 140–41
flame acanthus, 98–99
flor de la candelaria, 174–75
Fouquieria diguetii, 162
Fouquieria macdougalii, 10, 162–63
Fouquieria splendens, 164–65
four-o'clocks, 214–17
frutilla, 204–5
fuchsia-flowering gooseberry, 272–73

G

Galvezia juncea, 166
Galvezia speciosa, 166–67
Gambelia juncea, 166

Gambelia speciosa, 166–67
gardening with native plants, 55–63. *See also* habitat creation; hummingbird plants
   fertilizing, 60
   finding native plants, 61–62
   further information, 63
   heat tolerance, 60–61
   knowing the local landscape, 57
   microclimates and, 56–58
   planting basics, 62–63, 311
   reasons for choosing native plants, 55–56, 312
   soil types, 60
   time to plant, 62–63
   watering, 58–59, 63
gender and hummingbird behaviors, 4
giant hummingbird mint, 70–71
giant hyssop, 68–69
giant red paintbrush, 132–33
Gilia aggregata, 178–79
Gilia subnuda, 92–93
gilias, 92–93, 178–81
golden columbine, 102–3
goldenflower century plant, 76–77
golden-flowered agave, 76–77
gooseberries, 270–73
granny's bonnets, 110–11
Gregg salvia, 280–81
Grossularia speciosa, 272–73

H

habitat creation, 43–53. *See also* gardening with native plants
   accounting for other visitors, 48–49
   bloom seasons, 48
   choosing which hummingbirds to attract, 44–45
   hummingbird calendar, 47–48
   important features, 43–44
   knowing the local landscape, 44
   layout of, 45
   nectar feeders, 50–51, 312
   need for, 43
   nesting locations and materials, 46–47
   roosting spots, 46
   safety concerns, 51–52
   sentinel perches, 45–46
   water features, 49–50
hackberry beardtongue, 254–55
Havard's agave, 80–81
Havard's penstemon, 236–37
heartleaf keckiella, 188–89
heat tolerant plants, 60–61
helping hummingbirds and their flowers, 311–12
Henry's sage, 282–83
Hesperaloe parviflora, 42, 168–69
Heuchera sanguinea, 170–71
hierba de la cucaracha, 206–7
hierba de la virgen, 198–99
hierba de sapo, 134–35
hierba del piojo, 206–7
Hoitzia coccinea, 198–99
honeysuckles, 94–101, 200–203
Huachuca Mountain paintbrush, 134–35
hummingbird mint, 218–19
hummingbird plants. *See also* gardening with native plants; *specific kinds*
   at-a-glance information, 65–66
   avoiding invasive plants, 56, 312
   dependence on hummingbirds, 1–2
   drought tolerant, 58–59
   flower colors and shapes, 7, 9
   insect control for, 52
   nectar concentration in, 8, 9
   need for variety of, vi
   for nesting, 46–47
   relatively recent evolution of, 7
   for roosting, 46
   for sentinel perches, 45–46
   switch from bee pollination to, 7
   ways to help, 311–12
hummingbird sage, 292–93
hummingbird trumpet, 158–59
hummingbirds. *See also specific kinds*
   aerial feats of, 2–3
   availability for viewing, v
   backyard havens for, v
   energy-conserving torpid state of, 3
   feeding by, 3–4
   flowers solely dependent upon, 1–2
   habitat creation, 43–53
   humans a mixed blessing for, 2

life span of, 5
male and female behaviors, 4
memory skills of, 5–6
migration by, 3, 4–5
number of species of, 1
organization of profiles, 13
pollination by, 7–9
predators of, 5, 52–53, 312
primer, 1–12
safety concerns, 51–52
speed of wing and heart beats, 3
territoriality of males, 4–5
ways to help, 311–12
Hylocharis leucotis, 30–31
hyssops, 68–75

I

Indian paintbrushes, 8, 120–39
Indian warrior, 220–21
insects
   controlling in the garden, 52
   feeding upon by hummingbirds, 4, 8
   pollination by, 7
invasive plants, avoiding, 56, 312
Ipomoea arborescens, 172–73
Ipomoea bracteata, 174–75
Ipomoea chilopsidis, 173
Ipomoea coccinea, 177
Ipomoea cristulata, 176–77
Ipomoea rubriflora, 177
Ipomopsis aggregata, 11, 178–79, 181
Ipomopsis aggregata ssp. *arizonica*, 180–81
Ipomopsis arizonica, 180–81
Ipomopsis tenuifolia, 182–83
irrigation, 58–59, 63
island bush snapdragon, 166–67
Isomeris arborea, 264–65

J

jaboncillo, 162–63
Jacobinia ovata, 186–87
jarritos, 226–27
Justicia californica, 184–85
Justicia candicans, 186–87
jútuguo, 172–73

K

Keckiella antirrhinoides, 189
Keckiella cordifolia, 188–89
Keckiella ternata, 190–91
Kunth's penstemon, 238–39

L

Lady Bird Johnson Wildflower Center, 61
Lamourouxia coccinea, 192–93
Lamourouxia longiflora, 193
Lamourouxia viscosa, 192–93
Lampornis clemenciae, 32–33
lanceleaf beardtongue, 250–51
larkspurs, 150–53
lavender thistle, 146–47
lechuguilla, 82–83
Ledebour's honeysuckle, 202
Lemmon's sage, 284–85
licorice mint, 74–75
life span of hummingbirds, 5
limita, 94–95
little beardtongue, 254–55
Lobelia cardinalis, 194–95
Lobelia laxiflora, 196–97
Loeselia coccinea, 198–99
Loeselia mexicana, 198–99
Loeselia tenuifolia, 182–83
Lonicera arizonica, 200–201
Lonicera involucrata, 202–3
Lonicera involucrata var. *ledebourii*, 202
loose-flowered lobelia, 196–97
Lucifer Hummingbird, 20–21
Lycium andersonii, 204–5
Lycium exsertum, 204–5
Lycium pallidum, 204–5
Lycium parishii, 204–5
Lycium species, 204–5

M

Madera Canyon, 10
Madrean beardtongue, 260–61
madreselva, 200–201
madrone or madrono, 112–13
Magnificent Hummingbird, 28–29
male hummingbird behaviors, 4

Mandevilla foliosa, 206–7
manzanita, 114–15
maravilla, 216–17
Maurandella antirrhiniflora, 208–9
Maurandya antirrhiniflora, 208–9
Maycoba sage, 276–77
meadow paintbrush, 132–33
Melandrium laciniatum, 300–301
Mexican campion, 300–301
Mexican catchfly, 11, 300–301
Mexican columbine, 110–11
Mexican false calico, 198–99
Mexico, birding trip to, 312
microclimates, 56–58
migration, 3, 4–5
migratory corridors, 9–11, 12, 43
Miller Canyon, 10
mimbre, 142–43
Mimbres figwort, 298–99
Mimulus aurantiacus, 154–55
Mimulus cardinalis, 210–11
Mimulus eastwoodiae, 212–13
Mimulus longiflorus, 154–55
Mimulus puniceus, 154–55
Mimulus species, 154–55
mints, 68–71, 74–75, 218–19
Mirabilis coccinea, 214–15
Mirabilis multiflora, 216–17
mirto, 278–79
Mojave beardtongue, 248–49
Monardella macrantha, 218–19
monkeyflowers, 148–49, 154–55, 210–13
morning glories, 172–73, 176–77
mosquito plant, 68–69
mountain bugler, 240–41
mountain figwort, 298
mountain sage, 288–89
mulch, 59

N

najicoli, 192–93
narrowleaf desert-honeysuckle, 96–97
narrowleaf fireweed, 140–41
narrowleaf paintbrush, 130–31
nectar concentration in hummingbird plants, 8, 9
nectar feeders, 50–51, 312
nesting locations and materials, 46–47
New Mexico figwort, 298–99
New Mexico thistle, 146–47
northwestern paintbrush, 120–21

O

ocotillo, 164–65
ocotillo macho, 162–63
orange bush monkeyflower, 154–55
orange gooseberry, 270–72
organizations, 311
Oxybaphus coccineus, 214–15
Oxybaphus multiflorus, 216–17

P

painted red penstemon, 238–39
pale giant hyssop, 70–71
Palmer's agave, 84–85
palo adán, 162
palo blanco, 172–73
palo del arco, 304–5
palo santo, 172–73
Parish's thornbush, 204–5
Parry's agave, 86–87
Parry's penstemon, 244–45
Pedicularis densiflora, 220–21
Penstemon alamosensis, 222–23
Penstemon baccharifolius, 224–25
Penstemon barbatus, 11, 226–27
Penstemon bridgesii, 252–53
Penstemon cardinalis, 228–29
Penstemon centranthifolius, 230–31
Penstemon cordifolius, 188–89
Penstemon eatonii, 232–33
Penstemon fasciculatus, 234–35
Penstemon havardii, 236–37
Penstemon kunthii, 238–39
Penstemon labrosus, 240–41
Penstemon lanceolatus, 250–51
Penstemon miniatus, 242–43
Penstemon parryi, 244–45
Penstemon pinifolius, 246–47
Penstemon pseudospectabilis, 248–49

Penstemon ramosus, 250–51
Penstemon rostriflorus, 252–53
penstemon sage, 286–87
Penstemon species
    adaptation to hummingbird pollination by, 7–8
    as great starter plants, 48
    profiles, 188–91, 222–63
Penstemon subulatus, 254–55
Penstemon superbus, 67, 256–57
Penstemon ternatus, 190–91
Penstemon utahensis, 258–59
Penstemon wislizenii, 260–61
Penstemon wrightii, 262–63
perico, 138–39
periquito, 134–35, 138–39
Peritoma arborea, 264–65
Peritoma serrulata, 266–67
pesticide poisoning, 52, 312
pichelitos, 244–45
pine paintbrush, 122–23
pineapple sage, 278–79
pineleaf penstemon, 234, 246–47
pine-needle penstemon, 246–47
pinky anisacanth, 97
pitcher sage, 292–93
pointleaf manzanita, 114–15
pollination, 6–9
predators, 5, 52–53, 312
purple sage, 296–97

R

rama del toro, 186–87
Ramsey Canyon, 10
red bush monkeyflower, 154–55
red bush penstemon, 188–89
red four-o'clock, 214–15
red justicia, 186–87
red lousewort, 220–21
red morning glory, 177
red mountainbalm, 218–19
red umbrellawort, 214–15
red yucca, 42, 168–69
redbirds in a tree, 298–99
redflower false yucca, 42, 168–69

Ribes malvaceum, 268–69
Ribes pinetorum, 270–72
Ribes speciosum, 272–73
Rincon Mountain paintbrush, 124–25
riparian migratory corridors, 10–11, 43
rock penstemon, 224–25
Rocky Mountain bee plant, 266–69
Rocky Mountain larkspur, 152–53
Rocky Mountain migratory corridor, 11
Roemer's sage, 290–91
romero, 306–7
roosting spots, 46
rosebay willow-herb, 140–41
rough paintbrush, 136–37
roving sailor, 208–9
royal sage, 288–89
Rufous Hummingbird, 3, 5, 38–39
Russelia sonorensis, 274–75
Russian olive, 56

S

Saccularia juncea, 166
safety concerns, 51–52
sages, 8, 276–97
salt cedar, 56
Salvia apiana, 297
Salvia betulifolia, 276–77
Salvia clevelandii, 297
Salvia davidsonii, 282–83
salvia de montaña, 288–89
salvia del monte, 284–85
Salvia elegans, 278–79
Salvia greggii, 280–81
Salvia henryi, 282–83
Salvia lemmonii, 284–85
Salvia leucophylla, 296–97
Salvia mellifera, 297
Salvia microphylla, 281, 284–85
Salvia microphylla var. *wislizenii*, 284–85
salvia peluda, 290–91
Salvia penstemonoides, 286–87
Salvia regla, 288–89
Salvia roemeriana, 290–91
salvia roja, 278–79
Salvia rutilans, 278–79

Salvia spathacea, 292–93
Salvia species, 8, 296–97
Salvia townsendii, 294–95
San Gabriel beardtongue, 240–41
San Luis giant hyssop, 73
Santa Catalina paintbrush, 138–39
scarlet betony, 102, 302–3
scarlet bouvardia, 118–19
scarlet bugler, 226–27, 230–31
scarlet creeper, 176–77
scarlet four-o'clock, 214–15
scarlet gilia, 11, 178–79, 181
scarlet hedgenettle, 302–3
scarlet keckiella, 190–91
scarlet larkspur, 150–51
scarlet lobelia, 194–95
scarlet locoweed, 116–17
scarlet milkvetch, 116–17
scarlet monardella, 218–19
scarlet monkeyflower, 210–11
Schott's agave, 88–89
Scrophularia coccinea, 298–99
Scrophularia macrantha, 298–99
Scrophularia montana, 298
Scrophularia neomexicana, 298–99
seed harvesting, 61–62
Selasphorus calliope, 34–35
Selasphorus platycercus, 36–37
Selasphorus rufus, 3, 5, 38–39
Selasphorus sasin, 40–41
semandoque, 168–69
sentinel perches, 45–46
shindagger, 82–83, 88–89
shooting star columbine, 106–7
showy greenbright, 166–67
Sierra Madre cordilleras, 9–10
Sierra Madre lobelia, 196–97
Sierra Madrean penstemon, 242–43
Sierra woolly Indian paintbrush, 128–29
Silene laciniata, 11, 300–301
Skinner's columbine, 110–11
skyrockets, 178–83
slenderleaf skyrocket, 182–83
snapdragon vine, 208–9
snapdragons, 166–67, 208–9

soil types, 60
Sonoran firecracker plant, 274–75
southern bush monkeyflower, 154–55
southwest coral bean, 89, 160–61
southwestern paintbrush, 126–27
Stachys coccinea, 302–3
star glory, 176–77
Stellula calliope, 34–35
sticky monkeyflower, 154–55
subalpine larkspur, 152–53
sugar for feeders, 51
sunset hyssop, 74–75
superb penstemon, 67, 256–57
supporting hummingbirds and their flowers, 311–12

T

taperosa, 100–101
Tecoma stans, 304–5
Tecoma stans var. *angustatum*, 304–5
Texas betony, 302–3
Texas madrone, 113
Texas rose, 262–63
thistles, 144–47
thornbush, 204–5
threadleaf giant hyssop, 74–75
time to plant, 62–63
torote verde, 162–63
tosa huira, 174–75
Townsend's sage, 294–95
Trans Pecos morning glory, 176–77
transplanting wild plants, 62
tree morning glory, 172–73
tree ocotillo, 10, 162–63
Trichostema lanatum, 306–7
trompetilla, 118–19
tronadora, 304–5
twinberry honeysuckle, 202–3
twinflower, 202–3
twining snapdragon, 208–9
two-lobe larkspur, 152–53

U

Utah agave, 90–91
Utah firecracker, 258–59

Utah penstemon, 258–59

V
varita de San José, 244–45
Violet-crowned Hummingbird, 11, 16–17

W
wand penstemon, 190–91
wash willow, 142–43
water conservation, 312
water features, 49–50
watering plants, 58–59, 63
waterjacket, 204–5
wavy-leaf paintbrush, 122–23
western columbine, 108–9
White Mountain beardtongue, 228–29
white sage, 297
White-eared Hummingbird, 30–31
white-woolly paintbrush, 128–29
wholeleaf paintbrush, 126–27
whorl-leaf penstemon, 190–91
wild jícama, 174–75
willowleaf catalpa, 142–43

window collisions, 51–52
Wislizenius' penstemon, 260–61
wolfberry, 204–5
woolly blue curls, 306–7
Wright's beardtongue, 262–63
Wright's desert-honeysuckle, 98–99
Wright's penstemon, 262–63
Wyoming paintbrush, 130–31, 134

X
Xylocopa (carpenter bees), 48–49

Y
yant, 90–91
yellow bells, 304–5
yellow penstemon, 189

Z
zampantla, 160–61
Zauschneria californica, 158–59
Zauschneria cana, 158–59
Zauschneria latifolium, 158
Zion paintbrush, 136–37

PHOTO CREDITS

© Wynn Anderson: ii, 10, 64, 68, 71, 80, 84, 96, 99, 103, 104, 108, 111, 112, 115, 116, 119, 120, 124, 127, 128, 131, 132, 135, 136, 139, 148, 159, 163, 164, 171, 172, 175, 176, 179, 180, 184, 187, 192, 196, 199, 207, 208, 215, 223, 224, 235, 236, 239, 243, 247, 259, 263, 275, 276, 279, 283, 284, 287, 288, 291, 295, 296, 300, 303

© Scott Calhoun: 79, 91

© Christopher L. Christie: 123, 140, 183, 231, 240, 252, 272, 292, 307, 311

© Richard Ditch, www.richditch.com: 22

© Aaron Downey: 267, 304

© David J. Griffin: 54

© W. Ross Humphreys: 195

© Neal Kramer: 155, 188, 203

© Max Licher: 76, 160, 255

© Lisa Mandelkern: 83, 87, 100, 107, 143, 147, 227, 228, 248, 251, 271

© Steve Matson: 220

© Timothy McKimmie: 9, 204

© Charles W. Melton: Cover

© Keir Morse: 151, 191, 219

© Mountain States Wholesale Nursery: 13, 58

© Al Schneider, www.swcoloradowildflowers.com: 92, 152

© Jon M. Stewart: 167, 200, 212

© Tommy Stoughton: 264

© Robert Villa: 95

© Lynn Watson: 268

© Ron Wolf: 41

© George Yatskievych: 260

© Jimmy Zabriskie: vii, 6, 17, 42, 49, 72, 156, 168, 244, 280, 336

© Barry R. Zimmer: 3, 308

© Dale and Marian Zimmerman: viii, 14, 18, 21, 25, 26, 29, 30, 33, 34, 37, 38, 67, 75, 88, 144, 211, 216, 232, 256, 299

MARCY SCOTT is a birder, botanizer, former wildlife rehabilitator, and garden consultant. With her landscape-designer husband, Jimmy Zabriskie, she operates Robledo Vista Nursery near Las Cruces, New Mexico, specializing in southwestern native plants, plants for wildlife habitat, and other resource-efficient landscape plants. Together they have developed a mini-refuge at their home along the Rio Grande, where they now host thousands of migrating hummingbirds each summer.